*Heino Nyyssönen*

**SoPhi**
University of Jyväskylä 1999

SoPhi publishes social sciences at the University of Jyväskylä, Finland, and it is located at the Department of Social Sciences and Philosophy. It provides a forum for innovative studies in social policy, sociology, political science and philosophy. SoPhi publishes 10–15 titles per year, both in Finnish and in English. Manuscripts are selected for publication on the basis of expert opinion.

Correspondence should be sent to publications editor Juha Virkki, Department of Social Sciences and Philosophy/Publications, University of Jyväskylä, P.O. Box 35, FIN-40351 Jyväskylä, Finland, tel. +358-(0)14-2603123, fax +358-(0)14-2603101, e-mail jutavi@dodo.jyu.fi.

Books can be ordered from Kampus Kirja, Box 377, FIN-40101 Jyväskylä, Finland, tel. +358-(0)14-2603157, fax +358-(0)14-2611143, e-mail kirjamyynti@kampusdata.fi

Visit SoPhi home page at http://www.jyu.fi/sophi

ISBN 951-39-0426-1
ISSN 1238-8025

Cover Kimmo Lehtonen
Original Photo Heino Nyyssönen,
Imre Nagy at the Square of Martyrs in Budapest
Layout Juha Virkki

"The past is never dead, it is not even past"

– William Faulkner

# CONTENTS

# FOREWORD

In the opening scene of the Hungarian film *Csinibaba* (Pretty Baby, 1997) the new lottery numbers are read on the block radio. The caretaker, portrayed as a sympathiser of the ruling Hungarian Socialist Workers' Party, begins to announce the numbers: "4, 23, 28, 19... . What on earth... 56... How could this be possible... . This is not... ." Hence, he makes his decision instantly: "Urhm... The fifth lottery number, good tenants, will be published in *Népszabadság*".

The contextual code to the aforementioned scene is found in a film which in fact was one of the first public attempts to portray the Hungary of 1956 in an ironic sense in the 1990s. The comedy referred to Budapest in the beginning of 1960s, when the Space Age was about to emerge and science and progress were conquering the world. At that time *Népszabadság* was the organ of the Central Committee, and the caretaker was represented in order to avoid pronouncing a clear cultural icon.

For a political scientist the scene raises at least two questions: *How* to represent a certain event from the past, and *when* to represent the past. The year 1956 has had a different significance in Hungarian public life of the 1990s than it has over the previous decades. In 1989, '1956' was resurrected from the past and became a part of the current change of the system.

Naturally, I have to admit that this study, too, has been written in a political context. When I began to research recent Hungarian history in 1992, the euphoria of 1989 had turned into cautious pessimism and political critique against the centre-right government formed following the 1990 elections. Now, several years later, that government is also part of 'history', as its successor as well. Since the spring of 1998, all of the parties which crossed the threshold in 1990 have already participated at some point or another in the government of the young Hungarian democracy.

I would particularly like to thank the following Hungarians: György Litván, János M. Rainer and Csaba Békés in the '56 Institute, who despite their own busy schedules had the patience for a foreign newcomer and his peculiar questions. Additionally, I would like to thank László Szarvas, whom I have known since 1992 and István Vida, who was my tutor during my MA-thesis and my first longer visit to Hungary. Moreover, I must mention George Schöpflin, as well as two younger Hungarian or partly Hungarian friends of mine, the two Árpáds, Welker and von Klimó.

Of the others who have commented on my text, I would especially like to mention Seppo Hentilä and Ilmari Susiluoto, Holger Fischer, Anssi Halmesvirta, Juhani Huotari, Jukka Kekkonen, Jussi Kurunmäki, Pekka Korhonen and Kari Palonen, who has been my professor at the University of Jyväskylä and commented the thesis from the beginning. Moreover, I am grateful to Elisabeth Moulton, who has checked the language, Anitta Kananen, Saara Vattulainen, Kimmo Lehtonen and Juha Virkki. I have mentioned these individuals by name, however there are numerous other people whose support has been extremely important in many ways. Thanks to you all!

For their financial support, I must name and thank Väinö Tannerin Säätiö, the Europa Institute in Budapest, the Hungarian Academy of Sciences, the University of Jyväskylä, and within the University the Department of Social Sciences and Philosophy. I have had the opportunity to teach at the department since 1992, and in 1998 I also worked there as an assistant professor. Moreover, I must mention Vesa Saarikoski, whose project, The Europe Between, financed by the Finnish Academy of Sciences, I had the opportunity to participate in. Finally, in 1999 the Finnish Graduate School of Political Science and Internal Relations has helped me to finish my doctoral thesis. I am also grateful to SoPhi for publishing this book.

Furthermore, I must thank my parents. And last but not least, I wish to thank the most important person of all, my wife, Hajnalka Makra, who day after day has seen what it means to construct a doctoral thesis in practice. Indeed, research seems to be an art of politics, but at the same time it is comforting to realize that a researcher cannot be aware of all of the interpretations and consequences of his work.


At the Fodor utca in Budapest
In summer 1999

*Heino Nyyssönen*

# I INTRODUCTION: PROBLEMATIC AND SOURCES

## The Idea

George Orwell wrote the most famous slogan dealing with time and power. According to the thesis, he who controls the past also controls the future. Hence, control of the past was the magic word to the future. However, the whole thesis is rarely cited, and it raises the present to the fore: "Who controls the past,... controls the future: who controls the present controls the past" (Orwell 1949, 31). Although Orwell's maxim is usually understood as state control over an individual and as being connected to political systems, another reading is possible, i.e. an individual in terms of his or her own past.

The principal question in this research will be to analyze what the past means in the present and how it is interpreted in current politics. On the basis of the experiences of the 1990s, it is neither self evident that the past is merely something already gone nor that history belongs to the past. Since after 1989, metaphors such as 'the end of history', 'the rebirth of history' or 'awakening' have became famous. Moreover, metaphors such as 'returning', 'reckoning', 'nostalgia' and 'the rise of nationalism' have become common. It could be said that the past is a part of present political life and that history is not merely linear time which is left behind. In German there are even two concepts, *Geschichtsaufarbeitung* and *Vergangenheitsbewältigung,* used to describe getting on with the past, particularly the Nazi past[1].

In this study I deal with the question of how the Hungarian 'uprising' of 1956 has been present in Hungarian politics.[2] It is considered self-evident that in the Hungarian context the year 1956 had been taboo, beginning with the free research of the late 1980s which was a result of the system change. Another axiom was that the ruling Communist Party has consistently used history in its politics. Thus, in the 1990s the focus and the expectations in Hungary have mainly been to uncover the 'truth' from documents, to describe how things really were and to some extent to finally 'solve' the puzzle.

However, while the focus has generally been on the birth of the representative democracy and how to 'clear up' the past, I would like to reverse the question and question how '1956' has been both 'used' and 'misused' in politics. According to István Deák, Hungary offers an excellent example in the study of political justice and the political instrumentalism of history; how the past has been used, misused and constructed as a part of memory (1998, 60). This point of view solely offers the political use of history, and the demand to "open the archives" and "reveal the truth" appear not only as a means to 'solve' a problem, but also as a means for new legitimation.

In the case of Hungary, my thesis is that the most political debates since the end of the 1980s have not concerned the future, but the past. Thus, my thesis is that the collapse of communism did not undo the political use of the past, and that particularly in the case of '1956', politics has continued the war "by other means". In this sense, the debate of the recent past has set the tone for the transition as a whole. Moreover, contrary to common belief, the political usage of history in Hungary was not a phenomenon that was specific to communism. In this study there are several examples from earlier periods as well, which tend to suggest that the question has also been one of political culture in general.

My point is to question through the use of contemporary sources the way in which the understanding of 1956 has been transformed, which is both a political condition and political consequence in this case of the rewriting of history. My primary concern is the 'transformation' which took place during the transitional period of 1988-1989 and continued in the 'post-communist era' until the end of 1994. A few remarks on the discussion after 1994 will be done in the epilogue.

One of my points of departure for this volume is the idea that in the 1990s, history is partly made, but is also written and discussed in a new political situation. Particularly this is true in the former Eastern Bloc and countries, like Finland, which geographically was next to the Soviet Union and had a peculiar foreign policy during the Cold War. Thus, problems connected to the past have also been present in the political agendas of the 1990s. This is especially true when we are dealing with such tragic experiences as war or disputes, which might influence political thinking for decades to come.

The Truth Commission in South Africa, Cambodia struggling with the ghosts of the Red Khmers and the controversy surrounding the extradition of Augusto Pinochet are recent well-known examples of such problems. Central to these problems is the fact that it would have been impossible to solve them before the occurrence of a radical political change. Moral and political problems can also be found, for example, in dealing with the opening of archives, 'purges' of, or the restriction of 'men of the past' from participating in present political activity. Thus, the handling of a difficult past has been of immediate political significance.

Although my study deals with Hungary, it has similarities to other former state socialist countries, too. One of my general aims is to also contribute to the understanding of the history of political changes and transitions in general from the perspective of dealing with the past. Clearly, one way of dealing with such problems is to 'forget' the past, i.e. to draw a black line over the past as the first non-communist Polish Prime Minister Tadeusz Mazowiecki argued. However, in most cases the past has been reopened following a political change, as was also later the case in Poland.

When we are dealing with the past, we might ask: in what sense should politicians concentrate on injustices which have taken place in the past and which are frequently even referred to as "historical injustices"? In what sense were these issues later formulated or politicized in another political context, and in what sense did these problems already exist during the time in which there was no public discussion surrounding them? We certainly cannot speak in the name of the problems of a silent majority, because it has been silent as Murray Edelman (1977) formulated it.

My argument is that these phenomena include an inherent question of past oriented politics. Traditionally, i.e. since Aristotle's *The Art of Rhetoric*, the future has been seen as the tense of politics *par excellence*; political speeches were directed towards the future, whereas the juridical or forensic rhetoric concentrated on the past (Aristotle 1358b). However, not all courts judge equally, and the possible alternatives do exist, i.e. there is also room for political thinking in past judgements.

Thus, in principle, all forensic rhetoric also has a moment of politics, in that it deals *ex post* with the past. However, in a more concise sense I define past oriented politics as an attempt to reopen the past. Hence past oriented politics has much in common with history politics (*Geschichtspolitik*) (Wolfrum 1996) and history culture (*Geschichtskultur*) (Hardtwig 1990). Past oriented politics refers not only to the writing of history, but also to the experience that over the course of time 'time is turned into history', i.e. an issue is played out of the daily political agenda into a controversy of historians. However, turns like this are not final. Rather, any past events can, in principle, be reopened and returned to the agenda.

Thus, dealing with the past evidently includes political dimensions, and is not merely a question of writing history. It is a juridical, moral and political question, which could potentially possess many other dimensions that would be impossible to define in advance. Although analogies can be found between different countries, the past oriented politics is primarily connected to the peculiarities of each specific political culture, but also influences its international relations. The "weight of the past" (Welsh 1996,41) as its glory can be dealt with differently in various political cultures (cf. also Lowenthal 1988, xviii).

## Objectives

The Hungarian 'uprising' in 1956 was one of the most significant conflicts in Cold War Europe, and has also influenced political thinking. According to Péter Kende (1996), both a political scientist and participant in 1956, Hungary shook the Soviet Empire, ending its political illusions and serving as a model for forthcoming revolutions (Kende 1996, 165-181). The case of Hungary provides also an excellent example of history politics. As early as 1960, Leslie Bain argued "no event in recent history had been so much lied about, distorted and besmirched as the Hungarian Revolution" (cf. Lomax 1976, 17).

Thus, among different political groups and researchers, the case of Hungary in 1956 can be found, for example, in the argumentation of anarchists (*1956 Die Ungarische Revolution der Arbeiterräte* (1977)) and the New Left (Bill Lomax 1976). In addition, various conservative groups and extreme right wing authors (David Irving 1981) have used the case in their writings. With regard to political theorists, the role of, for example, Hannah Arendt (1963) may also be mentioned. Harshly speaking, as early as the 1950s, the interpretations have varied from that of repelling an attack of 'fascism' in Hungary to building some kind of 'national communism' or 'western democracy'.

The Hungarian 'rebellion' also took place in the middle of the Cold War but its central role in the political changes that occurred in Hungary during the end of the 1980s is less known. Moreover, the Hungarian case reveals a particular type of rhetorical argumentation: *what would have happened if?* In other words, a counter-factual analysis of an unfulfilled possibility, for which the consequences of its realization necessarily remain unknown. In the Hungarian case, this concerns the future which could have followed had the Soviet Union not intervened for the second time on November 4th, 1956. A counter-factual argument is also presupposed when János Kádár posed arguments in favour of the idea of a lesser evil, which implied that interference at the right time prevented the situation from worsening. This has correspondingly been the same argument that General Jaruzelski used in court in the 1990s (cf. also Rosenberg 1995, 178-222).

Although there are hundreds of books dealing with '1956', no one has thoroughly analyzed its connection either to the events which took place in 1989 or to present day Hungary. There are a few articles but even in the quite comprehensive handbooks published by a Hungarian research institute, The 1956 Institute, the story ends with the first free elections in 1990. Although my approach is new, it is not entirely unknown in Hungary: "1956 in relation to 1989" was one of the topics of a round table held during an international conference organized in Budapest in September 1996, i.e. close to the 40th anniversary of 1956 (cf. Évkönyv V 1996/1997, 305-308). Moreover, the tradition of 1956 in the transition was one of the themes in a congress held in June 1999, "Political Transition in Hungary 1989-1990".

Thus, my primary objective in this study is to make a basic analysis of the various existing interpretations of '1956' and their connections to present-day politics in Hungary. My aim is to deal with a broader basis of primary sources, as they are presented in their contemporary context, than any of the existing interpretations of the case have done. It is my view that by considering the current newspapers on a broader basis, I will be able to more aptly avoid the dangers of anachronism and *ex post* justification, which are clearly visible in the use of '1956' in daily political debates, but which are also by no means absent from Hungarian historiography. Although no 'source' speaks for itself, and although there are limits to the selection and analysis of the primary sources, my aim is to write one of the first comprehensive analysis of the transformation of the interpretations of '1956'. I consciously try to use my situation as a Finnish scholar who has lived in Hungary for several years, but whose academic frame of reference is still mainly based in Finnish political science, as a perspective in sketching a relatively detached view on this highly contested topic.

At the second level, the analysis of '1956' in Hungary will be used in this study as an example of a political culture, which is strongly connected to the past and in which the past is regularly used in political argumentation. The relationship between old and new is not only a question of post-communism, but is an acute question of political identity everywhere. On this second level I will also deal with the notions of time. According to many historians, changes in mentality occur more slowly than institutional alterations (cf. Le Goff 1978; Vovelle 1990). Hungarian state socialism largely relied on an idea of linear 'progressive' time, but in addition to this we can also speak of a cyclical notion of time as a strong element in Hungarian politics. It looks like that the mythical picture of '1848' has been a certain ideal pattern to interpret the present and even to 'repeat' history.

Thirdly, my study also deals with the collapse of communism in East Central Europe. The 'history of winners' is not unknown in the 1990s either and thus, there is one more level in this research. On the third level, I focus on the relationship between political argumentation, the writing of history and historical research. Indeed, historians, too, participated in the system changes that took place, new parties needed new ideologies and rehabilitated old ones.

Hence, on the basis of the Hungarian example I will concentrate on analyzing the means by which the various Hungarian political agents constructed the system changes in their argumentation. Those who participated in the system changes acted as historical beings through both their own experiences as well as those of others. Thus, my analysis differs from the 'mainstream' of studies on the transition from communism because of my use of a kind of 'rhetorical' approach. More specifically, I am using the perspectives of the 'rhetoric of history' or 'history politics' as a means of thematising some of the new aspects in the study of transition.

Therefore, I do not compare 1989 primarily as being horizontal to other transitional countries, but rather as vertical to earlier rapid changes in Hungary. However, I do also hope to say something about these other countries through this inter-cultural perspective. In fact, the experiential space of all three of the East Central European countries, Poland, Czechoslovakia and Hungary, includes 'interrupted revolutions' (cf. also Horváth 1992). These events surely influenced people's thoughts, although only two of them 'tolerated' critical conclusions of their recent past, as early as since 1988.

It is neither my intention to argue that '1956' in Hungary ultimately led to the change of the system (cf. NSZ 15/10/1996) nor that the collapse of communism would not have been possible without these 'rebellions'. Still, many other legitimate perspectives do exist. For example, the Gorbachev factor (Brown 1996) and a new history of winners is lurking behind any declarations concerning the decisive relevance of any given single factor, such as who threw the first stone.

After all, these 'rebellions' reminded communist leaders of their hazardous politics, and in most cases they led to a policy of raising the standard of living as opposed to the granting of political freedoms. Moreover, in Hungary, '1956' aided in the reorganising (szanálás) of the system as Melinda Kalmár (1998, 12) has formulated it. In spite of this, the memory of doing otherwise existed as an historical experience and was used by various political actors. Therefore, I argue that the reopening of '1956' was an essential part of the change in the Hungarian political system, and that it was also helpful in the realization of one of the easiest system changes in Europe.

There are some simple reasons to support this thesis. Firstly, the past, '1956' in particular, had been the main unifying factor between various dissident groups since the mid-1980s (Litván 1995, 5-12). Secondly, in February 1989, two issues were linked together when the Hungarian Socialist Workers' Party (Magyar Szocialista Munkáspárt, MSZMP) revaluated '1956' at the

16

same Central Committee session in which the decision in favour of a multi-party system was made. Thirdly, former Prime Minister Imre Nagy was symbolically reburied in June 1989. Finally, there is a direct connection to the present, because on October 23rd of 1989, i.e. on the anniversary of '1956', Hungary was declared a republic, which has since become one of Hungary's national holidays.

Hence, at this point I would like to introduce two theses which play a crucial role in this study. Firstly, after more than three decades, '1956' still played an essential part in the system changes which occurred in Hungary. Secondly, political legitimation with history did not vanish with the Kádár regime, but also existed in the multiparty system in the 1990s. A certain cyclical time with experiences and expectations has also played a part in political struggles after 1989.

This theme has not been limited to epideictic rhetoric, speeches for solemn occasion. For example, it was also included in debates regarding financial compensation following communist rule. Similarly, in post-communism '1956' was linked with the creation of screening laws, the policy on memorials, was used in the struggle of the electronic media etc. Since 1989 there have even been metaphorical attempts to continue political life from the point at which it was left on November 4th, 1956.

However, as a basis of legitimation, '1956' also faced resistance in the post-communist era, and references to it had to compete with other 'pasts' as well. Certain political groups and parties broke with the consensus and delved even further into the idealized past than 1956. In political debates, the "return to history" (Wolfrum 1996) became an issue, and in Hungary included the Horthy era, i.e. Hungary between the World Wars (cf. Litván 1993). These unfortunately and even dangerous historical divisions were politically essential in defining both expectations and, for example, the new positions of the new parties in the left-right spectre.

Although I systematically follow the Hungarian debate until the end of 1994, it does not mark the end of this discussion. Rather, we are dealing with a question of an ongoing argument, and even from the viewpoint of 1999, political debate has continued, although not with the same intensity as during the first years of the system change.[3] However, the system change of political institutions was mainly carried out at the end of 1994. In addition, the second democratic elections took place in 1994, in which the Hungarian Socialist Party (*Magyar Szocialista Párt*, MSZP) won an absolute majority. At that time a few different expectations concerning the country's future were also presented, including those concerning the fate of '1956'. To some extent, Rudolf L. Tőkés might be correct in referring to an 'end', when he argued that on October 23rd, 1994:

17

"... the revolution... was laid to final (?) rest... in the Budapest municipal cemetery on a macabre note. The principal speaker at the official commemoration was newly elected prime minister Gyula Horn – a self-confessed and unrepentant veteran of the postrevolutionary *pufajkás* armed vigilante squads. He called for national reconciliation and shared honour for all, communist and anticommunist, victims of the revolt." (Tőkés 1996, 419.)

Far-sightedly, Tőkés has put a question mark after the word final. Until now the Hungarian 1956 has belonged to recent history, i.e. to the time period in which contemporaries are still living. In this sense it is still "history living with us", which is only slowly becoming material solely dealt with in history books. Primarily, my thesis deals with the problems of understanding politics, although in a broader sense than in mainstream political science. My approach also makes use of some important elements of both cultural studies and historiography.

Regardless of whether or not we can speak of a particular Hungarian political rhetoric, there do exist some jargon and expressions which are culturally related, both in a general sense and with regard to the specific political culture, and which contribute to the creation of an ethos of 'being Hungarian'. In English translation, these expressions often lose much of their original emotional colour. For example, without further explication it might be quite difficult to grasp the meaning of the word *pufajkás*, which Tőkés used above in italics, as it lacks a direct counterpart in English. A *pufajkás* is an emotional term, because he was a man dressed in a Soviet type quilted jacket, a *pufajka*, and who helped the Soviet army after November 4, 1956.

## Sources

For a study like this, in which the main interest is in the 'rhetorical' analysis as opposed to the history of events, published sources are the most interesting type of primary sources. In my analysis of rapidly shifting views I have concentrated on newspapers, which have an 'obligation' to report on current events, whereas weeklies and monthlies can be more selective about what they report. Politicians' diaries and governmental White Books related to my topic have only been published fragmentarily, and parliamentary records only gain significance following the 1990 elections. The views expressed in newspapers are 'real', in the sense that they contribute to the debate and setting the agenda of political controversies, and they also offer the most precise venue for chronologically following the changes in the naming of events, streets and other symbols. I have also used newspapers as informational sources in the background chapters, however, their primary role has been in the formation of opinion.

I have read newspapers from three periods. The first deals with the crucial weeks of the 'uprising' in late October and early November of 1956. The second period, in which I have done a more selective reading, concerns the years 1956-1986. While my reading of the third period, from 1988-1994, was more intense and systematic.

With regard to the period of 'revolution' in 1956, I have read through all of the central Budapest newspapers as well as documents on radio programmes of the period, which have been published since 1989 in Hungary (cf. 1956 a sajtó tükrében... 1989; 1956 sajtója 1989; Kenedi 1989). As a background material, I also have used handbooks published in 1996 by the 1956 Institute.

Moreover, I have chosen the party organ *Népszabadság* as the main source of my analysis of how 1956 was present in certain anniversaries during the Kádár era. To keep the source material manageable, I have selected the October-November issues from the years 1961, 1966, 1971, 1976, 1981 and 1986. I have extended my research strategy to include three prominent Hungarian newspapers and one radio newspaper in dealing with material after May 1988. My systematic reading begins from May of 1988 because it was the year in which one of the oldest European leaders, János Kádár, was forced to resign from his position. As I mentioned earlier, I restrict my research to the end of 1994, primarily because the institutional system change was complete by then, but also because the period contains two elections. Thus, whether or not politics was present previous to May 1988 is not relevant here, because based on the source material the Kádár era cannot be thoroughly analyzed through these newspapers.

*Népszabadság* was an organ of the Central Committee of the Hungarian Socialist Workers' Party until October 1989. At that time the party changed its name to Hungarian Socialist Party (*Magyar Szocialista Párt*, MSZP) and at the same time the newspaper redefined its position to the newspaper of the Socialist Party. The second and present definition, 'national daily', was timed to coincide with the 1994 elections.[4] On the same day, when the Socialist majority in the newly elected parliament was confirmed, the new and thus more independent definition was made public. Moreover, *Magyar Nemzet* also became an independent daily in January of 1990. Until then it was the newspaper of the Patriotic People's Front (*Hazafias Népfront*), which was a "non-communist" social and cultural organisation closely related to the party. The third newspaper, *Magyar Hírlap*, was the organ of the Council of Ministers. It became an independent political daily in October-November of 1989.

19

Finally, *168 óra* is a weekly whose roots were in a radio programme broadcast on Saturdays. The first number was published in April of 1989.[5]

Thus, newspapers also emancipated themselves during the system change, although the same journalists continued to edit them. At that time they had to face the challenge of political credibility: was it better to have 'the long competence' obtained under the old system or less competence and new 'democratic faces'? In general, a new view of journalism seems to have emerged following the MSZMP's watershed conference in October of 1989; long speeches were no longer automatically published from A to Z, edited in order of importance and accompanied by a half-length picture.

However, as a result of their background, there is some question both as to whether the Hungarian newspapers were capable of providing a reliable picture of events, and whether they were the most appropriate representative channel for the mediation of information to the people. Indeed, according to an opinion poll from February 1992 (N=1000), the majority of Hungarians, 57%, did not read any nation-wide newspaper (NSZ 20/03/1992). In this sense, television and radio may be more representative, however, as opposed to the fleeting electronic moments of television or radio, written texts provide the reader with the opportunity to return and 'savour' the information contained in it.

According to the U.S. Freedom House, the Hungarian media reached the 'free' category up until 1993, after which it regressed as a result of the 1994 "media war" and the monopolization of the electronic media. Although the situation was corrected in 1995, Hungary remained three points short of the required level. (NSZ 18/05/1996).

In my analysis of the opinion formation, the concepts and rhetoric used in it, and the ideological criteria of the 'freedom', 'truthfulness' and 'representation' of the press are of minor significance. With regard to the day by day documentation of the political processes occurring during the system change, newspapers are an excellent source of material. They are representative of public opinion and frequently provide the initial interpretation and even construction of certain political events.

The contemporary material contained in the newspapers thus illustrates "the turn to the 21st century" as it was seen from the perspective of everyday political struggle. Although the specific focus here is '1956' and the system change, the text can also be read as a history of Hungarian system change in general, and is also illustrative of the history of newspapers, or, how the newspapers emancipated themselves from political guardianship. They also contain numerous references of political issues which have had political significance in Europe throughout the 1990s, such as anti-Semitism, the rise of nationalism, the extreme right, the "media war", the relativisation of the concepts 'left' and 'right' etc.

Hence, my analysis of the debates on '1956' also contains a narrative of the way in which newspapers began to form different views and opinions on how the non-conformist activities were visible in the public. When read 'between the lines', the picture since 1988 is supposed to be more significant than in underground *samizdats*. Although *samizdats* probably encouraged journalists to become more open, they belonged to small circles. For example, in September 1989, less than one percent of Hungarians were members of opposition organisations (Bruszt 1990), – or even less – although support of these organisations was much broader as will later become clear.

In general, the picture of the system change might be closer to more critical views; views which were more closely aligned with those of the opposition parties in 1990-1994. On several occasions government parties criticized influential newspapers for their partisan opinions (cf. also MN 07/03/ 1994). In addition, speculations on their political 'lines', such as those of *Magyar Nemzet*, which shifted closer to that of the government (NSZ 05/04/ 1993), can be read from he competing newspapers. Indeed, *Magyar Nemzet* understood the viewpoints of the government better than other newspapers. However, here the point is how to read newspapers, and I have compared them to each other in my rhetorical analysis. My conclusion is also an interpretation, and if one were to go through the some 7,000 newspapers which I used in my analysis, he or she might stress the argumentation differently.

In addition to my primary sources i.e. newspapers and published documents I of course also had to go through the most significant literature and articles published in Hungary in the 1990s. In this respect, I would like to mention here only a few of the many particularly valuable documents and studies. In 1992, Hungarian scholars published the studies resulting from the first underground conference dealing with 1956, held in Budapest close to the thirtieth anniversary of 1956: *Ötvenhatról nyolcvanhatban. Az 1956-os magyar forradalom előzményei, alakulása és utóélete című 1986. december 5-6-án Budapesten rendezett tanácskozás jegyzökönyve* (On fifty-six in eighty-six. The minutes of the meeting organized in Budapest on December 5-6th under the title: The Antecedents, Formation and Impacts of the 1956 Revolution).

Moreover, documents were also published in 1995 dealing with the Hungarian Democratic Opposition: *A Magyar Demokratikus Ellenzék (1968-1988). Dokumentumok* (Hungarian Democratic Opposition (1968-1988). Documents). Furthermore, two collections contain decisions and debates of the ruling party. Already in 1993, party resolutions from 1989 were published in: *A Magyar Szocialista Munkáspárt központi bizottságának 1989 évi jegyzőkönyvei. 1 kötet* (The 1989 Minutes of the Central Committee of the Hungarian Socialist Workers' Party. First Volume). In 1993 and 1994, more light was shed also on the early Kádár era when the minutes of the provisional Central Committee were edited and published in four volumes: *A Magyar Szocialista Munkáspárt ideiglenes vezető testületeinek jegyzőkönyvei I-IV* (The Minutes of the Provisional Leading Staff in the Hungarian Socialist Workers' Party I-IV).

To sum up, I am grateful to these studies and other primary sources, most of which have only become available to scholars in recent years. Still, I think that the value of this study is not dependent on them at decisive points for two reasons. I have used a huge amount of primary newspaper sources, which have helped me to gain a kind of inside view into the contemporary debate and which have been distinctly absent from the Hungarian discussion on the post-communist period. More importantly, my focus on the changes in political argumentation in the interpretations of '1956' allows me to sketch a detached 'rhetorical' perspective through which the debate can be used for the more general purposes of this study.

## The Story

In this study, my argument will be outlined and discussed in several steps which are illustrative of the multiple levels on which '1956' was thematised during the Kádár era and in post-communist Hungary. In practice, the levels are often strictly connected to each other, however, in order to sharpen the argument I have distinguished them from one another. Furthermore, in order to emphasize the points of my arguments concerning the interpretations and assessment of '1956', I have dealt with the history of each 'event' in a separate background chapter (see chapters three and six). The main function of these background chapters is to help those who are not specialists of Hungarian politics and history to comprehend the context within which my main arguments are located.

In the second chapter, I will present methodological remarks focusing on the relation between change, time, history and politics. Moreover, there are a few remarks on the crucial characters in earlier Hungarian history culture, which strengthen the later argumentation. Moreover, the Hungarian vocabulary on the concept revolution is contextually compared to the European vocabulary on the concept. The methodological background has been especially inspired by the works of Reinhart Koselleck, Chaïm Perelman and Hayden White, which I have used in order to specify my particular approach to a kind of 'political rhetoric of a past time'. In addition, two other studies also provided methodological inspiration. One was *Bastille*, written in 1990 by Rolf Reichardt and Hans-Jürgen Lüsebrink, in which they followed the symbolic dimensions of the French fortress from the 17th century up until recent decades. The other was Seppo Hentilä's (1994) analysis of the ideological debates between East and West Germany with regard to German history during the Cold War by utilising Hardtwig's concept of *Geschichtskultur*.

Thus, the main idea in the second chapter present the idea that Hungarian political culture contains specific strategies of rhetorical argumentation which utilise the past, particularly certain years, such as 1848, 1918 or 1956. These spaces of experience are not only linear but also cyclical, and there are many peculiar ways of dealing with the past. It seems as if in many ways there is an attempt to keep the past and the present joined, and that certain interpretations of the past also divide politics in the present, which is visible in the debate of '1956'.

In the third chapter, I will present a chronology of events in 1956 as they were discussed in the contemporary media. I follow the events from October to November day by day, and in particular concentrate on political speeches and newspapers, which attempted to define what was quite an unexpected political scenario. On the whole, my rhetorical and historical analysis of the day-to-day presentation of the events in the media constructs the background to which I relate later argumentation.

In the fourth chapter, I concentrate on the portrayal of '1956' as a counter-revolution during the Kádár regime. Using Reinhart Koselleck's (1988) triadic division of historiography, I pay particular attention to the time perspective in the argumentation. The first level of analysis deals with the White Books, i.e. official surveys published by The Information Bureau of the Council of Ministers of the Hungarian People's Republic in 1957. This material is frequently viewed as propaganda, however, I have methodically reread them by analyzing historical practices and discourses. Thereafter, I have chosen to analyze four history books published in Hungary between 1967-1986. In addition, two grammar school textbooks are included as an excursion.

In the fifth chapter, I also deal with further methods of remembering and forgetting in the historical writing of the Kádár regime. I have focused on several traces of the history culture, such as memorials, anniversaries, media etc,. The first subchapter focuses on the phenomena from the view of the government, and the other from the view of dissidents and non-conformists. In the sixth chapter, the focus shifts to the period following the time of János Kádár. I present in it an overview of the political developments from 1988 to 1994. For the sake of brevity I have chosen to focus on only certain points of the system change.

In the seventh chapter, we will begin by focusing on the results of the special history committee. In 1988, the ruling party appointed a committee whose task was to interpret the history of the previous four decades for the draft of the new party programme. The chapter also focuses on the political context and direct influence of the report on the multiparty system. Frequently, the reburial of former Prime Minister Imre Nagy in June of 1989 is seen as a decisive turn in the narrative. However, I would like place more stress on earlier events. It is essential to note that along with history, politicking also influenced the multiparty system. At first, one of the reformers in the MSZMP, Imre Pozsgay, used the report in the public against more conservative forces and single-handedly declared '1956' – the basis of the legitimation of the ruling party – an (popular) uprising. Secondly, the legalisation of the first democratic multiparty system in the former state socialist countries had distinct a connection to the revaluation of 1956. Here, the idea is that the 'premature' and surprising publication of the report finally persuaded the doubters in the Central Committee to accept the argument in favour of the multiparty system.

In the eight chapter, we will analyze the way in which political identity was construed through the past. After the free elections of 1990 the new political winners agreed about the symbolic naming of the past (the first law enacted in May 1990 dealt with the symbolic naming of '1956'). However, here the point is that they later disagreed about its nature and content. Thus, in this newly emerging political scenario the present was defined with the help of conceptions of the past. The new political actors, such as both new and revived parties, needed to create an identity of their own. The primary focus of this chapter is on the usage of the past in the elections of 1990, as well as the identities of the new members of parliament with regard to '1956'.

In the ninth chapter, I continue to expand the temporal perspective and discuss the analogies and symbols which were actualized during the system change. I would particularly like to stress the resurrection of the past through different symbols and analogies, which also influenced political expectations. Like national holidays, coats of arms are also symbols which have frequently been challenged during political upheavals. Moreover, reburials as a special Hungarian political tradition will be focused closer in this chapter. Imre Nagy's reburial in 1989 has its roots not only in 1956, but patterns could already be seen in the Austria-Hungary period. Memorials are also included in the category of analogies and symbols. In 1996, a statue of Imre Nagy was finally unveiled in Budapest, and since the system change a total of ca. 400 memorials have been built in the memory of 1956 (Boros 1997). Hence, I will analyze the debates and discussions surrounding the topics of both the erection of new memorials and the abolishment of certain old ones. Finally, I focus on the significance of street names as symbols, which have faced several political changes prior to the state socialist era, in 1956 and also during the Kádár era.

Contemporaries play the main role in the tenth chapter, which deals with disputes after 1989. In the late 1980s, organisations were born, which in one way or another were connected to '1956' and which appealed to political memory. The most important of them was *Történelmi Igazságtétel Bizottsága* (Committee for Historical Justice, TIB), which, above all, represented participants and the close relatives of people who had been executed. They played a role in the reburial of Imre Nagy, in the rehabilitation of other 'non-persons' and issues. Moreover, in Hungary it is quite striking to note that these organisations not only played a role as interest groups, but also piloted the system change on a more general.

The most controversial issue in the struggle about the past has been the question of historical and social justice. The question has been actualized in several former People's Democracies, but in Hungary it is mostly connected to the reprisals after 1956. The *Pufajkások* were neither accused nor punished of manslaughter during the Kádár era, and as they had occurred some twenty years earlier in 1971, the statute of limitations on the crimes had run out and the cases had become obsoleted. A difficult moral and juridical problem emerged as to whether or not these cases should be reopened following the system change. There were several options with regard to dealing with the past, ranging from naming the guilty persons to the enactment of retroactive laws, and these alternatives have essentially divided the government and the opposition since 1991.

This debate also had to address the more principal question facing a changing system; those who supported stricter means connected the question to the completion of the change, i.e. punishment equals and means system change. I will focus on two concrete examples and their consequences in more detail: the *Justitia* plan (1990-1991) and the screening law (1994). Moreover, another discussion is focused on this chapter; not only did the subject of punishment divide Hungary, but the future of the electronic media did as well.

In the eleventh chapter, the analysis of the past in relation to politics is put under the magnifying glass. As I have argued earlier, both the recent past and even earlier history were construed as a part of political identities and debates. These debates on history were not found exclusively on the level of contemporaries, veterans or politicians, but also on the level of research and researchers. The change of the system provided a 'once in a lifetime' opportunity, in which those roles were combined in several cases. Politicians interpreted history, but prominent historians also became politicians and members of parliament. In this chapter, I focus on the political role of research and researchers, and argue that research work also facilitated a sense of trust in the new democracy. In a separate subchapter, I will further illustrate research work in connection to the demands of punishment and researchers' views surrounding this debate.

In the twelfth chapter, I will begin by making some concluding remarks. The past must be made history, which is a far broader question than merely writing history. In this study I have also located other issues, such as the naming of the past and the present, repetitive anniversaries, identity and, in a sense, both positive and negative remembering. In the conclusion, I have analyzed the political use of the past in general as well as its significance in writing history. I will also assess in more general terms my initial theses, as well as the potential significance of the 'results' to my problematic at the different levels which I have sketched above.

# II FROM THE PAST TO THE PRESENCE OF POLITICS

In this chapter, I make a few crucial remarks on the concepts of change, time, history and politics. It is important to note that, time is no longer an entity in which politics only takes place *in der Zeit*, but also occurs in different experiences of time *durch die Zeit* (cf. Koselleck 1989, 321). In this study, what this implies is that not only did the Hungarian '1956' lack 'enough' time, but also that this past experience later comes to be valued from several political contexts by various political agents.

Thus, my study concentrates on two specific changes: the year 1956 and the tradition of '1956' as a part of the Hungarian political transition since the late 1980s. Secondly, there is time itself, which has both quantitative and qualitative dimensions. In this sense, time is not only linear but also cyclical, which on the one hand refers to how to value experiences and the past, while on the other hand pertains, for example, to certain TimeSpaces (Boyarin 1994). In Hungary, political dimensions can be found in concrete situations and in how people deal with the past: whether they attempt to dissociate themselves from it, build continuities, remember, forget or even attempt to repeat and return to the past.

Historical writing also implies the valuing and signification of the past in certain temporal political contexts. Fourthly, I examine the presence of politics, because the past is valued not only by historians – who are also political agents – but is also valued judicially, symbolically, artistically, by politicians and citizens, etc. In such contexts, the concepts of reconciliation and forgetting are significant. Thus, in this chapter I also shift to the topics of history culture and history politics, a certain 'use' and 'misuse' of the past, which I classify as belonging to a particular past oriented politics.

## Change

According to Timothy Garton Ash, the change in 1989 took ten years in Poland, fell to ten months in Hungary, then to ten weeks in the former German

Democratic Republic and finally ten days in Czechoslovakia (1990, 78). Thus, the duration of change can vary considerably, and gradual changes can also occur within such a short period of time; history books describe a six-day war, and John Reed wrote about the "ten days that shook the world" in the context of the Russian Revolution.

When discussing political changes, it is evident that they can take place slowly as 'reforms' or 'evolution', or more swiftly in the form of 'revolutions'. Revolution primarily refers to a concrete historical event. However, it is impossible for this concept to remain analytically pure; it collects different cognitive turbidity as emotions and enthusiasm of it. Nor does there exist a consistent theory of modern revolution although there are classical examples as Russia and China on the 20th century (Dunn 1989).

In late medieval times, the Latin word *revolutio* referred to the transmigration of souls and to turning over. The original 'turn over' refers to the tombstone of Jesus. The operation itself, the resurrection, was referred to as an uprising (cf. The Oxford English Dictionary 1989). In politics, *revolutio* referred primarily to the constant circulation of systems of governments and secondly to turning back (*re*) (Koselleck 1979; Arendt 1963). Through the French Revolution the concept acquired the meaning of consciously aspiring to a new and better future. The concept also became fragmented as a result of the emergence of counter-concepts such as 'counter-revolution' and 'reaction' (Koselleck 1984). Although the counter-concepts were frequently connected to political restoration, they do not necessarily refer to counter-revolution in the Arendtian sense. Through the concept of counter-revolution, Thomas Paine wanted to return to an earlier period, when political rights and freedoms still existed in America (Arendt 1973, 43-45).

Thus, hereafter the first problem deals with name changes, and can begin with the separation of current names and names assigned later. There are, for example, several current names used to describe 'the change' which has taken place in the former Soviet Bloc throughout the last ten years. In western literature the terms vary from rebirth and refolution (= reform + revolution) to reformation and transformation, negotiated revolution, revolutionary change and revolution (cf. Bozóki 1993). Also, the terms velvet revolution and transition have appeared in western vocabularies to define the ongoing process. Thus, it is impossible to locate one representative term to define the wide variation in the former Eastern Bloc.

However, in Hungary, not only was it necessary to name the present, but here the argument is that the entire process culminated in the naming of past events. In western literature 1956 in Hungary is most commonly referred to as an uprising or revolution, although other terms such as revolt, rebellion, crisis, incident, affair and fight for freedom were also used. For example, in a

United Nations report (1957), Hungary was defined as a "...spontaneous uprising, caused by long-standing grievances." (Report of the special... (I) 1957, 34). The most commonly used name in the report is uprising, although the term revolution is also hinted at to some extent.[6] On the whole, the term that would most precisely describe the Hungarian events would be an 'interrupted revolution' (befejezetlen forradalom), which, however, has not become established in public use.

Whether or not we can also unambiguously refer to the Hungarian '1956' as a revolution is dependent upon the decision regarding whether a failed revolution can also be considered a revolution. If we conclude that only a successful revolution can be considered a revolution, then 1989 can be referred to as a revolution. However, this does not apply in the present Hungarian logic: the revolution occurred in the past, while the question was one of a system change in the present. The concept is a direct translation of the Hungarian word rendszerváltás[7] and is the most commonly used term in current newspapers. Although other words are included in the vocabulary of system change (A rendszerváltás szótára, 1992) such as "negotiated revolution" (tárgyalásos forradalom), "quiet revolution" (csendes forradalom) and "breakthrough" (átmenet), their use has not become established.

Thus, when a political system is changed an actor must define it, although this can only be done through concepts of the past, in historical terms and by recognizing analogies and variations. Thus, names are not intrinsic, rather they must be chosen and assigned. Frequently, the naming of events belongs to the rhetorical struggle of power, in which event are valued, signified and symbolized on the basis of past experiences[8]. In this sense they not only define, but also oust political agents and even canonize events. Although some names seem to be more acceptable than the others, individuals have the right to use different names on the basis of their own experiences.

Secondly, there is the question of the temporal location of a change, in which the beginning and the end of the change are often problematic. In 1968 in Prague, it is said that the "normalisation" began on the seventh day, because it was on that day that parking fines began to be collected again (Karjalainen 1969, 23). When the Hungarian parliament legally enacted the new national days (VII/1991), it simultaneously defined them. According to the law, the revolution and fight for freedom began on 23rd October, when students took to the streets in demonstration of their solidarity with Polish students. Moreover, the same law defined the 23rd of October as the day on which Hungary was declared a republic in 1989, although there had already been political activity both in 1956 and 1989 previous to these days. The same problem emerges in defining ends. In Hungary, the day of the second Soviet invasion on November 4th has became a symbol, although armed struggles continued after that.

Nevertheless, in 1989 it still took more than sixth months for the first freely elected parliament to assemble in May of 1990. However, even this does not necessarily imply change, and it leads us to the third problem, i.e. *when* and *in what sense* the system has changed. This completion of the system has acquired current political significance since then and also deals with the question of *what* has actually changed.

Thus, symbols and political institutions such as laws and parliament have the potential to change quite rapidly, while changes in mentality occur much more slowly. Generals frequently fight previous wars and, according to Jacques Le Goff, the vocabulary of a car driver resembles that of a horse driver. Similarly, factory workers share the mentality of their peasant fathers and grandfathers (Le Goff 1978, 244-262). Following *risorgimento*, Italians also had to be 'created', and Hungary did not become "a land of iron and steel" overnight. The mentality of the Horthy era was still present during the period of state socialism (cf. also Schöpflin 1977).

Following the same logic, the communist era did not completely end at the turn of the decade, but rather a new temporal definition came into being: *post*-communism. On the one hand, it has been added to former state parties, but in a broader sense it refers not only to a party and a time, but also to a space. Thus, it is assumed hereafter that change progresses from names and naming, to symbols, to elites, and then finally – if we are freely permitted to adapt Bertold Brecht's cynical comment – to the changing of the people. In this sense I have found Bozóki's notion of politics too narrow, when he argued that the political system change had already been accomplished, while the social and economic changes had not (MN 12/06/1991).

# Time

Until now we have attempted to problematize change *in der Zeit*, although it also occurs *durch die Zeit*. An adult is well acquainted with the limitations of time, and a year is 'shorter' for an adult than, for example, for a seven year old child. Thus, in attempting to get 'into' the change I have first separated quantitative time (*how long ago, how soon* or *how much remains*) from quantitative time, i.e. how time is experienced and valued. New generations were born in Hungary after 1956, and since 1989 '1956' has primarily been a matter associated with the middle-age and ageing population. However, in politics there is a general 'delay': until 1998 all Hungarian Prime Ministers and Presidents have had personal experiences from the year 1956.

Secondly, there is linear and cyclical time, in which a given past event increasingly fades with every passing second. Historian Donald Cameron Watt uses the metaphor of a fast car, i.e. a person looks backwards toward an immobile object, which quickly fades away (Watt 1991, 15). Moreover, in cyclical quantitative time various anniversaries and celebrations occur and are repeated, which to some extent keeps the past in the present. Finally, on a subjective level, we can cyclically return to the past or linearly attempt to keep it at a distance, as the 'past'.

Hence, when we are discussing an individual, the past might come to mind or (s)he may metaphorically attempt to return to the past through memories. When a person *would like to* return to the past, the question surrounds the willingness to recall and call the past back to mind. On the other hand, the past could also come to mind despite the fact that it may be unwelcome or an attempt to dent it may have been made. Secondly, on a public level the question is frequently present through metaphors like 'returning to the past' or 'the past is returning'. The first metaphor frequently refers to a romantic ideal or an unattained "Golden Age".

In a sense, political activity includes the idea that a community is reminiscent of, rehabilitates or canonizes a given event or political period. However, there are inherent risks in this thought, which is expressed in an English proverb: "don't dwell on the past, think to the future". In these cases a person might already be 'behind the times', dramatically facing the future.

In this research, the metaphor of 'returning to the past' requires more political activity than 'the past is returning'. In the latter case, political expectation concerns more the 'other' people', 'them'. Thus, those, who 'return to the past' might already be 'restoring the past'. This restoration might be expressed as a threat, although it is frequently directed at political 'mud-slinging'.

On the whole, a unique singular experience is impossible to repeat or to resurrect (Koselleck 1988, 19-22). The past does not return as such, but rather belongs to political argumentation as a component of temporalization. Expectations of the future are sufficient for making analogies with 'returning' and 'restoring'. Here, political dimensions are found in the way in which people deal with the past in concrete situations; whether they attempt to free themselves of it and dissociate from it, build continuities, remember and forget or even attempt to repeat and return to the past.

Thus, in linear time October-November of 1956 was merely a few days in autumn of 1956, while on a personal level the days varied from a watershed, to an original state, to a fleeting disorder, a basis for the new democracy and so on. Furthermore, we may suppose that the value of October-November of 1956 from the perspective of the "peep-holes" of 1957 has quite a different significance than it did, for example, forty years later.

31

In the constructions of human time, the past can both be present in the present moment and also influence expectations of the future. According to Reinhart Koselleck, experiences belong to the present, "experience is present past, whose events have been incorporated and can be remembered" (Koselleck 1985, 272). The present past is not necessarily conscious, because rational reworking can be included in unconscious modes of conduct, which do not necessarily have to be present in awareness. Koselleck defined this category as the "space of experience" (*Erfahrungsraum*), which also includes an element of alien experience contained and preserved in experience by generations or institutions. (Ibid., 271-272). Thus, our experiences are not only 'ours', but are also learned and filtered through other people and institutions, such as the media and education systems.

However, expectations of the future are a part of the present, too: "person-specific and interpersonal expectation also takes place in the today; it is the future made present; it directs itself to the not-yet, to the non-experienced, to that which is to be revealed." Hopes, fears, wishes and desires etc., enter to into expectation, the "horizon of expectation" (*Erwartungshorizont*), and constitute it. (Ibid.). Experience and expectation are inter-linked, because there is no expectation without experience and *vice versa*. These two concepts are categories which are appropriate in the treatment of historical time. (Koselleck 1985, 269-270).

Hence, when we focus on the Hungary of 1956, we are dealing with an event of brief duration, but which has been commemorated and has remained a memory for over forty years. Dramatic historical events 'last' even longer. In France, the Revolution of 1789 influenced French politics for centuries, through the Bourbon restoration of 1815, extending even until the Fourth Republic in 1946 (Watt 1991, 13).

Thus, experiences of the past appear in the present and have to do with expectations of future. Hungary has experienced several political setbacks, and I suppose that this space of experience has also influenced cyclical political thought. Moreover, we might assume that especially rapid changes also include the expectation of 'turning back'. Hence, we must also face the problem of how to evaluate and deal with the past in a given present. Two post-1956 political contexts can be identified. First, the period of 'frozen socialism', which after 1956 continued in 'a reformed form'. Secondly, I have systematically focused on a more turbulent period, beginning in 1988. Hence, it is evident that both contexts have influenced ways of dealing with and reacting to the past.

The ongoing discussion also includes temporal limits which particularly refer to the state socialist era, such as *félmúlt* ('half-past') and *befejezetlen múlt* ('unfinished past'). In addition, the Hungarian language does not include the perfect tense, but only has one past tense, i.e. imperfect. Nevertheless, a translation from one dictionary is not sufficient: *félmúlt* means imperfect and *befejezett múlt* is the past perfect (cf. Országh 1998). On the contrary, there is no past as perfect, not as finished and 'perfect', and the space of experience remains open in peoples' minds.

## History

Traditionally, current or contemporary history has also been separated from other histories. In France, *histoire contemporaine* could refer to a time span encompassing over 200 years, while British contemporary history is frequently seen as beginning in 1832. In this sense, the Hungarian '1956' can hardly be considered current history and includes several peculiarities. The German *Zeitgeschichte* can be seen as analogous, in that the *Institut für Zeitgeschichte* was founded in München in 1952. In Hungary, a special Institute of 1956 was founded during the system change, and a specific Historical Office (*Történelmi Hivatal*) was established in 1997.

History itself is a broad concept (cf. Koselleck 1975, 593-594). For example, Gordon N. Carpenter compiled some 3,000 definitions of the term history from the perspective of politicians, researchers, writers etc. in a dictionary entitled *The Meaning of History* (Carper 1991,xii). Frank Füredi (1992) separates History and history, the first also including the future oriented broad narrative, while the latter refers to critical historical thinking (from different levels of history, see also Karlsson 1999). It is generally assumed that history repeats itself, teaches or absolves, as Fidel Castro noted following an unsuccessful assault on the Moncada Barracks. Nor is it a coincidence that the Hungarian word *kormány* (government) is synonymous for steering wheel. Rear admiral Miklós Horthy, *kormányzó* (regent, governor), was presented at sea (of history) strongly clutching the rudder (cf. A magyarok krónikája 1996, 568).

The primary definition of the word history, *történelem*, found in a Hungarian dictionary (1962) is a successive series of most important events. Secondly, it means a story which is loyal to facts. Thirdly, it refers to science and fourthly, is a school subject. Finally, it means the future, posterity, from which history as a tribunal is given as an example.[9] Moreover, subjects in history were found rather supreme and sublime level: "mankind, some people, nation, country or bigger than that". Thus, a series of past events, research and its results were combined (cf. Koselleck 1975). In this sense, this old view it does not differ from, for example, the definition found in a Finnish encyclopaedia from the same time period (Uusi tietosanakirja 1961, 820-821).

Hereafter the word history refers solely to the written and thus signified past. Everybody and everything has a past, although not necessarily a history that is constructed from sources. Thus, history is selected from the past and written down, and historians are an essential part of this process, in which history will be constructed from the past.

According to Reinhart Koselleck (1988), every *Historie* is either directly or indirectly related to experience. The first type, primary experience, (*Urerfahrung*) contains a moment of surprise and characteristically appears differently than thought. However, people can have previous experiences and are not easily surprised, i.e. an experience is also cumulated when remembered and brought to mind. Koselleck argues that the biological generations exist in addition to political generations. Thus, whatever the *Zeitgeist* may be, it is connected with generations. However, it would be wrong to limit the writing of history only to living generations, because the experience (*Erfahrungswandel*) changes more slowly than it does through single events and generations. In addition, there is the possibility that the whole system might change, such as the collapse of the Roman Empire (Koselleck 1988, 19-25).

In Hungary, a particular '1956' generation can be distinguished, comprised of individuals who personally participated in the events. As György Marosán notes in the title of his 1989 memoirs, the "witnesses are still alive". Thus, the problem becomes how to write a history, which on one hand is able to surpass all three types of experience, while integrating them on the other hand. Therefore, Koselleck separates three categories of writing history: *Aufschreiben*, *Fortschreiben* and *Umschreiben*. *Aufschreiben*, writing down is the first act, which is eventually corrected and completed by *Fortschreiben*, writing forward. Finally, *Umschreiben*, re-writing history corrigies both and allows for a new type of consciously re-written history (Koselleck 1988, 26).

The first phase of writing history is constructed from stories and writings, for example, from contemporary chronicles, which were predominant until the 18th century. In the Hungarian case, oral history belongs to the category of, for example, the 'four reasons', published in December 1956 by the Central Committee of the MSZMP, and the White Books published the following year. According to Koselleck, the basic theme has frequently dealt with preserving experience and memory; methods came into the picture only when specific questions were answered. Since Antiquity, questions of 'what was the case' and 'how did it happen' were asked. However, in searching for singularity (*Einmaligkeit*) the hypothetical question of 'how something might happen' must also be asked, i.e. the uniqueness in relation to the larger temporal base (*langfristige Gründe*) (Ibid., 29-32).

Secondly, temporal perspective could be extended and other sciences included in order to strengthen the argumentation. Comparison, analogies and parallels become tools when history is written forward. People easily forget details and allow their own experiences to influence the sources they use. The simplest way is to write, to 'copy' history to an end (*Ab-* and *Ausschreiben*). (Ibid., 32-37). The third stage is the re-writing of history, which is as unique (*einmalig*) as the first phase. It is an innovative protest to previously written history and corresponds to a change in the experience, which also directs us to new experiences.[10] It is impossible for everything to be revised, however, to the extent to which it can be done, new methods must be used. In addition, the first two methods will simultaneously be revalued. For example, Thucydides completed as opposed to changed the picture of the Persian Wars, but more importantly, he indicated the way in which history can be re-written. He was the first to illustrate the difference between doing and saying, between *logoi* and *erga*. Even the most comprehensive sources fall short of the argumentation regarding this. (Ibid., 42-43).

According to Koselleck, there are three possibilities, motives to re-write history:

1. New evidence could offer new information or bring old information to light.
2. New questions are opened and aid in the location of new perspectives.
3. Evidence can be re-read and re-interpreted.

All three of these possibilities are frequently combined in the present praxis. Evidence is found and new questions asked. With regard to the change of a system, the past will be re-written or there will be the possibility to re-write it. New history attempts to also explain new experiences (Ibid., 47). In Hungary, the re-writing of history was initiated in 1988 by the Pozsgay Committee, which re-researched the period of socialist Hungary for a new party programme draft.

According to Reinhart Koselleck (1988), the question of *who* is writing history involves the history of winners, which I also use to describe the attempts to interpret 1956 during the Kádár era. According to Koselleck, the *Geschichte* of 'winners' (*Sieger*) exists, but *Historie* comes from the 'losers' (*Besiegten*). Somehow 'winners' make history, but the history of the 'losers' will survive in the long run. Longer structures remain less analyzed but historians, who tend to come from the circle of 'winners', are more easily inclined to find longer ex-post-teleology to short successes. On the contrary, the primal experience of the 'losers' is to find out why everything went otherwise than was planned or expected. (Ibid., 51-52).

A potential objection has to be explicated, which may come from an historian who denies being either a 'winner' or a 'loser'. Still, a great deal of

Koselleck's examples, such as Herodotus, Thucydides, Polybius, Augustine of Hippo, Machiavelli and Marx did not belong to the winners of their time. As a result, they were able to develop long lasting methods (Ibid., 53-60). For an historian, the history of winners is a threat, which professionals attempt to avoid. Still, part of the work of a professional is to reflect upon and weigh his or her own acts in connection to the *present* webs of political power.

For example, Frank R. Ankersmit, who in the 1980s supported a radical linguistic interpretation of narrative, has stressed the distinction between research work and other writings of history. Ankersmit himself used the term historical writing, which is separated from historiography (Ankersmit 1992; cit. Mylly 1995, 57). Historical writing can be based on imagination, while historiography with source material. Literature can also be quite well-based on sources and thus, the division is not absolute. However, there is more professional control in historiography than there is in historical writing in general (cf. also Kalela 1993, 261-262). In state socialist Hungary, control was pursued particularly through a party, its guardianship and its publishers.

Merely separating historical writing and historiography does not exonerate proper historians from responsibility either. They also deal with texts, language and interpretation, and construct plots in the narrative as well. According to Hayden White, there is no proper history without metahistory and interpretation. Metahistory is a web of commitments, which "the historian makes in the course of his interpretation on the aesthetic, cognitive and ethical levels..." (White 1978, 71). In White's notion, the metahistoric view justifies strategies of interpretation as emplotment and modes of explanation. Thus, also narrative itself is a certain ideological instrument (White 1989, 81), although the writer not necessarily use it in that sense.

Therefore, narrativity becomes problematic when the researcher fails to explicate his or her methodological starting points, hypotheses and what has been incorporated into and excluded from the research. Hence, the text is rather an argumentation, which deals with a certain defined question. The researcher construes a line of argumentation which is based on reconstruction (cf. Mylly 1995). Thus, history is written on the basis of interpreted documents, and this interpretation, or 'reading', takes place at a certain time through the experiences of writers.

Moreover, historians agree that the contemporary context is one of the crucial elements of their reconstruction. However, the work is not limited to the reconstruction of the contemporary world, in that the other role of the work is to reach the present context. The argumentation must also be presented to a specific audience (cf. Kalela 1993). Thus, on the basis of the new rhetoric (Perelman 1982), I would like to argue that there is a struggle between the writer and audience regarding persuasion. Proper research of propaganda has also moved from the dichotomous concept of an active speaker and passive recipient toward the concept of an audience (Propaganda…1987, 3-4).

The argument does not consist merely of logos, but also includes ethos and pathos, and thus the breadth of the acceptance of the results is not completely dependent upon the historian. Rather, the question is one of what a given audience accepts in a particular moment of time. For example, in Hungary, political language has changed rapidly over the past ten years. Could present audiences understand the past or do they read it with the language of their own time?

There is a gap between the past and the present, and a tension emerges in regarding the attempt to turn the past into present audiences and language. The work of an historian is to explicate the dialogue of this tension, as well as to analyze the *present* context of his or her own writing. Thus, the historian not only researches the past, but also the present. Hence, I consider historical writing and research to be political acts which have (inherent) political significance and influence. When forensic rhetoric deals with history, an historian acts not only in the capacity of judge, but also as prosecutor and defender of an argument. One of the questions I shall address below is whether this presents a limitation or possibility.

## The Presence of Politics

As I have already mentioned in the introduction, dealing with the past is a far more complex problem than the question of historiography. Moral and political problems can be found, for example, in dealing with opening archives following political changes, 'purges' or the restriction of 'men of the past' from participating in present politics. Certainly all countries have skeletons in their closets, and debates on dramatic events and being 'right' last for decades.

Thus, we have now come to the judgement of the past, which always takes place in the present and in a certain political context (cf. also Collingwood 1963, 242). History as a tribunal was already mentioned, and in Aristotelian rhetoric, only a particular kind of forensic rhetoric deals with the past. There are two arts of forensic rhetoric: defending and accusing, which both also utilise arguments such as justice, injustice, honesty and disgracefulness. In addition, there is the judge, who possesses the right to settle a given question (Aristotle 1358b).

However, historians themselves also play a role in this rhetorical discussion. According to David Cameron Watt, current history always contains a political element which is written by proper historians as well. This element could weaken over the course of time, yet it still belongs to current history as long as there are researchers who choose to rattle these skeletons for their own purposes (Watt 1991, 13).

Watt defines the category of proper historians as also including those eye-witnesses who document 'the first stories', such as civil servants, political commentators and the participants of political disputes (1991, 15). In Hungary, this not only includes 1956, but also the system change in general. In Watt's theory, secondly, the memories of participants emerge following temporal distance. At this point, guilt and innocence become essential to the authors, who frequently defend themselves and accuse their opponents. Watt's second period is also a period of real trials and legal proceedings. Among these debates, an historian more often occupies the role of political prosecutor and defence counsel than impartial researcher (Ibid., 15-16).

Thirdly, current history loses its polemic character while myths, misunderstandings and moral arguments frequently become commonly accepted truths and 'orthodoxy'. Opening the archives is the fourth step following the testimonies of memories and eye-witnesses. Arguments such as "the truth must finally be revealed" are quite common. This phase also includes the emergence of 'instant historians', who are interested in publishing the most recently found documents as soon as possible. On the fifth level come those with more scientific ambitions, who burrow through the archives searching for contradictions between generally accepted interpretations and these new documents. Their aim is to liberate the past from earlier misunderstandings, mistakes and myths. Finally, the most scientific level, the sixth level, includes a deeper understanding of where earlier interpreters and interpretations have gone awry (Ibid., 16-18).

The point here is that most of the writers who participate in the first four phases research the past from a point of view that is connected to their immediate present. Watt argued that first narration, memories, accepted truths and instant histories focus on the past from a perspective which is tightly bound to their immediate present. The past is not read using its own specific terms, but through concepts of the present (Ibid.). Watt describes the phenomenon as 'present politics projected into the past', which is also analogous to Pokrovsky's notion of history.

Thus, both historical writing and the work of historians possess political significance. On one hand, historians as specialists gather events from people whose use for them is based solely in remembrance, and who 'misuse' them, i.e. treat historical events like they continue to be a memory of living men (cf. White 1989, 79-80). On the other hand, historians are also occasionally politicians, who are an integral part of the ongoing discussion and who can create politics in their studies. Moreover, historians are able to more openly participate in politics as active citizens. During the system change, dozens of Hungarian historians found new careers as politicians.

However, historians do not have 'exclusive rights' to the past, in that, for example, politicians also interpret history and the past in their speeches. For example, Dieter Langewiesche (1992) noted that all six presidents of the Federal Republic of Germany informed about and interpreted the German past in speeches made to the public (1992, 42-45). Thus, when we discuss the connection between the past and politics, it is evident that it is not only related to historians and politicians, but to all human beings.

Although the past has been used in political argumentation since Antiquity, modern 'historia magistra vitae' has offered a utilitarian political usage. The struggle of supremacy and the duration of domination remain struggles over history (Wolfrum 1996, 376; Langewiesche 1992; Habermas 1986). According to Hayden White, the way in which "one makes sense of history is important in determining what politics one will credit as realistic, practicable, and socially responsible" (1989, 73). Thus, I would say that yes, history does educate, but the problem is how to interpret the adaptations into practice; the paradigm of Munich was not merely a dilemma faced by Anthony Eden to interpret Suez in 1956. Historical analogy remains a current rhetorical figure to interpret the present at the end of the 1990s as well.

Moreover, not only does the past influence present politics, but the political use of the past (öffentlicher Gebrauch der Historie) in the sense of identity is also influential. In the 1980s Jürgen Habermas noticed changes in attitudes, which concerned political stands against the Nazi-past in the Federal Republic of Germany. Habermas noted new attitudes toward certain anniversaries, and above all toward the official state visit of US President Ronald Reagan, who commemorated fallen soldiers at the Bitburg Cemetery (Habermas 1986). Habermas' point connected the past to present politics: with the help of a few historians, the right-wing government attempted to revise the controversial picture of the recent German past (Ibid.; Hentilä 1994, 269-279).

The debate was not solely carried out amongst historians, but also occurred in public as part of history culture (Geschichtskultur). According to Wolfgang Hardtwig, the concept refers to undefined and various forms of keeping the past in the present.[11] For Hardtwig himself, Geschichtskultur is a general, superior concept, and his book contains articles dealing with history as a science, images of history, political symbols, mentality or memorials and anniversaries (1990, 5).

Moreover, in this study I use a concept history politics (Geschichtspolitik). The concept deals with history as politics (Geschichte als Politikum) and was used by Edgar Wolfrum (1996). According to Wolfrum, in history politics the past is used to achieve mobilised, politicized or legitimized effects in the public.[12] These effects might be found, for example, in discussions surrounding identity, nation, rituals, memorial days etc. (Wolfrum 1996, 377). In Kádár's Hungary, this concerns not only the first, 'official' public, but also the second, 'unofficial' public (Hankiss 1989, 121).

My study concerns Hungary, and according to Welsh, "the weight of the past" is particularly significant true in the 'transitional' countries (Welsh 1996, 419). Particularly in those societies dealing with recent past, the political question is broader and more complicated than mere historical writing. There are also obvious consequences, such as whether the policy of reconciliation will work, and if so how soon it will begin to work. Reconciliation requires not only remembering, but also forgetting. There are, however, always individuals who are eager to remember, reminisce over and commemorate the past.

In this study, I also separate the *strategies of remembering and forgetting*, in other words, how the attempt is made to keep a particular event in the present. An individual has personal memories, could remember and forget, recall, nostalgize or even idealize these memories, which influence on situations of choices, including politics. Next, individual memories and experiences can be narrated and mediated, after which they become stories which are told to different audiences. As White (1987) noted, these audiences can themselves be based on memory or commemoration, and their sole purpose is remembrance.

On the one hand, remembrance and commemoration are (tools) used in order to unite audiences. For example, jointly divided experiences of the past and a shared, common history are still one of the main ideals of a nation state.[13] However, remembrance (memories) and commemoration can potentially have the effect of separating people as well. An individual memory might contradict collective memories, and as such remembering becomes a social and political act done by various collectives and communities. Not only do 'ideological state apparata', such as schools, participate in the act of remembering, but so do unofficial networks, such as home and friends.

In general, remembering and forgetting (cf. Middleton and Edwards 1990) have to do with the politics of memory, a concept used by Comay (1990), Rappaport (1990) and Boyarin (1994). According to Boyarin's hypothesis, the politics of memory can be identified with identity, as they are almost conceptually identical (Boyarin 1994, 23). Habermas, too, concluded in *Historikerstreit* that the question was one of identity building (Habermas 1986; Hentilä 1994, 269-279). In Germany, the government was expected to build a new identity, which was also done through the politics of memory and 'forgetting'.

Hence, although they are more difficult to define, there are more or less counter-concepts, 'forgetting' and 'forgotten', to the concept of 'remembering'. Something is always 'forgotten' for someone. Here, however, we are

40

discussing politics, in which matters which have been 'forgotten' or silenced could also be the result of persuasion and coercion. Therefore, another distinction is made: 'reminding' and 'making to forget'. 'Reminding' attempts to open and re-open experience, while 'making to forget' consciously does the opposite through denial and censorship, for example. However, these two concepts require more significant political activity and thus are not as accidental or arbitrary as 'remembering' and 'forgetting'. The acts of commemoration and remembrance might already belong to reminding.

In addition, I also separate and distinguish between positive and negative remembrance. Depending on the subject, numerous rewards, such as decorations, pensions or compensations, can be granted following remembrance. On the other hand, negative remembrance includes the possibility both that earlier rewards may be revoked and legal proceedings may be taken against an individual. Thus, it is better to ask *who* wants to remember and reminisce; *who* wants to forget, and finally *why* one would like to forget.

Finally, 'forgetting' could also be a part of compromise and reconciliation. On the one hand, compromise and reconciliation need 'forgetting', but the question is, in what sense is this forgetting voluntary and in what sense is something 'made to be forgotten'. It is not time itself which heals 'pain', but rather different measures which take place in time, for example, politics. The question of whether the policy of reconciliation works, and if so during what temporal period, has implicit current political consequences. Hence, not only are notions of the past political, but there are also concrete situations in which individuals have to decide how to deal with the past.

All in all, I will argue that '1956' has not only existed in the Hungarian space of experience, but it was also used in politics. Not only was it used to legitimate the Kádár regime, it was also utilised by the dissident groups in the 1980s. This usage did not cease in 1989, but lasted in a range of forms until; the end of the period focused on in this work. Moreover, I argue that past experiences also influenced people's expectations during the system change. 'Historia magistra vitae' was once again used, and a few individuals even attempted to 'repeat' their past experiences (from the criticism of *historia magistra vitae,* see Koselleck 1979). Politically, the question surrounded how 'far' the 'negotiated revolution' could reach/return. In this sense, in another research context one might find similarities to the French republicans, who used the memory of 1789 in their politics.

Thus, I hesitantly suggest that the use of the past is purely political, to which I also connect historical writing and research work. Also, they are both public literal acts, which use publicity to change people's attitudes and views. Whether or not they are ultimately successful in this activity cannot be answered here. However, expectations of political usage are frequently even more essential than the actual political usage, which cannot always be taken seriously. However, expectations deal with the future, and among them there are also the aforementioned 'returns' and 'restorations'.

To summarise, we are dealing with a phenomenon that is not only a inherent to historiography, but is also a question of politics. I have named my case as past oriented politics, which is thus a broader and more temporally oriented concept than history culture and history politics.[14] Thus, I have connected to past oriented politics also different attempts to solve these difficult problems, such as juridical debates, history writing, historical writing and historiography. Thus, 'politics' and 'truth' are not positioned against each another, but 'revealing the truth' also requires political activity. Here political activity does not mean party interests but the knowledge of the idea of chances and possibilities of doing otherwise.

In principle, all forensic rhetoric deals with past oriented politics, although in the strictest sense of the word past oriented politics means an attempt to reopen a given case. An objection could be raised, for example, that a criminal case revealed decades after the crime has been committed does not yet fall under that definition. However, the case had been 'forgotten' until then and 'made to be forgotten' by an individual. The case of Imre Nagy presents a clear example of past oriented politics: he was sentenced to death and executed in 1958, but was exonerated and exhumed in 1989.

Here, the various ways of dealing with the past are primarily connected to particular culture and political culture. Although my main focus is on juridical and political reopening, there are several ways of attempting to reopen a given case. However, it is almost impossible to know and define in advance what, when and how something will be reopened. Therefore, the reopening stems from the sources, and in addition to historiography and juridical opening I have included art and phenomena such as reburials, street names, medals and bank notes (cf. also Andreas Dörner's (1995) book on the Hermanns-myth in Germany).

Somehow the idea of the thesis resembles *Bastille*, a symbolic history published by Hans-Jürgen Lüsebrink and Rolf Reichardt in 1990. In France, the usage of this collective symbol had its active, militant dimensions in internal political struggle. These dimensions were found on several levels: *Graphisch*, *argumentativ*, *erzählerisch*, *theatralisch* and *plastisch*. In addition, *Bastille* was a tool in the hands of the internal opposition during the last decades of the *Ancien Régime*, between 1815 and 1870. It also helped the resistance of the *Pétain-Régime* and particularly legitimated the republican tradition during the first years of the Third Republic.

# Remarks on History Culture in Hungary

Geographically, Hungary lies partially on the south and north banks of the Danube River, one of the most essential boundaries since the Roman Imperium. However, the area also represents a 'geography of the mind'. According to emigrant writer Milan Kundera, all of the citizens of Central Europe are connected by the history of conquerors. Constantly recurring conquests, attacks and occupations have created common memories, problems and traditions, which Kundera considered unique to Europe (Kundera 1984).

Moreover, in the 1920s, R.W. Seton-Watson argued that while the past is a key to the present in every country, particularly in Central and South-Eastern Europe the present is a key to the past (Seton-Watson 1922, 16). Thus, in order to inform readers who are unfamiliar with the Hungarian historical context, I will present a brief recapitulation of key events. These events have been selected in order to present the narrative of past events during later occasions, thus illustrating both the sense of continuity and returning to the past.

Moreover, among conquered countries, Hungary also belongs to the category of countries with a past as a conqueror and 'Great Power'. Thus, whether the Hungarian conquerors descended from the Turul bird or Huns of Attila – as the chronicles later legitimated the right to the crown – in the ninth century, seven nomadic tribes under the command of Árpád settled and divided the land amongst themselves. The next prominent figure in the 'national pantheon' is the first King, Stephen, who was crowned in the year 1000. In everyday jargon, Stephen is "the 'founder' of the state", although in the Georgian ideal it was a realm in which the church and the rule were part of the body of Christ (Szűcs 1974; Schlett 1996, 19-24; Szabó 1996, 61). In present day Hungary, Stephen continues to be a symbol of traditions that are over 1000 years old, especially within Catholic circles.

After the House of Árpád fell in 1301, the chronological narrative includes many periods of rule by 'foreign' houses, leading up to the house of Matthias Corvinus (1458-1490), which is frequently seen as one of the 'Golden Ages' in Hungary's history. Contrarily, the period following Matthias is seen as having been less prosperous; in an attempt to increase their own power they chose weaker rulers. A 'peasant rebellion' – or properly an example of a revolution (ÉrtSz 1960, 899) – broke out a decade before the more famous Thomas Münzer's in Germany. The story of how the former leader, György Dózsa, was burned at Timisoara (Temesvár), in what is currently Romania, is well-known in Hungary.

Finally, in 1526, the 'final tragedy' of the ancient Apostolic Kingdom occurred in Mohács. It was at this point that the region lost its independence to the Turks, due in part to the suppression of the earlier peasant movement. Even nowadays, the word Mohács is synonymous to the word catastrophe or the expression of a biblical Golgata. For example, Mohács even belonged to the vocabulary of fascist Arrow Cross leader Ferenc Szálasi, who argued in favour of restoring the role of the leading nation, which was lost at Mohács (Nagytér, élettér... 1943, 49).

During the 16th and 17th centuries, the former kingdom was divided into three parts and was more or less in a constant state of war. In 1686, Buda was re-conquered from the Turks, and peace in Karlowice secured the hegemony of Habsburg de facto until 1918. However, there were *kuruc* 'revolts' led by Imre Thököly during the 1680s and 1690s, and by Ferenc Rákóczi II in 1703-1711.The first revolt against Habsburgs took place in 1604 and was led by István Bocskai, whose attempt was the attainment of an independent kingdom.

Thus, we have already encountered difficulties limiting the historical background to the frames of 1956 and past oriented politics. However, the main argument is that these figures and events *later* have been used in political argumentation. Moreover, Budapest provides a prime example of this chronological history culture. In the late 19th century, the forthcoming millennium became essential in the horizon of expectation, and the parliament decided to build a memorial (Law VIII/1896) to codify Árpád and the whole historical past of the nation[15]. In the *Millennium Monument*, a construction of continuity *par excellence*, there are statues of fourteen individuals in chronological order. Among them are the aforementioned Stephen, Matthias, Bocskai, Thököly and Rákóczi. An obelisk with archangel Gabriel on top and Árpád and seven leaders at the pedestal stands in front of the monument (cf. Prohászka 1994, 28-36). Since 1932, this essential square in Budapest has been Hősök tere (Heroes Square) and the unknown soldiers is also located there, thus connecting the ancient past with the First World War. In 1989, the reburial ceremony of Imre Nagy also took place in the square.

However, Imre Nagy is not the first person in Hungary to be reburied. The French Revolution was initially viewed with enthusiasm, however, the nobles soon realized its disadvantages. A radical group of Jacobins, led by Ignác Martinovics, organized a conspiracy and were subsequently executed in 1795. Following their executions, their corpses were often searched for and were found in 1914 and reburied in 1919. This is merely one example, yet the number of Hungarian politicians who have been reburied over the past century is striking, as I will later discuss in greater detail.

The execution of the Jacobins ended radical political activity for thirty years to come. The decades after 1825 are frequently referred to as the "reform era" or, in Marxist terms, a break from feudalism to capitalism. These years significantly influenced the reforms made by Count István Széchenyi, who is frequently honoured by being assigned the title of the "Greatest Hungarian". In direct contradiction to contemporary views, the reformer argued in favour of shifting the focus from the past to the future, stressing the view that "Hungary was not but will be", thus breaking from past identity.

One crucial idea regarding the 19th century Hungarian metahistory has been a radicalisation of the reform, revolution and eventual compromise. Hence, the lawyer Lajos Kossuth is the next person in the Hungarian pantheon of 'great men', following in the footsteps of Stephen, Matthias and Széchenyi[16]. Kossuth represented more radical republican ideas, and is frequently seen as occupying a dichotomous position in relation to Széchenyi's moderate reforms. Both ideas were actualized on 15th March, 1848, when a revolutionary wave from Paris and Vienna reached Pest. The significance of this day in Hungarian political culture becomes clearer when one becomes aware that it is also a national holiday in present day Hungary.

The tradition of 1848 was also considered important during the socialist dictatorship. Hungarians might remember the occurrences of 1848 from a film made in 1953, and also from the many rhetorical analogies to 1956, which will later become clear.[17] The narrative itself contains radical youngsters, who planned their demonstration from the Café Pilvax. On 15th March, poet Sándor Petőfi played an important role by publishing his new poem, *Nemzeti dal* (National Song). People took to the streets in support of twelve essential points published under the title "What Does the Hungarian People Want". The first demand was for freedom of the press, and the second paragraph called for a responsible government in Buda-Pest. The other most important points surrounded the establishment of a national bank, national guard and unification with Transylvania.

Count Lajos Batthyány, to whom Imre Nagy was later politically analogised, was appointed Prime Minister and the first parliamentary government was established. The King recognized a constitutional monarchy for Hungary, with a parliament and an army of its own. In fact, Austria and Hungary shared a union, which implied Hungarian domination over various minorities on her territory.

However, Kossuth eventually lost the support of the minorities within Hungarian territory after they joined forces with the Austrian monarchists, a phenomenon which is vividly present in present East Central and South-Eastern European politics. In October of 1848, Ferdinand declared war on the Hungarian regime. At first Hungarian troops were successful against the Austrians, however they could not join forces with the Italian or Viennese rebels. Hungary declared its independence in April of 1849, electing Kossuth as Regent. When Czar Nicholas I sent his troops into battle their fate was sealed, and in August of 1849 they surrendered at Világos near Arad.

The period following the defeat is known as 'the Bach era', which was named after the new Austrian Minister of the Interior. During Bach's neo-absolutist period, Hungary reverted back to its pre-revolutionary Constitution based on feudal estates. The administration was re-organized and German became the official language. The first anniversary of the Viennese riot is the most famous in Hungary, because it was on that day that former Prime Minister Batthyány was executed in Pest and thirteen generals were executed near Arad. Since then, 6th October has become a national day of mourning for Hungarians (A magyarok krónikája 1996, 413).

After the Solferino defeat Francis Joseph seemed ready to make concessions. The February Patent of 1861 offered a central parliament, although it was rejected by the Hungarian aristocracy, whose goal was to restore the laws enacted in 1848. The diet was dissolved in 1861, and during the next four years the majority of the *Magyar* agrarian élite pursued a policy of passive resistance (Hoensch 1996, 15). The next new character in the narrative is Ferenc Deák, "the Fatherland's wise" and Minister of Justice in 1848, who was prepared to come to some kind of compromise, in which the previous demands would be rejected in part. The solution became easier to achieve, because Deák did not change his compromise proposal following the defeat of Königgrätz.

Thus, after 1848 and the Bach-era came the year 1867, which was known as a compromise (*Ausgleich*). The Austro-Hungarian Dual Monarchy was established, in which only portfolios dealing with foreign affairs, defence and finances were maintained with Austria. In Hungary, the political power fell into the hands of liberal noblemen, and, depending on the point of view, the era is remembered as a period of non-crucial political reforms, or as peaceful decades of moderate development. During the last third of the century Budapest grew to be the eighth largest city in Europe (cf. Lukacs 1991, 77).

The ruling Liberal Party supported the present union with Austria, but the memory and tradition of 1848 appeared frequently in political life. A crucial division emerged between those who supported the union and those who favoured full independence. The first party, whose name, The Party of '48 (*48-as Párt*) was based on the year 1848, was founded not but a year after the Austro-Hungarian compromise. It demanded independence based on democratic principles, full civic rights and a progressive franchise. In 1884, the Party of Independence and '48 emerged (*Függetlenségi és 48-as Párt*). It functioned under various different names until 1918 and was led also by Kossuth's son Ferenc. Moreover, as late as 1947, The Hungarian Freedom Party (*Magyar Függetlenségi Párt*), which argued of supporting the ideas of Lajos Kossuth[18].

46

Thus, both Kossuth and his memory have become key figures in Hungarian political culture. Kossuth's name is probably found in street names in every village, and the word 'kossuthing' (*kosutozik*, transl. HN) has even been used as a synonym for politicking (*politizál*)[19]. Kossuth himself did not accept the new policy of his countrymen and did not return to Hungary before his death. Some of those who emigrated along with Kossuth looked to England and France for help in encouraging another political 'uprising'. Thus, Kossuth belongs to the long line of emigrants in Hungarian history, serving as a political role model to later emigrants as well. In However, the passive resistance movement had rallied around Deák, and the antirevolutionary conservative aristocracy had begun searching for a compromise as early as the 1850s.

Rhetorically, 1848 was present in the nationalistic demonstrations which took place when Kossuth's corpse was brought from Turin to Budapest for burial in 1894. Furthermore, the memory was present during the years 1918-1919, and also during the Horthy era. Firstly, in 1920, when the government chose the regent, they fell back on an institution revived by Kossuth in 1849. Secondly, in 1927, the "everlasting merits" of Kossuth were codified in law and another commemorative law dealt with 15th March. Moreover, in 1926 Prime Minister Batthyány was commemorated by the lighting of a memorial flame at the site of his execution on 6th October (Magyarország történeti... 1982, 901).

However, Kossuth is not the only worshipped hero from 1848 to be used in the everyday vocabulary of Hungarians. Sándor Márai wrote about a Petőfi-cult in the 1930s, in which "a legend, genius and half-God had already been an example for three generations" (Márai 1937, 185-186). For example, Petőfi was even one of the five individuals whose likeness adorned stamps launched by the short-lived Hungarian Soviet Republic in 1919. The Soviet Republic itself came into being quite by accident, as it was a successor of the 'Chrysanthemum Revolution' of 1918. The first People's Republic, i.e. 'Bourgeois Republic', was established in November and included several basic liberal reforms. It was followed by the establishment of the Soviet Republic in March of 1919, a pattern which would later be followed by state socialist Hungary.

If we continue to use the *Millennium Monument* as an example of past oriented politics, here, the point lies in a contradictory recent past. The last five of the fourteen statues in the monument have been changed three times. First, they were removed in 1919 in part because they were representative of the Habsburg House. The Soviet Republic made a clear break with the past: on May 1st the entire memorial was shroud in red, hidden from view. On the other hand, an attempt was made at locating historical roots; the statue of

Marx was moved to the front of the obelisk, replacing the angel and seven leaders. It is quite astonishing to consider the swiftness with which several new monuments were erected within the span of only a few weeks of enthusiasm in 1919 (see the pictures, for example, Siklós 1978, 340-345).

The five Habsburg statues were restored during the second half of the 1920s. However, the statues were once again removed following the Second World War, in part because of damage incurred during the war (cf. Prohászka 1994, 28-36). The present order is from the 1950s, and thus, *Austrian* Ferdinand I, Charles III, Maria Theresia, Leopold II and Francis Joseph I were replaced by the more progressive *Hungarians*: István Bocskai, Gábor Bethlen, Imre Thököly, Ferenc Rákóczi II and Lajos Kossuth. Moreover, another canon of Hungarian rebels is seen in one of the long main streets of Budapest, which was named after three insurgents in chronological order: Kossuth-Rákóczi-Thököly.

Chronologically, the People's Republic and the Soviet Republic were followed by the regime of admiral Miklós Horthy, who ruled Hungary until 1944 and a short period of a fascist Arrow Cross rule. Horthy began his era by opposing leftists and liberals, and this "Christian course" also partly included opposition to Jews, who fell victim to it.[20] Also, the right to universal and secret ballot, which was introduced in 1918, was restricted in 1922; until 1939 75-80% of votes were cast through open election, which was unparalleled in the context of contemporary Europe (Parlamenti…1994, 5).

However, not only were the franchise, former statues and various street names restored, but the entire past oriented politics was based on revision. The old swanky kingdom lost two-thirds of its former territory to neighbouring states with the signing of the Treaty of Trianon in 1920, although some of the land was re-acquired from 1938-1940. Hence, at the end of the 1930s 'the newly triumvirate' Hitler-Mussolini-Horthy also found their names on the streets of Budapest. Thus, the cult of personality already existed before Mátyás Rákosi, whom is said to have brought the phenomenon to Hungary (the significance of Horthy rules tenth anniversary was also enacted in law in 1930 (cf. 1930. évi törvénycikkek, 1931)).

A few other examples of past oriented politics, which was familiar from revisionism and the slogan *nem nem soha* (no, no never), could also be mentioned. In Budapest, for example, a principle of street naming was accepted in 1928, according to which locations having been surrendered to successor states should receive priority (Deigner 1988, 10). Since January of 1921, a group of statues the *Irredenta* Memorial, has been a reminder of the territories lost in all cardinal points. Since the Second World War, a new memorial has stood at the same place in remembrance of the Soviet liberation. Nowadays, after 1989, the monument, in front of the US Embassy at Szabadság tér

(Freedom Square), is the only monument of its kind to remain standing in its original location.

Thus, both in Hungary in general and Budapest in particular, the past is present in several cultural political stratums, which could be 'erased' one by one. This phenomenon is evident in many other countries as well, although the rapidity with which several changes have taken place throughout the 20th century is quite specific to Hungary. Several of the public rituals in Hungarian political culture have been funerals and reburials as opposed to victory parades, as István Rév has formulated: "histories of battles lost, and consequently a continuous history of executions, exiles and political suicides" (Rév 1994, 21). Another specificity of Hungary is that, as Iván Vitányi has noted, only three men have ruled Hungary in a total of 126 years, Francis Joseph, Miklós Horthy and János Kádár, all of whom came to power in violent circumstances (NSZ 30/08/1993).

These numerous illustrations of the continuity and the return to the 'great moments' of the past suggest an horizon of interpretation of both the forms of history culture that were expressed in 1956 and the future implications of '1956'. I contend that this past oriented political culture has influenced people both in and after 1956. In 1956, the years 1918-19, the Horthy era, the Second World War, the coalition government between 1945-48 and the state socialist period were still all on the level of memory and the experiences of living generations. For example, it is common knowledge that Mátyás Rákosi and György Lukács themselves had personal experiences in the high ranks of Béla Kun's administration in 1919. For Rákosi, with the Horthy era came 15 years in prison, as was later the case for many of the Kádár supporters during the Rákosi era. Still, this 'tradition' has also been in the 1990s, as, for example, the President of the Republic, Árpád Göncz, was imprisoned for life as a result of 1956 (1956 kézikönyve (II) 1996, 192-220).

Therefore, the crucial question will not be if the past and past experiences have influenced an individual, but rather how they have had an influence. Iván Völgyes (1987), who has researched Hungarian political culture, separated several political generations. According to him, political generations are those whose "world views, values or political culture were formed by such cataclysmic events that they left a permanent mark on the individual". Völgyes argued that the identification of political generations takes place at a rather young age, between 13 and 20 years (Völgyes 1987, 191-197).

Hence, until the 1970s, plenty of communist leaders still belonged to the first generation, whose watershed had been in the First World War and the enthusiasm of the decline of the old Europe. The second generation was born during the second decade of the 20th century, and in 1956 they were around 35-45 years of age. Their basic memories and experiences dated back to the Horthy era, and they already held significant positions in society during the 1950s. However, according to Völgyes, the generations born between 1926-1940 were in a key position. Their permanent marks also included the experience of 1956: an idea of something better, fear of the police state and the perception that everything remained only an ideal (Völgyes 1987, 191-197).

On the contrary, Völgyes argued that children born after 1950 do not have the same kind of cataclysmic memories as their predecessors (Ibid.). Thus, when the focus will be moved to 1989, there are several generations who to interpret the past and the present through their own experiences. Individuals who are under 40 years of age were raised and educated in the current state socialist system. However, there is still also the older generation (1926-1940) present in political life since 1989.

Thus, it is not sufficient to limit our discussion to "permanent marks" or "deep imprints" on individuals (cf. Tőkés 1996, 411) without questioning *how* the past influences people as well as *how* it is sustained in the present. Freely, I would re-shape the old Marx's thesis about people acting within given circumstances, i.e. Hungarians were born with a certain past, although the question of whether these experiences are remembered and how and by whom the past is sustained in the present is quite separate.

As a whole, it seems that a national minded space of experience has been entirely remarkable in Hungarian political culture and the history of ideas. Even at the end of the Second World War, when the question was about the politics of new allies, arguing with the distant past was extremely important: "The Hungarian Communist Party went so far as to expel from its ranks a member who declared that St. Stephen was a feudal king", as Mihály Károlyi sarcastically later pointed out in his memoirs (1956, 309). Thus, the future was strongly connected to the experiences of the past and even used for political legitimation. For example, Ernő Gerő used the centenary as legitimation to finish the restoration of the oldest of the bridges in Budapest, the chain bridge, which was damaged during the war.[21] It is no wonder that the new *Népstadion* (People's Stadium) was opened on August 20th, 1953, on Saint Stephen's Day, which since 1949 has been referred to as the day of the new socialist Constitution.

As Toma and Völgyes (1977) noted, an air of cynicism was dominant in the politics of the Kádár era. On the other hand, Hungary was considered as an historical state, which had a great past and valuable culture. The existence of communist rule was accepted as long as it did not conflict too seriously with Hungarians basic sense of national pride (Toma & Völgyes 1977, 152). George Schöpflin argued that the tactic of the Kádár regime was to de-politicize and keep the people calm and content through economic recognitions (1991, 60). Thus, in 'gulash communism' the party state was to some extend

50

parallel to the head of Plato's state body and people, 'the stomach' belonged to the private realm.

To summarise, one can identify many sudden changes within the political culture of the 20th century. These changes were not only oriented to the future, but also provided a perspective for dealing with the past as well as for comparing the present to times prior to the changes. Therefore, it is difficult to characterise Hungarian notions of time 'linearly'. Questions of continuity and discontinuity, restoration and returning have not been senseless either in the Hungarian context or in Europe in the 1990s, although, surprisingly, they more or less framed political thinking and intellectual history. Instead of unambiguously branding these peculiarities only as 'nationalist', I would speak about a strong 'cultural nationalism'.

For example, in the late 1940s, Hungarian politicians debated whether the policy of Communists could be considered analogous to 1848. Those who denied the analogy argued that Communists (earlier Jews, also) were aliens, a non-national (*nemzetietlen*) element, and non-representative of Hungarian traditions. When Miklós Gimes replied to these accusations in March of 1948, he argued that if a People's Democracy fails to fulfil and continue the traditions of 1848, it alienates the Hungarian national past (Standeisky 1987, 120).

Therefore, it also seems that radical political groups have argued with 'continuity' and built their own 'continuities' with the past. A strong sense of both historical continuity and a return to the 'great moments' in history, as opposed to radical breaks and new beginnings, is to some extent also characteristic of radical or leftist politics, as well as of critical historiography in Hungary. Words such as 'history', 'historical pride' and 'historical' are particularly pertinent to Hungary – a tradition unbroken by radical politics or critical historiography, as was not the case, like for example, in France (cf. Enzensberger 1987).

## The Hungarian Vocabulary of Revolution

In Hungarian, the word for revolution (*forradalom*) does not refer to the direction of motions, as the Latin word *revolutio* does. In the Hungarian etymological dictionary (1967), *forradalom* is a basic word for being surging, of being boiling. Ferenc Kazinczy, a reformer of the Hungarian language, has used the word in this context, and is possibly its inventor around 1815. (TESz 1967, 955-956).

The word *forradalom* was constructed from the verb *forr*, which means boiling, and an artificial suffix, *dalom,* was added to it. Similarly, the word

51

*birodalom* (empire, realm) derives from the word *bír* (possess) (Ibid.; Nyys-sönen 1997, 27). In English *forradalom* is not always translated to revolution: one dictionary only knew the word revolution (Magay-Ország 1990). However, in another dictionary the definition was "revolution,[kisebb] rising, revolt" (Országh 1985), i.e. smaller is a rising or a revolt. The same definition is found in Országh (1998).

Although the Hungarian *forradalom* differs from its Latin origin, it primarily became established in use as a result of the naming of the 1848 (TESz, 955-956). For example, *Az Athenaeum kézi lexikona* (1893) provided two examples of significant revolutions, France in 1789 and Hungary in 1848. In a political revolution, some or all inhabitants of a given territory turn against the state or social organisation and overthrow it (1893, 628).

However, prior to the Second World War, several Hungarian dictionaries referred to the events not a revolution but as *szabadságharc*, which in English could be translated as a war of independence or fight for freedom.[22] Frequently, only Hungary 1848-1849 is given as an example from *szabadságharc* in the dictionaries but, contrary to others, *Az Athenaeum kézi lexikona* also mentioned Ferecz Rákóczi and Germany between 1812-1813. Thus, it seems evident that both in the Dual Monarchy and during the Horthy era revolution was not a positive concept, although 1848-1849 was considered positive as a war of independence. For example, when Communist leader Mátyás Rákosi was extradited to the Soviet Union in 1940, he was exchanged to the military flags of 1848.

Moreover, it seems that the 1848 only began to appear as a revolution after the Second World War (Nyyssönen 1997, 27). One of the most important events of that time was the centennial anniversary in 1948 (cf. also Gyarmati 1998). It was at this time that the significance 1848-1849 both as a revolution and war of independence became codified in law. The parliament also considered itself the heir and achievers of these ideals (Law XXIII/1948). Thus, the commemoration and canonization of events through the enactment of laws was an attempt to elevate. The traditions of 1848 were also found in the law, when Hungary was declared a republic in 1946.

Although different events can be referred to by the same name (cf. Koselleck 1972), we must face the problem of 'analogy', which also has inherent political dimensions in the Hungarian sense (cf. also chapter nine). In Hungary, both Law XXIII/1948, which concerns 1848, and Law I/1990, which concerns 1956, defined the events as *forradalom és szabadságharc*. However, in the book *The Hungarian Revolution of 1956*, '1848' is defined as a revolution and war of independence, whereas '1956' is characterised as a revolution and struggle for freedom (1996, x). Hereafter, I also use the translation 'fight for freedom' in connection with '1956', although it seems that these analogies have incorporated the past in the present and, depending on the individual interpreter, either similarities or differences between the two events have been highlighted.

When the content of these concepts is defined in dictionaries, *forradalom* was described before the Second World War as "bloody" or "bloodless", it has the potential to fail, succeed or be the basis of a new beginning or short interruption in legal continuity. For example, in 1938 *forradalom* was defined as a movement which aimed at changing the Constitution through violence. In this sense, it denied lawful continuity (*jogfolytonosság*) (Új idők lexikona 1938, 2522).[23]

On the contrary, the task of the counter-revolution (1937) was to secure a prior legal order and to restore judicial continuity. Moreover, a counter-revolution meant a movement that was directed against a government or state structure and which came to power by means of some kind of revolution, thus through violence or a *coup d'etat*. At that time, the dictionary provided a domestic example of a counter-revolution, describing it as a movement which was directed against the proletarian dictatorship of 1919. The counter-revolutionary government in Szeged had successfully "restored legal order swiftly and without any major shocks" (!). (Új idők lexikona 1937, 2011).[24]

Thus, in the period between the two World Wars, counter-revolution was not a concept with a solely negative connotation. In the history of the Hungarian parliament (1927), the beginning of the Horthy era is considered as a counter-revolution, because it was "natural that a counter-revolution follows revolution" (A magyar országgyűlés... 1927, 425). Later, in the 1950s, Horthy still occasionally used the concept in his memoirs, which were originally published in 1953 (Horthy 1993, 122-128).

However, in the beginning of the 1960s another dictionary was written in Hungary, and it already altered the definition of the term counter-revolution. Here, the counter-revolution was seen as "a reactionary struggle of the exploiting classes... an armed rebellion against the achievements of revolution in the interest of restoring pre-revolutionary conditions in order to increase their own rule." (ÉrtSz 1960, 217).[25] Conversely, revolution was seen as "an attempt at or an accomplished violent, generally armed rebellion against the existing government, or the overthrowing of a (social) order by a suppressed class or classes; generally a majority of the society".[26] Secondly, revolution also meant a complete turn, break or upheaval in economy, technology literature or art (Ibid., 899).

It is interesting to notice that both revolution and counter-revolution were armed rebellions (risings, revolts) (*fegyveres felkelés*), although their tasks were understood quite differently. The former was rhetorically justified and included 'the suppressed' or 'the majority', whereas in the latter 'the exploiters' were the subjects themselves, thus 'good' was pitted against 'evil'. It is important to note that neither definition necessarily had to be successful in order to be defined as they were.[27]

However, when the second edition of the dictionary came out in 1966, the concepts of (*felkelés*) and (*forradalom*) were revised and redefined. Revolt was no longer directed against a ruling power or system. In the new edition, the word 'oppressive' replaced the word 'ruling', i.e. the concept of a rebellion against rulers became impossible to fathom. In the new edition, revolution meant "the forthcoming phase in the development of a class society, in which there was a more advanced social-economic configuration... overthrow and change of an obliged social order."[28] Thus, the Leninist vanguard had replaced 'attempts' and earlier Luxembourgist 'deviance', and a revolution began to turn into 'an historical law of nature'.

Moreover, political revolution no longer existed in the book, and there were also fewer words to define the examples: revolutions no longer failed (*elbukik*), gained the upper hand (*felülkerekedik*) or was 'knocked out' (*kiüt*). These words were removed but instead appeared a new meaning, which was connected to the creation of a nation state. Also, one of the examples was replaced by one with a more local context: György Dózsa's 1514 peasant revolution replaced the earlier Bolivian example.

All in all, a significant transformation in Hungary from 1938 until the 1960s can also be seen on the level of concepts. A certain dichotomy between various notions of revolution already existed, although it seems as if the concept of revolution is not turned to historical laws of nature until the mid-1960s. If the change since late 1930s is understood widely, it also correlates with Völgyes, who considered that people born between 1926-1940 were in a key-position. The experience of '1956' also plays a role here, and the chronology of 1956 will be focused on in greater detail in the following chapter.

# III BUDAPEST 1956 IN THE CONTEMPORARY HUNGARIAN MEDIA

Although chronologically the year 1956 began on 1st January, on personal levels of experience its timing is more difficult to pinpoint. Several phenomena remembered and reminisced about as taking place in October-November actually took place years earlier: Stalin died in March of 1953, the singleparty system was established in the spring of 1949, the first Soviet troops crossed the Hungarian border in September of 1944. Struggles for freedom had already taken place centuries earlier, in 1848 as in 1918 people made also a revolution.

Political narratives dealing with 1956 frequently begin with the years 1944-1945 (cf. 1956 kézikönyve (I) 1996; The Hungarian Revolution... 1996). The chronology published by the 1956 Institute divides the periods before the 'uprising' into four phases: from 1944 to June of 1948, from June of 1948 to March of 1953, from March of 1953 to October 6th of 1956 and finally from October 6th to October 23rd of 1956. On the whole, the first phase can be characterized by the coalition government comprised of four parties that ruled Hungary at the time. In June of 1948 the Communist Party merged with the Social Democrats, creating a new party called *Magyar Dolgozók Pártja* (the Hungarian Working People's Party, MDP).[29]

The second phase, which lasted until March of 1953, was dominated by the creation of a Soviet type state socialist system. The culmination of Stalinist policy was the selection of the first secretary of the MDP, Mátyás Rákosi, as Prime Minister in 1952. Particularly, the third phase, 1953-1956, was framed by the party struggle between the supporters of Rákosi and supporters of Imre Nagy. Before 1949 Nagy had fulfilled the posts of Minister of Agriculture, Minister of the Interior and Chairman of the Parliament. Following Stalin's death, Mátyás Rákosi was forced to leave the post of Prime Minister, which was then occupied by Imre Nagy. The new government revaluated the previous policy, which favoured heavy industry, to include emphasis on the areas of agriculture and consumer goods. Political prisoners were released, and, for example, a special organization called *Hazafias Népfront* (Patriotic People's Front) was established in 1954. In Nagy's political thought, the front represented the function of the multiparty system in socialism.

The premiership of Imre Nagy lasted until April of 1955, at which point he was succeeded by then 32 year old András Hegedüs, one of the youngest Prime Minister in the world. The Soviet leadership had also criticized Nagy, although he refused to criticize himself, as was demanded of him by the Rákosi wing of the Hungarian party. In April of 1955 Nagy was forced to leave the Political and Central Committee of the MDP, and in May of that year his 'de-canonization' began to reach his published works, after which he was finally expelled from the party in December of 1955 (cf. Horváth 1992; Magyarország története 1995; Hoensch 1996; 1956 kézikönyve (I) 1996).

In May of 1955 Austria regained its neutrality, the Warsaw Pact was ratified, and in December of that year Hungary became a member of the United Nations. Moreover, diplomatic relations between the Soviet Union and Yugoslavia also improved during this time. Rákosi was one of Tito's arch enemies, but his policy finally began to become obsolete when Krushchev denounced Stalin's crimes at the 20th Party Congress of the CPSU. Rákosi, however, interpreted the speech as concerning only the Soviet Union, noting that Hungary had acted in this spirit since 1953. In 1955, Rákosi and his supporters did not restore the premiership to Rákosi, but rather to his close ally Hegedüs.

Although only Yugoslavia was mentioned by name in Khrushchev's masterpiece of forensic rhetoric (cf. Hruscsov 1988), the speech especially encouraged political debate in Poland and Hungary.[30] By the end of June, 100,000 people participated in riots in Poznan, causing the Polish political leadership to begin negotiations. In Hungary, Rákosi was ousted from both the Political Committee and from the post of First Secretary in July. In a meeting of the MDP's central leadership, at which Anastas Mikojan was present, member of the Politburo and Vice-Prime Minister Ernő Gerő was chosen to replace Rákosi as First Secretary. In September, Rákosi's name was removed both from the award which previously bore his name (currently The Award of the People's Democracy) and from the factory (named after Manfred Weiss before him and from now Csepel Works) (1956 kézikönyve (I) 1996, 59).[31]

In May and June, the *Petőfi-kör* (Petőfi Circle), an intellectual group affiliated with the party youth organization *Dolgozó Ifjúság Szövetsége* (Alliance of Working Youth, DISZ) organized several meetings. These debates concerned the second Five Year Plan, problems of philosophy and Hungary's economy.

In one of the debates, Rákosi's concept of party history and the spirit of history teaching were condemned. In his first speech, the newly elected First Secretary Gerő condemned the activities of the Petőfi Circle. However, the Writers' Union also activated its policy; In September, the union's leadership was revamped and it demanded that the criminally liable former leaders take responsibility for their actions. Other clubs were also established in university towns throughout the country.

The fourth phase finally began on October 6th, with the reburial of László Rajk and three other politicians who had been executed in 1949. Temporally, the reburial occurred on the anniversary of the execution of 13 Hungarian generals in 1849. Ca. 100,000 people gathered for the reburial, and also a demonstration took place at the Batthyány Memorial Light at Pest. At the memorial lantern, demonstrators demanded the full rehabilitation of Imre Nagy, as the Writers' Union had done earlier. Negotiations were already in progress, and Nagy was finally re-admitted into the party on the 13th of October (Magyarország története 1995; 1956 kézikönyve (I) 1996).

In mid-October, university students began to take political initiative. Students in Szeged resigned from the party's youth organization, DISZ, and established the independent MEFESZ. Although a previous student organization functioned under the same name between 1945-1949, the organization was not its successor *per se* (1956 kézikönyve (1) 1996, 65). Thus, the political debate had commenced, and late on Monday the 22nd the Radio Kossuth reported that university students had already held meetings in two Budapest universities. Reporting from the University of Technology, a reporter described the atmosphere as "hot in March" (1848, HN), noting that the students had concluded discussions on some points while others were still under discussion. According to the radio report, the discussion points dealt with the national economy and politics within the university. The reporter noted that the students demanded that Imre Nagy be given a position in the highest party leadership, that they supported solidarity with the Poles and were likely to establish a MEFESZ. They also demanded that March 15th, a normal working day since 1951, be made a national holiday.

In the following chapters we focus on the events which occurred between Monday, the 22nd of October and the 4th of November, as seen daily in the Hungarian media. It is not a full analysis and reconstruction of the 'event' but is made to clarify the later argumentation. In 1956, television did not yet exist and portable radios were not readily available but the living room receivers could reach the most people (The Hungarian Revolution... 1996, 123). Although we will concentrate on contemporary media first, a few background details must already be explicated in this subchapter. These background details are intended to help the reader and are made on the basis of the handbook *1956 kézikönyve* (I) (1996). Particular attention is paid to rhetorically defined and commented on political life based on contemporaries space of experience and horizon of expectation. Political conflicts are also conflicts of argumentation, and Budapest in 1956 provides an extraordinary example of rhetorical persuasion, which during a very brief period had several concrete impacts of politics.

## Tuesday, 23rd October

On Tuesday, newspapers focused on Poland, reserving several pages for Wladyslaw Gomulka's entire speech. The return of the Hungarian delegation from Yugoslavia was another 'first page' political event in the morning press. The party organ paper, *Szabad Nép* (Free People), put the establishment of the 15th March Circle on its front page. The inner pages of the paper comment on the university meetings with the heading: "The Student Movement Cannot be Used in Restoration". The students' main focal points were briefly reported on, however, their content was not described in detail.

At 1.00 p.m., the Minister of the Interior, László Piros, announced that the demonstration, which students had planned for the afternoon, would not be permitted to take place. Later, at 2.23 p.m., Piros released a new statement allowing the demonstration to take place as planned. The paper of the party youth organization, DISZ *Szabad Ifjúság* (The Free Youth), supported the demonstration and published a special number dedicated to reporting on it. Traditionally, relations between Poland and Hungary had been friendly, and DISZ reminded its readers of this by quoting the poet Sándor Petőfi' and slogans: "Long Live Hungarian Freedom" and "Long Live the Fatherland", which were used to support the demonstration of solidarity with the Poles.

The newspaper of the Technical University, *Jövő Mérnöke* (The Engineer of the Future), published all ten of the students' points. In addition to the demands broadcast on the radio, the students also demanded the implementation of free elections with secret ballot, the withdrawal of Soviet troops and the Kossuth coat of arms, which was used in the republic prior to 1949. Moreover, a special edition of *Irodalmi Újság* (The Literary Gazette) was published and the text began with the notion of coming to an historical turning point. The present situation was described as revolutionary, and writers argued that it would be impossible for them to be acquitted unless the entire Hungarian working people rallies in a disciplined camp. In the special edition, writers outlined seven focal points and sent greetings to their Polish counterparts.

At 3.00 p.m. demonstrators gathered in Pest at the statue of Petőfi. There, the demands were read, as well as Petőfi's poem, *Nemzeti dal* (National Song). The statue was the same one that, for example, was used in 1942 as a space for political demonstration against the war.[32] In 1956, the demonstrators had the pattern of 1848 in mind, as they marched from Petőfi's statue to Buda. At the Bem tér, demonstrators sang *Szózat* (Appeal), which was written by the Hungarian romantic 'national poet' Mihály Vörösmarty, and was also described as the Marseillaise of Hungary.[33]

By the late afternoon people had already begun to gather at Kossuth tér (Kossuth Square) in front of the parliament building, where they demanded that Imre Nagy come to the fore. At that time, Nagy did not have any official position in the party leadership. He had returned to Budapest from the countryside and met with members of the party opposition that same morning. However, Nagy did agree to speak to demonstrators in front of the parliament.

At 8.00 p.m., the First Secretary, Ernő Gerő, made a speech on the radio. Gerő had also returned to Budapest that same morning, although with the delegation of Yugoslavia. In his speech Gerő interpreted the party decisions in July, during which time he came to power and admitted earlier mistakes. Gerő's strategy in the argumentation was based on the lack of time, i.e. that it was impossible to implement the decisions in such a short period of time. Gerő did not make any concrete promises to the demonstrators in his speech. The most frequently cited point of the speech is:

> "Our people's enemies' most important aspiration today is to sway the power of the working class, they are trying to loosen the ties between workers and peasants, to undermine the leading role of the working class in our country, to undermine people's faith to the party... good relations to other socialist countries are undermined.... Therefore, we condemn those who try to spread the poison of chauvinism among our youth, and who use the democratic freedom which our state has assured the working people for nationalistic demonstrations." (cf. Gadney 1986, 34).

In actuality, Gerő did not specifically refer to counter-revolutionaries, but rather used the expression 'people's enemies', which was coined by Stalin during the 1930s. Gerő saw the people's enemies as hidden amongst the demonstrators, and viewed them as attempting to use the demonstration for their own purposes. Moreover, the twenty-minute speech is not only representative of communist-bureaucratic language, but uses also 'us'-rhetoric on several occasions. Gerő frequently repeated expressions such as "our party", "our working class", "our people" etc. Communists were also considered patriots, which in Gerő's mind also included the experiences of Horthy's prisons, underground activity and the Spanish struggle for freedom (!). For

Gerő, patriotism differed from nationalism, which was directed at the enemies of the people, who used the demonstration as a means to their own end.

The demonstrators also demanded the right to voice their points over the radio, although that demand was denied by the director of Radio Kossuth, Valéria Benke. Beginning in the afternoon, troops from the Ministry Council's *Államvédelmi Hatóság* (The Office of State Security, ÁVH) began to arrive at the radio station, and by the evening a battle ensued between them and the demonstrators. The large statue of Stalin, which was unveiled on the dictator's 72th birthday, was torn down that same evening. The first three casualties, however, were in Debrecen, where some 20,000-30,000 people demonstrated in front of the local headquarters of the Ministry of the Interior (1956 kézikönyve (I) 1996, 77-80).

## Wednesday, 24th October

Newspapers reported on a large demonstration of university students in Budapest. *Népszava*, the paper of the Trade Unions, referred to the events with the brief headline: "The Story of 23rd October." According to the paper, some 10,000 people had gathered at the statue of Bem. The subheading of the front page article continued: "With the People on the Road to Socialism." Journalists wrote that could not comprehend Gerő's speech, which mocked the working class, repeating old phrases while the workers waited for a responsible attitude toward their demands. *Népszava* was briefly sympathetic to the demonstration, although it also emphasized its counter-revolutionary elements. The demonstrators had legitimate aims, and the masses were concerned about socialist construction, which counter-revolutionary elements aspired to misuse.

*Szabad Nép* published the slogans: "We Want Socialist Democracy" and "Onwards toward Socialist Democracy." The paper encouraged the people of Budapest to help to develop and renew socialist democracy through the publication and distribution of a special leaflet. However, the organ of the Patriotic People's Front, *Magyar Nemzet*, was more cautious, dedicating half of its front page to the homecoming of the party leadership from Yugoslavia. One of the inner pages reported on the demonstration with the headline: "Huge Demonstration of Budapest Youngsters".

However, at 4.30 a.m., radio reports began for the first time to use the terms "fascist" and "reactionary" in describing the events taking place. It was also at that time that the Council of Ministers' statement was read on the radio. In the first lines of the broadcast were the words: "Fascists, reactionary elements have organized an attack on our public buildings." Merely an hour after this broadcast, the expressions used to describe the demonstration shifted from "fascist" and "reactionary" to "counter-revolutionary" and "reactionary". This notion of counter-revolution continued to be repeated in statements broadcast later that day.

An announcement of the Ministry of Interior was read at 6.30 a.m. According to the text, the cleansing of counter-revolutionary groups would continue until 9.00 a.m. Citizens were urged to stay off the streets as much as possible. Moreover, it was reported in the afternoon that the pancels and soldiers in Budapest were troops who were mandated to be in Hungary in accordance with the Warsaw Pact, and had come to restore order by the invitation of the government. Moreover, there had already been radio reports that morning regarding the implementation of personnel changes within the political leadership. There were new members in the Central Committee of the Hungarian Working People's Party: Ferenc Donáth, Géza Losonczy, György Lukács and Ferenc Münnich. Imre Nagy had been appointed the new Prime Minister, and the former Prime Minister, András Hegedüs, had been appointed Nagy's deputy.

The new Prime Minister made a speech at 12.10 o'clock. Nagy did not define the situation as counter-revolutionary, but rather argued that there were hostile elements among the mainly peaceful demonstrators, who misled the workers into opposing the People's Democracy. The general aim of the speech was to persuade demonstrators to cease the struggles in the streets and instead implement the principles of Nagy's 1953 government.[34] The speech was repeated throughout the day, and the cease-fire deadline was extended.

Thus, on 24th October, the predominant goodness of the demonstration can be seen in the comments made, although they frequently ended with the idea of the political use of the movement. This interpretation can be read, for example, in the statements and leaflets published by the Patriotic People's Front, the Central Committee, István Dobi and the DISZ.

At 8.45 p.m., János Kádár, a member of the Politburo, spoke on the radio. Again, the current situation was described in the first sentences of his speech:

"At first, the university students' march had mainly acceptable demands, however, it quickly degenerated into a demonstration against the People's Democratic order. An armed attack broke out under this umbrella. One can only speak of this attack with ardent contempt, in which counter-revolutionary, reactionary elements rose up against the capital of our Fatherland, against our People's Democratic order, against the power of our working class."

Based on these characterisations, the goals of the demonstration itself began to be in the background of the counter-revolutionary and reactionary elements, as well as the element of 'turning back'. In the views of the ruling party, the demonstration began to become the backdrop for a proper attack, which could potentially produce a dangerous vision of the future. Moreover, in the province of Bács-Kiskun, Brigadier-General László Gyurkó expressed an analogy of the white terror of 1919, stating that a similar scenario must by all means be prevented (1956 kézikönyve (I) 1996, 86). During the night rebels had taken weapons from factories, carried out several attacks, and finally occupied the radio station on Wednesday morning. In the early hours of Wednesday morning, more troops had been dispatched to Budapest, and later Mikojan and Suslov, members of the Soviet Politburo, arrived from Moscow to engage in negotiations with Hungarian politicians (Ibid.).

## Thursday, 25th October

On the morning of the 25th, the Minister of the Interior demanded a cease-fire until 10.00 a.m. on Friday. It was also reported at daybreak that János Kádár had replaced Ernő Gerő as the First Secretary of the MDP. According to a special edition of *Népszava*, "the democratic will of the Hungarian people had won". That afternoon the new party leader made a speech on the radio, which he began by defining the current situation:

"In this difficult situation… it is characteristic that many different elements have become involved. A group of our youngsters began the peaceful demonstration, and the great majority's… honest demonstration degenerated after a few hours into a counter-revolutionary… attack against the People's Democratic state order…. The leadership of our party were in agreement when they stated that… the armed attack must be quelled by any means necessary."

Although Kádár surmised that the situation had become more complicated than it had been the previous day, restoring order was still the first thing on the day's agenda. Military logic was beginning to become the prevalent line of thought: an attack must be suppressed, regardless of who was to be blamed.

Following Kádár's speech, Imre Nagy continued by stating that Hungary had survived a string of tragic events during the past few days. Next, he defined the situation more closely, stating that: "The small number of counter-revolutionaries grew and began an attack against the order of our People's Democracy, which a portion of the working class in Budapest supported as a result of the bitterness toward the situation in the country."

Thereafter, Nagy sited an analogy to political and economic mistakes made over the past few years. Nagy promised that the new party leadership and the government would learn from the present tragic events. Nagy also stressed the importance of the restoration of order to the country. In addition, he mentioned that the government would like to begin negotiations regarding the relations between the Soviet Union and Hungary. He noted that the withdrawal of Soviet troops would be one of the issues on the agenda of these negotiations.

The secretary of the Petőfi Circle and the presidium of the Patriotic People's Front supported the new party leadership. The radio broadcasters were also in agreement, and they followed the progress of the decisions. The experience was enhanced on the radio through the Marseillaise and the Hungarian *Himnusz*, which had already been played earlier that day, and were replayed following the broadcast of Nagy's speech. In addition to other news, the broadcast reported on Thursday, for example, that life in Hungary continued to go on, there were potatoes in the shops and the trams were running once again. The Ministry Council encouraged people to return to work and assured them that the restoration of order was progressing well.

Among others, a group defining itself as a revolutionary youth group printed leaflets in both Russian and Hungarian. The writers demanded a cease-fire and referred, for example, to Karl Marx's thought that a nation is not free as long as it is suppressed by another nation. Youngsters from Kilian, the former Maria Theresa Barracks, printed their own leaflets, referred to themselves as freedom fighters and wanted to restore order in a sense that Russians troops could not stay longer in the name of restoring order. Contrarily, the local party division from the 13th district described the events as an attack by counter-revolutionary bandits. Although "counter-revolutionaries speak about democracy and freedom, in fact they robbed, burned and killed patriots who had fought for workers' power". In this statement, the goals were separated from the actual results, and according to them the reality seemed not to correspond with the sublime ideas.

## Friday, 26th October

A special edition of *Magyar Nemzet* was delighted at the playing of *Himnusz* and the flying of the Hungarian colours. The front page donned the text of the *Szózat* by poet Mihály Vörösmarty. In addition, a new metaphor for describing the current situation came into being, as the events were interpreted as a struggle for freedom in another special edition. A publication used the pseudonym *Magyar Ifjúság* (Hungarian Youth) and argued that Gerő had branded the Hungarian people's struggle for freedom as counter-revolutionary. Moreover, the edition also introduced "the demands of the

Hungarian people", which were condensed into fifteen points published by the student organization MEFESZ.

*Szabad Nép* referred to the interpretations of counter-revolutionaries and stressed the importance of restoring order. According to the views expressed in the paper, Hungary should be an independent, democratic country, which progresses in its own way and at its own pace toward socialism. In the news, the situation was defined as a tragic armed conflict, which had been going on for three days. In *Népszava*, journalist Tibor Méray appealed to the fighting youth and the 'majority', because on the basis of his own experience the great majority of demonstrators had taken to the streets in support of the Fatherland, its people and freedom. In addition, Zsuzsa Szegő wrote about her own experience of participating in the demonstration, noting that she had not noticed the presence of anti-Semitism, chauvinism or any attempt at a bourgeois restoration.

The Central Committee made a statement in which it no longer referred to counter-revolutionaries, although it did warn of possible repercussions. According to the announcement, Hungary had not experiences as tragic since the Second World War; civil war destroyed the city of Budapest.[35] Now the party promised the establishment of a new government, negotiations with Soviet troops and amnesty for those agreeing to lay down their arms until 10.00 p.m. that evening. The previous deadline had expired at 10.00 a.m. that same morning.

Until this point, political leaders had used words like "the people's enemies", "counter-revolution", "reactionaries" and "tragedy" in defining the situation at hand. However, the first attempt to define the present through the unambiguous rhetoric of revolution is found in the first issue of *Igazság* (Truth), which was published on October 26th. Until this point, Hungarian newspapers had usually defined themselves and their editorial policy under the logo of the paper. Now the new paper, *Igazság*, was an organ of the "Revolutionary Hungarian Youth". In the paper Petőfi was once again brought to the fore, as the title of the front page article was the name of a Petőfi poem, *A nép nevében* (In the Name of the People).

> "...the paper was born in the flames of a revolution... it is not fascist bandits who are fighting on barricades with weapons in their hands, nor is it a sympathetic mob in agreement about what they are fighting for, but rather the people themselves... the people are politicking [*politizál*]... this is a revolution. Revolution. Not against the system or socialist ideals... but against those who have tainted... the sublime ideas of socialism. The people want socialism, but a pure and honest socialism."

Thus, the example of Petőfi had already begun to encourage the use of the rhetoric of revolution. The writer(s) understood the people as a single unit, and the journalists spoke in its name and interpreted its will. At the bottom of the page was another Petőfi slogan, which was widely used in Hungarian schools: "With the People through Fire and Water."

Among the leaflets from Friday was one published by *Egyetemi Forradalmi Bizottság* (the University Revolutionary Student Committee), which put its trust in Imre Nagy. In another leaflet, the glorious revolution was described as being far from over, since Soviet troops had not yet left Hungary. Instead of supporting narrow party interests, the committee urged that the revolution and struggle for freedom progress to victory in all strength. The leaflet signed by the Hungarian people fighting against tyranny stressed the need for the implementation of elections through secret ballot, with the 1947 parties having the right to participate in them: "Such a traitor did not exist in 1848, who summoned the Cossacks of Nicholas as Imre Nagy did." Hungarians were also asked to be worthy successors of the 1848 national army *honvédség*.

By that evening, the interpretation of the revolution had also reached the radio, when reports began to be broadcast about the revolutionary councils in Szolnok. At that time the first workers councils also began to appear. Moreover, on Thursday and Friday, communist symbols such as red stars were removed in several smaller towns (1956 kézikönyve (I) 1996, 92-110).

## Saturday, 27th October

In the morning, the Minister of the Interior announced that the majority of fighters had laid down their weapons. The ridding of provocative elements from Budapest was said to be progressing well. A new government was formed; a national government, which was said to be national, democratic and Hungarian. In the late forenoon the new Ministers were introduced: Prime Minister Imre Nagy (Vice Prime Ministers Antal Apró, József Bognár and Ferenc Erdei), Minister without portfolio Zoltán Tildy, Minister of the Interior Ferenc Münnich, Minister of Agriculture Béla Kovács, Minister of Justice Erik Molnár and Minister of Education György Lukács. It was reiterated in a special leaflet that Kovács was the former Secretary of the Smallholder's Party. Both Lukács and Minister of Health Babits were university professors.

Altogether, five of the Ministers were not members of the ruling party: four had been members of the Smallholders and one belonged to the National Peasants' Party. Thus, on Saturday, the Hungarian audience was not only persuaded by specialists and the notion of social harmony, but in part also by the coalition government of 1945. Both Tildy and Kovács were among the most prominent members of the Independent Smallholders' Party, which in 1945 had won a majority in the parliament. Zoltán Tildy was also chosen to be the first President of the Republic, although he was ousted in 1948. Béla Kovács was arrested by the Soviet military and extradited to the Soviet Union in 1947, after which he was returned to Hungary in 1955.

*Szabad Ifjúság*, an organ of the DISZ, welcomed the new appointments with the slogans: "Long Live Sovereign, Democratic Hungary" and "Long live the new Hungarian government, which was born out of a broad national united front!" In addition, there was the slogan: "Long live the government, in which the Hungarian peoples' skills are embodied and its will represented!" In contrast, the Political Committee of the MDP continued to focus on the notion of counter-revolution in a leaflet dated the 27th. One of the statements in the leaflet was directed toward the future:

> "The struggle over power continues. Those who now fight against us are counter-revolutionaries.... . The party has gone to the ultimate lengths to fulfill [the peoples'] demands. Those who consider this insufficient do not want a People's Democracy but a counter-revolution."

At noon, there were news reports that armed rebels had mostly laid down their weapons until 10.00 p.m. the previous evening. Still, three important objectives were occupied by the counter-revolutionaries and the liquidation of those resistance centres was told of still going on. Rebels seemed to be those, who had already laid their weapons but counter-revolutionaries fought still on the streets.

## Sunday, 28th October

In the editorial, entitled *Híven az igazsághoz* (Faithfully toward the Truth) *Szabad Nép* expressed its lack of comprehension of those who considered the events of the last few days as a counter-revolution. According to the newspaper, although the demonstration was initiated by university students, it would be a mistake to view it merely as a university movement. According to *Szabad Nép*:

> "...a thorough and unifying national democratic movement [*nemzeti demo-kratikus mozgalom*] developed in our Fatherland, which the despotism of the past few years had suppressed, but which during the past few months had been sparked into flickering flames by the first breeze of freedom. This movement expressed workers' desire to become owners in the factories in which they work... the struggle of communist and non-party intellectuals strength-

ened the movement, a crucial task in the purification of our system."

Now, the demonstration and the events which followed were redefined on the level of the party organ. The majority of the demonstrators now belonged to a national democratic movement. However, while there was still an insistence of the existence of real opponents, they were assumed to be few in number. According to the leading article, university students attempted to persuade the extremist faction that the fight should not continue against the system, but rather in support of socialist democracy and the securing of national sovereignty. Although there continued to be struggles, the writer(s) found that they had decreased since Thursday afternoon, because the rebels saw their democratic demands as having been fulfilled.

On Sunday, the complexity of the situation increased in the interpretations, because, according to the writer(s), it was difficult to differentiate between the counter-revolutionaries and those loyal to the system. Those who were misled or infatuated should lay down their weapons and dissociate themselves from the counter-revolutionaries. They should trust the national government, because it was the 24th hour to dissociate from the path, which leads to a counter-revolution. In addition, the party organ attempted to locate those individuals responsible for transforming the great and patriotic demonstration into a civil war (testvérharc).

At 5.25 p.m. the new Prime Minister, Imre Nagy, spoke on the radio, and he, too, redefined the significance of the past few days. Nagy initially directed his words to the Hungarian people, after which he commented on the swiftness with which the events of the past week had occurred. According to Nagy, fate has not spared our people and nation "over the course of our thousand year history, but perhaps never has our Fatherland lived through such a shock". The proper definition of the situation began in the fourth sentence:

"The government condemns the view that the great peoples' movement [népmozgalom] is a counter-revolution. Clearly, as in all great movements of the people, there were destructive elements who have used the last few days for committing crimes. It is also a fact that the reactionary counter-revolutionary elements connected and aspired to use the events as a means to overthrow the People's Democratic system. However, it is indisputable that the basic power of this movement has developed into a great and overall unifying national democratic movement."

Thereafter, Nagy specified the aims of the national democratic movement, which attempted to secure national independence, the sovereignty of the country and to democratize the society, economy and politics. All of these goals were understood as basic aspects of socialism. Moreover, Nagy also announced that negotiations were to begin regarding the withdrawal of Soviet troops from Hungary. Furthermore, the government recognized workers' councils and initiatives to broaden democracy in the work place. Imre Nagy also mentioned that the government would take initiative both with regard to reverting the Kossuth coat of arms back to the Hungarian coat of arms, and declaring March 15th a national holiday.

Generally speaking, Imre Nagy confirmed the view already expressed by the party organ and in the session of the Central Committee at dawn. Now, the national democratic movement represented the majority and the movement. Gerő's "enemies of the people", an unknown unspecified audience, were seen as a less significant minority.

Next, the Minister without portfolio and former President of the Republic, Zoltán Tildy, came to the microphone. First, Tildy referred to his eight years house arrest and also outlined the reasons for his participation in Imre Nagy's government. The argument was based on the notion of being Hungarian: "Imre Nagy is a Communist, which I am not. However, I and all of the other members of the government are Hungarians first and foremost." For Tildy, there was only one possible destiny for the future: to put an end (felszámol) to past mistakes and crimes and build a solid base for the free life of the nation.

Later that same evening, the Patriotic People's Front went even further than the party and the government had by beginning to define the present situation as a revolutionary struggle. At 10.48 p.m. an appeal was read on the radio, in which it was said that national unity was born "in the revolutionary fire of our youngsters and people... the national government was created by the revolution and by Prime Minister Imre Nagy... ." Moreover, the radio reported about new National Revolutionary Committee, how rebels at Széna tér had stopped fighting following the presentation of Nagy's speech. News also reached Budapest that revolutionary councils had been established in the provinces. Moreover, the Yugoslavian news agency Tanjug reported that the name of Stalin Street in Warsaw would be reverted back to its previous name. At the United Nations, the United States, Britain and France requested an investigation into the situation in Hungary. It was also reported that history textbooks would immediately be removed from schools. The government's actions would be overseen by the Minister of Education and the existence of personal cult in the books was the given argument for the decision.

## Monday, 29th October

In the leading article of *Hétfői Hírlap* (Monday News), Editor-in-Chief Iván

Boldizsár defined the present situation with the headline "Bloody Paper". Boldizsár also referred to Petőfi and interpreted the present situation as a revolution led by Imre Nagy. The newspaper also created its own future expectations by changing the name on the front page from the Patriotic People's Front to the Independent Hungarian Daily.

Szabad Nép and two other newspapers were published with the Kossuth coat of arms on the front page. The term revolution could not be found in the headlines of Szabad Nép, although several appeals written by revolutionary committees were published, in which they spoke of a revolution or struggle for freedom. Now, the radio described itself as the Kossuth and Petőfi Radio. Moreover, it was described how people had returned to work and how the United Nation's Security Council had dealt with the situation in Hungary. The Belgrade newspaper Politika wrote that the tragic events of the past few days were not initiated by Kádár or Nagy, but rather by Rákosi's guards, who were still in power i.e. in their positions. Moreover, on Monday, the Minister of the Interior suspended the ÁVH and began to organize the establishment of a democratic police force.

In Budapest, Stalin Street was renamed the Street of Hungarian Youth. In addition, the Stalin Bridge was renamed the Árpád Bridge, and Stalin Square became György Dózsa Square.[36] Furthermore, Néphadsereg (the People's Army) published the order given by the Minister of Defence, that from now on members of the military would revert back to addressing one another as bajtárs (companion in arms), as opposed to elvtárs (comrade).

That afternoon the DISZ published an announcement, in which it encouraged revolutionary youth to establish revolutionary committees. According to the statement, our struggle for freedom has been won and this struggle will reform socialism:

> "Our people's fight for freedom has been won. The new independent national government will declare a program to renew our People's Democratic system ... . Our revolution has reached a peaceful phase. Young workers, its time to consolidate the achievements of our revolution... ."

At midnight, a letter from Josip Broz Tito was read on the radio. The letter had been dated the previous day and was addressed to the Hungarian party leadership. In the letter, the Yugoslavian people and the Alliance of Communists were described as following the situation with strained the attention. Tito was worried about the news of tragic clashes in Hungary. Tito described the present situation as "events", arguing that they were the result of past mistakes, and denied that Yugoslavia had any intention of intervening in the Hungarian situation. Earlier, the radio had also broadcast a similar statement by Gomulka, whose made an appeal to the Hungarian people to stop fighting and to support the national government. Imre Nagy was quickly becoming the Hungarian version of Gomulka or Tito.

## Tuesday, 30th October

Imre Nagy had referred on Sunday to a national movement, and by Tuesday the terms generally varied in different newspapers. For example, the university staff demanded freedom for the universities and wrote about revolution, the struggle for freedom and rebellions. In black frames, *Népszava* demanded eternal glory for our dead heroes. Events were now also compared to 1848, because in both cases the struggle for freedom began on the desire for both internal and external freedom.

Another issue of *Magyar Nemzet* came out a few days after its Friday release, now describing itself as an Independent Daily. The name of the Patriotic People's Front was replaced with the name of its founder, Sándor Pethő. In the first leading article, "Do Not Risk the Fatherland", it was described how the paper was found again following the past dangerous, bloody and glorious days. The freedom fighters were honoured in the leading article, and it was frequently mentioned that Fatherland must not be put at risk. Hungarians formed a small nation, and there was now the possibility of a future international conflict. Moreover, *Szabad Ifjúság* redefined itself from the organ of working youngsters to the organ of the Revolutionary Hungarian Youth. Imre Nagy's interpretation of the national movement identified it as a revolution. *Szabad Ifjúság* reported that it could not comprehend how the Soviet radio could report about the "rebellion of counter-revolutionary groups".

Three 'new' newspapers came into being: *Függetlenség* (Independence, Hungarian Independence the following day), *Magyar Szabadság* (Hungarian Freedom) and *Magyar Honvéd*[37] (The Hungarian Soldier), which had previously been *Néphadsereg* (The People's Army). *Függetlenség* was edited by a Hungarian Revolutionary National Committee, which was led by engineer József Dudás. It went further than the other papers, because it did not accept the government, a topic which was focused on in greater detail in the second issue. "We Do Not Accept the Present Government". There 25 points under the headline, one of which was that the demand that the UN Security Council declare a state of war in Hungary and send help to the region. The writer demanded the establishment of democratic parties, full civil liberties and freedom fighters to the government as members of the National Committee and János Kádár, Imre Nagy and Béla Kovács. The writer also demanded the release of Roman Catholic Cardinal József Mindszenty, which was carried out that same evening.

The most important event on Tuesday was Imre Nagy's speech on the radio at 2.28 p.m. At first, the Prime Minister dedicated his words to working people, workers, peasants and intellectuals. In the second sentence Nagy defined the situation and now the most important, as a revolution:

> "In our Fatherland there is a widely unfolding revolution, an enormous movement of democratic forces has placed our Fatherland at a crossroad.... .In the interest of the continuing democratization of life in the country, including the suspension of the singleparty system, we set out to govern on the basis of the 1945 coalition and democratic cooperation among parties."

Next, Nagy announced the establishment of a closer cabinet within the national government. The cabinet was represent by Imre Nagy, Zoltán Tildy, Béla Kovács, Ferenc Erdei, János Kádár, Géza Losonczy and an individual to be nominated by the Social Democratic Party. Moreover, the national government would contact Soviet troop headquarters to demand the immediate withdrawal of troops from Budapest, and to begin negotiations with the government regarding the eventual withdrawal of all Soviet troops from Hungary. Nagy finished his speech with the words: "Long Live Free, Democratic, Independent Hungary!"

Thus, the situation had once again been redefined, and the return of the multiparty system was declared on the basis of the principles of 1945. Following Nagy, Zoltán Tildy and Ferenc Erdei also supported the decision and interpreted that the will of the people and the national revolution had been victorious. Erdei wanted to defend the victory both from those who wanted to revert back and those who wanted to throw it into anarchy or oppose the achievements already made. Tildy expressed his gratitude to the Hungarian youth, workers and soldiers, whose actions had been as commendable as those of March 1848. Above all, Tildy's speech included the promise of free elections, although the date was not specified.

Minister of State János Kádár also announced his support of the government and his concurrence agreement with Erdei and Tildy. However, as opposed to the other speakers, Kádár refrained from explicitly using the term revolution, referring instead to a civil war (*testvérháború*). Although his use of the expression might have been purely coincidental, it may in fact be descriptive of his own view, and the task of directing his words to a specifically communist audience. In fact, Kádár made his speech as the leader of a party which had lost its dictatorial power. When compared to the statement from Saturday, both Kádár and Nagy had crossed the Rubicon and joined those whom they had earlier considered counter-revolutionaries.

In the evening, an announcement was made stating that the National Peasants' Party and the Smallholders' Party had resumed their activity. The situation was embraced in the countryside as a "glorious revolution", and the radio station changed its name to *Szabad Kossuth Rádió* (The Free Kossuth Radio). In the foreign news, AFP, for example, reported that Ferenc Nagy, former Prime Minister of Hungary, had returned to Paris from a visit to Vienna. Moreover, in a produced by the Hungarian Revolutionary Youth, they demanded the resignation of the government and their replacement by freedom fighters, as well as the implementation of free elections, in which the parties from 1947 would be represented.

In the evening, József Értavi attempted to persuade rebels still fighting in the ninth district of Budapest to stop, warning them that there was a possibility that some might misunderstand their motives. At 10.43 p.m., a statement was released on the radio, its most famous signatory being Colonel Pál Maléter. According to the statement, October 23rd was the greatest day of our people and our fighting movement. An independent and sovereign Hungarian Republic was beginning to be established through the maintenance of the present achievements and the restoration of order. The establishment of the Revolutionary Youth Committee in the ninth district was also announced. It was argued that the decision was necessary in order to prevent resistance movements and bandits from endangering the welfare of the people or their property, and therefore indirectly also the nation's entire development.

On Tuesday, the new First Secretary of Budapest also made an appeal to Communists to accept their obligation to join the National Guard in order to defend workers' power. The radio also reported, for example, that over the previous week more than 50% of the world media and western radio stations had dealt with the situation in Hungary.

# Wednesday, 31st October

Several newspapers published an announcement made by the Soviet government, in which it stated its inclination to begin negotiations. In a moderate tone, it was also reported in the *communiqué* that an order had been given to military commanders to withdraw from Budapest. In the statement, the name "events" frequently described the Soviet attitude. Unlike other newspapers, *Magyar Függetlenség* published the whole statement, which also contained the notion of counter-revolutionary forces. They used the situation as an attempt to restore the previous estate capitalism.

According to the headline of *Népszava*, a decisive turn had taken place in domestic politics after the victorious struggle for freedom. The question of what had actually happened at Köztársaság tér (Republic Square) was also addressed. There was a brief report about a siege, which had ended in the occupation of the party headquarters located at the square. In the last sentence it was reported that the people's hate and anger was unleashed against the representatives of the ÁVH, who had defended their building during the siege. *Magyar Függetlenség* also reported on the event, as a statement was released in which the square was mentioned and the pseudonym "fighters" was applied to all freedom fighters. The "fighters" argued that the members of the ÁVH should not be killed, but instead should be prosecuted before a court of law.

Representatives of the revolutionary forces and the delegation of the Revolutionary Council of People's Army broadcast their demands on the radio at 10.55 a.m. They included the nullification of the Warsaw Pact, the implementation of an armed resistance and establishment of revolutionary tribunals. Elsewhere, the Students' Revolutionary Committee demanded the expulsion of the old Stalinists from the government. The radio reported that foreign broadcasts should no longer be interrupted or altered. *Magyar Honvéd* published new the new military ranks and noted that the Hungarian flag to be flown at the Melbourne Olympic Games would be the Kossuth coat of arms. The first issue of *Szabad Szó* (Free Speech) was published with the words of the Hungarian National Anthem, *Himnusz*, on its front page. Although the issue was the first number for a long time, 24th annual volume was printed on the front page. Later, this 'continuity' was constructed, for example, in the catholic *Szív* (Heart), because on the first issue on November 3rd the annual volume was XL.

Several newspapers were read on the radio; it was reported that some people felt that the great star should be removed from the top of the parliament. In Pécs, the former Party Secretary of the Smallholders, Béla Kovács, said that no one should dream about the past world, because the world of counts, bankers and capitalists was gone forever. For Kovács, a real Smallholder had now neither 1939 nor 1945 in mind. Christian parties also began to organize themselves. Moreover, in a leaflet published by the Smallholders, they argued that the revolution had been successful and that a new life was expected to begin. The second leaflet referred to the spirit of Kossuth, and the third included the slogan "God, Fatherland, Family". A radio report from the road between Vienna and Budapest noted that medicine and fruit were being brought into Hungary and that an SS-soldier was spotted reconnoitring the border.

# Thursday, 1st November

The newspaper survey on the radio began with a description of the tenth day of our glorious revolution, which was characterised as the first peaceful morning after a peaceful night. Several new and 'old' newspapers started to appear: the independent daily *Magyar Világ* (The Hungarian World), *Magyar Ifjúság* (The Hungarian Youth) from the Revolutionary Council of the Working Youth, *Népakarat* (The People's Will) by the free trade unions and *Paraszt Függetlenség* (The Independence of the Peasants). After a long hiatus, the organ of the Smallholders' Party, *Kis Újság* (The Small News), was once again published. In *Magyar Nemzet's* leading article *Ismét a magyar úton!* (Again on the Hungarian Road!), writer András Kemény once again followed the suit and the ideas of the Smallholders, i.e. the same policy earlier supported by Sándor Pethő's paper. *Népszava* declared that "We Are Social Democrats", and once again became an organ of the Social Democratic Party.

In Budapest, reports circulated that Gerő, Piros and Hegedüs had escaped to the Soviet Union. At dawn, Colonel Pál Maltér became the Deputy Minister of Defence and Major General Béla Király was appointed to the military command of Budapest. Király began to organize a Revolutionary Defence Committee comprised of members of the army, police and National Guard. Király located an analogy from the past in this reorganization, because the National Guard was "the heir of the heroic national guards of the glorious revolution and struggle for freedom in 1848." Moreover, Király also connected the National Guard the troops "who in the spring of 1849 squashed the aggressive forces." The task of the Defence Committee was to coordinate separate armed forces groups until the election of the new government.

The idea of 1848 can also be found in the words of a wounded freedom fighter who was interviewed on the radio. When the 16-year-old boy was asked why he joined the freedom fighters, he argued that just as they had in 1848, our freedom fighters rose against both domestic and foreign oppression. The connection to 1848 can also be seen in the name of the Peasant Party, which now operated under the name Petőfi instead of its former name, The National Peasant Party. Writers Gyula Illyés, László Németh, Áron Tamási and Péter Veres were among its organizers. All of these writers also signed a statement published by the Writers' Union, in which they stated that the revolution should be kept pure and criminals should be prosecuted in front of a free Hungarian court. A long text by László Németh was read on the radio, in which he also speculated on the dangers of the future and negative remembering:

"I saw only what radio and events in the country side allowed me to see, clearly there was danger before me... . While the full attention of the armed forces turns to the withdrawal of Soviet troops, those who aspire to new positions, who expect the return of the old glory, occupy these positions and create a counter-revolution from the revolution, follow the '19 course in the '56 struggle for freedom."

Two days earlier, on 30th October, the Hungarian Revolutionary Youth had demanded the resignation of the present government, the appointment of freedom fighters to government positions and elections based on the 1947 parties. Now, on 1st November, the Reformed Church began to reorganize itself and the Democratic People's Party announced that it would stand behind its old program. It was announced on the radio that the following day *Keresztény Front* (The Christian Front) would hold a meeting after ten years of illegal activity. On the radio, Endre Varga, the leader of the *Katolikus Néppárt* (The Catholic People's Party) referred a bitter eight year long underground struggle and dealt with the promise to rebuild the *Regnum Marianum* Church.

At 7.50 p.m., Imre Nagy spoke briefly on the radio and announced the neutrality of the Hungarian People's Republic. According to the Prime Minister, the Hungarian people desired the consolidation and further development of the achievements of their national revolution without having to join any power blocs. Nagy estimated that the century-old dream of the Hungarian people was now being fulfilled. After the speech, *Himnusz* and other sublime and elevating music was played on the radio.

An hour later, the radio broadcast the speech of First Secretary János Kádár. Kádár also defined the situation on many different occasions in many different ways: "the glorious revolt of our people" (*népünk dicsőséges felkelése*), "a rebellion" (*felkelés*), "an armed revolt" (*fegyveres felkelés*) and the peoples' revolt (*a nép felkelése*). Although possibly purely coincidental, the expressions revolution or struggle for freedom remained unmentioned. He referred to the pure ideals of socialism, which were tainted by Hungarian representatives of stalinism, Rákosi and his clique. Then the glorious revolt of the people was directed toward overthrowing the Rákosists' supremacy. It also aimed at the attainment of the freedom of the people and the sovereignty of the country, without which socialism could not exist. Next, Kádár dealt with the horizon of expectation:

"Will there be enough power to strengthen the achievements of the Hungarian democratic parties or will we face an open counter-revolution. The blood of Hungarian youngsters, soldiers, workers and peasants did not flow so that Rákosi's type of despotism could be followed by the despotism of counter-revolution."

Kádár did not clearly define either negative expectations or the content of counter-revolutionary autocracy, although he referred to the possibility of its occurrence. The present achievements had to be defended and the present cross-roads had to be faced, because the class struggle evidently did not end victoriously. Kádár's reference to the role of the United Nations in the Korean War alludes to the fact that he did not interpret it as an independent organization:

"We did not fight so that mines and factories would be ripped from the hands of workers and land from the grasp of peasants. Whether the revolt secured the crucial achievements of our People's Democracy, the freedom of association, personal freedom and security, the establishment of a free juridical system, freedom of the press, humanitarianism and humanity, or we sunk back to the captivity of the old world of autocracy... . There is a serious and alarming danger that foreign intervention would threaten our country with the same tragic fate of Korea... the achievements of the Hungarian Republic must be defended, as must land reform, the social ownership of factories, banks, mines and the unchallenged social and cultural achievements of our people."

Next, Kádár called working people to the party called *Magyar Szocialista Munkáspárt* (The Hungarian Socialist Workers' Party, MSZMP). All those who were not responsible for the criminal policy of Rákosi and his clique were welcomed into the party. Kádár also mentioned a committee, which had prepared a congress. In addition to Kádár, its members included Ferenc Donáth, Sándor Kopácsi, Géza Losonczy, György Lukács, Imre Nagy and Zoltán Szántó. In addition, Kádár introduced the party organ *Népszabadság* (People's Freedom) by name, which in fact had recently been changed from *Szadad Nép* (Free People). The concrete adjective 'free' had become the more abstract substantive 'freedom'. On the basis of the name, the party itself became more of an interest group: 'working people' were substituted with the narrower term 'worker', including the specific term 'socialist'.

Cardinal József Mindszenty had been freed two days earlier and received a telegram from the Pope. Mindszenty spoke briefly on the radio at 8.24 p.m. and defined the situation as a struggle for freedom. According to him, a struggle for freedom was taking place, in which admirable heroism had liberated our Fatherland. The Cardinal had literally been freed from house arrest in Felsőpetény in Northern Hungary.

## Friday, 2nd November

A new group of newspapers were published in Budapest: *Népszabadság, Új Magyarország* by the Petőfi Party, *Forradalmi Ifjúmunkás* (The Revolutionary Young Worker) by the Revolutionary Committee of the Working Youth and

*Esti Hírlap* (The Evening News). The general sense of delight at the neutrality and independence which had been achieved in Hungary were visibly present in the headlines.

There was an significant increase in the amount of foreign news that was reported in the newspapers, and most of the focus was on the situation in Suez, the role of the United Nations and the situation in Hungary. On October 29th, *Népszava* was the first newspaper to print foreign comments on the situation in Hungary, with the headlines: "The Reception of the Events in Hungary" and "World Newspapers On the Hungarian Struggle for Freedom" (October 30th and 31st). In *Igazság*, President Eisenhower assured that the United States was prepared to help achieve freedom in Hungary without any obligations. *Magyar Nemzet* warned that the Fatherland was in danger and that the arrival of new Soviet troops was in direct contradiction with the statement made by the Soviet Union on October 30th.

*Magyar Világ* focused attention on the same Soviet announcement and asked "Still 'counter-revolutionaries'?" The writer pointed out that, according to the Soviet interpretation, those who were opposed to the singleparty system were classified as counter-revolutionaries and were viewed as being in favour of the secret ballot. According to paper, no one could undermine the base of the People's Democracy. Hungarians would achieve a real democracy, and if the Soviets' understanding of a People's Democracy was a bureaucratic clique dictatorship, they wanted to dissociate themselves from it. It was also stressed that in the future factories would not be given capital, nor would land be given to the big landowners. The writer persistently used quotes when referring to counter-revolutionaries.

The organ of the Petőfi Party (The National Peasant Party), *Új Magyarország*, argued that the Party's ideology was based on poets Sándor Petőfi, Mihály Vörösmarty and also books by Endre Ady and Zsigmond Móricz. The definition was based on a speech given by the writer Gyula Illyés, but was not commented on in greater detail. Culture had also defined the space of experience elsewhere, for example, there were several poems published by *Irodalmi Újság*. Petőfi's poem *Ismét magyar lett a magyar* (Hungarian Became Hungarian Again) was printed on the front page of the paper.

The renamed party organ, *Népszabadság*, shifted somewhat behind the rhetoric of revolution. As an adjective, the word revolutionary made frequent appearances. Furthermore, the expression "Our Revolution Has Won" was used in the front page article written by Commander Béla Király. One party leaflet described the conflict as a "glorious revolt", and in another the revolution was said to have begun on October 23rd.

In Hungary, All Souls Day (*Halottak napja*) had been celebrated on the previous day, 1st November. The reporter on the radio described that a million candles had been lit in the city, resembling one enormous cemetery. Moreover, the radio reported on *Keresztény Ifjúsági Szövetség* (The Christian Youth Association) and that on October 31st, *Magyar Függetlenségi Párt* (The Hungarian Independence Party), which had been dissolved in 1947, had been reestablished. There were also reports of both a visit to Rákosi Villa and a Rákosi membership card, which one should always carry with them, according to party rules. A statement by *A Magyar Egységes Ifjúsági Szövetség* – a new non-party youth organization – was read on the radio, in which it distinctly rejected the restoration of the Horthy system.

Moreover, shortly after 7.00 p.m., an announcement directed to the Secretary General of the United Nations, Dag Hammerskjöld, was read on the radio. In the statement, Prime Minister and Minister of Foreign Affairs Imre Nagy pointed out that new Soviet troops had crossed the border and were moving toward Budapest. Imre Nagy asked Hammarskjöld to vocally support the recognition of Hungarian neutrality. Hammarskjöld should instruct the United Nations Security Council to immediately begin negotiations between the governments of Hungary and the Soviet Union. The government had also reminded Soviet ambassador Juri Andropov about withdrawal of the troops.

After midnight a telegram was read on the radio, in which it was stated that the situation in Hungary would be on the daily agenda of the Security Council. Nine countries had voted for, and one against focusing on the problem; more specific details of the meeting would be broadcast the following morning. Earlier on Friday, Colonel Pál Maléter had showed Molotov cocktails in an international press conference. Soviet troops will be considered to be a part of the Warsaw Pact and resisted.

## Saturday, 3rd November

The meeting of the Security Council occupied the front pages of all of the newspapers. According to the radio, United States Delegate Henry Cabot Lodge argued that it was impossible for the United Nations to remain a disinterested spectator with regard to the unfolding events in Hungary. The western representatives in the Security Council were mistrustful of Hungarian Ambassador, and requested that Imre Nagy send an envoy from Budapest. A delegation, which investigated the situation later on Saturday, estimated that the reason for the increasingly strained relationship between the Soviet Union and Hungary was the Gerő-Hegedüs clique, who had originally requested the presence of Soviet troops in Budapest. In the statement, the Hungarian revolution was characterised as being directed toward the withdrawal of Soviet troops, as opposed to being directed against the Soviet Union as a state. The delegation denied that the revolution would clear the way for fascism.

*Népszabadság* published a TASS report from Beijing, in which the People's Republic of China considered the moderate October 30th statement by the Soviet Union as the correct decision. In the leading article *Megtisztultan* (Purification), it was reported that The Hungarian Socialist Workers' Party MSZMP wanted to be faithful to the Hungarian revolutionary workers' movement and its traditions. It also was loyal to the battalions who in 1919 had defended the country against foreign countries and had finally become dissociated from the catastrophic politics of the MDP leadership. The situation was defined twice as a national democratic revolt and once as a national revolt, however, the word revolution was not used in the leading article.

A Soviet soldier was interviewed in *Magyar Függetlenség* and told how he and the other troops were instructed to fight against the fascists. In *Népszava*, Anna Kéthly, who participated in the meeting of Socialist International in Vienna, speculated that Hungary would become a socialist country. In the paper of the university youth, *Magyar Jövő* (The Hungarian Future), university students argued that they had taken pen in hand in a moment of crisis, during a time in which the existence of their free and independent country was threatened by great danger. Moreover, several newspapers were interested in the rumours that ÁVH's prison had been located under the party house at Köztársaság tér. When Ottó Végh reported about the ongoing excavations in *Magyar Nemzet*, he used the name Kálmán Tisza Square, which was the name of the square before the declaration of the republic in 1946.

The composition of the Ministry Council changed for the fourth time. Imre Nagy also assumed the post of Foreign Minister, and there were ten other Ministers in the government. The Socialist Workers' Party, Social Democrats and Smallholders, each held three posts, and two were given to the Petőfi Party. There was still a socialist/communist 'majority' within the government, and including Pál Maléter, the socialist parties now had seven ministers and the other two parties five.

At 8.00 p.m. Cardinal József Mindszenty made a speech on the radio. Initially, Mindszenty acknowledged that by the grace of God he was the same person he had been prior to his imprisonment. Next, he briefly interpreted Hungary's history, noting that although Hungary was a small nation, "in one matter we are first. No other nation has suffered as much during its her thousand-year history." Mindszenty also referred to the first King, Saint Stephen, as well as the nation's constant fights for freedom, which, according to the Cardinal, were mainly fought in defense of western countries.

When Mindszenty dealt with the present domestic situation, he highlighted the suspended production and the imminent threat of famine. According to

Mindszenty's experience, the struggle for freedom was fought by the people, who by this time were becoming emaciated as a whole. As such, he viewed the restoration of production as the primary task, after which, according to the Cardinal, "everyone has to know that the fight was not a revolution but a struggle for freedom." The implementation of free elections was necessary, in which all parties had the right to participate and which would be carried out under international supervision. The Cardinal declared that, based on the nature of his position, he would remain non-partial.[38]

In Mindszenty's view, Hungary should be a cultural nationalist state (kultúr-nacionalista szellemű nemzet és ország) with a restriction on private property. Moreover, Mindszenty did not mention the People's Democracy by name, although he referred on several occasions to "a fallen system". According to Mindszenty, legal responsibility should be carried out to its fullest extent within independent courts, and personal reprisals should be avoided. Specifically addressing the 6.5 million Catholics in the country, Mindszenty noted that "we will put an end [felszámol] to all the violent and distinct traces of the fallen system through a course [vonal] guided by the church. This derives voluntarily from our ancient religion and the moral and church laws of the same period." In the end of the speech, Mindszenty anticipated the free teaching of religion and the restoration of the institutions, associations and publications of the Catholic Church.

Following Mindszenty's speech, Minister of State Ferenc Farkas argued that the present government does not stand on the basis of the debates of 1945. The Minister listed seven tasks, of which the maintenance of socialist achievements was the first. However, he also added that included in these tasks was "everything which can and must be used in a free, democratic and socialist country, in accordance with the will of the people". The next points dealt mainly with friendly relations to other socialist countries and the withdrawal of Soviet troops. In addition, in an international press conference, Minister of State Géza Losonczy denied rumors that planned land reform would be cancelled or that factories were not going to be returned to their previous owners; the land belongs to the peasants and the factories to the workers.

## Sunday, 4th November

At 5.20 a.m., Imre Nagy spoke on the radio and announced that at dawn Soviet troops had begun an attack against Budapest. According to Nagy, the aim of the attack was to overthrow the lawful Hungarian democratic government. Nagy declared that Hungarian troops were now in combat. Following the speech, both the national anthem, *Himnusz* and also *Szózat* were played on the radio.

Religious newspapers were also published on November 3rd and 4th. On November 3rd, *Szív* published a picture of Mindszenty on its front page. Among the demands outlined were the establishment of relations with the Vatican, the right to strengthen social institutions, the institution of the family as the base of society, complete freedom to act and the return of church schools from the state. In a smaller news clip it was reported that the national committee of the neighbouring town of Martonvásár was preparing to change the name of Voroshilov Street to József Mindszenty Street.

The organ of the Democratic People's Party, *Hazánk* (Our Fatherland), came into being, and the first issue contained slogans such as "With God for Our Fatherland and Freedom" and "Do Not Harass a Hungarian". The latter was based on the famous pamphlet by Miklós Zrínyi, who in 1660 wanted to create a permanent Hungarian army. In addition, the writer interpreted that the Democratic People's Party had received the greatest amount of votes in 1947, and remained the second largest party in the parliament as a result of falsified election results. Although the aims in the paper were parallel to the aims in Mindszenty's speech, writer Vid Mihelics was opposed to any restorative attempts or to the return of mines and key factories from the state. However, he noted that compensation should be paid to ex-owners, and regular companies and apartments should be returned. In the article, Mihelics did not mention the word socialist at all, but rather defined future with the words "democratic, social Hungarian state".

*Népszabadság* joined the camp of the revolution in its leading article. Moreover, the organ suggested that former Minister of Defense Mihály Farkas and the entire bureaucratic, pseudo-Communist clique be brought before a court of law. The paper opposed the armed searches of the private homes of innocent people.

A few hours after Imre Nagy's announcement an open letter written by Minister of the Interior Ferenc Münnich was broadcast. According to Münnich, Ministers Antal Apró, János Kádár, István Kossa and Ferenc Münnich had broken their ties to the government of Imre Nagy. They had also started to form The Hungarian Revolutionary Workers' and Peasants' Government. Münnich argued that Nagy's government had become incompetent when faced with the increased influence of reaction. Inside the government there was no possibility to act against the danger posed by the counter-revolutionary danger. Moreover, it had become clear that "glorious fighters of the workers movement... had been killed". Imre Mező and two others were specifically mentioned by name. In addition, Münnich stated that "masses of honoured sons of the working class and peasants were murdered." Münnich came to the conclusion that "we can no longer watch idly while counter-revolutionary terrorists and bandits kill... our best workers and peasant brothers under the guise of democracy."

Moreover, the group also defined the situation in a leaflet entitled "An Appeal to Hungarian People". The writers dissociated themselves from both Rákosi's and Nagy's governments. At first, one of the main tasks had been to rectify the crimes committed by Rákosi and to defend national independence and sovereignty. However, Nagy's government was considered weak and penetrated by counter-revolutionaries, who endangered socialist achievements, the power of workers and peasants and finally the whole existence of the Fatherland.

The new government defined itself as patriotic and promised to secure the country's independence and sovereignty. In addition, they promised to put an end to the civil war (testvérháború) and to ensure the implementation of elections to revolutionary councils. It was also told how the government had, acting in the interest of our people, working class and our Fatherland, turned to the Soviet military commander to help our nation to quell the sinister reactionary forces. At the end of the leaflet it was mentioned that after restoring order the government would begin negotiations regarding the withdrawal of Soviet troops.

Later on Sunday, Hungarian radio stations sent requests for help in Hungarian, Italian, French and in English. In the English language broadcast, a request was made that the United Nations send paratroops to West Hungary. Over the following days, radio stations reported serious struggles between Soviet and Hungarian troops. For example, Radio Free Rajk argued on 5th November that we are once again dealing with a question of traitors, who lie about having liberated the country from counter-revolutionaries, and that the communist fight will continue both on the ground as well as underground.

* * *

Thus, in 1956 the present was frequently defined and important years repeated in the argumentation. On the level of the ruling party, MDP, and the Central Committee, the expectation of "counter-revolution" turned at first to "tragical events", to "civil war" and to different definitions of a "rebellion". Finally, on 4th November "revolution" was also found in the front page article of Népszabadság. It was only after this that it can be found on the level of the government; definitions were frequently more moderate in the statements of Imre Nagy. On 28th October, which later has been interpreted as a Rubicon, Nagy spoke about a "national democratic movement", and the 15th March and the Kossuth coat of arms were also reestablished. Later "revolution" appeared in the same speech than the restoration of the multiparty system.

However, various organizations spoke about a "revolution" prior to the government and the MDP. Writers defined the situation with the vocabulary of revolution already on 23th October, and DISZ interpreted the views of the government as a "revolution" the day after Nagy's reference to a national movement. For the first time, the clear definition of a revolution appeared on October 26th, when it was taken from 1848 and from the poetry of Sándor Petőfi. "Fight for freedom" also appeared on the 26th, i.e. before Nagy's speech.

Of the various years referred to, 1848 is the most common, although 1919, 1939, 1945 and 1947 were also present. Contrarily, it is interesting to notice that particularly the Horthy era was not used in the argumentation, for example, as the year of the compromise 1867. In fact, medieval and feudal history were not present either, although on 28th October Imre Nagy referred to one thousand year old history. King Saint Stephen and the constant fights for freedom were used by Cardinal József Mindszenty, who was also the only one who openly dissociated from the interpretation of a revolution.

* * *

Although the traces (1989), i.e. newspapers and radio programs, ended on November 4-5th, the 'uprising' itself continued. There were struggles and resistance, strikes, emigration, arrests, death sentences, demonstrations and consolidations of power etc., which will later be temporally located in chronological order and interpreted historically. In 1996, the writers of the handbook *1956 kézikönyve* (III) (1996, 7) called the period after 4th November one of the darkest and least known in Hungary's history, and divided the period into two periods. The first period spanned from 5th November to 12th December, and the second period began with the introduction of martial law and lasted until the end of March, 1963, with the attainment of general amnesty (1956 kézikönyve (I) 1996).

A broader armed resistance continued until mid November and 'passive' resistance until the first months of 1957. On 23rd November, a month after the student demonstration, it has been said that the streets of Budapest emptied as an act of demonstration between 2.00 and 3.00 p.m. On 4th December, on the first 'monthly anniversary' (*hófordulo*, cf. anniversary = *évforduló*) of the second intervention, the symbolic demonstration was followed by a march of women clad in black in honour of the memory of those who had fallen (Ibid., 265).

In mid-November, a Central Workers' Council of Greater Budapest was established in the electrical plant Egyesült Izzó. The Workers' Council organized a general strike on November 22nd and 23rd. Strikes were especially common in Salgótarján in Northern Hungary, where the great steel factories were located. It was there that the most serious clash took place on 8th December, in which 131 people were killed. Martial law was declared on 11th December by a decree, and it lasted until the end of March 1957. Internment camps were established and military tribunals judged people until November 1957. The first death sentences were pronounced already in mid-December. (cf. 1956 kézikönyve (I, III) 1996; Felkay 1989).

According to secret official statistics from 1957, 2652-2700 people had died before 11th November (1956 kézikönyve (III) 1996, 303-312; The Hungarian Revolution... 1996, 103). Imre Nagy and ca. 40 of his companions fled to the Yugoslav Embassy. There, Nagy refused to resign and, thus, refused to recognize the new government, which was sworn in on 7th November. Although Kádár promised his safe return home, he was extradited to Romania, after which he was brought before a Hungarian court and eventually executed on 16th June, 1958. Some 200,000 people fled from Hungary, and Cardinal Mindszenty remained in the American Embassy until 1971.

Thus, between 1957-1962 ca. 22,000 people were sentenced in courts, 13,000 were interrogated and some 35,000 were questioned (Az 1956-os... 1991, 130). In the beginning of the 1980s, emigrant historian and 1956-veteran Péter Gosztonyi made an historical analogy by noting that these numbers were higher than following 1848 or 1919 (1989, 206). The number of death sentences received is estimated at 250-350 (cf. also The Hungarian Revolution... 1996, 144).

# IV THE INTERPRETATION OF COUNTER-REVOLUTION IN 1956 DURING THE KÁDÁR ERA

In the former chapter the focus was on current newspapers. However, innumerable books have been written about the situation in Hungary in 1956, and the first bibliography was published already in 1963, in Toronto. In 1996 the 1956 Institute collected a bibliography consisting of more than 250 pages. The handbook *1956 kézikönyve* (II) is the most complete as yet. This handbook deals not only with events, but also contains portraits, memories, diaries, interviews, etc., as well as fiction, novels and short stories, drama, poetry, documentary and short films, and TV programs. However, the films, for example, were not necessarily written in 1956, but in some way refer to the 'uprising'.

The following chapter deals with the '1956' in the context of the Kádár era. To evoke the atmosphere of the era, I have first chosen a *samizdat* chronology *1956 a forradalom kronológiája és bibliográfiája* (Chronology and Bibliography of the 1956 Revolution (1990)), the first edition of which was published in 1986. According to the bibliography, 155 titles had been published in Hungary up to that time. Two thirds of the material dealt with monographs of the contemporaries, memories and documents. The writers argued in the preface that they tried to give preference to publications, which were available to the Hungarian audience regardless of the content.

The following table is comprised of nine categories, which were mentioned in the *samizdat* bibliography. I have headed each column with the year of publication. The first category of dates is before 1988, and it formally describes the Kádár era. The second category contains material from 1988, i.e. both before and after May 1988, when János Kádár was removed from office. In the third column there are publications from 1989. Finally, there is the total amount of all literature both inside and outside of Hungary.

85

| | Before 1988 | 1988 | 1989 | Outside Hungary | Total |
|---|---|---|---|---|---|
| 1) Contemporary history after 1944 | 7 | - | 3 | 2 | 12 |
| 2) General literature from 1956 | 7 | - | 8 | 19 | 34 |
| 3) Monographs and studies of contemporaries | 10 | 4 | 16 | 20 | 50 |
| 4) Document and source material | 6 | 2 | 25 | 7 | 40 |
| 5) Autobiographies | 2 | - | 6 | 10 | 18 |
| 6) Eyewitnesses accounts | - | - | 2 | 12 | 14 |
| 7) Memoirs | 15 | 5 | 21 | 21 | 62 |
| 8) Domestic propaganda | 12 | - | - | - | 12 |
| 9) Anniversary publications | 1 | - | 3 | 16 | 20 |

In Kádár's Hungary, most commonly available were memories (15), and monographs and studies by contemporaries (10). Outside Hungary these two categories were the most popular. In Hungary there were also a striking number of works of propaganda (12). Most of them (10) came into being in the late 1950s. Here, the so called White Books from the provinces are read as one unit. Secondly, the 'resurrection of 1956' in 1989 can be seen in the table. In 1989, 25 new document and source publications came into being. Memories (21) and new monographs and studies by contemporaries (16) were also published in 1989.

Seven titles from the category of memories before 1988 were published after 1985. In the category of documents and sources the only writings were two volumes (1958 and 1987) of writings of János Kádár, and decisions and documents of the Hungarian Socialist Workers' Party (1964). Another collection of documents was available from the years 1956-1957 (1981) in the form of the statements of other socialist countries concerning Hungary (1957). As a whole, it must be stressed that after 1989, the situation changed dramatically. A special institute, the Institute for the History of the 1956 Hungarian Revolution, exists in the Hungarian Academy of Sciences and has published more than 50 books in the 1990s (cf. Boros 1997, 284-286).

When tracing a typical example from '1956' in the historiography in Kádár's Hungary, I shall eliminate the small number of memories and anniversary publications. When more general representation is focused on, the emphasis will be on analyzes and studies. Thus, documents and memories as the monographs and studies by contemporaries are left out. Hence, I have left out of the table categories one, two and eight – contemporary history after 1944, general literature from 1956, and domestic propaganda.

Furthermore, the first criterion was timing the focus on different anniversaries, since after the 1950s, the printing of several publication was frequently timed to anniversaries: 1966, 1976, 1981 and 1986 (cf. Az 1956-os... 1991; Litván 1992). Since this was not possible in every case, the publications primarily centre on the years 1957, 1967 and 1986. The first example will be *Ellenforradalmi erők a magyar októberi eseményekben I-IV* (The Counter-Revolutionary Forces in the October Events in Hungary I-IV, 1957), which was placed in the category of domestic propaganda from 1957. Secondly, there is János Molnár's *Ellenforradalom Magyarországon 1956-ban* (Counter-Revolution in 1956) from 1967. According to the *samizdat* chronology, Molnár's book represented the first attempt at an "independent scientific analysis" (1990, 121) – by a member of the party. In addition, there are two books, which belong to the general literature of 1956 and represent the late Kádár era: *Counter-Revolution in Hungary* (1969/1981/1986) by János Berecz and *Drámai napok 1956 október 23 – november 4* (The Dramatic Days from 23rd October, 1956 – 4th November), 1986 by Ervin Hollós and Vera Lajtai.

In the bibliography there is only one general work from contemporary history after 1944: *A magyar népi demokrácia története 1944-1962* (The History of the Hungarian People's Democracy 1944-1962) by Balogh-Birta-Izsák-Jakab-Korom-Simon. However, here the aim is to focus on the literature directed toward a more international audience, and to emphasize the late Kádár era. Therefore, instead of the aforementioned book, I have chosen to use the book by Sándor Balogh and Sándor Jakab, *The History of Hungary After the Second World War 1944-1980* (1986). The book is not mentioned in the bibliography, which mostly concentrates on literature in Hungarian language. However, it is one of the few books published in English from the period.

## The Analysis of the Provisional Central Committee

The Provisional Central Committee of the MSZMP held a meeting between December 2–5th, 1956. Although it was noted that more material would be needed, four reasons or determining factors, were published. In the resolution published on 8th December it was argued that these "four basic reasons or determining factors, which for a long time before October 1956 had already been simultaneously effective, side by side, interlinked and in interaction with each other, and had jointly led to the tragic development of the events" (Balogh & Jakab 1986, 161). The analysis was written during a situation in which rear-guard struggles were still going on and passive resistance still existed. Later, it also dealt with the fact that these four reasons evidently formed a cornerstone of the policy of János Kádár. (cf. A Magyar Szocialista... II 1993, 12-13 & IV 1994, 9). The first sentences quoted below are the first sentences in the numerically corresponding chapters and are cited by Balogh and Jakab (1986, 161).

1. *"From the end of 1948, the Rákosi-Gerő clique, which had a decisive influence in [sic] the Central Leadership of the HWPP [MDP, HN] and the Government of the Hungarian People's Republic, had started to deviate from the fundamental principles of Marxism-Leninism... ."*

If the order of the factors matters, the past domestic mistakes would be the most significant. Marxism-Leninism was supposed to have a fundamental and true basis, but it was abused by political leaders. The clique was blamed for dogmatism and aggravating circumstances, dishonest economic policy, violating socialist legality, copying the Soviet model and finally of mis-understanding national interests. It was also considered a mistake that the leadership did not change its policy after the 20th Congress of the CPSU.

2. *"In the precipitations and tragic climax of the October events, a major role was also played by that wing of the Party opposition which had developed in earlier years and had since been playing a continually increasing role, which rallied around Imre Nagy and Géza Losonczy... ."*

The second factor is also connected to the ruling party. The activity of Nagy and Losonczy was considered positive insofar as they fought united in the ranks of the whole party opposition. The change occurred during spring-summer of 1956, because it was at that time that criticism was brought outside the party and into the streets, where reactionary elements were also included.

3. *"...The counter-revolution of the Horthy-fascists and Hungarian capitalists and landowners was a basic factor in the preparation and unleashing of the October events... and they had significant forces which operated illegally in Hungary."*

The actual counter-revolution itself can be found in the third determining factor of the unfolding of these tragic events. In addition to "significant forces", the original Hungarian language text also contains the term "main forces" (fő erői), which gathered and operated in West Germany (A Magyar Szocialista... 1964, 15). Internal forces were considered significant. However, the most important villain in the plot seemed to be external; the supposed threat of German revisionism. In 1955 the Federal Republic of Germany had also joined NATO. The aim of the Hungarian counter-revolution was interpreted to have been the restoration of the capitalist system of land ownership.

According to the Central Committee, counter-revolution had been defeated in 1945, after which time the former aims remained the same.

4. "... finally, international imperialism, whose objectives naturally extended much further than the Hungarian question, also played a decisive and fundamental role in the events in Hungary."

International imperialism was understood as a decisive factor of world politics in the 1950s. Hungary was considered to have been an integral part of the provocation of international imperialism, as were Suez, Vietnam, Korea and Taiwan. On the basis of these examples, it was concluded that international imperialism had not abandoned its aims of subduing people, its role in local wars and potentially in the Third World War. This was a particularly prevalent view on US radio stations, such as Radio Free Europe and The Voice of America. These stations began their activity in 1945 by opposing land reform.

With the exception of the first point, the recent past was defined in every case as a counter-revolution. However, the expressions "events" and "October events" were used synonymously in every paragraph. Thus, in the first quickly made December analysis, the significance of the recent past was not unanimously classified as a counter-revolution.

When the minutes of the Provisional Central Committee were published in 1993 and 1994, they revealed the first weeks of hesitation, and contained two possible scenarios. According to the stricter view, the counter-revolution began on 23rd October. The supporters of the more moderate view argued that although the counter-revolution had been present also on 23rd October, its momentum increased only from the beginning on 30th October, the day of the abolition of the party monopoly. Secondly, on November 11th the party leadership still had the idea, for example, that Imre Nagy could form a party of his own. At that time Nagy continued to reside at the Yugoslavian Embassy and refused to resign. Moreover, at the December 17th meeting of the Executive Committee, the implementation of a certain multiparty system was considered a possibility, on the condition that the parties recognized the idea of building on 'socialism'. The Smallholders and the Petőfi Party were explicitly named as such parties, i.e. the parties which had participated in the coalition government of 1945. (A Magyar Szocialista... I 1993, 270).

However, the term "national democratic movement", which the party leadership accepted in the end of October, did not have any legitimate place in the discourse of the party leadership (A Magyar Szocialista... I 1993, 17-20). Among party members, professor Erik Molnár had represented this viewpoint in his study, which was dated February 20th, 1957. At that time his study *Nemzeti-demokratikus felkelés vagy burzsoá ellenforradalom?* (National Democratic Revolt or a Bourgeois Counter-Revolution) had not yet been published (Molnár Erik..., Társadalmi Szemle 4/1989). However, it was brought to light in April of 1989 (Ibid.) in a situation in which the multiparty system had been reestablished and a struggle over the content of the past was occurring in Hungary.

In January of 1957, the Soviet, Bulgarian, Czechoslovakian and Romanian party leadership had already held a meeting in Budapest on the initiative of the Hungarian Provisional Central Committee. There, Communist leaders concluded that a counter-revolution had taken place and Imre Nagy was considered as a traitor. In February, the notion of Nagy the traitor was included in a speech given by Kádár, and on 23rd February, Ferenc Münnich surmised that the counter-revolution had already begun on 23rd October. Moreover, based on minutes of one specific day, April 9th was the day on which the notion of counter-revolution was sealed. On that day the Executive Committee held a meeting, at which they changed the name of Gyula Kállai's lecture. The Executive Committee corrected the original title "The Events of the Hungarian October-November in the Mirror of Marxism-Leninism" to "The Hungarian Counter-Revolution in the Mirror of Marxism-Leninism" (A Magyar Szocialista... III 1993, 52). Also, when an exhibition was opened on 22nd June, it defined the significance of the days, as: "Hungarian Counter-Revolution 23rd October–4th November" (NSZ 21/06/1957).

Although János Kádár was the Chairman of the Provisional Central Committee and led the Hungarian party, his position was also unstable at first. Kádár lacked 'canonized' experiences from 1919, as opposed to Rákosi, Gerő, Révai and Münnich, nor had he participated in the Spanish Civil War like Münnich or Gerő. In the Soviet Union Molotov had opposed him, but Khrushchev assured Kádár of his support against Rákosi and Gerő. On 19th February, the Provisional Central Committee decided that Rákosi and Gerő could not return from Moscow for five years, but József Révai's return was accepted, partly because of his earlier disagreement with Rákosi. On 7th March, Révai published an article in *Népszabadság*; in both Yugoslavia and the West its strict tone was expected to forecast the return of the past, i.e. Rákosi. (A Magyar Szocialista... II 1993, 13-20).

In the party organ, Révai's arguments were parallel to those in Kádár's February speech. Both also analogously used the space of experience when referring to the period following the dismantling of the Soviet Republic in 1919. Both saw the future as a threat, and argued that in 1919 the situation had only gradually become radicalized to Horthy. In his conclusion, Kádár also argued that in October of 1956 neither the bourgeoisie nor landowners expressed their goals honestly, but rather insisted that it was a struggle against stalinism. In addition, Révai also mentioned symbols in his criticism. He paid particular attention to the looseness of the leadership and gave as an example that the party's publishing house had changed its name from *Szikra* (Spark, compare Lenin's *Iskra*) to *Kossuth*. (NSZ 02/02; 07/03/1957).[39]

Symbols and traditions, thus, played an important role, and György Marosán commented on them when he spoke at Republic Square in 29th March. According to Marosán, "the wheel cannot be turned back", the dictatorship of the proletariat existed in the country. Marosán reverted counter-revolution to symbols; when he mentioned "a million metres of national ribbon", "a million Kossuth coats of arms", *The Hymn* or *Szózat*, they were actually referring to the counter-revolution. According to him a national revolution was not possible, because every revolution includes the task of altering property relations (168 óra 17/10/1989).

At that time, the Provisional Central Committee had changed and annulled Imre Nagy's declaration that 15th March would be a national holiday. When on 5th March the Provisional Central Committee prepared for the anniversary, they had already 'forgotten' the promises in the previous November. Also, Kádár had shared this view in a public speech, and in December the day was still accepted as a national holiday (1956 kézikönyve (I) 1996, 284). On the basis of a decree they returned to a former practice and March 15th became no longer a red letter day, but simply a school holiday. Rumours had circulated that the resistance would start again, particularly on 15th March. The act was a strict countermeasure to these rumours.

However, although Lajos Kossuth and 1848 contained 'reactionary traditions' for the Communists, it was an important TimeSpace. The Central Committee primarily considered itself to be the legacy of Sándor Petőfi and former serf Mihály Táncsics. However, members argued that keeping Kossuth in the fore would also prove the Communists maintained the traditions of 1848 (A Magyar Szocialista...II 1993, 249). When the theses were published (NSZ 10/03/1957) history was seen as bravely serving the present aims, i.e. "Communists and Working People Building Socialism Are the True Legacy of 1848." Moreover, Kádár wanted to time the appeal for the creation of the new Communist Youth Organization, KISZ, on 15th March. It was finally published on 21st March, which was the anniversary of the establishment of the Soviet Republic in 1919. (A Magyar Szocialista...II 1993, 19). According to the minutes, the anniversary should be used to increase confidence in MSZMP and to show the connection between 1919 and recent events (A Magyar Szocialista... V 1998, 110-114).

All in all, Kádár had not only accepted the 15th of March already in November, but also publicly accepted the Kossuth coat of arms. In spite of this, the new coat of arms was presented in the party organ during the parliamentary meeting (NSZ 12/05/1957). The new colours of the flag replaced the sickle and hammer also in the coat of arms, thereby replacing class symbols with nationally minded symbols. In May, another new symbol also came to being when the former *Sztálin útja* (Stalin Boulevard), which became the Street of Hungarian Youth during the 'uprising', was renamed *Népköztársaság útja* (The Boulevard of the People's Democracy).

Symbolic street naming was also mentioned in the first White Book (see the next chapter). There was the story of how counter-revolutionaries had torn down the street sign *Lenin körút* (Lenin Boulevard) and replaced it with a sign reading *Teréz körút* (Theresia Boulevard), which the street had been called prior to the Soviet 'liberation'. However, the tension between the old and the new was so obvious that on 1st May, 1957, the party organ published an article with the headline *Visszatér a múlt?* (Will the Past Return?). The article revealed that not only enemies but also allies were discussing the possibility that the past could return. Some members of the party leadership also supported the restoration of both the 1949 coat of arms and the name of the Communist Party to the ruling party (A Magyar Szocialista... IV 1994, 8).

However, the question of *which* past would return was less 'evident'. At the end of May, the government renewed an agreement, which dealt with the present situation in Europe and legitimized the provisional presence of the Soviet troops. News articles reporting on the trials of counter-revolutionaries appeared in the party organ in the spring; until the 1st of May there had been 33,704 arrests. Ideological teaching was brought to schools, and the study of the Russian language became compulsory. In November, workers' councils were suppressed by a decree. (NSZ 1957; A Magyar Szocialista... II 1993, 23 & III 1993, 10-12).

## The White Books

In 1957, The Information Bureau of the Council of Ministers of the Hungarian People's Republic published the so-called White Books in four volumes. Already on 30th December, 1956, the Executive Committee had accepted an initiative that party activists should collect memories from events occurring since 23rd October. It was pointed out that these memories should present the events from many sides and particular attention should be paid to the role of Communists, the army, youngsters, workers; councils etc. According to the Executive Committee, the material should be available for scientific research and propaganda. According to the minutes, even a car was ordered to The Institute of Party History, and it should be used for the collection of material. (A Magyar Szocialista... V 1998, 47-48, 57-58).

On February 2nd, *Népszabadság* reported that the second volume had been published, and the third came out on 5th July, 1957. The full name of the books, *Ellenforradalmi erők a magyar októberi eseményekben I-IV* (The Counter-Revolutionary Forces in the October Events in Hungary), contained both the words "events" and "counter-revolution". The first volume was directed toward an international audience and has been translated into many languages. Although the books cannot convince present readers, they still represented the first broad report of the events of October-November 1956 in Hungary.

In the first three volumes western and emigrant newspapers searched for credibility (the first book includes a specific chapter dedicated to western newspapers). Conversely, newspapers from socialist countries were only rarely utilised. For example, an article in *Le Monde* was cited for its mention of United States support for the Free Europe Committee. The *Reuters* news agency speculated about the witchhunts that were occurring and the possibility of Horthy's return (at that time he was living in Portugal, where he died in 1957). *Berliner Zeitung* (!) was also connected to western newspapers, and it illustrated how Hungarian refugees were being trained in American camps.

Photographs published in western newspapers were frequently used, although the reprints were often quite poor quality. All of the books also contain photographs by John Sadovy, whose photographs were published by *Life* Magazine (cf. Gadney 1986). Particularly Sadovy's photographs of Republic Square, in which a group of capitulated ÁVH members were lynched, are unique and astonishing historical evidence, and are also evidence specifically against the individuals in the photographs. There are close-up shots of lynched human bodies accompanied by tales of murder, mutilation and torture (the *samizdat* chronology (1986/1990) recognized a total 24 cases of lynching). The first book documents in great detail the attack on the party headquarters, which was supposedly based on a deliberate military plan.

In several cases the books are based on different eye-witness accounts. For example, in the case of the struggle at the radio station, there are interviews with people who used pseudonyms such as K.I. and M.L.. Officers' accounts were also referred to, for example, with regard to the attacks which took place on the night between the 23rd and 24th of October. However, it is important to notice that in comparison to contemporary newspapers, the White Books already contained information, for example, on the events at Kossuth Square, at which people were shot on October 25th. In western sources the amount has been estimated at between 300-600; the White Books mentioned only 22 victims; and in 1996, *1956 kézikönyve* reported 60-70 deaths and 100-150 wounded. However, in the White Books it was told how seven officers signed a statement in which their interpretation of events was that counter-revolutionaries had organized a confrontation in order to agitate the people against the ÁVH. Officers had defended the parliament, and mentioned shooting towards the parliament on October 24th, but argued that the real confrontation began the following day.

In the first book, the writers launch a narrative of certain events, which were considered a result of an active operation. The writers crystallized the activity into specific 'tactics': At first there was a witchhunt against the security forces, based on the crimes of "a few hundred at most", but initiated against thousands. Secondly, counter-revolutionaries had freed fascists as well as other criminals, after which a general witchhunt was directed against the dissolution of the party of the working class. Moreover, counter-revolutionaries attempted to penetrate administrative organizations, and once they had successfully accomplished this goal they "shed their 'socialist' masks". The tactics was interpreted in the concepts of 1945: fascist emigration started to return from the West. Finally, the incompetence of the government led to the counter-revolutionary activity and the bourgeois voices prevailed during the last week of the Nagy government.

Thus, in addition to a specific conspiracy theory, the argument 'what you did before', i.e. the use of forensic rhetoric, is essential in the argumentation. The idea becomes clear through the example of armed groups, which were presented in the first leaflet. For example, in the case of the combat group at the *Corvin* picture house, it was pointed out that one member had been Horthy's Lieutenant, one had been condemned 16 times and one's father had escaped to the West in 1945 but had since returned to Hungary.

To some extent the analysis had similarities to Berlin 1953, in which the SED called as fascist provocation and even named the Federal Chancellor, the Chairman of the SPD, one Minister and the Mayor of West Berlin responsible for it. Moreover, in Hungary the writers reminded from family relations: For example, it was argued that Béla Király, who commanded the National Guard, was a relative of fascist leader, Gyula Gömbös. In the chapter "The Activity of the Traitor Béla Király" his autobiography was referred to as describing the activity during the Horthy and the Arrow Cross era. Moreover, his imprisonment for espionage was mentioned, although his joining the Communist Party after the Second World War was not. On October 31st, 1956 Imre Nagy had rehabilitated Király (1956 kézikönyve (I) 1996, 151)[40].

The parties were described in greater detail in the fourth book and there the continuity to Hungary between the wars is found. They found a member from the ranks of the Christian Democratic Party who had belonged to *Magyar Élet Pártja* (The Party of Hungarian Life), which had ruled Hungary during the Second World War. Moreover, one of Horthy's Ministers was said to be a member of the Catholic People's Party and a high-ranking individual in the Revolutionary Youth Party was a former member of the Arrow Cross Party etc. Moreover, the writer reminded that one of the sons of a member of the Arrow Cross Party was a member of the Christian Hungarian Party, etc. However, it was forgotten how after the war, former members of the Arrow Cross Party also joined the ranks of the Communist Party.[41]

Cardinal Mindszenty's entry into political life was interpreted as an attempt to supersede Imre Nagy's government. Mindszenty's speech was not considered the act of an individual, but was influenced by Horthyite forces. Although the White Books made a few concessions to the content of Mindszenty's speech, it was argued that the Cardinal visualised the tasks of the counter-revolution. Despite the fact that he did not directly mention the restoration of the system capitalist landowners, his open declaration of the restoration of private property was interpreted as sufficient proof of his 'real' intentions.

The existence of spies and espionage were current problems during the Cold War, and the third book also dealt with the specific problem of foreign espionage. The United States was blamed for preparing to have ideological, politico-military and armed forces act against Hungary. Reports of judicial proceedings were published in the book, one of which involved one man, Imre Molnár, admitted to having received money and conceded that he had visited Hungary in the interests of the former Prime Minister Ferenc Nagy. One emigrant described in *Newsweek* how the western radio had given instructions on how far to go and what to demand.

In general, Hungarian emigrants were estimated to be to the strongest elements in the policy of the West. The diversity of the emigration was characterised through the slogan "An American In Spirit, A Hungarian by Language", an advertisement in an emigrant newspaper. These papers were read somewhat 'tongue in cheek': first there is a quotation from an Arrow Cross paper. Right after Imre Kovács, a former Party Secretary of the National Peasants' Party demanded the initiation of economic reorganization, which was interpreted as a restoration of capitalism.

In the fourth book there is already a polemic against the United Nations' Research Committee, which had been launched in January of 1957. The Special Committee on the Problem of Hungary had representatives from Australia, Ceylon, Denmark, Tunisia and Uruguay, who, although they were unable to enter Hungary, interviewed 111 individuals in New York and Europe. The committee completed its report in June, in which it concluded that it supported the theory of "a spontaneous uprising", and on 14th September the General Assembly accepted the report with a vote of 60 for, 14 against and 10 abstaining. For Hungarian intellectuals the report became somewhat of an inconvenience, and in September of 1957, 276 writers and other intellectuals bent to sign an appeal disputing its content.

In the White Books, discrepancies in the UN report were located and

95

discussed. For example, more than a hundred people disagreed with the description of the attack at the radio station. According to United Nations report, a few prisoners had been released from the Hungarian prisons, however, the White Books revealed that thousands of criminals had served in the counter-revolution. The argument was strengthened with numbers, as it was reported that 9962 convicts and 3324 political prisoners had been released.

The activity of János Kádár is not an issue in the White Books. The writers argued that the Presidential Council had stayed ahead during the counter-revolution and had nominated, according to the Constitution, a government with János Kádár as its head. This is partly true, because on the basis of the Constitution, the Presidential Council had the power of authority between the two annual sessions of parliament. The last session had been held in August of 1956, and on 9th May, 1957 the parliament accepted the actions of the Council after 4th November. The Constitution obligated the government to publish decrees on official bulletin. But the next issue of *Magyar Közlöny* after 20th October was not published until 12th November. On 12th November, there were two decrees without a date: the first was unnumbered and its purpose was to remove Imre Nagy from office, and the second (28/56) concerned Kádár's election as Chairman of the government (Report of the special... (I) 1957, 129). No information was given, as to whether the Presidium Council had fulfilled *all* formal details in Nagy's nomination on October 24th, but at least Nagy's formal resignation was lacking before the new government swore its oath.

The end of the book contains information, which tries to prove that the situation had calmed down since November. Pictures illustrated large mass gatherings: on 29th March, people gathered in front of the Budapest party headquarters, on 1st May and on the Day of the Constitution. The last picture illustrated the march of the Workers' Militia and was accompanied by a text, according to which several tens of thousands had joined the militia. The Provisional Central Committee had established the militia in February 1957 by decree. According to the decree, privilege in the new militia should be granted to red soldiers from 1919, Spanish veterans, partisans, Communists and trade unionists before 1945 (A Magyar Szocialista... V 1998, 346).[42]

In conclusion, the White Books were written during a time of active resistance, and the new government attempted to win the confidence of the people and new members to the party. The books were based on eye-witness accounts, newspapers and attempts to revise notions in the West. Compared to the report by the United Nations, the White Books contain 'white spots' and forgotten aspects, especially after 4th November. Although the books could not persuade a present reader, comparing to current newspapers they told *also* what had happened. In Hungary, they represented the first phase of

Koselleck's history writing *Aufschreibung*, in which there are many different stories available. Moreover, it seems that the White Books did not merely construct the background for the reprisals, as had frequently been said. It is possible that the historical analogy from 1919 also led to more direct reprisals.

## Politician as Historian and Vice Versa?

In 1965, Harry Hanak in *The English Historical Review* divided western literature concerning 1956 into three categories of authors: journalists, victims of the system and historians (The English... 1965, 874-875; cf. also Molnár 1967). As early as 1957, several publications had been created in the United States and Western Europe.[43] Among the first pieces of research work are Paul Zinner's *Revolution in Hungary* (1962) and Paul Kecskemeti's *The Unexpected Revolution* (1961). The latter does not focus exclusively on October–November of 1956, but concentrates on the period before and ends with the last week of October.

Elsewhere, Hannah Arendt and Ferenc Fejtő were among the first to put 1956 in historical contexts. Andy Anderson's work (1964) represents a clearly left-wing critique, in which the situation in Hungary was characterised as a social revolution, in which the people had wielded their own power in beginning to create an autonomous system (1975, 141-146). Moreover, *Die Ungarische Revolution der Arbeiterräte* connected Hungary to broader revolutionary movements in the 1950s. Moreover, for Bill Lomax (1976), the situation in Hungary was neither a national rebellion against communism, as in the West, nor an attempt to restore capitalism, as in the East, but a social revolution, which would be more democratic than the West and more socialist than the East.

Thus, western literature also evidently seemed to have been content with the political argument and could more or less be connected to the writer's political views. In general, conservative writers have argued over history, and connected '1956' to other historical analogies, while leftist writers have tended more to see the unfulfilled potential possibilities in 1956. In addition to the aforementioned books, I would like to mention three others. In 1981, David Irving, who is notorious for his connection to the extreme right, classified the uprising in Hungary as anti-Semitic. That same year, the 25th anniversary, Ágnes Heller and Ferenc Fehér published *Hungary 1956 Revisited*, in which they found leftist ideas in Hungary and also revisited the western picture of János Kádár. Conversely, the conservative Emil Csonka (1981) argued that the real changes in Hungary would take place only after the elections, which he believed had led to a Christian Democratic victory (Litván 1992, 11).

As a whole, the Hungarian 'conflict' was an issue that effectively united politically diverse emigrants and strengthened their political views (cf. Borbándi 1989, 417-418). Politically, emigration was rich in colour: for example, the Foreign Group of the Revolutionary Socialists of Hungary (1963-1964) could be described as Trotskyist. Moreover, there were also centrist and right-wing elements in the emigration to whom '1956' was of highest importance. (Ibid., 483; Az 1956-os... 1964). The position of the extreme-right, however, could be described as being between a rock and a hard place: their increased activity would prove Kádár's arguments of counter-revolution correct. Their right-wing publications, *Út* (Road) and *Cél* (Destiny), were published first in Salzburg and later in Münich, Buenos Aires and Australia (Ibid.).

One of the first acts of the new emigrants was to form the Hungarian Revolutionary Council in Strasbourg, on the initiative of Béla Király. In the first congress, held in January of 1957, the participants condemned Kádár and confirmed the former principles of the revolution. Moreover, a year later, a group of emigrants established a political and social institute in Brussels and named it after Imre Nagy. The Institute concentrated on leftist movements, the history of socialist movements and wanted to open possibilities for humanism and principles of democratic socialism. (Borbándi 1989, 456; Litván 1992, 7). At that time, Bad Godesberg was not yet a common experience and socialism as an ideology still had a competitive future. The institute ceased its activities in 1963, because American and other financiers declined to provide financial support, eventually forcing it to close (Ibid.).

The question of naming mainly surrounded the debate of whether '1956' was a revolution or a fight for freedom. According to Gyula Borbándi, the latter was rooted in the right side of the political spectrum and was supported by people to whom the idea of revolution was alien and who did not hesitate to voice their doubts about the revolutionaries. With regard to the idea of '1956' having been a fight for freedom, so-called national emigration, *szabadságharc*, was a more sublime concept than it was for the idea of revolution or uprising (Borbándi 1989, 417; cf. also Molnár 1967, 17-18). However, this did not mean that the October-November of 1956 revolution or fight for freedom had completely divided Hungarians on the basis of the left-right axis.

Thus, by focusing on Hungary and expanding the time perspective to include the ten years after 1956, Minister of Culture, Professor János Molnár, began the second phase in history writing. Of the books which I have chosen, the first is Molnár's, with its subtitle "A Critique of Bourgeois Literature" (1967). Molnár argued as an historian that western writers failed to use sources, baseing their books solely on interviews (the method of questioning and the value of the answers were also criticized in *The English Historical*

*Review* (1965, 874-875)). When referring to emigrant historian Péter Gosztonyi, who had written that emigrants were paid to recount their stories in the West, Molnár himself listed many archives which he had used as sources: television, radio, the Ministry of the Interior, the Central Committee, the party organ and Trade Union. In his strategy of argumentation, a writer began each chapter by briefly discussing western material, after which he began his own research. Molnár's sources contained ca. 80 foreign books and ca. 20 periodicals, and he commented on, or actually criticized, Méray, Arendt, Kecskemeti, Zinner and Sartre.

János Berecz's *Counter-Revolution in Hungary* was published in Hungarian in 1969, completed in 1981, and a third print came out in 1986. Berecz's doctoral thesis was written during a period in which Vietnam was penetrating living rooms, and in the second editions (1981), the writer also referred to recent events in Poland and their lessons. Moreover, the writer had a long career in the MSZMP, for example, since 1985 he has been the secretary responsible for ideology and propaganda. Berecz did not add specific literature to his bibliography, although the book includes a total of 131 footnotes including documents, memories, minutes, magazines, the experiences of the Brussels emigrant in the form of speeches and self-made interviews. Berecz also used material derived from United States sources, for example, the defense of Radio Free Europe by its leader Robert Holt (1958).

Sándor Balogh was working as a university professor when *The History of Hungary After the Second World War 1944-1980* was published in 1986. He also held a trusted position in the Academy of Sciences, and in 1988 he became the Chairman of the Institute of Party History. The historian Sándor Jakab had also participated in the activities of the party. For example, he had been the deputy Minister of the Interior in the 1960s. As a whole, Balogh's and Jakab's book differs from the others, because they condense period of October-November 1956 to a mere 20 pages. There are more than 70 Hungarian books in the bibliography, but anyone of them focuses on the events from an international or non-Hungarian perspective.

*Drámai napok* (Dramatic Days) by Ervin Hollós and Vera Lajtai also came out in 1986. Lajtai had edited the Central Committee's periodical *Pártélet* (Party-life) in 1960-1982 and Hollós belonged to the high ranks of the Ministry of the Interior after 1956. In addition to Hungarian literature, Hollós and Lajtai cited the stories of the Brussels emigrants, as well as western research and magazines. There is also archival material: Newspapers from 1956, court decisions, interviews and documents. There is also material from outside Budapest in the 1950s, which also referred to the White Books and other literature published in 1957.

Thus, in spite of the archival material and other primary sources, all of the named Hungarian writers also held positions within the existing system. Their positions dealt either directly with political decision-making, or more indirectly with higher education or communications.

## Before October 23rd

According to János Molnár (1967), the main differences between western and Hungarian research were not found in the events themselves, but more in the character, preceding activity and consequences of those events. One of the most crucial question has been: How spontaneous was the demonstration on 23rd October?

Contrary to others, János Berecz (1969) placed greater emphasis on international and western activity. At first Berecz reminded of the *containment doctrine*, connecting it to George Kennan and Harry S. Truman. When the nuclear monopoly collapsed, Eisenhower and Dulles had the idea of *peaceful liberation*. Berecz enumerates the consequences of United States tactics against the *captive nations* through examples such as the training of guerrillas in Albania, Radio Free Europe and various balloon campaigns. In Hungary, a specific Free Europe Committee organized Operation Focus in two phases, 1954-1955 and again in 1956. In Berecz's analysis, the balloon campaign was aimed at giving moral and psychological support to the underground resistance. It was not intended to supersede Nagy's government, but to aspire to more radical demands. Thus, Berecz did not directly argue that the West planned the conflict in Hungary, but claimed that it had encouraged it and supported the strive for more radical demands.

After the changes in Hungary in the spring of 1956, a *signal* once again came from the United States encouraging the resumption of subversive actions. For Berecz, this second phase of Operation Focus meant preparing for revolt, although public opinion forced imperialists to speak out about peaceful liberation. Berecz also connects to this activity the visits of former Prime Minister Ferenc Nagy and Károly Peyer to Vienna in the summer of 1956. Moreover, according to Berecz, there was also a third phase in the offensive which was finally launched on the basis of the Hungarian party leadership's inadequacy.

For Berecz, politics consisted of offensives and interventions, which continued the war through various other means. However, in the late 1990s, it seems that the fears of foreign intervention and of the political usage of 'weaknesses' seem to be based on exaggerated exceptions. According to Csaba Békés (1996), the United States employed rather peculiar double tactics: in principle they argued for peaceful liberation, however, contrarily, they tried to avoid an armed conflict with the Soviet Union at any price. Nevertheless, the US bipartite policy caused the United States government to be responsible for the armed revolt; young workers and students were convinced that the USA would offer armed assistance (Békés 1996, 35-38).

The role of Radio Free Europe spawned a heated discussion in the West, and its leader, Robert Holt, was forced to resign (Holt 1958, 199). During the 'revolution', the radio criticized Imre Nagy and, for example, on 29th October argued that no weapons should be laid down, because the goal of eventual peace also had to be won (1956 kézikönyve (I) 1996, 148). However, János Berecz argued that Radio Free Europe was already an executive organ at an early stage. On the basis of the transcripts from a Budapest court, Berecz provided a list of eight underground military organizations, which had operated since 1949 and received orders from Radio Free Europe. In Berecz's Marxist interpretation, Operation Focus was a decisive last resort, and he connected the demands of Imre Nagy, Radio Free Europe, and the students at the end of this operation.

However, János Molnár (1967) had already argued that no significant assistance was received from the West. Hollós and Lajtai surmised that an internal reaction could not have provoked the crisis with external support. Radio Free Europe raised the hopes of those who would not have taken arms without its influence. But there were also those who would have fought without the radio, too. Later Balogh and Jakab estimated that Radio Free Europe also occasionally encouraged co-operation. For example, in July 1956, it demanded purges against the Hungarian Stalinists and Rákosists. Therefore, under "such circumstances, the sincere wishes and urgings of those who wanted to improve socialist construction became almost inevitably 'mixed up' with the voice of those who strove for a fundamental change... and in the final resort for a fundamental bourgeois restoration" (Balogh & Jakab 1986, 143-144).

In general, the domestic political situation is taken more to the fore and in comparison to the White Books, Hungarian scholars began to place Hungary into specific contexts, such as the attempt to locate 'the road', 'the development which led' to the counter-revolution. Balogh and Jakab located '1956' as a component of the narrative beginning with 1944, and Hollós and Lajtai also reverted back to 1945. Thus, the coalition government, the establishment of the singleparty system, and the purges and power struggle between Nagy and Rákosi supporters are all an inherent part of the narrative.

Rajk's reburial on 6th October was not connected to an historical space of experience. Balogh and Jakab wrote how László Rajk and other *martyrs* "who had fallen victim to the 'show trials' should be transferred to an honorable place of burial in a fitting manner". In the background, there is a theory of the political misuse of the burial: For Molnár (1967), the reburial created a psychological background and were used politically. According to Balogh and Jakab (1986), revisionists and groups in favour of the bourgeois restoration used the funerals and the accompanying moral shock to whip up emotions and to incite rebellion against socialism.

János Berecz argued that domestic preparation was based on the class which had lost its power and property, and on the social stratum of the former power elite and other elements, who he considered to be fascists. Secondly, there were groups who identified themselves with Imre Nagy. Berecz did not argue that these groups prepared armed rebellion, but that they waited for someone else to carry it out. Also, Christian and liberal organizations were interpreted as planning to take power, some of them merely verbally and others in a more organized fashion. According to Berecz, the offensive also had possibilities, because the growth of the working class and the party had brought in petite bourgeois elements.

The 'revisionist group' received less attention in the White Books. However, Molnár had already estimated that among right-wing illegal groups, both the revisionists and the Petőfi Circle prepared demonstrations directed against the system. This position of being 'against' was argued in meetings held outside Budapest, at *MEFESZ* and in illegal youth organizations. Berecz reminded of analogies to 1848 in the meetings, and later Balogh and Jakab (1986, 145) stressed the atmosphere: "...a feverish atmosphere ruled in the universities and colleges, which soon spread to students in the younger age-groups."

Thus, before 23rd October, dissatisfaction had increased in Hungary, which is evident in the works of all writers. However, interpretations vary as to the level of importance which should be placed on circumstances or individuals and organizations in the shaping of these conditions. For János Berecz, who most obviously seemed to represent the theory of different 'offensives', a conclusion was reached – that under the influence of the erroneous politicy and the enemy activity there was a growth of dissatisfaction and indignation among working people.

# The First Week

Imre Nagy is an antihero throughout the entire plot, and none of the writers questioned his guilt and responsibility. Nagy's inconsistency is indicated, for example, by illustrating the idea that earlier he had to be self-critical regarding revisionism and opportunism, but had not expressed self-criticism in the beginning of October of 1956. János Berecz surmised that Nagy constantly denied the dictatorship of the proletariat and therefore the leading role of the working class. Balogh and Jakab pointed out that Imre Nagy was respected by peasants and intellectuals, but that he did not have direct contacts to proper workers, but only to professionals and the lumpen elements among the workers.

All of the books contained the concept that Imre Nagy also supported the idea of requesting assistance from the Soviet troops on 23rd October – a statement, which on the basis of the latest research work, has been found to be untrue (cf. 1956 kézikönyve 1996). Balogh and Jakab (1986, 147) wrote that the central leadership accepted Imre Nagy and several members of his group as members "after they had promised to cooperate in putting down the counter-revolutionary uprising". Thus, the concept 'uprising' was already accepted in late Kádárián literature, although it was complemented by the adjective 'counter-revolutionary'.

Kádárián historians tend to agree that the proper demonstration was begun by students. Also, according to János Berecz, while the majority of people felt that they had spontaneously made history, this did not necessarily mean that there had been no preparations made in advance. János Molnár re-postulated that the demonstration did not begin as a coup, but rather as a mass movement, in which Communists also participated. However, right-wing elements were present from the beginning, and their demands became more radical when they began to insist that Imre Nagy be included in the central leadership. The crowd described by Hollós and Lajtai did not become counter-revolutionaries, nor did they necessarily demand capitalism or counter-revolution. Rumours and contingent aspects come to the fore as more of a moving force in their book.

In general, the meaning of the mass movement and its metamorphosis into an armed collision were problematic, because writers attempted to distinguish 'corn from chaff', i.e. conscious counter-revolutionaries from those who were simply misled. The clumsiest attempt is made by Balogh and Jakab, who divided the demonstrators into the categories of Dr. Jekyll and Mr. Hyde:

"...it was no longer the university students who were calling the tune in the crowd but various bourgeois, right-wing groups, who by then had begun to organize openly. They started to burn and to destroy red flags and red stars and coat-of-arms of the People's Republic. They hooted down Imre Nagy, who spoke to them from Parliament in the evening hours, because he addressed the crowd as comrades... . From 28 October on... majority of students and young people who had been misled – suddenly realizing who were controlling them – left the armed rebel groups. Their place was now taken by thousands of those freed from jail and other lumpen elements turned 'revolutionaries'." (Balogh & Jakab 1986, 150.)

Nationalism and anti-Semitism can also be seen as elements of the October 23rd demonstration, because Béla Kun, Trianon and the experience of Auschwitz also existed in Hungary. For example, nationalism was reduced to the Kossuth coat of arms. János Molnár referred to a Yugoslavian newspaper when arguing that the Kossuth coat of arms belonged also to others. Molnár connected slogans such as "he who is Hungarian belongs to us" to nationalism, because those who did not join were considered 'un-Hungarian'. Hollós and Lajtai tended more often to mention anti-Semitic slogans which referred, for example, to the demand that no Jews be permitted to broadcast on the radio. There were beatings outside of Budapest in Hajdúnánás (26th October), and in Győr (28th October) it was demanded that Jews be dismissed from the Council (1956 kézikönyve (I) 1996, 107, 132).

There was also a campaign against nationalism in MSZMP's policy during the 1950s. In Yugoslavia, Milovan Djilas had developed a concept of national communism, while Gomulka did not agree completely with the treatment of Imre Nagy after 1956. Moreover, on 31st October, 1956, the United States National Security Committee argued that the Polish pattern of national communism as the first step toward freedom corresponded to United States aspirations (1956 kézikönyve (I) 1996, 171-172). Hence, in 1959, the Hungarian party constructed a thesis that denied the existence of a national communism belonging to bourgeois nationalism, attempted to dissolve the socialist camp and restore capitalism. They interpreted that the ruling classes had already betrayed national independence in 1867, but that the working classes would have been proud of the years 1848 and 1919 and, thus, of socialist patriotism. Bourgeois liberties were progressive in 1848, but in 1956 they would have merely pitted bourgeois power against the people's power (A burzsoá nacionalizmusról... 1959, 10-35).

However, in the history books which we have focused on the reconstruction and argumentation of the first evening is clearly more complex than it is in the White Books. János Molnár argued that Ernő Gerő's speech on 23rd October was a textbook example of political schematism, in that Gerő did not understand the complexity of the situation. Hollós and Laitai pointed out that he had been out of Hungary for only ten days; that the speech was taken from the work room; and that speech was the cause of his expulsion. Moreover, the picture of the struggle at the radio station has become clearer, and the reconstruction of the first night is also quite detailed – although they value that 'the crowd' shot first. In critical parts of the plot the 'trustworthiness' of the sources is put to the fore. For example, with regard to the question of who actually requested the deployment of the Soviet troops to Hungary, there is a quote from a party decision, the reliability of which was not questioned.

When Balogh and Jakab dealt with the massacre at Kossuth Square, they wrote about the provocation on 25th October. First a "crowd of several thousand demonstrators marched to Parliament; there, an armed group hidden in the building of the Ministry of Agriculture opened fire... . The armed provocation, which claimed many deaths was then blamed on the State Defence Authority and used to provoke a new wave of hatred." (Balogh & Jakab 1986, 148). They leave open the question of who first opened fire and thus, over the course of time, pinpointing the exact number of deaths became increasingly difficult. Often times the number of casualties was simply generalized as "many". Thus, even in the 1990s, the details of the incident remain unclear, although according to 'public opinion', ÁVH began shooting at people from the roof of the Ministry of Agriculture (1956 kézikönyve (I) 1996, 92).

There is a polemic against the United Nations report, for example, criticizing its contention that workers' councils spontaneously came into being. In general, the argument is still that the former activities of their members be revealed and that their democratic or progressive character be denied. Although the mass movement was significant, the writers say that the first councils were established from an initiative of party members.

Naming is essential in every book. While the emigrants had referred to 'revolution' and the 'fight for freedom', the term 'counter-revolution' could already be seen in the headlines of János Molnár and János Berecz. In the eighties, however, the title by Hollós and Lajtai became "Dramatic Days" and Balogh's and Jakab's title was changed to "The Events of October 1956". However, there are no changes in Berecz's book (1986), and thus the nuances can be interpreted as being more between the writers than a temporal sequence. Although all of the books include synonyms, such as 'revolutionaries', they are subjugated by the 'correct' name and systematically put in quotes.

Molnár (1967) argued that during the first days, bourgeois literature concentrated on Imre Nagy's statement on 24th October, Kossuth Square on 25th October and the massacre in Magyaróvár on 26th October. According to Molnár, through these examples, western literature attempted to shift attention away from the idea of civil war. As a whole, the illustration attempts to portray the first days as a civil war, in which workers also defended the factories. Although several of Molnár's examples are taken from a brief period of time, i.e. the period before the first intervention by Soviet troops.

Moreover, Balogh and Jakab mentioned that on 26th October, Imre Nagy attempted to suggest that the conflict be named a "national democratic revolution", however, the party leadership did not accept the initiative. More essential, however, is the redefinition of 28th October, which is interpreted as a revolution, although János Molnár noted that Nagy did not use this particular expression. Suslov and Mikojan had also accepted the formula of a national democratic movement on the day before, i.e. on 27th October (1956 kézikönyve (I) 1996, 115).

Berecz's category is sharper than the others. Nagy's declaration paralysed both parties, and thus counter-revolutionaries, fascists, criminals, reactionaries and murders became revolutionaries. According to Berecz, this meant that every worker, peasant and soldier who had defended the people's power became a counter-revolutionary. Balogh and Jakab defined renaming as an act that "struck a serious blow" to the defenders of the existing powers, who were now labelled as enemies of sorts. On 28th October, the party approved the "declaration that the counter-revolution was a national democratic revolution, and at the same time also agreed to meet several of the demands of the rebels. After this, Prime Minister Imre Nagy declared in the radio address that the 'revolution' had achieved its goal...". (Balogh & Jakab 1986, 145-147). Thus, there is the idea that redefining also had to do with new policy and concessions.

## The Second Week and After

In the White Books, the counter-revolutionary activity and the bourgeois organizations were characterised as having operated more openly during the last week of Nagy's government. Balogh and Jakab (1986) wrote that the party leadership hoped that the October 28th concession would restore order, although it had exactly the opposite effect. When the rebels saw the demoralisation and division within the party, they began their offensive in order to achieve their real aims. These 'real aims' were the aspiration for power and bourgeois restoration.

Behind the lines, there seems to be the idea of classical theory of revolution in which the ranks first face a common enemy, after which time reckoning begins within the ranks of the revolutionaries themselves. Imre Nagy's continuous retreats are admitted and the yielding of his supporters is still present in late Kádárian literature. Balogh and Jakab took the view that the forces of the bourgeois restoration began to show their hatred of the revisionists by declaring that they were Communists or that they were Communist supporters. Although there were signs pointing to the substitution of Nagy with Mindszenty – on the basis of Eisenhowers' memoirs, Berecz found that Dulles, too, expected this to happen – the generalization is still based on only a few days. Thus, the argument that Imre Nagy was still the Prime Minister was an argument which could be used both to support and oppose him.

For János Molnár, the multiparty system itself was not counter-revolutionary, however, every party included anti-Communist tendencies. Also, the coalition government had a different position in 1945-1948, when the parties were allies of the Communist Party, but then turned against it. Contrary to others, Hollós and Lajtai were more interested in the Christian parties. They connected them to the counter-revolution of 1919 and also found examples of there having been former Arrow Cross leaders and National Socialists within the parties. They reminded that the National Guard, too, was a product of 1944 as opposed to 1848. Thus, pluralist groups might have connected themselves to the past, and the poetry of Ady, Széchenyi and Vörösmarty could even be found in the texts of Ferenc Szálasi. However, this does not mean that these persons necessarily had anything to do with Arrow Cross, but the Hungarian space of experience offered a multitude of material for later interpretations.

The writers interpreted Cardinal Mindszenty's radio speech 'as the devil would interpret the Bible'. For example, Balogh and Jakab argued that all individuals having to do with the government of the People's Republic should be ousted and dealt with. Hollós and Lajtai refer often to the speech, and the Cardinal's obsolescence is stressed through a western newspaper. The book also includes a picture of a paranoid Mindszenty speaking behind a microphone. In addition to Mindszenty, there is an admirable statement from Otto von Habsburg. It later become known that on 31st October, Otto von Habsburg had suggested to Eisenhower that Saint Stephen's crown be returned to the freely elected Hungarian parliament (1956 kézikönyve (I) 1996, 171-172).

When focusing on workers' councils, János Molnár examines both Arendt's view and the Brussels institute. According to Molnár, the West only began to remind workers' councils to keep the Hungarian problem on their agendas after 4th November. Molnár also referred to the conclusion reached by the United Nations, that instead of the councils the parties took the task to represent the revolution. Molnár noted that not even the revisionists took the councils seriously, and as such they merely represented a dangerous illusion to western workers. In this sense, Molnár's notion is more independent than Berecz's or Hollós' and Lajtai's, who argued that the councils merely fell into the 'wrong hands', as was the case in Kronstadt in 1921.

The period after 4th November is the most questionable in every book. The *samizdat*-chronology from 1986 paid attention to how newspapers and history writing in the Kádár era did not practice reprisals following the revolution. The writer(s) of the chronology also pointed out that there were 'white spots' in the events outside Budapest and in the sentences after 1956 (1956 a forradalom... I 1990, 15-18). For example, János Kádár did not speak in public about the first months of his government. Rather, he quite casually noted the idea of 'the time to intervene', as seen, for example, in László Gyurkó's portrait of Kádár (1988). An 'urban legend' has surfaced surrounding how the memory of Kádár's hesitation has been stifled. Namely, his expressions of hesitation have become destroyed issues of the party organ, in which he also expressed his support for the multiparty system.

However, it is not unique that an inconvenient past takes time to be dealt with more objectively, for example, Vietnam in the United States or the civil war in Finland. However, none of the writers criticize the present leadership. János Molnár referred to the Kádár era very briefly, mentioning only in passing that there are few sources, many living witnesses, and that the research includes subjective elements. If Molnár had difficulty documenting the events, he had paid quite a bit of attention to János Kádár, dedicating more than half a page to his speech from 1958.

In addition, when the minutes of the Provisional Central Committee became available in 1993, researchers tended to refer to problems which were still quite obscure; the founding of the MSZMP was timed between 30th October and 1st November. Also, the trip to Moscow was still shrouded in shadow until 3rd November, at which time Kádár flew from the Ukraine to Szolnok (A Magyar Szocialista... I 1993, 10-12). However, there is evidence that Kádár participated in the session of the Presidium on 2nd and 3rd November (Döntés a Kremlben, 1996, 75-95). Kádár may in fact have received certain orders upon his return to Hungary, evidence of which can be found in the so-called "Yeltsin File", which confirmed in 1992 that the first announcement of the new government was translated from Russian.

Thus, in the books written during the Kádár era, the textual style is casual. Historians use expressions like a "growing group", the "working masses", which hardly reveal Kádár's popularity. János Berecz wrote that following the party split, the Communists stepped aside and allowed the organization of a new power centre or, as was literally noted in the first announcements, that the Soviet government had followed the Hungarian people's wishes that the counter-revolutionary forces be crushed. In the third edition, Berecz added a chapter entitled "The Founding of the Socialist Consolidation", in which he refers to Kádár's own notion and then to his own interviews. The last subchapter deals with political jargon and is entitled "With the Working Masses for Socialist Consolidation" – as politics is seen as having ended on 4th November.

The Soviet leadership, too, was divided with regard to the intervention decisions. It seems that French, British an Israeli politicians planned their attack on Suez (29th October) already on the 22nd, i.e. prior to the demonstration in Hungary (Békés 1996, 62). Secondly, it seems evident now that before Suslov and Mikojan left Hungary, they also expressed their support for the multiparty system on the 30th, although in Moscow on that same day they had already another intervention in mind. At this phase, Khrushchev answered with a more moderate statement, which Hungarian newspapers also published on the next day. (1956 kézikönyve (I) 1996, 151-160). However, on 31st October, Krushchev argued in favour of halting the withdrawal, because it occurred to him that, following in the footsteps of Egypt, they were also giving Hungary to imperialists (cf. Döntés a Kremlben 1996, 62). Thus, the Soviets, too, had their own 'domino theory'. In addition to Egypt, reference was made to the possibility that Czechoslovakia might also crumble (Ibid., 72).

Hollós and Lajtai were able to partially avoid the problem, because 'the dramatic days' were temporally located between 23rd October and 4th November. However, they support the legitimacy of Kádár's government with the argument that Nagy's government renounced the Warsaw Pact, thus acting unconstitutionally. Moreover, Balogh and Jakab wrote that the government made a strict distinction between conscious counter-revolutionaries and those who and those who had been misled, and the former were faced with strict punishments. János Berecz counted 70 death sentences until the end of July, 1957. Hollós and Lajtai did not write specifically about death sentences, but estimated 2,505 deaths.

On the basis of the Soviet declaration of 30th October, the conclusion is drawn that the only acceptable development would be a socialist. Berecz argued this view with the idea of a repetitive past, i.e. neutral Hungary had threatened its socialist neighbours, because Hungarian nationalism had always been directed against its neighbours. According to Hollós and Lajtai Hungarian neutrality would have threatened the status quo in Europe and European peace in general.

As I mentioned earlier, naming is essential in every book. Now, János Berecz argued that, in fact, the founding of the Kádár government under extremely difficult circumstances was a revolutionary move. The government was created in order to suppress a counter-revolution and to restore social order. The definition "Revolutionary Workers' and Peasants' Government" was used in the name of the government until 1971. Moreover, the first years in the Kádárian history writing were described as consolidation. After 1989, a few researchers have used another name, "soft dictatorship", which began with the restoration (cf. Horváth 1992; Seifert 1992; Gombos 1993; Magyarország... 1995). Thus, after 4th November, there were two competing notions of revolution in Hungary, neither of which belonged to the category of modern restoration or counter-revolution. However, both notions attempted to restore and return to the past, in the sense of Thomas Paine: Imre Nagy to 'the forties' and Kádár to 'the fifties'.

As a whole, the second phase of Koselleck's history writing, *Fortschreibung*, began with the publication of János Molnár's book in 1967. Although the authors could have expanded their illustrations of the situation, they do not exceed the party resolution of December 1956. Mistakes were also found in their own ranks, although it is quite typical to reiterate people's previous activities and 'provocations', as well as to defend the present leadership. Moreover, the authors also treat the past as living memory. Hollós and Lajtai, for example, mentioned how difficult it was for them to write, because the counter-revolution still completely ruled the first half of the century.

Thus, when read from the perspective of the late 1990s, the logos in the argumentation could potentially be even more 'credible' than I had expected. However, the argument also contains an ethos and pathos, which can be seen in whether different audiences discerned the 'history of winners' and were able to locate the logos under the ethos and pathos. Not all intellectuals had the possibility of using history or studying western literature, because such literature was branded with the letters "Z.A." (closed material) and those wishing to view it needed special permission. The restriction of western material was lifted at the end of August, 1989 (MPÉ 1990, 306).

## An Excursion into Text-Books

Below, we focus more closely on other traces of political history, textbooks. I begin with a textbook written by *Ágota Jóvérné Szirtes: Történelem a gimnázium IV. osztálya számára. A legújabb kor története* (History for the Fourth Grade in Senior High School. Recent History). The book was published in 1976 and, here, the fourth edition will be used for the 1985-1986 school year, and the sixth edition for 1989-1990. In the first book the narrative "Counter-Revolution in 1956" contains five semi-full pages. The following titles, represented below in italics, are the chapters in the textbook.

*"Counter-Revolution Break Out."* The demonstration is first ascertained as having been organized by the revisionists, after which time it was out of their hands and eventually ended up as an armed counter-revolutionary revolt. After Imre Nagy had promised to cooperate in the eradication of counter-revolutionary acts, he and several members of his group were recruited into the central leadership of the MDP. Nagy's 'weakness' is illustrated by his gradual retreat from view in various events. On the contrary, the current leader, Kádár, is mythologized by the idea that, on the same day on which he was chosen to fill the position of First Secretary, he said in a radio address that the attack must be quelled.

*"An Attempt to Overthrow the People's Democracy."* In this chapter, armed groups were seen as having already attacked party headquarters on 26th October, in order to hinder the formation of Communist resistance. Reference

is also made to the same day in the caption under the picture referring to the lynchings at the Köztársaság tér. This does not hold true for other sources, but rather the impression was given of conscious and planned aggression already at the early stages. Furthermore, both Nagy's suggestion of a "national democratic revolution" and its subsequent rejection are also mentioned. In spite of this, *Szabad Nép* was of the opinion the following day – the date was incorrect.

However, the article is said to have caused a major setback to those elements defending the workers' power, because it branded them as enemies of the revolution, named rebellions as revolutionaries and paved the way for the liquidation of workers' power. The revisionists were also accused of preventing the possibility of the arming of the Communists. Then they briefly introduce events such as the establishment of the multiparty system, the overthrowing of communist rule, the following of a "Christian course" and Mindszenty's support of the restoration of great landowners and capitalists.

*"Setting Up the Hungarian Revolutionary Workers' and Peasants' Government."* There is a brief description of how Kádár, Münnich and other members of the central leadership broke from traitor Imre Nagy and his group, as well as how they and other fighters found a new revolutionary centre in Szolnok. In the representantive of the new counter-government, János Kádár made a speech on the radio and mentioning that they had requested assistance from the Soviet Red Army. The speech is quoted on more than half of the page, thus stressing Kádár's 'sovereignty' in the events. There are also other quotes in the text-book from Radio Free Europe, *Le Monde, Die Welt, Der Spiegel*, Mindszenty's radio speech and party documents.

*"The Liquidation of the Counter-Revolution"* also seems to be a mental watershed in state socialist Hungary, because this is the title of a chapter dealing with reinstating the power of the people. This chapter includes a description of how the units of the Soviet Army and other forces trusted for socialism disbanded the armed resistance groups in a matter of days. According to the book, the most serious battles took place in Budapest, where the material and human losses were also the heaviest.

*"The First Measures of the Hungarian Revolutionary Workers' and Peasants' Government."* Two specific sentences reveal the clear-cut division made between conscious counter-revolutionaries and those who were simply misled and influenced by them. Strict punishments were enforced on the former, while attempts were made to win over the latter through patient persuasion (cf. Balogh and Jakab in the former chapters).

*"The Reorganization of the Communist Party and the Mass Organization and Activity of the Parliament."* The name of the reorganized Communist Party is mentioned only now, although it played an important role in the consolidation

of the people's power. In this chapter, the four reasons of the Provisional Central Committee are listed in order, and it is also pointed out that the reorganization had primarily ended by the summer of 1957. Furthermore, the idea of a dual struggle against dogmatism and revisionism can be found in the textbook as the MSZMP, a leading political force in the People's Democratic System.

There are four visual representations in the textbook: the mass demonstration at the Bem statue on 23rd October, a poster published by the Writers' Association, a lynching at the Köztársaság tér and the Workers' Guard march in March of 1957. As I mentioned above, the lynching image is accompanied by a caption referring to 26th October, which thus strengthens the notion of conscious anti-Communist activity at an early stage. Furthermore, the notion of counter-revolution is illustrated with quotes from western newspapers. On 2nd November, *Le Monde* seemed to write that the revolution, the counter-revolution, if you will, was successful in Hungary. Finally, the number of emigrants is estimated at 150,000, which is significantly less than is generally mentioned in western sources, 200,000.

Thus, the text-book indicates the same signs as other history books until then: there are parts with inaccurate details, which could be revealed with a magnifying glass. Keeping present positions was a value in itself, the current political leadership was glorified and Imre Nagy was branded an incompetent Premiere. The other visual aspects of the book are graphics, including statistics illustrative of the growing economy and increase in national welfare. The last image in the book really reveals everything of the socialist construction in a nutshell. It is the first and only Hungarian nuclear plant, the construction of which began in the early 1980s.

Regardless of the fact that the current temporal context is the years of the Cold War, recent history was 'successfully' documented up to the present, and the most significant contrast (1989-1990) is a clear break with the past. In the sixth edition, Hungarian history ended at the end of the Second World War, leaving out the entire communist period. Moreover, Hungary's entire recent history, since 1914, was revised in the new edition. The earlier "The Counter-Revolutionary System in Hungary Between the Two World Wars (1919-1939)" was now entitled "Hungary Between the Two World Wars" and was combined with the revolutions in 1918 and 1919.

Thus, in the text-books, a temporal perspective had not made the past more exact, but rather more 'obscure'. In the late 1980s not only the present, but also the past was in turmoil and it can be assumed that this turmoil also influenced future expectations.

# V   THE POLITICS OF REMEMBERING AND FORGETTING DURING THE KÁDÁR ERA

In the previous chapter I have discussed history writing and text-books, which as a part of history culture, keep the past in the present. However, there are also many other traces of how '1956' was present in Hungary after 1956. For example, in 1976, the date 23rd October, 1976, contained in a poem, was censored. The poem was written by István Eörsi, who was imprisoned after 1956 (168 óra 09/07/1991). Strategies of remembering and forgetting generally vary, but we have to particularly focus on different anniversaries. Hereafter, I would like to discuss other bits of history culture since 1956, which, on the one hand attempts to make us remember, and on the other, to make us forget.

The first anniversaries were widely used in commemorations and demonstrations outside Hungary. In particular, different emigrant groups reminded Western Europe, South America, Canada and the United States of the situation. On the third anniversary, for example, the Mayor of Los Angeles dedicated the day to Hungary, and a year later seven US States remembered Hungary by dedicating the day to the Hungarian Freedom Fighters. There were also protests against Hungary. In 1958, the British Labour Party protested against the execution of Nagy, as did the PEN, and in December of 1958, 37 countries condemned the execution in a United Nations Resolution (1956 kézikönyve (I) 1996, 316-345).

It seems that the foreign remembrances were once again strengthened on special anniversaries during the Reagan era. Among the western media, particularly Radio Free Europe, memorialized and reminded from the events. In 1983, the "Third World Congress of Hungarians Living in the Free World" dedicated the year to the memory of Imre Nagy. In 1986, New York State declared 23rd October "the day of Hungarian revolution and fight for freedom". In 1988, an Imre Nagy Memorial Committee was established in the United States, and a memorial session was held in the United States Congress of June 15th (1956 kézikönyve (I) 1996, 344-345).

The Hungarian problem began to vanish from the daily agenda after the Cuban crisis arose in 1962. As a result of secret diplomacy, an agreement was reached, and in December of 1962, the General Assembly requested that the question be made *ad acta*. As a response to this move, general amnesty was reached in Hungary on 21st March, 1963 (on the anniversary of the establishment of the 1919 Soviet Republic). However, it did not concern persons sentenced to prison for manslaughter. From 1963 onward, diplomatic relations with Hungary were reached with Britain, France and other western countries.

In August 1962, 190 persons were rehabilitated, and Rákosi, Gerő and 23 others were stripped of their party membership. Moreover, a committee was appointed and given the task of investigating the terror in the Rákosi era. The international background was favourable for this decision, because in the Soviet Union de-stalinisation had continued in the XXII Congress of the CPSU and, for example, in Bulgaria, Chervenkov had been dismissed following the meeting (Horváth 1992, 193-194; cf. Lomax 1985, 110-112.). In fact, these actions finally sealed Kádár's alliance to Rákosi's supporters. In 1972, Kádár was finally ready to admit that "a national tragedy had occurred, which was scientifically defined as a counter-revolution" (cf. also Seewann & Sitzler 1982, 16-18).

When studying various strategies of remembering and forgetting during the last half of the 1990s, we encounter several difficulties concerning '1956'. Since the 1980s, '1956' has been seen as having been an integral part of the system change, however, the period following the 1960s has yet to gain popularity among researchers. On the other hand, the last ten years have produced such significant societal change, that the Kádár era has already been left far behind. From the perspective of critical research work, there are two other points of value. First, since the end of the 1980s new experiences have come into existence, which have also influenced interpretations and memories concerning the past. Second, the period itself has its peculiarities and restrictions, because, for example, the freedom of association and the right to free speech did not exist.

Free and open public speech concerning '1956' was not advantageous. Therefore, the question of whether people kept the 'uprising' in their minds or tried to forget it, needs to be posed. Psychologist Ferenc Mérei has written about a "national amnesia" (The Hungarian Revolution... 1996, 147), in which the past was suppressed in people's mind. Moreover, in 1989, Miklós Vásárhelyi argued that the first generation wanted to forget, while the second generation simply no longer knew anymore (MN 30/05/1991). Thus, if the next generation no longer had memory of events, what were the roles of the ruling power and the party in this forgetting. In what sense did the rulers of

Hungary and their henchmen make people forget. Or did they instead provoke people into remembering? Whether also preventive actions, such as the locking up of typewriters and copy machines in factories prior to 23rd October (The Hungarian Revolution... 1996, 161) provoked people into remembering, or prevented them from political actions?

Remembering experiences other than 'winning' ones was not advantageous in public and could bring unexpected difficulties and troubles. Present day scholars (cf. Kalmár 1998) discuss oral memory, but there are problems with anachronism and inaccuracies in the evaluation of the memories of those who had later experiences. Oral history is valuable. However, whether people had fears to speak during Kádár regime, it is not self-evident that they do not have any political motives or expectations of the narratives in the 1990s. In this sense, everything that is said about experiences in '1956' and since 1988, is said in a new political context.

However, another approach to memory is also possible, because throughout the entire Kádár era, there were traces in history culture which revealed ways of dealing with the past. Thus, whether "everyone knew" (The Hungarian Revolution... 1996, 161) there were exceeded an individual like punishments, emigration, difficulties at work or general pessimism. The new economic liberties of the 1960s and the re-arrangement (*visszarendeződés*) in he 1970s also belonged to these traces; although someone might 'dwell in the past' and continue to remember the 1950s as a primary experience in the 1980s. Finally, there were several other traces, such as statues and street names, which both consciously and unconsciously left traces in human memory.

In the late 1980s there were mainly two generations involved in the remembrance of 1956: 'fathers and sons', i.e. people who had personal experiences of the events, and those who learned about the events through oral history. Moreover, by the late 1980s "the beat generation" had already occupied state bureaucracy and enterprise (Szalai 1990, 74). For them, the former cataclysmic memories were partly mediated through state-run apparata such as schools, the media etc., and partly by their own parents and other private channels, as far as they personally were interested in the past.

## Politics of Memory in the Kádár Regime

Around the time of the first anniversary in 1957, the Workers' Militia was on alert from 22nd October to 8th November; the mounted police patrolled the cemetery; and several hundred people were arrested. On 30th October, there was a mass gathering at Republic Square, where a plaque was unveiled honouring the memory of the defenders of the party headquarters building

(1956 kézikönyve (I) 1996, 302). Moreover, near the second anniversary a plaque was also unveiled at the radio station.

In April 1957, the party organ defended ÁVH's activities. Martyrs and fallen heroes – not only ÁVH's – were included in the White Books. Altogether, 51 fallen heroes were introduced in the second and third books, including pictures and personal details. Furthermore, during the spring of 1957, *Népszabadság* reported on the (re)burials of victims of the counter-revolution, some of whom were buried on the same plot of land as László Rajk and others in October of 1956. Among the various decorations was a medal awarded for 'workers' and peasants' power', which was established in April. With this medal "fallen heroes" were recognized as faithful supporters of Kádár, i.e. individuals who had supported the new government at the end of 1956.

In 1958, the construction of a special Workers' Movement Memorial got under way at the Kerepesi Cemetery. From then on, Communist politicians and other high officials were buried and reburied in the same cemetery in which the mausoleums of other important figures in Hungarian history, such as Lajos Batthyány, Lajos Kossuth and Ferenc Deák were located. There were also Soviet soldiers buried at Kerepesi, as well as tombstones, on which were inscriptions showing that the deceased had been victims of the counter-revolution. However, closer scrutiny also revealed the existence of unmarked graves and tombstones bearing only the text "1956". These unmarked graves have been restored in the 1990s, and the tombstones now mythically refer to those who "fell in the revolution and fight for freedom".

On the fourth anniversary in 1960, the fallen defenders of the party headquarters building were honoured with the dedication of a memorial at Republic Square, where many of the martyrs discussed in the White Books had been killed. For the MSZMP, the attack on the party headquarters meant an attack against the whole party. It was also the most important argument in the legitimization of the necessity of the second Soviet intervention, and was seen as proof of the rein of white terror. The notion that the party should be defended became a crucial part of communist thinking during the whole Kádár era. According to Molnár (1967), it was the first open attack meant to liquidate the party, and Hollós and Lajtai (1986) considered it as a destruction of an essential political centre.

The laying of wreaths annually at Köztársaság tér and the cemetery of Kerepesi, became a part of communist rituals and were regularly mentioned in the newspapers. For example, on every fifth and tenth anniversary, these commemorative actions were systematically noted in the party organ. Usually *Népszabadság* did not feature the events on the front page, however, they were mentioned on other pages. However, the commemoration of the 25th anniversary was featured on the front page. Five years later, the government

116

itself held a ceremonial meeting, in which '1956' was not hidden from view. By this time 30 years had passed since the formation of the Revolutionary Workers' and Peasants' Government in Szolnok. According to János Berecz, the party did not need to reevaluate its policy from December 1956 (1956 kézikönyve (I) 1996, 345).

Regardless of the fact that the last two anniversaries of the decade could be considered more important than the others, János Kádár did not usually participate in the rituals at Köztársaság tér or Kerepesi Cemetery. The task was given to other officials in the ruling party, although the first tenth anniversary seemed to be an exception. On the tenth anniversary, Kádár was seen at the commemoration. The party organ around the 23rd of October, 1966 is quite interesting. There was nothing in it about '1956', although there was a story dealing with the 30th anniversary of the Spanish brigades.

Thus, the anniversaries evidently also became an important part of expectations. In April 1981, MSZMP's Political Committee dealt with the forthcoming anniversary as a form of propaganda and agitation. It was noted that in the West, only hostile literature from 1956 had been published, and therefore a more authentic historical literature should be brought to developed capitalist countries. According to the Central Committee, the interest of journalistic teams who independently come to Hungary should be focused on present-day Hungary by selecting the appropriate locations and people for discussions and interviews. Those "requests, which directly concern the 25th anniversary of the counter-revolution had to be rejected. The travellers – with the exception of those on the prohibited list [tiltólista] – should not be rejected." (A Magyar Szocialista... 1988, 203-204).

On the 25th anniversary, different series started to appear. In September and October of 1981, Népszabadság published on series on weekends, "This Happened, the 13 Days of the Counter-Revolution". It was written by journalists and had a total of 13 parts. Five years later, a series, "The Facts Are Talking", was published in seven installments. In 1986, there was also a weekly television series called "History Living With Us". In this series János Berecz, János Molnár and Ervin Hollós, whose books have been analyzed in earlier chapters, played an essential role. In one sense, they were the most significant official authorities on '1956' in Kádár's Hungary, and they guarded the 'right' interpretation. (cf. also Seewann & Sitzler 1982).

On television, October 23rd was not paid special attention, nor was it especially remembered. A more serious programme was timed to the end of October and to the beginning of November, i.e. the same time the occupation of the party headquarters had taken place.

On the whole, two matters seem to be evident. First, the authorities attempted to shift people's memory from 23rd October to 30th October.

Secondly, the events in Hungary remained in the shadow of the anniversary of the Russian Revolution on November 7th. On the basis of the party organ, the great phallic symbols of the Kremlin and the image of János Kádár waving from a train occupied the Hungarian public consciousness. The anniversary was declared a holiday in 1960, and a central square in Budapest was named after this day.

Since 1945, there was another holiday which referred to the Soviets, April 4th the Day of Liberation. Also, the first amnesty in 1959 was timed to coincide with the 14th anniversary of this holiday. Moreover, the celebration of the anniversary was enacted into law both on the 15th and 20th anniversaries. In 1959, the same canonization was done to the memory of the first Soviet Republic on its 40th anniversary – thus, the old way of codifying certain events into law continued during the period of state socialism.

On the other hand, there was also ambivalence on the question of 'acceptable nationalism' in the party-state. Official policy stressed internationalism, but towards the mid-eighties the old communist rhetoric had vanished and for example Queen Elisabeth had returned to Budapest (1986), as did Frederic the Great to Berlin (1983). In Hungary, the government ordered the tricolour flown on 15th March, 1985, but when several thousands marched in 1986, the police responded with beatings. Nevertheless, several political symbols were reactivated during the Kádár era. As I mentioned earlier, a new coat of arms was created and the old one was removed from the flag. Moreover, Soviet type uniforms were rejected and were substituted with models which resembled uniforms used between the World Wars. The government also gained a moral victory when the crown of Saint Stephen was returned from the United States in 1978. In the critical years of 1849 and 1945, the crown had been hidden to avoid its loss to enemy hands (it was taken to Austria in 1945 and from there to the United States). According to political idea, the owner of the crown also had legitimate power.

Therefore, on both symbolic and mental levels, the Kádár era did not imply a clear break with the Hungarian past. Thus, 'discontinuity' was impossible either and both the Horthy era and Austria-Hungary viewed 'mystically' in history culture (cf. also Schöpflin 1977). In the tradition of 1848, Kossuth, Petőfi and others were now seen all over Hungary as "National Poet" Vörösmarty, "Military Hero" Hunyadi and "Counts" Rákóczi and Széchenyi. These were also the most popular street names; and the map of Budapest (1987) showed streets named after the noble Zrínyi family in twelve districts, as well as those named after the author Jókai, the peasant rebellion leader Dózsa and the poet Attila József. Only the communist martyr Endre Ságvári was able to complete with the former, as he was represented in eleven districts. Polish General Bem and Karl Marx were the first 'foreigners' to have their names represented nine times in the city text (Budapest térkép, Kartográfiai vállalat Budapest 1987).

However, this did not prevent central boulevards and streets from being named after Lenin, the Red Army or Majakovski. In addition, three of the fallen at the Köztársaság tér, Imre Mező, Sándor Sziklai and János Asztalos had streets in Budapest named after them. Various 'martyrs' from 1848, 1956, or other crucial years, were also strikingly visible, including the married couple, the Rosenbergs, who were executed in the United States in 1953. However, the number of national heroes commemorated is striking also in Kádár's Hungary.

As a whole, it is striking to note the position of earlier events, and how they label present actions. How, for example, the dead generals from Arad were remembered, particularly on October 6th 1966, which was also the 10th anniversary of László Rajk's reburial. Although the martyrs of Arad were remembered throughout the entire Kádár era in schools and by the Patriotic People's Front, in 1966 people were particularly reminded how on that day in 1941 Communists had opposed the war, and how partisans had blown up the statue of Prime Minister Gyula Gömbös three years later. Rajk's reburial was not done as a reminder, but the Communists also timed their political actions to important political days.

In general, there are numerous examples of timing political actions to different anniversaries prior to the communist era, and the value of these actions was also recognized in the socialist dictatorship. Hence, national values gained greater significance in political history, although the party had argued in 1959 that national communism did not exist. Several statues, memorials and plaques were unveiled; the births and deaths of national figures were remembered; and the parliament and the Academy of Sciences held ceremonial meetings.

Whether these were real signs of a compromise, or whether the whole compromise was fictive (cf. Gombos 1993), cannot be decided here. It is reasonable to conclude that these were attempts at both a compromise 'from above' and the creation of an eastern welfare state within the framework of a singleparty system. Attila Ágh has described the last decade of the state socialism as 'a crisis of crisis management'; the more the party attempted to solve the crisis, the bigger it became, because it was simply not prepared for the implementation of political reforms (Ágh 1991, 16; cf. Szabó 1991). According to Ágh, however, the masses accepted the offer, which meant that neither a "social conflict" nor political conflicts such as those in Poland emerged (Ibid.).

# Non-conformists and Remembrance

In December of 1961, János Kádár made a famous speech at the meeting of the Patriotic People's Front and defined allies by citing the Bible. Referring to the Gospel of Matthew, Kádár turned the slogan "he who is not for us is against us" to "he who is not against us is with us and welcomed by us" (cf. Hoensch 1996, 234). More accurately, the notion can be explicated as follows: "those who are not against the Hungarian People's Republic are with it; he who is not against the MSZMP is with it; and he who is not against the Patriotic People's Front is with it" (A Magyar Szocialista... I 1993, 18). That definition was used to try to win over and calm those who were not clearly against the system – contrary to the Rákosi era, in which 'everything' was considered as political.

According to Jenő Bangó, when we deal with the concept of resistance during the Kádár era, the term 'dissent' is too narrow, while 'opposition' refers to the post-Kádár era. Bangó suggested using the concept of non-conformism, which implies a critical and negative attitude toward official values, which can be found in every society. In Hungary, non-conformism was seen as encompassing economic, political, cultural and religious spheres (Bangó 1991, 191-194). In 1984, several non-conformist groups existed, and many of the former '56-ers' were members (cf. Gorlice 1986).

On the other hand, Ervin Csizmadia (1995) found that the origins of democratic opposition were as early as 1964, when social criticism began to increase. Moreover, in 1968, Ágnes Heller and four other Marxists argued that the intervention in Czechoslovakia would endanger the development of socialism and the present renewal of Marxism. (A Magyar Demokratikus... 1995, 13). However, it was more than a decade after 1968 that the *samizdat*-publication *Beszélő* appeared, on the same day as the declaration of martial law in Poland (cf. MH 15/03/1989). Between these events, 34 intellectuals signed a letter in support of Charter 77, which was interpreted as having been the start of the democratic opposition movement (1956 kézikönyve (I) 1996).

We are now faced with the problem of defining exactly what kind of activity should be interpreted as resistance. When Imre Nagy's face suddenly appeared in Márta Mészáro's film *Napló* (Diary, 1984) and was applauded by the audience, was it also a political demonstration? Did rock musicians make a political statement in 1980, when they traveled on "Bus 56" and asked how far they could go (cf. Vámos 1994)?

However, the Hungarian space of experience also included other periods in which political activity in the narrow sense of the word was impossible (cf. also György Konrád's notion of anti-politics). During the Bach-era, following 1848, stories and signs which could be interpreted as passive resistance were present (cf. Szabad 1977, 48-78). The date March 15th was used for the first time in a demonstration already in 1860 (Ibid.). Similar demonstrations occurred occasionally throughout the Kádár era. Black (mourning) flags first appeared on 15th March, 1957, and some people placed candles in their windows in the 1970s to honour the memory of '1956'. Moreover, in 1981, a secret commemoration had taken place at the grave of Minister István Bibó (168 óra 24/10/1989) following his death, intellectuals also composed a Memorial Book in his honour.

Thus, these were signs of commemoration, which also the party produced. But in what sense were these signs political? In other words, how do we judge whether memory is political activity? Hereafter, memory is considered political when it is possible to understand as a symbol, the meaning of which includes various interpretations or even expectations (cf. Edelman 1971; 1985; Pekonen 1991). Although the question could have been limited to the acts of remembering and commemorating, the rulers could have interpreted such acts as the act of reminding and thus, as a symbolic demonstration. In this sense, All Souls Day, celebrated on the 1st of November of every year, annually repeated in difficult time.

However, it also appears as if the question also included a 'culture of teasing'. The culture of teasing involved the testing of the limits of power, particularly around different anniversaries. For example, also Imre Nagy was briefly shown in the rock video of Bus 56, and the video was subsequently banned (Vámos 1994).

Secondly, the act of remembering also had political consequences. In 1983, Imre Mécs lost his job after referring to 1956 as a revolution in his speech at a funeral. Mécs also had a 'particular' level of status, because he had been sentenced to death following 1956, but his sentence was later reduced to a term of imprisonment. When Mécs later attempted to place flowers on the graves of his friends on 1st November, 1986, the police requested to see his papers and informed him that the Ministry had forbidden the particular Section of 301 at the cemetery of Kerepesi (MN 25/02/1989). Thus, on the one hand, the prohibition was based on political expectations, but on the other hand, Hungarian non-conformism was visible in the attempt to apology the memory of the revolution.

Thirdly, the memory of '1956' brought people together and created political demands for the future. In addition to a general sense of dissatisfaction, it is essential to notice that '1956' was the main factor in the unification in the mid-1980s of various groups, including former neo-Marxists (Litván 1995, 5-12). In 1985, Ferenc Donáth assembled the Democratic Opposition, the so-called 'people's writers', reform sociologists and veterans of 1956 for a meeting in Monor. This meeting took place on 14th-16th June, the 16th being the anniversary of Imre Nagy's execution in 1958.

The focus in the *samizdat* publication *Beszélő* had been on the issue of '1956' since 1983, thus the 25th anniversary of Imre Nagy's execution. At that time it was demanded that the bodies buried in unmarked graves be exhumed (on the basis of instructions given in December of 1954, the bodies of those executed were not given to relatives, and the following year the Minister of the Interior ordered that the graves remain unmarked, and he forbade the participation of relatives in the burials) (1956 kézikönyve (I) 1996, 46-56). Moreover, they circulated documents and demanded amnesty for those who had been imprisoned between 1947 and 1963. They also demanded pensions for those who had been imprisoned, since a law from 1975 did not allow pensions for those who had not worked for at least five years. (Csizmadia 1995, 275).

Four years later, in 1987, *Beszélő's* political agenda became even clearer. In a special edition entitled "The Social Contract", they were adamant that the Kádárian consensus had to be broken and that Kádár had to go. In the last chapter, "1956 in Current Hungarian Politics", the publication connected '1956' directly to daily politics; it was impossible to achieve a "contract" without the revaluation of '1956' (Beszélő 1987, 1-57). Thus, the argumentation included both a 'reason' and a 'consequence'. For example, during a private conversation with György Aczél in 1983, Ferenc Donáth argued that it was impossible to carry out a real reform as long as the basis of that reform is referred to as a counter-revolution (Csizmadia 1995, 273).

In December of 1986, non-conformist activists organized the first illegal conference in a private apartment. At that time '1956' offered a large basis to unite intellectuals. All in all, some 80 people participated in the conference and, when read from the present perspective, the participants included many future political leaders: Árpád Göncz (President of the Republic), Lajos Für (Minister of Defence), Gábor Demszky (Mayor of Budapest), Iván Pető (Party Leader of the Free Democrats) as well as several future members of parliament. The conference was organized in accordance with the 'the best communist underground traditions', because the Ministry of the Interior's "wagon" i.e. 'superviser' had also participated in the meeting in Monor in 1985 (Ötvenhatról... 1992, 9-11). However, among the participants were also historians like Tibor Hajdu and Miklós Lackó, who belonged to the ruling party MSZMP. There was also former Prime Minister András Hegedüs, who had been ousted from the party and had subsequently become a sociologist and opposition activist. As a whole, it seems that the Democratic Opposition was basically present. However, there were also people like Lajos Für, Csaba Kiss and Sándor Lezsák, who later became famous in the ranks of the Hungarian Democratic Forum. (Ibid.; Az 1956-os... 1991, 169).

The first lectures of the conference focused on the years 1953-1956 and were given by Ferenc Donáth and Miklós Vásárhelyi, who in 1956 had been Imre Nagy's Press Chief. Jenő Széll and Imre Mécs spoke about the revolution, and the main focus of János Kis's speech was on the restoration following 1956. The participants did not discuss naming at all, although they refer to the formulation of 'revolution'. Another word was also generally used: *megtorlás,* which means reprisal or revenge (Országh 1990). The expression had frequently been used, for example, in connection with 1849, and was later used by the Pozsgay Committee (1989), when it referred to the period immediately following the Second World War (cf. chapter seven). In addition, the expression had been used in connection with 1919. For example, Deputy State Prosecutor Dr. Albert Váry (1922) 'underestimated' the period following the collapse of the Soviet Republic by noting that "it was impossible for the reprisals to remain unfulfilled" ("*a megtorlás nem maradhatott el*") (A vörös... 1993, 1-2).

The Italian paper *l'Unita,* published a small article about the meeting. From the perspective of the party members, and in order to avoid marginalisation, the statement of the conference was given to foreign left-wing papers, but not to Radio Free Europe (Ötvenhatról...1992, 10). The bibliography and chronology of 1953-1963, which I have used in the fourth chapter, was also specifically prepared for this conference. In the preface of the third edition (1990), it can be read how the chronology had originally been published as *samizdat* and was written by "a cooperative acting in private circles in Budapest". Until then, the view of the 'losers' had been absent from published history books, and, for example, Pál Maléter's widow, Judit Gyenes, told how the information about the executions etc. had been spread orally as "folklore" (Tetemrehívás 1988, 51; cf. Szabó 1991, 989; A Magyar Demokratikus... 1995, 492-499).

In general, the underground activity seemed to have increased since the beginning of the 1980s. Around the time of the 25th anniversary a commemorative meeting was held in the apartment of György Krassó; a political prisoners' association, *Recski Szövetség,* named after the prison, was illegally established; and a few veterans began to record their memories on tape recorders. Also, the first *samizdat* publications were published in the beginning of the 1980s, ca. 1981 (1956 kézikönyve (I) 1996, 334). A great number of the 216 *samizdat* publications published in the 1980s dealt with 1956.

In Paris, a memorial at Père Lachaise Cemetery was unveiled in 1988 in memory of the executed. There were nearly two hundred people among the protectors of the statue, including intellectuals, politicians, authors and other artists. For example, Saul Bellow and Joseph Brodsky; Desmond Tutu, Haldor Laxness as well as Mario Soares, Raymond Barre, Yves Montand, Paul Ricoeur, Pierre Rosanvallon and Andrej Wajda. An appeal was sent to the Hungarian government demanding reburial, however, the government did not respond. The commemoration has been recorded in the book *Tetemrehívás* (Invitation to Corpse), which in old folk tales refers to God's Judgments. In Hungary, János Arany wrote a famous ballad with the same name. (Tetemrehívás 1988, 76-80; Tóbiás 1989, 531-537).

In Paris, a representative of the Italian Communist Party also laid a wreath and reminded of the Prague Spring. Delegates also represented Italian and French Socialist Parties and made a speech in which they noted that socialism with a 'human face' did not originate in Czechoslovakia in 1968, but in Poland's and Hungary's intelligentsia in 1955-56. (Ibid., 127-129). However, United States President Ronald Reagan also sent greetings and thus, from the perspective of the 'conservative' MSZMP, the activities of the non-conformists were 'aligned' with the position of the United States.

At the same time, the question of reburial also became significant in Budapest. On 16th June, the demonstration took place in which 317 persons signed an appeal and claimed that the police had brutally broken up a quiet and peaceful commemoration. The paper of the government, the Council of Ministers, *Magyar Hírlap*, published a small article, which was written from the point of view of the police. However, at the same time the demonstrators also received publicity. In the article "What Happened on Thursday Afternoon Downtown?", it was reported how 350-400 persons who represented movements against the system had attempted to carry out a demonstration, but police had arrested several people. The article also mentioned that these same groups had appeared the previous year, and that they aimed at using the 30th anniversary of Imre Nagy's death as a means of attaining political goals (MH 18/06/1988).

Of the demonstrators' demands *Magyar Hírlap* mentioned the revaluation of the events of 1956, the rehabilitation of the participants, the distribution of pensions and the erection of a statue. Moreover, the demonstrators tried to demonstrate in several other places, such as Batthyány tér (Batthyány Square), Hősök tere (Heroes Square) and at the cemetery and in church. The paper mentioned eight demonstrators by name (among them were János Dénes, Jenő Fónay, György Litván, Imre Mécs, Elek Nagy and Gábor Demszky) and the memorial in Paris, finally concluding that the question had been one of provocation (Ibid.).

A little earlier, on 5th June, 1988, The Committee for Historical Justice (*Történelmi Igazságtétel Bizottsága*), hereafter TIB, was founded illegally. In the founding document, TIB demanded "the full moral, political and juridical rehabilitation of victims, both alive and dead, from the revenge which followed the revolution." Moreover, they demanded history writing after the 1945 period, documents from 1956 to be published, and national memorial as the reburial of the executed persons.

Among an estimated 40 signatories were the widows of Pál Maléter, József Szilágyi, Miklós Gimes and Géza Losonczy as well as the daughter of Imre Nagy and many prominent intellectuals (cf. Az 1956-os... 1991, 170-171). The document barely mentioned "the Prime Minister of the revolution, Imre Nagy, who was executed 30 years ago." The four others, i.e. Maléter, Gimes, Szilágyi and Losonczy, were also mentioned, as were "the hundreds of victims in the restoration, which began on 4th November." An historical analogy was used to strengthen the argument, as it was mentioned that "not even Habsburgs, Haynau and Horthy combined, vilified, judged, executed and forced to the extent that the political power born on 4th November, 1956 did" (Tóbiás 1989, 523-527; Az 1956-os... 1991, 169-171).

All in all, the present was bound to the past, historical analogy used, and over the course of the 1980s everything began to crystallize: 15th March, '1956', democracy, the politics of remembering, analogies etc. In 1987, *samizdat* demanded that János Kádár be superseded. On the whole, the politics and political expectations of the government with regard to the memory of '1956' can be characterised by a certain ambivalence. At first, new martyrs were created and memorials built for them. Secondly, the government attempted to shift the focus from 23rd October to the 'more convenient' 30th October. Contrarily, the entire month of October remained shadowed by other political events. Politics was linearly directed toward the future; '1956' was the past, and there was no 'reason' to dig up such complex event.

# VI  HUNGARY 1988-1994

In the fourth chapter I argued that although the students started the 'uprising' with their demonstration, it was far more difficult to pinpoint precisely when '1956' began on the level of experience. The same is true for the 'system change': Mihály Bihari (1993) argued that several "model changes" had occurred before the "system change". Moreover, Rudolf L. Tőkés (1990) listed several single events: 1956, the Kádár speech in 1961, the New Economic Mechanism in 1968, the economic disaster in the late 1970s, the elections in 1985, the establishment of new parties, pluralism, nomenclature and the dissolution of the party in October of 1989.

A few other signs could also be added. In 1982, Hungary had joined the IMF, it became possible for citizens to make one annual trip to the West, and even the first McDonalds in a former Soviet Bloc country opened in Budapest already in 1987. Moreover, it could also be mentioned that in 1987 both the first income tax and a new passport were introduced, and the youth organization of the party demanded "socialism but in a different way." In addition, 100 intellectuals had boycotted the new programme of Károly Grósz's goverment and, for example, the first Public Opinion Polling Institute was established in July of 1988.

However, we are not interested here in signs of 'westernisation', but in a presence of the past in politics. From this point of view, we could focus on the words of Charles Gati (1990), who estimated that in Poland and in Hungary the change started both on the basis of the domestic situation, and different signs from Moscow in 1988. The Polish and Hungarian governments understood Gorbachev's message to be that they should reevaluate their past and continue radical, even indefinite reforms (Gati 1990, 162; cf. Schöpflin 1989; Lundestad 1991).[44] Thus, it seems evident that the general discussion about the past became livelier toward the end of the 1980s (cf. also the chronology1956 kézikönyve (I) 1996). However, one crucial question is whether we can locate certain factors which 'led' to changes in the system.

The next section begins in 1988 and includes a systematic reading of newspapers from May of 1988. I have chosen the following headlines from

Hungarian political yearbooks. Political scientist Attila Ágh wrote an article in all of the yearbooks, the headlines of which define the previous year.

# The Year of a Half Turn, 1988

According to the news agency MTI, aside from the country-wide festivals on 15th March, "smaller groups had made unsuccessful attempts to win over youngsters for their own political purposes at the Petőfi statue." Eight persons were mentioned by name, since house searches had taken place on the basis of their disturbing attitude on 15th March (MPÉ 1988, 431). Moreover, on 8th April, the police told five students and young intellectuals to cease their activities, since they had made initiatives to establish an illegal organization (Ibid. 432).

However, in the spring of 1988, János Kádár was already one of the oldest political leaders in Europe. In May 1988, the national convention of the MSZMP created a new post, an honorary chair and, superseded Kádár de facto. Prime Minister Károly Grósz was chosen as First Secretary (cf. Schöpflin, Tőkés & Völgyes 1988). In addition to his trip to Moscow, Grósz was the first Prime Minister to negotiate with the British Prime Minister, and became the first Prime Minister to visit the United States since 1946. Grósz made a 'positive' impression abroad and, among other questions, his relationship to 1956 appeared in several interviews with him. For example, he answered a question dealing with passports by saying that those people who had received prison sentences as a result of 1956 were not given passports. In an interview in *Newsweek,* Grósz argued that a counter-revolution had taken place and that Imre Nagy would have to answer for it in court. "It is unacceptable for the Prime Minister to break the law or the constitution. Imre Nagy did that" (MH 12/07/1988).

Moreover, Grósz stated that many of the people involved in "this national tragedy" had been misled, and he also noted that those people who died at Köztársaság tér were considered martyrs (NSZ 26/07/1988). Grósz did not consider the Nagy's rehabilitation possible, since he had broken the law. However, Grósz did state that the "time has come for the mortal remains of Imre Nagy to find lasting peace" (MH 26/07/1988). Thus, the new First Secretary offered a new interpretation of Imre Nagy, although he continued to connect the concept of revolution to the party. Moreover, Grósz did not exclude the possibility of a multiparty system, as long as it functioned within the framework of the socialist system. In the Central Committee meeting János Berecz made the statement that a singleparty system had been legally confirmed, and he considered it as the political basis of the whole system (NSZ 15/07; MH 27/07/1988).

In general, Grósz's statements, especially those concerning the possibility that Imre Nagy might be reburied, included few signs of something new. Grósz admitted that from a *human* point of view, reburial might take place (1956 kézikönyve (I) 1996, 353-355). In September of 1988, the Council of Ministers dealt with amnesty for people involved in the events of 1956, and promised to eradicate legal consequences for people who had been punished earlier (MH 05/09/1988). When sentences were revoked until the end of December, it had no bearing on those who had committed crimes during the struggles, for example, on Köztársaság tér. According to *Magyar Nemzet*, the majority of those persons lived abroad.

Moreover, since the summer of 1988, Hungarian newspapers had begun to raise their voices regarding Ceausescu's plans in Transylvania, and in June political demonstrations took place to defend the rights of the Hungarian minority in Romania. Other essential issues were problems concerning the proposed building of a dam in the Danube River and strikes going on in Poland. Moreover, on August 20th, the 950th anniversary of the death and canonization of Saint Stephen was commemorated widely. A small, although not insignificant change also took place when *Magyar Nemzet* celebrated its 50th birthday in August: it once again (as it had in 1956) placed the name of Sándor Pethő next to the name of the Patriotic People's Front, in its logo.

Reform and socialist pluralism had been the slogans of the party convention, and toward autumn these 'heretic ideas' began to appear more expansively. New concepts began to appear in newspapers, such as "socialist market economy" (MH 11/10/1988), "markets if socialist" ja "market economy on the birth" (MH 13/10/1988). On television, Rezső Nyers characterised himself as a 'Reform Communist', which for him included the democratization of the party, as well as reconciliation and living with parliamentary democracy (NSZ 22/10/1988). Thus, reform was an acute concept, in which even obscure content was argued under the concept of socialism.

Moreover, countless organizations were born in 1988, and little by little newspapers began to report on them more openly. Great numbers of organizations began to appear with such descriptive terms in their titles as: society (*társaság*), association (*egyesület*), circle (*kör*), alliance (*szövetség*), forum (*fórum*), council (*tanács*), club (*klub*), network (*hálózat*), trade union (*szakszervezet*), committee (*bizottság*) and front (*front*) (programmes see MPÉ 1988). Several organizations participated in the demonstration on the anniversary of Imre Nagy's execution, in which TIB was one of the main organizator. Among the participants were, for example, the Association of Young Democrats (FIDESZ) and The Network of Free Propositions, and later the Alliance of

Free Democrats (*Szabad Demokraták Szövetsége*, hereafter SZDSZ).

The Hungarian Democratic Forum (*Magyar Demokrata Fórum*, hereafter MDF) was founded in Lakitelek, where the national-minded intelligentsia and reformers of the MSZMP met in the Autumn of 1987. The MDF started to appear in the newspapers in September 1988. It wanted to "progress in its own way and did not embrace either government [*kormánypártiság*] or opposition titles." Nevertheless, the MDF wanted to spread throughout the country as an idealist-political movement, but did not have a specific or concrete programme (MH 05/09/1988). One of the founders, Sándor Lezsák, surmised that sooner or later, a multiparty system would be the norm in Hungary (MH 20/10/1988).

In October, close to the anniversary of the 1956 demonstration, *Népszabadság* published a statement by the Budapest police. According to the police, "FIDESZ and other groups announced plans to organize a commemorative procession to memorialise the events of 23rd October, 1956... . However, the police will not allow any kind of public meeting, processions or demonstrations in the streets... . The police are prepared to do whatever was necessary to prevent any act which would go against the Constitution of the Hungarian People's Republic, disturb the peace, or cause disorder" (NSZ 22/10/1988).

Hence, after the anniversary, *Népszabadság* reported that "there was no disorder on 23rd October", and *Magyar Hírlap* wrote that "thorough complete peace and order reigned", although five persons were arrested. The MDF and "other responsible representatives" had obeyed the order, but small groups of about 8,000 gathered to follow the lead of a few overly-excited (*túlfűtött*) people in a few places in the capital. (MH; NSZ 24/10/1988.)

A few days later *Magyar Hírlap* published an interview with Károly Grósz and, among other questions, the demonstration was dealt with. According to Grósz, they "were not allowed to commemorate the memory of a counter-revolution." Grósz had no basis on which to believe that the former viewpoint would change in principle. Grósz did not mention details, but he did mention that a scientific analysis had begun. The sources must be restudied, and this research would likely benefit both society in general and all political leaders (MH 28/10/1988).

Another anniversary came to the fore in autumn of 1988. In a government organized press conference, a journalist indicated that "the people have spoken in Budapest, and that western newspapers had written" about a particular demonstration in which some two dozen individuals had demanded that 7th November be a regular work day and that the proper anniversary was 15th March. The spokesman for the government agreed with the information and speculated that in the future, the day might not be celebrated as it had been up until now. Furthermore, *Magyar Hírlap* published a correction sent in by a participant of the demonstration, who stated that he had been beaten by several policemen. On the next day, however, a high-ranking police officer replied that there had been 19 arrests, but that no "equipment of force", such as rubber truncheons, had been used (MH 26/11/1988).

However, since November, not only had new organizations come into being, but the Independent Smallholders' Party had also been reactivated. Inside the ruling MSZMP, for example, Imre Pozsgay had postulated that a multi-party system does not depend primarily on the government, but on the will of the people (MH 24/11/1988). On the contrary, First Secretary Károly Grósz rejected the idea of a multiparty system in front of 10,000 party activists who had gathered in Budapest at the end of November. In a long speech, Grósz also noted "the aggressiveness of a few, but noisy, elements of the bourgeois restoration and counter-revolutionary elements." Grósz's interpretation was that a class war was taking place, but that the result was solely dependent upon "us, our self-esteem and whether we would be able to win the moderate forces to our side." If this were to occur, order and safety would be maintained and it would be possible to overcome economic difficulties and create a better functioning Hungarian socialism. If this were not the case, according to Grósz, anarchy, chaos and – this would not merely remain an illusion– white terror would rule (MH; NSZ 30/11/1988).

Thus, Grósz also dealt with the possibility of the establishment of a multiparty system, and eventually concluded to oppose the idea. The fate of socialism was not dependent on whether there was a multi- or singleparty system, because, according to Grósz, while it was possible to operate well within a singleparty system, and badly within the multiparty system. The first secretary concluded that 'we' must continue to build socialism and that 'we' appeal to Hungarians to participate in it. (Ibid.).

Furthermore, on 24th November, the new government was sworn in, led by Miklós Németh, and before Christmas it declared that 15th March would once again be a holiday (MN 21/12/1988). Elsewhere, *Népszabadság* reported earlier in December about a new radio bridge between Budapest and the Voice of America, in which political scientists discussed current political problems – the first of such discussions having taken place in June. Moreover, on 5th December, the Hungarian News Agency, MTI, reported on a two-day conference organized by student clubs, which dealt with "the social and political processes taking place in 1956" (for more on the debates, see Hegedűs & Baló 1996).

An extensive article by the president of the Hungarian Academy of Sciences, Iván T. Berend, was published in *Magyar Nemzet* on 24th December, and it dealt with the fate of socialism in Hungary. The article contained a chronicle from the 1950s, and its conclusions were quite similar to the report by the Pozsgay Committee, which will be analyzed in the seventh chapter. This particular article no longer contained the term 'counter-revolution', but instead referred to a new term, 'uprising', which has inherently humiliating overtones regarding the human dignity and pride of a nation. It is worth noting that the new term had been used by a high-ranking member of the party prior to the events which took place in the end of January, 1989.

A two page spread was given to the alternative movements as "a Christmas present" in *Magyar Hírlap* – as the headline formulated it. Among other themes, FIDESZ and SZDSZ both took up the question of 1956. A member of the Free Democrats demanded the revaluation of 1956, and the abolition of the Workers' Militia. In addition, István Hegedűs (FIDESZ) was of the opinion that Károly Grósz's speech had been directed at them. Beside the claims already made by the SZDSZ, Hegedűs demanded a "dignified celebration of 15th March", and a public debate regarding the withdrawal of Soviet troops. (MH 24/12/1988).

In conclusion, on the one hand, the ruling party had made a few concessions towards the end of 1988. However, a public commemoration of 23rd October, for example, was forbidden. Moreover, the country's economy was in a deep crisis and reform, although obscure in its limits, was generally considered necessary. On the other hand, the revaluation of 1956, as rehabilitations and the payment of pensions, belonged to the demands of the new groups and united them against the existing government and the party. Finally, there was a demand for research work, which, for example, Miklós Vásárhelyi defined as the first step (MN 31/12/1988).

## The Year of Party Formation, 1989

On 11th January, the parliament accepted a law based on freedom of association and assembly. In principle, the law made it possible to found other parties. As mass organizations, parties were mentioned by name, however, a special law specifically governing parties was scheduled for August 1989. On 24th January 51 out of 97 non-party members formed their own faction within the 386 seat parliament.

A new coat of arms, the so-called 'Kossuth-Emblem', first appeared in the newspapers on 23rd January. According to this piece of news, the idea had been in the works since July and, on the basis of the article, the coat of arms was used by Ferenc Rákóczi (with a crown), in 1848, 1918 and between 1945-1949. Its usage also in 1956 was not mentioned at that time in the newspapers.

On 20th January, the ruling MSZMP and the MDF met in public for the first time, and on the following day, Pozsgay interpreted that the necessary conditions were not yet in place for the multiparty system (MH 23/01/1989). The New March Front supported a multiparty system and suggested the establishment of a national committee to carry out the transition to representative democracy. A few days later, on Thursday the 26th, the Central Committee decided to permit the private reburial of Imre Nagy and his companions. Already in the next issue of *Magyar Nemzet*, the TIB, the Committee for Historical Justice, welcomed the decision with pleasure. However, it was only the first step, because all the names of the executed were yet to be published. (MN 27/01/1989).

On 28th Saturday, 1989, *Népszabadság* briefly reported that the Pozsgay Committee had dealt with the report of a particular history committee. The task of the committee and the contents of the report were briefly mentioned. However, the real 'scandal' would unfold on the next day, because following the meeting, the leader of the committee, Imre Pozsgay, gave an interview to a radio programme, 168-Hours, which was to be broadcast on Saturday afternoon. In that programme, Pozsgay interpreted the recent past, and declared that an uprising had taken place in 1956.

On 11th February, *Magyar Nemzet* briefly reported that the Central Committee had dealt with questions concerning socialist pluralism and the transition to a multiparty system, and that the session would continue that throughout the day. The result of the meeting could be read in the *communiqué*, which was published on the front page of all the three newspapers on Monday, 13th February. In the first part the principle of the multiparty system was accepted. In second part, the Central Committee concentrated on the results of the recent piece of research. The Central Committee considered it important to put the study into the focus of discussion, and needed a versatile evaluation of the "national tragedy of 1956.... A revolt, an uprising took place, in which elements of democratic socialism played a role." (MH; MN; NSZ 13/02/1989).

However, between February 20th and 22nd, the Central Committee made a statement to be included in the new draft of the Constitution: Hungary should be a free, democratic, socialist state, yet it should remain a People's Democracy. Conversely, on 10th March, the parliament accepted an amendment to the Constitution abolishing the leading role of the party, and Mátyás Szűrös was chosen as the President of the People's Republic. On 15th March, now celebrated as a red-letter-day, both the government and the opposition held their own ceremonies, in which the opposition managed to gather people "for peaceful demonstration" (cf. MH/20/02/1989).

Soviet troops began their withdraw on 25th April, and on 3rd May, the Ministry of Foreign Affairs reported that the barbed wire at the Austrian border was removed. On 8th May, Kádár was forced to resign from the chair of honour, and in June the study of compulsory Russian was abolished from school curriculums. Moreover, in May-June, the large statue of Lenin was removed from Pest for restoration, and it was promised that it would be brought back when the reparation was completed (NSZ 01/06/1989).

By March, the opposition groups had founded their own roundtable and were ready to negotiate with the MSZMP. An agreement was reached on 10th June, merely five days after the election in Poland in which Solidarity won all of the seats in the *Sejm* and all but one in the Senate (Bruszt 1990, 379; Bozóki 1990). In a press conference given by the roundtable on 13th June, Imre Kónya, who represented independent lawyers, defined three aims of the revolution of 1956, which were to be peacefully implemented: national committees and workers' councils, which were suppressed by the domestic reaction, the freedom to travel, and free elections (NSZ 14/06/1989).

Although the Council of Ministers had agreed in January to rebury Nagy and his compatriots, on 14th February, *Magyar Hírlap* wrote that the location of the body was still unknown. At the end of March, however, a coffin was recovered, which in all probability contained the mortal remains of Imre Nagy (MH 30/03/1989). The coffin was found with an old map from 1908 and with the help of old cemetery labourers who were able to estimate its location. The coffin had been wrapped in tar paper, and thus it was well preserved.

The reburial of Imre Nagy and his companions was timed to the 31st anniversary of the execution, and the invitation to the burial was distributed by the new political parties and organizations. In attendence were relatives of those buried, five out of the six parties to win seats in parliament in the 1990 elections, members of TIB, former political prisoners of *Recski Szövetség*, members of the People's Party, various Social Democrats, Republicans and members of the New March Front.

However, the government also announced a declaration in which it recognized Imre Nagy as an excellent statesman, who wanted to change policy which varied from Hungarian tradition. An agreement between the TIB, the government and the parliament was reached (NSZ 09/06/1989), and President Mátyás Szűrös and Prime Minister Miklós Németh also attended the funeral. In an interview with ABC television, Németh commented that the era of doctrines was over, and that the Soviet Union would not intervene to Hungarian reforms (MH 17/06/1989).

Moreover, before the reburial it was reported that six charter flights would arrive from the United States. At the airport, Béla Király stated that his opinion about 1956 had not changed. When a journalist used the expression uprising, Király argued that the revolution had won outright. The Minister of the Interior had suspended ÁVHs, the party itself, and only eight or ten lynchings took place. (MH 02/06/1989). Elsewhere, the party organ interviewed, for example,

József K. Farkas, who had survived Köztársaság tér despite the fact that twelve bullets were recovered from his body. Farkas' face became famous through a series of photos appearing in *Life* magazine, and he now claimed to have merely been a soldier, stating that he now supported the efforts of national reconciliation (NSZ 10/06/1989).

Following the reburial, the headline of the front page article read: "The Grieving Nation Bids Farewell to Imre Nagy and the Martyrs." Several veterans of 1956 were in attendance at the burial ceremony: Miklós Vásárhelyi, Imre Mécs, Béla Király, Tibor Méray and Tibor Zimányi, (the Chairman of the Pofosz) and Sándor Rácz (leader of the Central Workers' Council in 1956), all of whom used the ceremony as an occasion on which to speak. In addition to the veterans, a representative of the younger generations was allowed to make a speech. The leader of FIDESZ, Viktor Orbán, stated that only once, in 1956, was there enough courage to attempt to attain the goals of national independence and political freedom, the groundwork for these tasks already having been laid down in 1848. According to Orbán, "our aims have not changed from those of 1848 or 1956" (MH 17/06/1989).

The rehabilitation of Imre Nagy and his companions was hurried, and in May a special committee was appointed to plead the cause in court (MH 29/05/1989). On 23rd June, Mátyás Szűrös announced that there was a faction within the MSZMP, which was not forceful enough in pushing the rehabilitation of Imre Nagy. Finally, on 7th July, it was reported in the newspapers that Imre Nagy, Ferenc Donáth, Miklós Gimes, Zoltán Tildy, Pál Maléter, Sándor Kopácsi, József Szilágyi, Ferenc János and Miklós Vásárhelyi were rehabilitated, on the day of János Kádár's death.

After the funeral, the First Secretary of the party, Károly Grósz, was ousted. A new collective leadership (Grósz, Németh, Nyers, Pozsgay) was sworn in, led by Rezső Nyers (MN; NSZ 26/06/1989). They simultaneously announced that the forthcoming party convention would begin on 6th October. Moreover, on the same day, the MDF officially became a party which described itself as representing the legacy of the national popular movement, the national liberalism of the 19th century, Christian Democratic world views and the tradition of István Bibó's political philosophy (Ibid.). A few days later, the trial of Cardinal József Mindszenty became a reality, because on 11th July, Miklós Németh gave the green light for the reexamination of the process.

Regarding foreign reception, the party organ wrote: "Prague Worried That the Opposition Had Been Given Free Reign in Hungary" (NSZ 20/06/1989). In *Novoje Vremja,* three historians estimated that in the recent past the Soviet Union had intervened strongly in Hungarian politics. They noted that in the 1950s, the intervention was necessary, that it had been requested by the government, and finally that offensive anti-Communist terror would have been the main line in 1956 (MH 06/07/1989). In October, the war historical review *Vojennoisztoricseszkij Zsurnal*, called 1956 in Hungary a counter-revolution, Imre Nagy a traitor, and presumed that the West had planned an intervention (NSZ 19/10/1989).

The roundtable negotiations, dealing with the most essential laws and the Constitution, ended in September, and a total of five parties signed the agreement. FIDESZ and SZDSZ refused to sign, and in November a referendum was organized on four issues. In the end, the President would be chosen following parliamentary elections (50.07%), units of the party would be abolished from the workplace, and party property would be distributed. In addition, the Workers' Militia, which played an important role in the beginning of the Kádár era, would be dissolved.

In a newspaper caricature (MH 15/08/1989), Erich Honecker ordered the suspension of the production of suitcases, as people were queuing at the border. Foreign Minister Gyula Horn opened the Austrian border on 10th September. In addition, since September, *Magyar Nemzet* published a series entitled "The White Spots of History" and the Smallholders demanded the rehabilitation of Béla Kovács. According to the representative of the Münnich Ferenc Társaság, socialism worked, although the leaders had made mistakes.

A new concept emerged on the horizon of expectation: Iván Vitányi, a sociologist and a member of the party, argued that a system change (*rendszerváltás*) was taking place. This all-encompassing system change – not merely a theoretical change as before – was a positive concept, if it included the possibility of getting rid of paternalism, which also existed in the current socialist system. In Hungary, socioeconomic systems had been liberal-paternalistic at their best. According to Vitányi, socialism could exist only if it was approximate to the Western European and US developed capitalism. Socialism had been the reason behind Columbus' voyage, and instead of India, he had found America (NSZ 13/09/1989).

In May, the reform circles in the MSZMP had supported negotiations with the opposition roundtable, and in September they held another meeting. Finally, the 14th Congress of the MSZMP began on 6th October, and the party was divided into at least three platforms: conservatives, the centre, which was closely aligned with Károly Grósz, and the faction close to Imre Pozsgay. The majority in the assembly changed the name of the party to *Magyar Szocialista Párt* (The Hungarian Socialist Party) by a vote of 1002 for, 159 against and 38 abstaining. In its programme, the new party supported parliamentary democracy, human rights, free elections and a market economy. Rezső Nyers, who had been a Social Democrat prior to 1948, was chosen as chairman of the party.

On 13th October, merely a few days after the party split, newspapers reported that the red star above the parliament had been switched off, and on the 24th, radio newspaper *168 óra* was issued with the 'Kossuth Emblem' on the cover. The interpretation of the minority in the MSZMP meeting was that a new party had been born. The official conference had still not been held, and Károly Grósz began to prepare for the 14th Congress of the MSZMP (in 1993 the party changed its name to the shorter *Munkáspárt* (Worker's Party) (cf. NSZ 22/03/1993).

Finally, the law which defined the free, multiparty election system, was accepted on 20th October and adapted on the anniversary of 1956, 23rd October. On the 23rd, President Mátyás Szűrös declared Hungary a republic. In his speech, Szűrös spoke about the free and democratic Hungary, which would be created by the end of the 20th century. The President used historical examples to clarify the present situation: Hungary was following in the footsteps of the previous republics, which he connected to the names of Lajos Kossuth (1848), Mihály Károlyi (1918) and Zoltán Tildy (1945), in the spirit of the democratic and national tradition, and he finally commented on the last 40 years. He specifically mentioned the uprising and the national movement, and the historical ideas on which the republic would be based. According to Szűrös, Hungary would be an independent, rule of law, in which the traditions of bourgeois (*polgári*) democracy and democratic socialism would be of equal value. (MN; NSZ 24/10/1989).

In conclusion, during 1989 both the transition to a multiparty system and the 'resurrection of 1956' were central and entangled issues. The adoption of the multiparty system was initially made in the Central Committee simultaneously to the redefinition of '1956'. Since March, the opposition had become united, wanted "one step to democracy", rejected compromises, and set free elections as a main goal(Bruszt 1990, 379; Bozóki 1990; Tőkés 1996, 346-347). This was followed by the reburial of Imre Nagy, which was not only the last human service for the former Prime Minister, but also a defining moment in political position and legitimization for the future. Finally, in October, the new democracy was symbolically connected to historical events from the past.

## The Year of Incomplete Changes, 1990

In the beginning of January, the MSZP dissociated itself from a few post-1956 leaders and erroneous policy of the 1970s. Pensions would be paid to both the participants in the uprising and to those who had been imprisoned thereafter (Ibid.). In addition to this, on 17th February the over 100,000 persons who had been illegally sentenced between 1945 and 1963, would be rehabilitated. In Esztergom, they commemorated the 41st anniversary of Cardinal Minszenty's trial and named a square after him (NSZ 09/02/1990) and stating that he should be returned to Hungary. Also, diplomatic relations with the Vatican were reestablished for the first time since 1945 (MH 10/02/1990).

On 11th March, Foreign Minister Gyula Horn signed an agreement on the schedule of the withdrawal of the Soviet troops. The last troops were to leave the country by June 30th, 1991 (in reality, the last soldier would leave on 16th June, 1991). In January, it seemed possible that in the future, Hungary might join NATO (NSZ 29/01/1990), and there was also speculation that a multiparty system would be established in the Soviet Union.

The first free elections were to be held in March, and in the beginning of January, the Smallholders' Party clearly dissociated itself from the possibility of cooperating with the Socialist Party. The leader of the party, József Torgyán, argued that they would demand the withdrawal of the Soviet troops, reckoning with the Communists and return land ownership to the level of 1947, if the party were to be part of the government (MH 22/01/1990). Later, the MDF unequivocally announced that the former Socialist Worker's Party, the Socialist Party, and the organizations close to them, would be considered their political opponents (NSZ 04/02/1990).

On 25th March, the first round of elections took place, and 65.77% of those eligible voted in single constituencies and 65.10% voted for regional candidates:

| | |
|------|---------|
| MDF | 24,73 % |
| SZDSZ | 21,39 % |
| FKGP | 11,73 % |
| MSZP | 10,89 % |
| FIDESZ | 08,95 % |
| KDNP | 06,46 %. |

(MPÉ 1991, 80-82; Körösényi 1990, 340-341)

From the 176 single constituencies, only in five had a candidate who won a majority and, thus, was elected in the first round. Therefore, the real power struggle for the major party's 171 seats was left for the second round. The rest of the seats, 210 would be divided on the basis of party and national lists (see also chapter eight).

In the second round on the 8th, the MDF enjoyed a landslide victory, winning 41,2 % of the votes and 114 seats (altogether 165 seats). Even though the SZDSZ had led after the first round in 65 constituencies, it ultimately won only 35 of them (altogether 91) (Körösényi 1990, 341; Hibbing & Patterson 1992, 442-444). The forum had also supported more moderate change than the SZDSZ (cf. Schöpflin 1991, 64). Finally, the MDF, Smallholders and Christian Democrats made an agreement in the period between the two rounds to support each other in the second round.

The opening ceremony of the newly-elected parliament took place on 2nd May, 1990. The occasion was honoured by the presence of the Speaker of the Parliament, Béla Varga and Otto von Habsburg, a descendant of the last king of Hungary. In the first session, the new parliament enacted a law which dealt with the symbolic meaning of the 1956. In the first paragraph, the memory was enacted into law, and the second paragraph declared 23rd October a national holiday. The new speaker of the parliament, György Szabad (MDF), an historian by trade, found '1956' to be the most important connection to the historical past, and the most important basis for the creation of the future in Hungary (see chapter nine) (MN; NSZ 03/05/1990).

The first months of the newly elected parliament were consumed by self-organization. SZDSZ and MDF had created a political cluster of laws, which needed a two-thirds majority in order to pass. They had agreed to chose the President of the Republic (Árpád Göncz, SZDSZ) and the Chairman of the Parliament (György Szabad, MDF) and, for example, the President would be appointed on the recommendation of the Prime Minister, leaders in the Hungarian radio and television and news agency, MTI. On 23rd May, József Antall's (MDF) government was formed, in which three parties, the MDF, the Christian Democrats and the Smallholders, were represented.

In June, Prime Minister Antall commemorated Trianon, and expressed concern about the fate of minorities in neighbouring countries. His words that "I wish in my soul to be the Prime Minister of 15 million Hungarians" became famous, because it also meant Hungarians living outside the Hungarian state (MN; NSZ 04/06/1990). At the end of June, the MPs discussed the possibility of disjoining the Warsaw Pact (NSZ 27/06/1990). In June, amnesty was also declared – in the discussion surrounding amnesty the name of Imre Nagy was also mentioned (MH 13/06/1990) – and the last political prisoners left prison in September (MH 08/09/1990). In July, thirty executed officers were promoted posthumously and, for example, Colonel Pál Maléter became a Colonel-General (vezérezredes) (MH 06/07/1990).

On 3rd July, the parliament voted to adopt a new coat of arms, which was made from other symbols. The parliament eventually selected the coat of arms with a crown, which had been used before 1946, i.e. during the Horthy era before the establishment of the republic. Moreover, in September, the government decided on the decorations for the new republic: several were taken from the period prior to state socialism.

By the end of the summer, there were already signs of differences, which cooled relations between the government and the opposition. In September,

SZDSZ demanded the resignation of Foreign Minister Géza Jeszenszky, because he had stated on two occasions that the government represents "more European type values" than the opposition (MH 14/09/1990). Secondly, the SZDSZ had a political advertisement (MH; NSZ 03/09/1990), in which the party evaluated the first hundred days of the new government. According to the Free Democrats, the moral, economic and social conditions of the country were worse than they had been prior to the elections. Moreover, the government found less and less continuity between the years 1956 and 1947, increasingly recognizing the great deadlock of Horthy's Hungary (MH; NSZ 03/09/1990).

Moreover, at the end of August, a detailed *Justitia* plan was made public (NSZ 28/08/1990). In the space of eleven paragraphs, the plan put forth broader settlement with the past, expressed a desire to locate responsible parties, and wanted to take legal measures against the leaders of the old system. Representatives of the MDF gave the plan to the Prime Minister in June, but it did not become public until August (MPÉ 1991, 277) (on the debate about reckoning with the past, see chapter ten).

The first anniversary came in October, and was described as "the first free national holiday" (MN 18/10/1990). The main celebration was held at the Technical University, and from there a procession marched to Bem Square. Parliament held an honorary session at which relatives of the 1956 martyrs and heroes of the revolution were present. Furthermore, commemorations took place in Section 301 and at the 'National Pantheon' at Kerepesi, Section 21, the Batthyány Memorial Light, the *Corvin* Theatre, the Kilián Barracks and Széna tér. Also, the first World Meeting of Hungarian Freedom Fighters was organized.

An incident took place on 23rd October, in which a group ripped down a plaque which had been unveiled at the radio station the previous year. At that time, a few hundred members of the Christian National Union (KNU), the Hungarian National Party and a number of skinheads had marched to the radio building and introduced 12 points, which contained, for example, a demand for the establishment of a "national government". (NSZ 24/10/1990). Moreover, KNU had also organized some 150 supporters in front of the parliament, where they argued that "the spirit of '56 still lives" and claimed that the system had not changed (NSZ 26/10/1990).

However, the first anniversary was shadowed by the gasoline crisis, when the government decided to raise prices by 65%. Taxi-drivers blockaded the streets and bridges of Budapest. The new government faced a situation in which it had to decide if it should "restore order by all legal means" (NSZ 26/10/1990). The blockade ended safely, however, partly thanks to the mediating role of President Göncz, and partly because the prices were reduced. (MN 28/10/1990).

All in all, the most important political processes in 1990 were the first free elections, and the inception of the new parliament. At first, '1956' was considered as the most essential basis for the new Hungary, although quite soon it became apparent that it had to compete with other pasts as well. To some extent, the first year of post-communism not only represented the present political problems, but also all the former spaces of experiences and symbolic time-periods, which began to appear in the public debate.

## The Year of the Structural Stalemate, 1991

In January, local peasants occupied their former land (MH 08/01/1991), which began a wave of occupations lasting for several weeks. Thus, swift compensation became a current matter, and the first constitutional version of the compensation law was accepted in June. The law restricted compensation to former owners who had lost their property after 8th June, 1949 (two other laws were enacted in 1992: between 1st May 1939 and June 1949, and between 11th March 1939 and 23rd October 1989 (cf. MH 21/04/1993)). In May 1991, the government also promised TIB that compensation would also be paid on the basis of 1956.

Moreover, the parliament accepted a law in July 1991, which returned estates, building-sites and cemeteries, but neither land nor hired houses to churches. Both 1991 laws were accepted by a majority vote in the government (MH 11/07/1991). The Free Democrats supported compensation for the general public, Socialists supported only partial compensation and FIDESZ was generally opposed to the idea (MH; NSZ 05/02/1991).

On 25th February, the Foreign and Defence Ministers of the contracting parties of the Warsaw Treaty signed an agreement in Budapest abolishing the treaty as of the end of March. Moreover, in February, the extreme right-wing Hungarian National Association planned to tear down the Soviet Memorial at Gellért Hill and replace it with the Crown of Saint Stephen (168 óra 23/03/1991). At that time, many of the old statues and street signs remained in place, and in October, Minister of the Interior Péter Boross argued that they should be changed by 23rd October (NSZ 10/10/1991) – rumours also circulated that they would be torn down on the 23rd (NSZ 18/10/1991).

Near the March anniversary, six parties agreed, on the initiative of the MDF, that the day should not serve individual party purposes (MH 05/03/1991). On the anniversary, both Prime Minister Antall and President Göncz cited analogies between the present, 1956, and 1848 in their speeches (NSZ 16/03/1991). However, criticism already arose by the next anniversary in June, "the second anniversary of the reburial of the martyrs", because Imre

Mécs wondered where the spirit of 1956 was (NSZ 15-17/06/1991). Christian Democrats, Smallholders and the MDF – i.e. the government – did not participate in the commemoration of Imre Nagy, nor did they partake in the laying of wreaths (168 óra 25/06/1991).

The Horthy-question also began to actualize. In February, *Népszabadság* had posed the question "Horthy to be Buried in Hungarian Soil?" (NSZ 01/02/1991). In November, Socialist Party also questioned whether the government was planning to rehabilitate and rebury Horthy. Prime Minister Antall rejected Horthy's reburial as a state event (NSZ 13/11/1991). In October, Minister of Justice István Balsai (MDF) had considered Horthy's political rehabilitation possible (NSZ 21/10/1991).

On 4th May, Cardinal József Mindszenty was reburied in the Basilica of Esztergom. Another landmark took place in August, when Pope John Paul II visited Hungary for the first time in Hungarian history. In September, a new movement, the Democratic Charter, was born, with prominent intellectuals joining, and thus openly challenging the present government (cf. MH 02/10/1991).

Near the 35th anniversary, on the initiative of the Prime Minister, the President granted decorations "for services rendered in the service of the nation and in the defense of the Fatherland during the 1956 revolution and fight for freedom." Among the decorated were some 30 of the important '56-ers, 25 posthumously, and also two Ministers of the present government. At that time, Mikhail Gorbachev stated that the Soviet military intervention in 1956 had been in violation of international law (MH; MN 24/10/1991). In November, a square in front of the Ministry of Foreign Affairs was named after Imre Nagy, and a memorial tablet was unveiled (NSZ 04/11/1991).

In the beginning of October, *Sajtószabadság Klubja* (The Free Press Club) had been founded within the Hungarian Journalist Association (MUOSZ) (MH 03/10/1991). After 23rd October, the club complained that radio, television and some newspapers had not paid enough attention to the events, and accused them of a lack of reverence with regard to the 35th anniversary of the 1956 revolution and fight for freedom. Moreover, István Csurka argued that radio and television had sabotaged its memory, and accusingly stated that reform communists ruled the newspapers (NSZ 30/10/1991).

Since the spring, reckoning with the secret police and lustration was a part of the daily agenda. In June, Minister of the Interior Péter Boross declared that the material would remain secret until parliament made a decision. In the discussion, Boross referred to a forthcoming law, the function of which was to discover whether a person had been a member in the III-III department of the Ministry of the Interior, the armed forces between 1956-1957, the ÁVH, or had something to do with the cases before 1956 (NSZ 11/05/1991).

In the summer, the *Justitia* plan once again became part of the political agenda of the MDF. The whole plan of punishment was revealed by *Népszava* on 5th September. According to the plan, it was time to speed up the system change, as well as to revitalise the spirit of Hungarian radio and television. At the end of October, the discussion entered the parliament, and it concerned homicide, treason and disloyalty between 1944 and 1990. Finally, the controversial Zétényi-Takács law was accepted in parliament on 4th November. The result clearly divided the government and the opposition: 197 for, 50 against and 74 abstaining. The three government parties voted for, one member of the MDF voted against, and seven abstained. On the contrary, FIDESZ and MSZP (one abstaining) voted against, and the majority of SZDSZ abstained (MH; MN; NSZ 05/11/1991).

Moreover, close relatives of the deceased made a statement in which they refused to accept the government's proposition. Instead, they were adamant that real criminals and their crimes should be named in the public with the weight of their actions. (NSZ 19/11/1991). In parliament, János Dénes (ex-MDF) demanded hangings in a speech he made, and Miklós Vásárhelyi (SZDSZ) believed that the law would bring uncertainty to society (NSZ 22/11/1991).

In conclusion, some type of compensation seemed to be both a political necessity in 1991 and a precondition of social peace. However, the November debate concerned punishment, and it widened the gap between the government and the opposition. Finally, on a more general level it could be said that since the last half of 1991, different positive views of the future had begun to remain in the shadow of the struggle of the past.

## The Year of Polarization, 1992

In March 1992, the Constitutional Court found all paragraphs of the Zétényi-Takács law to be unconstitutional (NSZ 04/03/1992). When politicians commented on the decision, the opposition argued that the rule of law had been victorious and the democratic state structure worked. Contrarily, Imre Kónya (MDF) said that one need not outline events to find other lawful means of carrying out historical justice (NSZ 04/03/1992). On 12th March, Tibor Füzessy (KDNP) said that the government would formulate a new bill (NSZ 13/03/1992). In April, Attorney General Kálmán Györgyi opposed the new bill, noting that retroactive punishment would be against the law (MN 29/04/1992).

According to a police announcement in January, a few well-organized, neo-fascist groups were also in existence in Hungary (MH 18/01/1992). On the day after the decision in the Constitutional Court, *Magyar Hírlap* hinted that the extreme right was planning actions on the 15th of March (MH 04/03/ 1992). On 15th March, skinheads also emerged at the celebration at the National Museum with, for example, the slogan "The Constitutional Court Betrayed Our Revolution". The Mayor of Budapest, Gábor Demszky (SZDSZ), felt "cold winds blowing": Political nominations, television and independent courts were all in grave danger. (NSZ 16/03/1992). The leader of Pofosz, Jenő Fónay, said that the tradition of 1848 had continued in 1956. Although now the revolutionaries did not have a forum in any sector, the Hungarian media showed ways of living, which were "alien to the nation", and said that the court had betrayed 1956 when it declared it impossible to punish perpetrators (Ibid.).

Moreover, József Torgyán (FKGP) had previously made the statement that the government should get rid of Communists, and gave until the end of February as a deadline (MH 13/01/1992). On 25th April, Torgyán organized "a day of anger" and demanded "a real system change" (NSZ 27/04/1992). The Smallholders had left the government in February, but the majority of their MPs promised to support the government from the opposition.

The debate over punishment and compensation reached the Committee of Historical Justice, TIB. Following the decision by the Constitutional Court, a committee, which held a meeting of the TIB, condemned it in the name of the entire organization. Finally, at the end of March, a split between the 'radicals' and the 'moderates' took place in the TIB, and the new leadership openly supported punishment. The organization lost several of its original members in 1992 and, for example, Erzsébet Nagy, the daughter of Imre Nagy left in autumn.

On June 15th, a memorial at Section 301 was unveiled, the day before the actual anniversary of the execution, the 16th. At that time, the national consensus which had existed three years ago, no longer existed. On 16th June, a silent commemoration took place at Section 301, and the majority of the politicians in attendance represented SZDSZ and FIDESZ (MH 17/06/1992). On the same day, a wreath was laid at Imre Nagy Square. Jenő Fónay (Pofosz) and two Ministers from the main government party, MDF, were representatives (MH 17/06/1992).

In September, *Népszabadság* reported that the government had prepared a new bill, which was based on Law VII/1945, having to do with war crimes (NSZ 22/09/1992). A few days earlier, the Hungarian Martial Court in Budapest, as had the local Martial Court at Győr, denied to prosecute since doing so would mean the death of rule of law. The crimes had become obsolete since manslaughter had a statute of limitations of fifteen years and, thus, should could be tried only until 1971 (MH 17/10/1992).

During 1992, the situation at the radio and television stations had become polarized. The government was dissatisfied with the directors, Csaba Gombár and Elemér Hankiss, who they had accepted in the summer of 1990. In February, the government proposed its own candidates for Vice President, who were opposed by the opposition. The President, however, proceeded to appoint them, hoping that their nominations would raise the standard of the media (MN; NSZ 03/03/1992). Both Gombár and Hankiss were heard in front of the Culture Committee of Parliament, and by the votes of the governing parties, their removal was proposed. Again, President Göncz refused (NSZ 21/05/1992), and the confrontation between the President and the government endured for the entire year. In December, the government ordered Hungarian television to be under surveillance by the government.

Elsewhere, Prime Minister Antall was once again Prime Minister of 15-million Hungarians (MH 17/08/1992), and on the 20th, St. Stephen's Day, the Vice President of the MDF, István Csurka, published a pamphlet. In this study, Csurka demanded radical changes; revealed that Prime Minister Antall was ill; and argued that Göncz was being told what to do by communists, reform communists, liberals and radicals in Paris, New York and Tel Aviv (MN 24/08/; NSZ 22/08/1992). In September, the case reached the US Congress, Senator Tom Lantos, who was of Hungarian origin, delivered the translation to the House of Representatives (NSZ 25/09/1992).

Towards the autumn of 1992, the political situation in Hungary had radicalised, and a group called the '56 Association threatened demonstrations if the radio and television leadership were not removed. Thus, on 19th September 1992, A Szabad Magyar Tájékoztatásért Bizottság (The Committee for The Free Hungarian Information) organized a demonstration against the media leaders, in which the resignation of President Göncz was also demanded (NSZ 21/09/1992). By February, the MDF had dissociated from both (NSZ 14/02/1992) and from the demonstration (NSZ 16/09/1992). However, members of the party were present, as was Csurka, one of the main organizers (NSZ 21/09/1992).

On 24th September, the Democratic Charter organized a counter-demonstration, which they argued was to be a referendum of Csurka's Hungary (MH 23/09/1992). Members of MSZP and SZDSZ themselves reported to supporters of the demonstration (NSZ 23/09/1992). According to Népszabadság, tens of thousands of people had gathered at the statue of Petőfi and marched from there to the parliament (NSZ 25/09/1992).

On 23rd October, an incident occurred on Kossuth Squre when a group of neo-Nazis gathered there. When President Göncz tried to speak, they whistled and shouted at him, and the President left the square. On 26th October, the issue was discussed for three hours in parliament, and it was debated whether the government or the opposition was responsible, and why the police did not prevent the action of the skinheads. On the basis of this incident, several members of the MDF created an initiative to prohibit fascist and bolshevist symbols (MH 27/10/1992) – the law was finally enacted in April of 1993 (cf. MN 22/04/1993).

In November, Boris Yeltsin visited Hungary and brought documents from the Moscow archives. In addition, he laid a wreath on Imre Nagy's grave, and apologised to Hungarians for the intervention in 1956 (MN; NSZ 12/11/1992). In parliament, Tibor Zimányi had condemned the idea of a joint memorial for both sides in 1956, because "nowhere in the world could defenders of a dictatorship and revolutionaries, be included in the same memorial" (NSZ 10/11/1992).

In conclusion, a general polarization and radicalisation came to the fore after the decision in the Constitutional Court. The strengthening of the extreme right was not unique to Hungary – in the autumn there were also demonstrations and counter-demonstrations, for example, in Rostock and Berlin. But from the point of view of this study, it became entangled with '1956', the electronic media and system change, in general. Also, the annual celebrations began to commemorate particular political days, and various actions were timed in accordance with these days.

## The Year of Incertitude, 1993

In the beginning of January, the directors of radio and television, Gombár and Hankiss, decided to withdraw, and the Vice Presidents took command. In addition, the government had begun to create another television station, and Tamás Katona (MDF) admitted that in January, the creation of a satellite channel, Duna-television, had been on the agenda (MH; NSZ 08/04/1993).

The incertitude in the electronic media continued for throughout the entire year, and the question was part of a specific videotape containing a report about the incident at Kossuth Square in 1992. It appeared as if the tape had been spliced and edited afterwards, and thus the question was whether the report of the square had also been manipulated. Also, the confrontation over the media issue continued between the President and the Prime Minister. Moreover, at the end of October there was a demonstration to defend the freedom of the press, and students gathered at the statue of Petőfi to defend free speech (NSZ 01-03/11/1993).

In May, the parliament ratified an agreement neighbourliness with the Ukraine, which was signed on 6th December, 1991. The agreement also confirmed the present borders, and it was accepted by a vote of 223 for, 39 against and 17 abstaining. Moreover, in February, the Zagreb newspaper *Globus* had insisted that Hungarian revisionism take back territory from the former

Yugoslavia (168 óra 02/03/1993).

In the beginning of 1993, the MDF held a national meeting, which was declared to be the triumph of Antall and the centrist forces (NSZ 25/01/1993). The countdown of Csurka, and the separation of the MDF were further strengthened when they founded the platform *Magyar Út* (Hungarian Road) in February – the flag with a hole in the center decorated the press conference of the new platform (MH; NSZ 15/02/1993). A few members of the platform had also belonged to those who had voted against the basic treaty with Ukraine (NSZ 12/05/1993).

In the beginning of June of 1993, István Csurka and two others were expelled from the party. However, at the same time, three other members, who had confessed to being national liberals, also had to leave the party. (NSZ 03/06/1993). A few days later "a national political group" was born, which included 28 members in the parliament. Later, in 1993, Csurka founded a new party, *Magyar Igazság és Élet Pártja* (Hungarian Truth (Justice) and Life).

In September, Horthy was reburied in Kenderes, and seven government Ministers participated in the occasion. In April, Horthy's widow had promised to organize the event strictly as a family affair (168 óra 27/04/1993), which the government supported. However, at the end of July, a memorial medal for Horthy was planned (MH 31/07/1993), and it was announced that "several members" of the government would participate in the ceremony as private citizens (NSZ 16/08/1993). Finally, the day before the reburial, the intelligentsia held a symbolic demonstration: The programme was directed by Miklós Jancsó "*Végsőbúcsú a Horthy-rendszertől*" (The Final Goodbye to the Horthy System), and it bid farewell to Horthyism (MH 04/09/1993). According to foreign comments, the funeral itself became a political event (NSZ 06/09/1993).

Beside official commemorations on March 15th, the Democratic Charter held a march of its own (NSZ 16/03/1993), and the '56-flag was again present during the events of March 15th (MH 16/03/1993). In June, some 500 members of the '56 Association, Pofosz and the skinheads commemorated Trianon (MH 05/06/1993). On 15th June, decorations were handed out again, and on the 16th wreaths were again laid "on the day of independence" (cf. NSZ 17/06/1993).

Finally, the Constitutional Court made its decision concerning the law enacted in October 1992. It concluded that there is no statute of limitations for a crime against humanity. In March, President Árpád Göncz again asked for a decision from the Constitutional Court before he would agree to sign the bill (NSZ 08/03/1993). At the end of June, the Court declared the bill unconstitutional (NSZ 30/06/1993). In October, it became apparent that the Geneva Convention from 1949, which protects the victims of war, defined international armed conflicts and forbade actions that were not international armed conflicts from taking place. According to the Constitutional Court, the first paragraph of the bill was unconstitutional, however, the second was not. (NSZ 13/10/1993). Despite its complicated sentences, the message was clear. Crimes committed in 1956 were not considered as war crimes, but as crimes against humanity, and on 22rd October, the President signed the bill.

The Minister of Justice called for the organization of a few dozen legal proceedings (MH 14/10/1993). A week later, the 1956 Association of Moson-magyaróvár demanded the arrest of István Dudás, who had commanded the frontier guards in 1956 (NSZ 21/10/1993). István Csurka proclaimed that if they were to seize power, "a whole process of reckoning and making justice would begin" (MH 29/10/1993). However, critical voices were also heard, because international agreements usually do not justify punishments, and international treaties are not understood as defining in the legal sense (MN 17/11/1993).

After a long illness, Prime Minister József Antall died on 12th December. On the 14th, parliament declared the day of burial as a national day of mourning, and a memorial medal was established (MN 17/12/1993). Antall would be buried at the cemetery of Kerepesi, beside the mausoleum of Fe-renc Deák (NSZ 16/12/1993). The new government of the former Minister of the Interior, Péter Boross (MDF), was sworn in on the 21st.

As a whole, 1993 seemed to be the of preparation for the elections in 1994. The electronic media, punishment and how to face the Horthy era, were also on the daily agenda. The MDF had been in deep, inner crisis, and in November, three prominent members of FIDESZ left the party. Until that time, FIDESZ had been the most popular party in the opinion polls, but in December, Socialists surpassed the popularity of FIDESZ (MH 29/12/1993).

## The Year of Two Elections, 1994

In February, the Minister of Justice, István Balsai, stated that the question of punishment was becoming more of a responsibility, and interpreted that "the whole system itself had come into being from war crimes" (NSZ 07/02/1994). Two suspects were arrested in Mosonmagyaróvár, and two in Salgótarján (MH; NSZ 12/02/1994). After 35 investigations, there would be proceedings in five cases: Berzence, Eger, Mosonmagyaróvár, Salgótarján and Tiszakécske. Except in the cases of Eger and Salgótarján, Military Courts would handle the trials (NSZ 01/04/1994).

On 8th March, 1994, a law "for controlling persons chosen to certain important positions" was enacted in parliament, and it entered into force on

July 1st, 1994. The law deals not only with official and secret members of the former counter-intelligence (III-III), but also with persons in the armed forces (1956-1957), and members of the fascist Arrow Cross Party. The bill, also known as the "Agent Law", was accepted with 177 votes for, 12 against and 50 abstaining.(NSZ 09/03/1994).

The "media war" had continued to escalate prior to the spring elections, and on "Black Friday", 129 journalists were fired from the Hungarian radio (NSZ 05/03/1994) – illegally, as the court found (MN 23/04/1994). Moreover, before the second round of the elections, Péter Hack (SZDSZ) stated that former Vice Presidents Csúcs and Nahlik could not remain after the elections (MH 12/05/1994). The MSZP was more patient: Csúcs and Nahlik could remain until further notice (NSZ 19/05/1994).

The first parliament finished its work on 7th April, by which time it had enacted 219 new laws and changed 213 (Mpé 1995, 349). The elections took place on 8th May; there was a 69% rate of voter turnout. The results of the first round were as follows:

MSZP 32, 96%
SZDSZ 19,76%.
MDF 11,74%
FKGP 8,82%
KDNP 7,03%
FIDESZ 7,02%

Thus, although FIDESZ had clearly been ahead in the opinion polls until the end of 1993, the Socialists eventually won 1,78 million votes in the first round, with FIDESZ only receiving 379,344 votes. The first round did not bring new parties to the parliament. In the second round, the Hungarian Socialist Party won an absolute majority with 209 seats, SZDSZ won 70 seats, MDF 37 seats, FKGP 26 seats, KDNP 22 seats and FIDESZ 20 seats. In December, local self-governments were elected on the municipal level and there, independent candidates won the largest number of seats (NSZ 13/12/1994).

The new government comprised of Socialists and Free Democrats was sworn in on 14th July, and Gyula Horn (MSZP) became the new Prime Minister. The Socialists could have formed a government of their own, however they preferred a coalition with Free Democrats. Socialists in fact agreed on the idea of cooperation, but the coalition question divided the Free Democrats: 479 of the delegates supported and 106 opposed the coalition with MSZP (NSZ 27/06/1994).

The changes at the television station took place in July, when a new person took over the leadership, and new logo was chosen. According to an opinion poll, in September, the new news show was "rather moderate", when their predecessors were considered "rather extreme" (MH 20/09/1994). The former TV-news leader commented about "new purges" and noted that "the news will be censored, also mentioning that a "political purge is continuing" (NSZ 23/07/1994). Moreover, when the leader of the National Bank resigned in November, he cited "political reasons" as the background for his decision (MH 23/11/1994), and the MDF considered the act a "purge" (Mpé 1995, 364).

The 16th of June, was one of the first appearances of the upcoming new Prime Minister Gyula Horn (MSZP). Horn laid a wreath with Erzsébet Nagy at the grave of Imre Nagy, in the Section 301. Horn, whose activities in 1956 were brought up prior to the election, signified the fact that there was no place for restoration attempts (MH 17/06/1994). Thus, Horn and Erzsébet Nagy had engaged in an act of reconciliation which, according to Béla Kurcz, astonished veterans and the relatives of '56-ers (MN 17/06/1994). The elections had drastically changed the political palette of Hungary and, for example, Jenő Fónay had expressed his bitterness about the results (MN 02/06/1994).

However, Zoltán Gál (MSZP) argued that there would be "no political interpretation" (MN 18/06/1994), and received the 1956 organizations the day after the commemoration. Gál promised that "national reconciliation" would be one of the basic pillars of the new government. Moreover, the government should stay away from evaluating politics, and stressed the hopes that there could be a unifying interpretation. Maria Wittner, who represented the organizations, commented on the meeting that the Socialist Party accepted the spirit of 1956 (MH; MN 18/06/1994). The dialogue between the party and the organizations continued in June (MH 23/06/1994).

In Salgótarján, on June 23, a trial began, and three out of twelve defendants were questioned. Attorney General Kálmán Györgyi commented that the ongoing slaughter was verifiable, and the actions were based on the Geneva Treaty. According to Györgyi, a juridical problem had emerged, which neither Hungarian nor European law had looked at head on until now. Homicides also occurred in Salgótarján, and it has to be decided whether the cases belong to the Geneva Convention, or were crimes against humanity. (MH 13/08/1994).

Moreover, the Budapest Court questioned several people, among them Béla Biszku and Gyula Uszta (MN 08/07/1994). Later, other high officials were questioned as witnesses: ex-Minister of Defense Lajos Czinege, and László Földes, then a member of the Central Committee. Both of them denied the existence of an order to open fire (MH 21/09/1994). In November of 1994, István Dudás and three other border guards were prosecuted at

Mosonmagyaróvár (MH 12/11/1994). At the end of the year, one more case was opened in Tata, against a Lieutenant-Colonel, who had retired from active service (MH 29/12/1994).

In October, Socialists and Free Democrats represented the government at the official ceremonies. For the first time, Gyula Horn, Zoltán Gál and Árpád Göncz laid a wreath together. (MN 22/10/1994). Conversely, at that time the opposition had their own memorials, and the idea of reconciliation was dubious (MN 24/10/1994). For example, Pofosz had its own commemoration, as did Csurka's party MIÉP. According to Viktor Orbán (FIDESZ), the Hungarian people in 1956 had demanded the return to their middle class (*polgári*) traditions and citizens' ('bourgeois') Hungary (*polgári Magyarország*) (MN 24/10/; 29/10/1994). Elsewhere, István Csurka interpreted the past and spoke about "the quiet counter-revolution" of the 1980s, which had been fulfilled in the elections of 1990 (NSZ 24/10/1994).

In conclusion, the most decisive event in 1994 had been the second round of free elections, in which the Hungarian Socialist Party finally won an absolute majority of the seats. To some extent, it also altered some of the expectations concerning the evaluation of 1956. However, the new government recognized and carried out most of the decisions and traditions of its predecessors. For example, at the end of December, the Minister of Justice personally argued that research work would continue, and the government would carry out the lustration laws (NSZ 28/12/1994). According to the Minister of Education and Culture, Gábor Fodor (SZDSZ), the base of the present consensus in the cooperation in the government was still the recognition of the revolution (MN 20/10/1994).

* * *

Historians Csaba Békés and Melinda Kalmár began speculating in October 1994, when 1956 would be considered "history". Current history writing was rendered more difficult because of the phenomenon that '1956' had become the focal point of comparison of everything before and after that date (NSZ 22/10/1994). I agree with this view, although I might add that '1956' had not only become a difficult historical and political problem, but also a symbolic figure, which was widely used in political argumentation.

Thus, it has now become evident how, during the system change, '1956' was renewed, and how certain phenomena returned and were restored to the present policy. In this sense, the system change has not only been a 'transition', but also an every-day political struggle, and particularly a struggle over different pasts. The system change was not the first in Hungarian space of experience since 1988. Therefore, in the following chapters I will attempt to enter 'into' to the system change and vertically relate '1956' to other Hungarian spaces of experience. In the first place, I will attempt to focus on how the earlier spaces of experience have constructed current political argumentation and expectations.

# VII NEW INTERPRETATIONS OF RECENT HISTORY

Although Charles Gati wrote about different signs from Moscow in 1988 (1990, 162), no evidence was found in this study that Gorbachev had explicitly told Hungarians to revaluate their past. However, a discussion on the past was going on during perestroika as well, although some held the view that there should be concentration on the future, and energy should not be wasted over the past. The turn toward reappraisal occurred slowly toward the end of 1986, and in spring 1988, it was openly recognized in the Politburo "that the reconsideration of the past was essential to perestroika" (Davies 1989, 129, 193). In February 1987 Gorbachev had spoken about filling "blank spots", and in October a commission began to research the Stalin era (Miller 1993, 95; Karlsson 1999, 97-150).

In the Hungarian Party Convention of May 1988, a committee was appointed which had the task of studying the recent history of Hungary. Properly, the aim was to focus on the last four decades and prepare a text as a background for the draft of the new party programme, which was to be discussed at the 14th Congress of the ruling party. A member of the Central Committee, Imre Pozsgay, led the work and had four special committees under his command. One of them dealt with history and was led by Iván T. Berend, the President of the Hungarian Academy of Sciences and a new member of the Central Committee. In addition to university professors, representatives of the Academy of Sciences and party historians (Sándor Balogh, Tibor Hajdu, Mária Ormos and six others) there also included MSZMP politicians like Gyula Horn, the future leader of the Socialist Party and Prime Minister.

Finally, the results of the report, "Our Historical Road" (*Történelmi utunk*), were published in the second half of February of 1989 in the special edition of *Társadalmi Szemle*, which had been since 1945, the scientific and theoretical journal of the MDP and later the MSZMP. In the report, the Central Committee added a short comment stating that the study did not reflect the views of the Central Committee (Társadalmi Szemle 1989, 80). Thus, the text is not a 'real' historical study with a special list of documents, footnotes or referenced literature. In spite of this, historians had participated in the work and, thus, documented history for the purpose of creating a party programme for a party, the legitimization of which was broadly historically based.

On the first pages, Iván T. Berend estimated that research work in domestic and foreign archives would probably take years. In spite of this, the author assured that the committee had attempted to go through all of the literature and read the most important unpublished documents (Ibid., 2). When we look at the committee now, ten years later, it seems evident that the committee had the potential to be the leader in trying to deal with the inconvenient past, particularly '1956'. The committee was nominated in spring of 1988, but until 1989, the newspapers analyzed in this study reported no special signs of its work. Later, in 1993, Pozsgay wrote that he had known about the reprisals that took place during the first years of János Kádár's leadership. However, Pozsgay argued that he had not known that between 1957 and 1963, every other week the Central Committee had received certain statistics which dealt with trials, prisoners at the camp and people who had been executed. According to Pozsgay, Kádár himself ordered that more death sentences should be pronounced instead of prison sentences (Pozsgay 1993, 92).

In the report, eighty pages, with four main chapters which usually had three to five subheadings, focuses on four decades. Sometimes the text is not exact, and although the narrative is chronological, events still might remain partly unclear. There, for example, the forming of People's Democracies, i.e. "plebeian revolutionary democratic social-political systems", is put in the Cold War context. As a whole, the period of 1948-1956 is seen as seriously contradictory in the most recent Hungarian history. For some it was a difficult, deformed period of mistakes and victims, and for others a period during which the wrong historical path was taken. (Ibid., 15-30).

The last subheading in the second chapter is "The Uprising in October 1956", and the text contains less than four full pages (Ibid., 31-34) out of eighty. The chapter begins with 23rd October and ends with the departure of János Kádár and Ferenc Münnich from Budapest. Contingency had 'increased' since the narrative began with spontaneous hopes, which surpassed the hesitation and resistance of party leadership. Spontaneity seems to be the main subject of the plot, and not conscious groups or conspiracies. Furthermore, students' demands of reforms were mentioned, as were the symbolic abolishment of the Stalin statue, the nomination of Imre Nagy, and the demands of a courtroom trial, *and also* the withdrawal of Soviet troops, as well as the restoration of the multiparty system.

As in earlier interpretations, the wolf, however, still lay in ambush for Little Red Riding Hood, because in the next paragraph there were elements which had more fundamental demands. According to a report, these narrow intellectual groups were quiet in the beginning, however they existed and were ready to stand firm. Nevertheless, the spontaneous demonstrators had the main role. With them, the power (*hatalom*), which had lost its connection to the masses, had, for a long time, not been reluctant to engage in dialogue and thus it united (*egybemosta* = wash together) different groups of the society.

## An Armed Critique Instead of a Critical Weapon

In the text presented to the committee, there is no clear picture of how the peaceful demonstration turned into a bloody uprising. There are no signs of who provided the weapons, where they came from, who fired the first shot, or what happened in front of the parliament on 25th October, 1956. The authors were able to avoid these detailed questions through the metaphorical reference to and play upon Marx's words; instead of a *"Waffe der Kritik"*, an *"Kritik der Waffen"* came into being (*" 'a kritika fegyvere' helyett már a 'fegyverek kritikájára'"*). Thus, this open criticism led to the explosion of an uprising against the existing political power.

The stalinist model of socialism was seen to be the most important factor leading to the uprising, and its overturn was the only common platform of the various groups. Thus, not the idea of socialism as such, but an existing and present model, was the common target of opposition. However, in comparison to the former "four reasons" of the Kádár regime, the origins were now clearly national and internal. As was argued in earlier interpretations, the Gerő-Hegedüs government was unable to deal with the problem, and therefore invited Soviet troops into the country. According to the report, this changed the masses, whose national feelings had already been hurt. They decided to fight for national independence.[45]

Instead of fascism and counter-revolution, the themes of pluralism and the mixed, multi-dimensional aims of '1956' were more the focus in the report. When in the previous interpretations the revisionists were considered to have joined with the counter-revolutionaries, and were superseded during the second week, it was claimed that until the end, an aim existed to reform socialism and aspire toward democracy and fundamental reforms. For the others, it appeared to be a reversion to the post-1945 'plebeian' People's Democracy. Moreover, besides this, elements in favour of restoring the old system existed, which had been overthrown not but a decade earlier, as well as those who tried to restore the western bourgeois democracy. Furthermore, the report listed the appearance of the conservative-nationalists and the extreme, anti-Communist Horthyite Christian national course. Finally, in the factories and on the streets, essential roles were played by factions who were set free from prison and were lynching people and demanding revenge.

In the report, there is no ranking of which groups or aspirations were the broadest or most essential. Although the reformed socialist ambition lasted until the end, the words used to define the relations between the groups were "beside", "to others", "in addition", "played a great role", "also" etc., i.e. at this time pluralism was acknowledged more in the aims of 1956 – perhaps simply because the power relationships between these groups were impossible to discern during such a short, temporal period. However, it is striking to note how the socialist direction is referred to. The ruling party was revising its programme, and also found positive traditions from the revolutionaries of 1956.

In addition to including social property, democracy and socialism in the same sentence, the authors also made more critical or 'negative' remarks. In addition to those three concepts, land reform was called in question (in Mindszenty's speech) as an unrealistic and dangerous idea of denying the current geopolitical situation, as did the lynching and pogroms taking place in the streets. Attention is also briefly paid to white terror, which is credited to put in the mouth of writer László Németh, who had warned about this possibility particularly in the countryside. As a whole, there seemed to be a chance of the return of the Horthy system, and the attainment of other aims also seemed to be possible.

Imre Nagy was no longer seen as a traitor. Although the writers understood the extreme difficulties of the situation, Nagy and his government were criticized harshly. According to the report, Nagy continually made concessions which not only did not satisfy the demands of those in the streets, but "added fuel to the fire". Nagy was drifting along with the events, instead of controlling them. Therefore, it now seems that the situation did not reach an end, but shifted chaotically to the right. Also, "foolish views such as if the masses would like fascism, there will be fascism," gained a foothold. In other words, they criticized Nagy for being excessively trusting of the rebels and not trying to control them. Imre Nagy was still seen as too weak to handle the situation, i.e. the Prime Minister should keep order and not join with others and capitulate to their demands.

The decision to engage in a second Soviet intervention is assumed to have been based on the shift on 30th October. Only the shift in policy was mentioned, but on the 30th, Nagy had restored the multiparty system, and rebels had attacked the party headquarters. Moreover, the report briefly touched on the international political situation following the Suez crisis, French-British intervention, the viewpoint of the United States, the Hungarian question and the propaganda surrounding it. Furthermore, the decision of Soviet intervention is dealt with in the same paragraph. The standpoints varied, and the decision was made after three days. Furthermore, the support coming from China and Yugoslavia, and how the consensus of opinion was reached, was stressed.

From the 1st November, both János Kádár and Ferenc Münnich were seen as independent and determined political actors, i.e. they "on 1st November... did not see any other solution than to leave the government of Nagy, and after the negations in the Soviet Embassy, to leave Budapest and to form the Revolutionary Workers' and Peasants' Government". Properly, these words led to the chapter that dealt with the uprising until 4th November, because the next big chapter deals with the years 1956-1973 under the headline "A Compromise Attempt to Renew Socialism".

According to the report, Imre Nagy had no chance to carry out the reorganization of power, because he, based on moral motivation, had declared Hungary's neutrality and the split from the Warsaw Pact. The reorganization was also impossible for the despised and compromised Rákosi-Gerő group. In the next chapter the report also recognized reprisals, which, particularly in the countryside, (the term *vidék* means usually outside Budapest, thus also includes smaller cities) were frequently based on subjective decisions. Imre Nagy's death sentence is connected to the shift in the Soviet Union and China, but also to Nagy himself, i.e. even in Romania, Nagy was reluctant to resign and legitimize the new government. The number of death sentences was mentioned at this point and was estimated to be around 300.

## Renaming 1956

In the history committee, a new name, 'uprising', '(popular) uprising' (*népfelkelés*) was given to the events. This name, which also refers to German *Volksaufstand* and has become established in use, for example in Finland, was also the most recent piece of news in the whole report. The term "uprising" was used throughout the entire text, with the exception of only one paragraph:

> "In spite of the hidden tendencies, which pushed the events to the right and strengthened counter-revolutionary traces during the first days of November... unambiguous clarifying, 'final' establishing cannot become... of the corrective [*korrektív*] revolution and counter-revolution... . The following has to be done: contradictory pair correct revolution – counter-revolution are mixed unexplainedly to each other, into which also the earlier debates could not create a successful solution."

In the report, the expressions 'revolution' and 'counter-revolution' were not defined in greater detail, and their meaning must be read and discerned from

156

the text. Although hidden "counter-revolutionary tendencies" existed, as a whole, revolution and counter-revolution were mixed. Thus, according to the report, the questioning of the monolithic socialist structure and the changes which had taken place during the second week of Nagy's government could equally and similarly be interpreted as an attempt to overthrow the stalinist model of socialism, *or* as an attempt to overthrow the whole idea of socialism. In other words, it was impossible to say whether it was the existing system or the rejection of a more abstract idea, which took place in 1956.[46]

As we have seen, the concept of revolution was not yet accepted, i.e. revolutionary and counter-revolutionary purposes were juxtaposed. Therefore, a new term, which exceeded the former confrontation, was given to the whole conflict. The background of the name was not explained, but it was closer to the expressions which Kádár used in his speech on 1st November, 1956. However, more important was that "uprising" was the term which the UN's Committee of Five report had predominantly used in 1957. Furthermore, in the Hungarian context *népfelkelés* had been used in the context of 1848. At that time, it meant the draft by which Lajos Kossuth gathered voluntary troops against the Austrians.

When applying Koselleck's categories of history writing, the party itself began the phase of rewriting (*Umschreiben*) by renaming or presenting a new expression for the event. Although all names could be said to be partial, the new name was a gesture of reconciliation. Moreover, in the former East European context, the ruling Hungarian Socialist Workers' Party was able to evaluate its past from an early stage. However, regardless of whether a party programme is the right forum in which to explain history, in Hungary it offered a possibility to deal with the inconvenient past. Evidently, party programmes are directed toward the future, where political actors try to keep to a stage which might need a modernized picture of the past. However, in Hungary, the reforms not only concerned the future, but also the past, and the naming challenged the 'historical' legitimacy of the ruling party.

The Pozsgay Committee had now prepared a new compromise with the notion of the recent past. However, it would be wrong to see it only as one link in a chain towards democracy, but rather, it should be seen as an ice-breaker to new positions. On the one hand, alternative movements had demanded a multiparty system. On the other hand, Imre Pozsgay had partly understood them, but clear limits to the discussion were laid by Károly Grósz at the end of November, and by János Berecz by mid-December. Therefore, the first months of 1989 and the reception of the report became more essential in this study. On the one hand, the new name was an attempt at compromise with the audiences outside the party. But on the other hand, it could be seen as a provocation, which would test the content of the word "reformer" within the ruling party. Those who had a multiparty system in mind had to force the fall of those who defined the change only within the frame of a single party.

However, in the course of events since February of 1989, even the programme draft itself becomes obsolete in 1989. At their last convention in October, the MSZMP tried its best to cut its connections to the past. Not only was the name of the party changed, but the entire early history portion of the draft was ousted from the programme (!). The new text began with the words "at the end of the 1980s, Hungarian society came to an historical turning point." No one was mentioned by name, and 1956 was no longer stressed (NSZ 10/10/1989). The draft of the party programme had been published in August (NSZ 19/08/1989), and in September, the party organ had already published specific changes to the draft (NSZ 30/09/1989). At the second national meeting the reformers demanded a new programme for the party (MH 08/09/1989).

## The Report and the Multiparty System: the Pozsgay Interview

In principle, the law on freedom of association and assembly on 11th January, 1989, made it possible to found parties. However, there was nothing in the law about how these parties could function during free elections; nor was there anything about elections in general. At that time, a special law for parties was scheduled to be voted on in August of 1989. However, even though parliament had activated itself, we must focus on the party, because in a party state, the Central Committee of the ruling party is the most important political organization.

On Thursday 26th, the Central Committee decided to permit the private reburial of Imre Nagy and his compatriots. On the following day, Committee for Historical Justice, TIB, welcomed the decision with pleasure, but said it was only a first step, since the names of all the executed should also be published. In practice, a short piece of news was hidden on the fifth page, with an uninformative headline "Communiqué". At that time, the term "revolution" seemed to appear for the first time in the newspapers. (MN 27/01/1989).

On Saturday the 28th, only Népszabadság briefly reported that the previous day a research report was dealt with in the meeting of the Pozsgay Committee. The session was briefly mentioned as the purpose and the content of the report. However, there was nothing about the new terminology, and when 1956 was mentioned once, it was defined with the word "events". The proper 'scandal' was to occur on the following day, when, after the meeting, Pozsgay gave an interview on the radio programme, 168-Hours, which would be broadcast on Saturday afternoon. The radio interview is documented in Pozsgays' book (1993), and the 'true' piece of news spawned from the second answer. The first question had dealt with the possible rehabilitation of Imre Nagy, because the Central Committee had given permission for his reburial.

Question: "What is thought about the role of Imre Nagy and his doings in 1956?"

[*Answer:*] There are ongoing debates on it. It is possible to discern internal and external connections, which make the evaluation more nuanced, for example, the fact that on the basis of the newest research work the committee considers what happened in 1956 as an uprising, as a revolt, against one oligarchy, and against the power, which humbled the nation.

Question: The change in the usage of the word shows that the thinking of politics is now totally different than in the year 1956. Earlier it was classified as a counter-revolution, later the events of '56 were a general formulation in the speeches of politicians, and now you are talking about an uprising. Why has the classification changed so rapidly almost within the space of a year, and could this change be considered final?

[Answer:] Nothing can be considered final when we go back in history. Even if facts are honoured, the facts both beforehand and those facts which might possibly be revealed in the future must also be honoured. Definitely at all events I would like to add that with this formula... politics, history and the public opinion have become closer to each other. Both in public opinion and in the opinion of the majority of the party members the existing relation was shown by an interpretation, which classified what happened in '56 with the single word counter-revolution. On the basis of the research work up until this point, it could be considered that this is not true." (Pozsgay 1993, 223-224). (Transl. HN).

In 1993, Pozsgay revealed in his book that he was of the opinion that a legal and formal multiparty system does not come into being by itself, but that the ruling party must also take action (Pozsgay 1993, 90). Pozsgay wrote that "until that day, an idea of what he should do matured in his mind, but he did not know how to do it" (Ibid., 94). On the next page, he focused on the idea that he had formed a plan to use the media "on the day before the session". Originally, the committee meeting was to have been held the previous week, on 19th January (Pozsgay 1993, 90-97). Now the interview was broadcast on Saturday, i.e. on the weekend, when offices were not open. Furthermore, specifically over that weekend the First Secretary of the Party, Károly Grósz, had traveled to a conference to Davos, Switzerland. (cf. also Dienstag 1996). In other words, the act looked like a one-man conspiracy against the system.

On the basis of his formulations of document politics, history and public opinion had been related to each other. In the first place, according to Pozsgay, the relationship of history and public opinion were supposed to have become closer to each other. However, when at the end of the interview the reporter questioned the possibility of preventing or stopping the work of the committee, Pozsgay used a metaphor about toothpaste: Cancelling the work is as absurd as pushing toothpaste back into the tube (Ibid., 227). Something irrevocable had been done. Pozsgay had put the 'cat on the table', i.e. he went straight to the point and the party, whether united or not, was obliged to answer.

Although the majority had supported the new viewpoint of an "uprising" in the meeting on Friday, they would have preferred to utilise party channels to publish the results, i.e. first the Political Committee and next the Central Committee meeting. In 1993, Pozsgay estimated that this alternative would have watered down the entire report (Pozsgay 1993, 94-95). Indeed, on the one hand, the party might have stopped the whole draft or watered down its content. But on the other hand, there was the more essential theoretical possibility that the MSZMP would 'claim' the whole report for its own use.

However, in 1993, Pozsgay wrote that he wanted to act alone, and that he also took full responsibility, because in January-February of 1989 there was no information available as to how the Soviet Union would react, or whether the Yalta or Brezhnev Doctrine still existed (Ibid., 94-95). Even if, for example, Bukharin and others had been rehabilitated in 1988, four reformers had been ousted from the party in Hungary as late as April of 1988, because they had participated in founding the New March Front.[47]

We could doubt that new history of winners was lurking in the Pozsgay's book but at least in 1993, Pozsgay was no longer one of the key politicians. He had left the Socialist Party in 1990, but remained a Member of Parliament with his small Alliance of National Democrats. Moreover, only a few weeks before Pozsgay's statement, a Soviet magazine still characterized Imre Nagy as a contradictory figure (NSZ 06/01/1989). Thus, in January, 1989, Imre Pozsgay had taken the political initiative and tested the practice of *glasnost*. At the same time, he had opened a new political space for himself, which had he succeeded, would also bring personal advantages. Thus, from this time on, a government Minister brought a political issue to public discussion and openly questioned the previous political 'basis' of the party, whether former 'fundamentals' should be broken at first in order to create a basis for new ideas, as in brainwashing. But now the party was forced to leave the safety of the trenches it had previously inhabited and enter into no mans land.

The significance of the question can be discerned, for example, in several international newspapers. On Monday the 30th, *Frankfurter Rundschau, Frankfurter Allgemeine Zeitung, l'Unita* and *Repubblica* all reported the interview. In the Hungarian party newspaper *Népszabadság,* the interview was modestly put only on the bottom of the left-hand page. When the party newspaper briefly referred to The Hungarian News Agency, MTI, they argued that *researchers* considered the events as an uprising. However, in the paper of the Council of Ministers, *Magyar Hírlap,* the article was in the best position on the front page. The headline was: "According to the History Committee of the MSZMP, the Events of 1956 Could be Considered as an Uprising".

On that Monday, Károly Grósz had flown back from Davos and, according to Pozsgay, had telephoned him from the airport. Later, Grósz accused Pozsgay of smashing the identity of the Hungarian Socialist Workers' Party and branding the Soviet intervention illegal, unjustified and meaningless, with this act (Pozsgay 1993, 96). On the following day, the 'scandal' reached the front pages of Hungarian newspapers. *Magyar Nemzet* published comments from foreign newspapers which had supported Pozsgay's declaration. *Népszabadság* carried the headline "Károly Grósz on the Party, '56 and Reform Debates", and *Magyar Hírlap* published the same interview. The journalist from *Népszabadság* speculated that Pozsgay "had used terminology, from which a consensus was not reached in the party". Grósz had read the article in an airplane and was of the opinion that the report was written for the party congress, and that it depended on the congress as to how far the concept would be worked up during the current year (NSZ 31/01/1989).

However, on Tuesday afternoon, the Political Committee, Politbureau, held an exceptional session. A *communiqué* of the meeting was not published in the newspapers. On the basis of Pozsgay's notes, Károly Grósz estimated that Pozsgay's act had served the purposes of the international anti-Socialist bloc. In principle, the supporters of Grósz did not argue that the new interpretation was wrong, but rather that the opinion of the Central Committee should have been solicited first (Pozsgay 1993, 96-102). On the basis of the document published in Pozsgay's book, the Political Committee "could not accept the means by which the results of the historical subcommittee were brought to the public and timed." Moreover, it would be "wrong to bring the results to the public before the decision of the official staff." (Ibid., 228-229).

Furthermore, they wrote in the statement of the Political Committee that the declaration promotes anarchy, weakens the position of the MSZMP and provides arguments to political opponents. It was urged that they strengthen the unity of the party and form a distinct programme by which they could keep the power. The solution of the Political Committee, however, was to ask the Central Committee first, and to define its own stand only after that (Ibid.). A day after, on Wednesday, *Magyar Hírlap* reported briefly that there would be a meeting of the Central Committee the following week. MTI had written the piece of news, which was comprised of only two sentences, the latter of which told only that the "daily agenda contained actual political questions" (MH 01/02/1989). According to Pozsgay, the meeting on 10th February would be a special session (cf. Pozsgay 1993, 99-102).

Thus, the train kept rolling, and on Wednesday, 1st February, *Magyar Hírlap* referred to international comments in which the AP, AFP, TASS, New China and the party newspaper of China, had noticed Prime Minister Miklós Németh's and Károly Grósz's statements. International media, thus, followed and probably even influenced events in Hungary and, for example, *Westdeutsche Allgemeine Zeitung* characterized Pozsgay's declaration with the word "sensation". Moreover, according to *l'Unita*, Pozsgay was the first politician, who dissociated himself from the casual expression "counter-revolution". Furthermore, *Magyar Nemzet* added that the *Independent* had described the day before the interpretation as a "revolutionary change".

Hungarian politicians commented on the situation and, for example, Prime Minister Németh thought it impossible to characterise the events with one word (MN 01/02/1989). Another member of the Central Committee, János Lukács, said that the statement represented only Pozsgay's opinion. The Secretary of the Central Committee, Mátyás Szűrös, argued that it was impossible to understand the existing situation with one word. Iván T. Berend, was more pessimistic and noted that the evaluation of 1956 was impossible, because of the existence of white spots (MN 02-03/02; NSZ 04/02/1989).

However, the new interpretation was also connected to other current political aims. For example, *Magyar Nemzet* carried the headline that the party was made to define its stand on the multiparty system (MN 03/02/1989), In addition, prior to the session of the Central Committee on 10th February, newspapers began to publish other statements which dealt with 1956, but which also had other current political aspirations of democracy. The most important of these announcements was signed by 16 different organizations. The signatories included Social Democrats and five out of six of the forthcoming parties, which were to win seats in parliament more than a year later. Also among the signatories were the TIB, the New March Front and nine other organizations.

On the basis of the document, the organizations wanted "to serve the purpose of creating a rule of law and democratic Hungary and to raise serious economic, social and moral concerns"(MH; MN 07/02/1989). Moreover, the declaration included appeals such as "party members trusted by Hungarians", "the great majority", "national responsibility" and "cooperation" from which position an opposition would be built (Ibid.). Once they referred to 1956 as an "uprising", as Pozsgay's Committee had done. Thus, the statement connected two entangled arguments, one dealing with the past and one with the future; and they also took history as a part of a political argumentation.

Among other comments, the President of the Hungarian Association of Writers mentioned that, within the concept of uprising, public opinion, science and politics had become closer. In addition, BAL, which considered itself as leftist, stressed the importance of reevaluation, and resisted the idea that the future should be bound with the past. Finally, the MSZMP's fifth circle from the XII district of Budapest had also sent a declaration. According to the section, "Communists and non-Communists consider *a slaughter* [italics HN] as an uprising" and pointed to single events like Republic Square, the withdrawal from the Warsaw Pact and counter-revolutionary parties. They had the opinion that if they would agree "with the committee, then almost a quarter of the party members would themselves be counter-revolutionary, because they had stopped and overthrown 'an uprising'". Thus, the definition was still significant more than three decades later, and the new interpretation also seemed to be related to the question of guilt.

## The Interpretation of 1956 and the Introduction of a Multiparty System

On 11th February, *Magyar Nemzet* briefly mentioned that the Central Committee "had dealt with questions dealing with socialist pluralism and the transition to the multiparty system". Furthermore, it was said that the discussion would continue that day. According to the newspaper, Pozsgay's declaration was not on the agenda but, as became apparent a few days later, it was one of the issues. The *communiqué* of the session was published on the front page of all three leading newspapers on 13th February. However, the debates in the Central Committee were published in 1993.

At first, Károly Grósz took the floor, and then the members of the Central Committee spoke in turn. According to the minutes, there was no special agenda in the meeting, but the members dealt simultaneously with '1956' and the idea of a multiparty system. Almost every speaker dealt with both the past experience (usually 1956), and expectations (the fate of the party in "a competitive system"). János Kádár himself was not present at the meeting, and at the end of the session, it was revealed that he would be on vacation until the middle of February (cf. A Magyar Szocialista Munkáspárt központi... 1993).

In his opening words, First Secretary Grósz said that he wanted to decide how to form a multiparty system in Hungary. The First Secretary interpreted the possibilities and limits of the session in such a way that the last party convention in 1988 had not forbid the multiparty system either – literally, the formula had dealt with socialist pluralism built under the leadership of the

163

party. Next, Grósz defined his view of Pozsgay's declaration, and said he felt it had been made prematurely. Hence, the First Secretary proposed that the Central Committee would not agree with the channel of publication, but did agree that the entire report should be published in *Társadalmi Szemle*, which took place at the end of February. According to Grósz's proposition, the Central Committee would not agree with Pozsgay's act, but indicated its confidence in Pozsgay (A Magyar Szocialista Munkáspárt központi... 1993, 10-11).

Thus, both the past and the future were present in the argumentation. Among the arguments, the following aspects were mentioned: the international publicity turned toward the session was mentioned (Iván T. Berend); Europeanisation – the fact that there were no singleparty systems among the developed countries in Europe (Gyula Horn); and that there were more than 100 poorly functioning and some 20-15 smoothly functioning multiparty systems (Frigyes Berecz). However, appropriately, history in politics came to the fore when, for example, György Aczél pointed out that in France, debates concerning the French Revolution continue even two hundred years after the fact. Moreover, in was common practice in the meeting to tie 1956 into one's own experiences and tell 'how it was'. Several members of the Central Committee disapproved of Pozsgay's declaration, which, for example, had brought the debate to the streets (A Magyar Szocialista Munkáspárt központi...1993).

The connection to daily politics became evident already in the words of Károly Grósz, when he estimated that the case of 1956 also included emotion stirring interests, which also serve current politics. However, Grósz did not define these current interests in more detail but, for example, when Imre Pozsgay defended himself, he said that "an acceptable expression helps us in the question of legitimization" (Ibid., 33). In the concluding analysis, Grósz pointed out that the party has twice been in crisis: in 1956 and now. The stalemate is crystallized in the words: "if we do not make our stand, we are Stalinists and if we do, we will drag out the events." They waited for the future mixed economy and socialism, but no one knew how socialism would function in the future (Ibid., 180).

In general, the domestic character of such an important meeting is striking. *Glasnost, perestroika* or other contemporary arguments of that time did not frequently repeat themselves. Mihály Korom mentioned Gorbachev and doubted the permanence of his course in the Soviet Union (Ibid., 61). However, in his concluding remarks Károly Grósz noted that Gorbachev had phoned him two days earlier. Grósz argued that a complete mutual under-standing had prevailed between Hungary and the Soviet Union, although he mentioned that the Soviet leadership had worried about the declaration (Ibid., 174-176). Moreover, a Russian academic stated in a Hungarian newspaper a few days earlier that sovereign Hungary would not endanger the security of the Soviet Union (NSZ 09/02/1989).

If international politics did not prevail in the discussion, a few analogies were found between the experiences of other countries. Prime Minister Miklós Németh was among the few who compared the current situation with the case of Spain. Spanish reformers were no longer remembered, yet without them the present welfare increase would not have been possible (Ibid., 165). However, Poland was viewed as parallel to Hungary at that time, although the Polish case was not present in the Central Committee. During the same week, on 6th February, roundtable negotiations had began between the government, Solidarity, The Communist Trade Union and The Catholic Church. In the Hungarian newspapers, these negations were reported on 13th February, i.e. on the same day as the *communiqué* on the multiparty system was published. Officially, the multiparty system was 'born' first in Hungary, despite the fact that the roundtable negotiations finished earlier in Poland and semi-free elections took place already in June of 1989.

At the end of the meeting the *communiqué* was put to a vote, and four members opposed party's confidence in Pozsgay. In addition, ten votes were given for the proposal of Mihály Korom, who wanted to change the content of the text: "until the first of November the character of the events changed to counter-revolution"("*november els napjaira az események ellenforradalmi jelleget öltöttek*") (Ibid., 185-191). In 1993, Pozsgay wrote that he was later informed that during a pause, Grósz had surmised that the majority would oppose his exclusion from the party and that he feared a party split (Pozsgay 1993, 108-109).

Thus, on Monday, 13th February, the *communiqué* was published on the front page of all the three newspapers focused on in this study. The first part of the declaration was given as the decision to implement a multiparty system. The decision was argued by a large ambition to develop democracy, people's sovereignty and the principles of a rule of law. Moreover, they argued that on the basis of historical experiences, a multiparty system could create better guarantees for controlling the government and the prevention of an abuse of power. In the second part, the Central Committee concentrated on the results of the research, which, according to the text, "attempts to give a touching and scholarly picture of the recent past." The Central Committee considered it important that the study be a focus of discussion, adding that a versatile evaluation of the "national tragedy of 1956" was necessary. Among other aspects, the elements of restoration and strengthening of counter-revolutionary events also existed in the text. (MH; MN; NSZ 13/02/1989).

Moreover, it was reported that the Central Committee had confirmed that the inability of the leadership had led to an explosion. "A revolt, an uprising took place, in which elements of democratic socialism played a role" (Ibid.). Finally, Pozsgay was also 'chastised', according to declaration, because it was held to be hasty to publish the results before the discussion in the Central Committee. Furthermore, they found it regrettable that a simplification provided an excuse for misunderstandings, and that Pozsgay had simplified past events. Separately, it was mentioned that the Central Committee confirmed its confidence in Comrade Pozsgay. (Ibid.).

Dealing with two such fundamental issues in the same meeting could naturally also have been coincidence, because the demands concerning the implementation of a multiparty system were already 'in the air', and several organizations had also demanded it. If the decision was not made now, would it have been realized in the very near future even without Pozsgay's declaration? The interview had influence, because both the sessions in the Central Committee and in the Political Committee had been exceptional, and had been published following Pozsgay's declaration. Moreover, according to commentator András Bozóki (1993), the new interpretation of history *helped* in dismantling the existing system. Charles Gati (1990) wrote that Pozsgay's declaration *helped to mobilize* publicity against Grósz and his supporters (1990, 171). Finally, György Litván, an historian, non-conformist activist and veteran of 1956, concluded that following Pozsgay's statement, the party had *lost the most important basis of its legitimacy*. (Litván 1991, 721).

However, if we study rapid and turbulent changes in society, there is the question of whether special Rubicons could be found at all. To some extent, not even the free elections might be a watershed, because the legacy of the communist period continues to influence people's minds. According to a current cynical interpretation, conservatives in the party might still consoled themselves with the idea that, in principle, there was a multiparty system in North Korea, too, and that a Constitutional Court will still be necessary in order to control the parties... (Bruszt 1990, 374-375).

Thus, as early as February, a breakthrough 'from above' took place, because the Central Committee was forced to do something in order to "save face". On the one hand, the MSZMP might stop the reforms and forget the jargon about being a reform party. On the other hand, the party might have continued reforms, in which case it would have had to admit that Pozsgay had gotten a feather in his cap. Thirdly, the party could be more radical and, thus, connect the question of 1956 with the multiparty system. It seems apparent that Pozsgay's declaration was the straw that broke the camel's back in persuading those who remained hesitant about the future. Parties existed *de facto* but not *de jure*, and now the question was solved peacefully and at an extremely early stage in the context of the former Eastern Bloc (cf. Bihari 1993). Finally, László Bruszt (1990) was the one who combined the naming question with the roundtable negotiations, i.e. to current politics. If the definition used was "counter-revolution", there was nothing to negotiate, because 'we' would have then been compromising with the heirs of the counter-revolution. On the other hand, in the case of a "revolution", there was nothing to negotiate either, because 'we' had served a counter-revolutionary government almost 35 years and would have no legitimate role within the government. Therefore, the formula "uprising" was invented as a compromise. It was not 'we' who suppressed it, but 'they', Muscovites, conservatives and enemies of reform, who forced "this system upon society" (Bruszt 1990, 370-371).

It is also possible that this argument reveals more about a Hungarian political line of thought in which decisions are "either-or". In an interview at the end of 1987, Grósz had estimated that a new interpretation of 1956, thus revolution, would mean that 'we' are guilty and counter-revolutionaries (Lendvai 1988, 164).

However, Bruszt tied the idea of naming to the roundtable, although the idea of a roundtable was proposed in the newspaper on 18th February, thus five days later than the *communiqué*. The demand was included in a declaration made by the opposition, and it was dated 17th February. As on the 7th, forthcoming party organizations were among the signatories, even if some of the former organizations were not represented at that point. When they discussed the "uprising" in the text on 7th February, the formula was now a "revolution and fight for freedom". In addition to 1956, the founding of the multiparty system and the demand for "historical truth" also had a place in the same declaration:

"We, independent political organizations, associations and parties, welcome the declaration of the Central Committee of the MSZMP from 11th February and consider this as an important step on the way to creating democratic Hungary.

1. We welcome the standpoint, which is connected to 1956. Finally, after 30 years, the party decision from December 1956 was rejected. This 1956 decision branded the democratic movement of the people as a counter-revolution, it was the unutterable constitution of the MSZMP's leadership, which was superseded last May.

The statement is seen as a progressive step, although completely un-satisfactory, because we abhor its failure to accept the fact [that '1956' has been] a revolution and fight for freedom, as well as failing to recognize its democratic character. We consider a unanimous positive evaluation of 1956 as necessary and reject that the current party stand, which still over-stresses those rare negative matters which can be considered only as a reflection of 40 years of Rákosist-Stalinist indiscretions. At the same time, MSZMP is silent about the bloody masses of victims caused by the ÁVH and the cruel reprisals after - 56.

We argue: it is an historical truth that after the cease-fire between the Imre Nagy government and revolting groups on 28th October until the intervention on 4th November, the country was moving in the direction of consolidation and the position of the government was strengthening. A decisive role in this was played by reborn parties, which are now once again coming to the fore. However, a similar statement was also made by the leader of the MSZMP, born during the revolutionary period, János Kádár, who spoke about the glorious rebellion of our people.

2. We consider it as an important presupposition of the democratic progress that the body of MSZMP accepted the multiparty system, which is the only democratic form of power. Therefore, we note:
a) We consider democracy, which is attained by the provision of human rights, as the principle basis of power apparata. Hence, even mentioning the leading role of the MSZMP is in contradiction to a principle of party competition mentioned by the First Secretary.

[...]

3. We are grateful that the reform wing of the MSZMP has been strengthened in the meeting and that the demands of the 'system party-wing' were not given a platform in the documents.

4. We stress that the Hungarian newspapers and other media played a significant role in the democratization of the last period. A few benevolent misunderstandings refer to the tragedy of our situation. At the same time, we point out that the Hungarian Radio and Television belong to the nation, to the society maintaining them and to the state, and no single party can own them.[48]

5. We recommend speeding up the democratic process and creating a more stable, stronger and broader basis. A national roundtable should be established, in which the government, the leadership of the MSZMP and democratic political organizations could participate. The task and the aim of this negotiation would be to prepare presuppositions for elections and for a Constitutional Assembly." (MH 18/02/1989).

Thus, the opposition publicly interpreted that 1956 was unanimously a democratic movement, even considering this kind of evaluation as a necessity. Secondly, the declaration strengthened the idea that history was used for political legitimization. Thirdly, the past and future were connected in the same political argument and concretely in the demand for a national roundtable. Therefore, the question seemed to concern much more than what actually happened in the past. The past was also made a part of the present, politicized, and 1956 had become a means of political discussion, which had culminated in the naming of a certain event which had taken place in the past but had not been openly studied.

## Counter-Revolution, Uprising, Revolution, Fight for Freedom and War

Thus, until the end of February, 1989 several terms to define '1956' had existed in the Hungarian public. By the end of 1988, Hungarian historians had introduced the term "uprising", which was also accepted in the Central Committee in February. The opposition had already used two other terms in February, "revolution" and "fight for freedom", which they canonized in the first law written following the free elections.

In 1989, a few opinion polls posed the question of what had happened in 1956, i.e. what 1956 was about. Hereafter, I use these polls in this study, although one has to keep in mind that they show only the direction of opinions; more or less the results depend on how the question has been formulated. In Hungary, public opinion polls were a new phenomenon and, as will later be clarified, their timing and questions created doubts surrounding their use in determining legitimate political opinions. However, not using such polls also creates different illusions of existing consensus on certain matters. Thus, in my opinion, these polls exhibited diversity, uncertainty and plurality on political issues.

The first poll was made by *Hírlapkiadó Vállalat* and published in February by the party organ *Népszabadság*. The inquiry contained the opinions of 398 readers of the party organ and was made between 14th February and 18th, thus immediately following the meeting of the Central Committee.

The results were as follows:

13 %   regarded the events as a counter-revolution
6 %    regarded the events as a revolution
40%    viewed it as having begun as an uprising and changed to a counter-revolution

(NSZ 20/02/1989).

Among the readers of *Népszabadság*, the concept "revolution" was not popular and the term "fight for freedom" was completely unknown in the poll. On

169

the other hand, the dogmatic alternative, the anonymous "counter-revolution" was not very popular either. More than a third (40%) agreed with the new party line or were acquainted with the 'new public opinion'. However, according to the newspaper, the majority considered that 1956 was still too close to be evaluated unanimously (NSZ 20/02/1989). No information was given as to why the rest 41% had not answered at all.

Between 24th February and 1st March, the Institute of Public Opinion Polls, *Magyar Közvélemény Kutató Intézet,* asked the citizens to describe the character of 1956. The term "fight for freedom" did not exist in these results either, which were collected from Budapest, Győr and a small village. At that time, among those who sent back the inquiry, "uprising" was the most popular (38-44%) term, the second was "revolution" (20-22%), and the third was "counter-revolution" (15-20%) (168 óra 13/06/1989).

The question of naming was present in Hungary until the declaration of the republic on 23rd October, i.e. on the same day when the 'uprising' had begun. The problem of naming was, for example, seen in an interview conducted by the radio newspaper in May; János Berecz did not want to name 1956 "an uprising, but rather as an event which should be examined in the spirit of tolerance and reconciliation" (168 óra 23/05/1989).

A few days prior to the reburial of Imre Nagy, broader discussion was taking place in *Népszabadság* concerning the essence of 1956, as well as its naming (NSZ 10/06/1989). The interview resembled a national roundtable of historians, because the MSZMP was represented by Mária Ormos and Mihály Korom. In addition, Miklós Szabó (SZDSZ), and archivist János Varga (non-party, later MDF), participated in the debate, as did Imre Mécs (TIB, SZDSZ). On the basis of the discussion, it became clear that an unambiguous name did not exist, but compared to the report of the Pozsgay Committee, a corrective (*korrektív*) revolution seemed to be gaining ground, and it was also made a headline of *Népszabadság*.

At the reburial itself, the reporter of *168 óra* interviewed Adam Michnik, who noted that 1956 lives as a legend in Poland, despite the fact that little is known of the actual events. Michnik paid attention to spontaneous movements, which had organized in Hungary during two weeks of 1956. In that sense, that meaning of the word "uprising" was, to him, the most important one (168 óra 20/06/1989).

Moreover, different names could also be seen in the third opinion poll, which was published in *Magyar Nemzet* on 9th November. 1000 people were polled, and the question was the same, i.e. how did they evaluate 1956. In the third poll, the question was asked in three phases between May and September: 8 May - 30 May, 27 June - 3 July and 23 August - 1 September.

|       |                                          | May   | June  | August |
|-------|------------------------------------------|-------|-------|--------|
| I     | Revolution                               | 21 %  | 24 %  | 22 %   |
| II    | Uprising                                 | 20 %  | 28 %  | 29 %   |
| III   | Started as an Uprising, ended as a Counter-revolution | 32 %  | 25 %  | 25 %   |
| IV    | Counter-revolution                       | 14 %  | 12 %  | 13 %   |

As of June, the most popular interpretation was of an uprising (II). Revolution (I) was now clearly more popular than its counterpart (IV), although neither changed significantly. However, the old interpretation, which better understood the acts of Kádár (III), evidently diminished after the reburial of Imre Nagy. On the other hand, the popularity of the pure uprising rose practically as much as the former had reduced.[49]

In April-May 1989, MSZMP was still the leading party (35,6%) in opinion polls. Then there were the 'new' parties: Social Democrats MSZDP (13,0%), The Hungarian Democratic Forum, MDF (11,4%), The Alliance of Free Democrats, SZDSZ (5,6%) and The Independent Smallholders' Party, FKGP (5,4%) (168 óra 09/05/1989). The MSZMP even increased its popularity in June, after which time it began to decrease steadily. At the same time, 'new' parties became more popular and, thus, in September of 1989 MSZMP's diagram crossed the rising diagram of the MDF (23%). In December the popularity of the MSZMP was equal to that of the Free Democrats and the Smallholders (Szabadon... 1990, 14).

There had been no opinion polls since August of 1989, but in May of 1990 the concept of uprising was also superseded. Thus, there was a long political rotation in which the new name "uprising", which was still in use in September, was superseded. The law recognized only the names revolution and fight for freedom. Therefore, it is possible to connect the names to the prevailing power struggle in the Hungarian public, which, thus, essentially dealt with the past.

A few weeks prior to the elections, TIB could conclude that the party, and all political forces, had recognized that a "revolution", which ended as a fight for freedom, began on 23rd October (NSZ; MH 10/03/1990). In careful reading, however, this was not the case, because, for example, in the programme draft of the new MSZP, there was an expression which dealt with "the revolutionary activity of Imre Nagy" (NSZ 26/04/1990). Nevertheless, in the party convention, the expression was changed to "uprising and fight for freedom" (NSZ 28/05/1990). In fact, the shift also reached the rhetoric of both the Socialist Party and the former party newspaper over the course of 1990.

Until then the political playing field had changed, new rhetorical approaches were needed, but the complex content of '1956' was still to be discussed. In spite of the new rhetorical language, 25% considered 1956 as an "uprising" in the last opinion poll taken in November of 1991 (Szonda Ipsos (N=1000)). Almost half, 48%, supported the new interpretation "revolution and fight for freedom"; 11% had the opinion that it had been a "counter-revolution"; 14% could not answer; and according to 2 per cent, the question was too complicated to define, i.e. for example, in the beginning it was an "uprising", and in the end, a "counter-revolution". "Revolution" tended to gain popularity among more educated persons, and those who were provided with more information of the transpiration of events. However, the term "uprising" became more popular, especially at the level of the most educated. (NSZ 27/12/1991). Even if the possible inaccuracies are taken into consideration, it seems evident that there was no consensus about the content of 1956 in the first years of the 1990s.

However, one more naming debate arose following 1992, when the government wanted to punish those who had participated in the reprisals after 1956. The plan was to punish them as war criminals, but in order to do that, what occurred in Hungary would have to be defined as a war. Immediately after the bill was passed, the Press Chief of the government interpreted that a war had taken place (NSZ 31/10/1992), and later, a member of the Christian Democrats, Miklós Gáspár, argued that the war lasted until 1963 (NSZ 28/12/1992). The punishment debate will be examined more closely in the tenth chapter.

# VIII IDENTITIES CONSTRUCTED WITH THE PAST

In the late 1980s, new organizations began to emerge inside Hungary. Most of their members had lived and worked in Hungary during the Kádár era. However, in the late 1980s, they needed to dissociate themselves from the ruling MSZMP, but on the other hand from their own rival organizations as well. The central point here is that the identity was constructed with the past, sometimes with certain continuities to the past, and the tradition of 1956 also belongs to this discussion. In general, '1956' was present in several new movements and their first programmes: MDF, FIDESZ, the Republic Circle, SZDSZ, TIB and the New March Front connected '1956' in one way or another to their policy. Frequently, the demands concerned the "revaluation" or "clarification" of the recent past (MPÉ 1988, 727-783). The Free Democrats, SZDSZ was the 'most poetic', because it considered three Hungarian revolutions as a 'model': 1848, 1918 and 1956. According to SZDSZ, parliamentary democracy was born in 1848, while in 1918 the central issues were political freedoms, the emancipation of the working class and the initiation of the first land reform. Finally, in 1956, the will of the people and political pluralism were fully revealed in the multiparty system. Next, the SZDSZ argued that the demands of 1848 had not been fulfilled, nor were they fulfilled in 1918 and 1956 either. (Ibid., 758).

The historian Lajos Für described the MDF as an organization which continued the tradition of Hungarian Jacobins, reformers from the 19th century and the democratic aims from the years 1945-1948 (MN 19/11/1988). The MDF, however, was not alone in its historical arguments, because, for example, also the New March Front defined itself as being based on the tradition of 1848. In addition, the goals of democratic socialism in 1956 were mentioned in the programme of the March Front – the name of the front was based on an anti-fascist, leftist organization which was founded in 1937, more precisely on 15th March (MPÉ 1988, 783; A magyarok krónikája 1996, 609). Thus, the present identity seemed to be the last 'link' in a certain 'chain of continuity', which was built on the traditions of periods decades or even as many as two hundred years in the past.

The founding document of the MDF was created in Lakitelek and dated 3rd September, 1988 and it, too, demanded "a truthful evaluation of 1956". The programme included two terms side by side, "revolution" and "national rebellion", and the latter (*nemzeti felkelés*) was put in brackets (MPÉ 1988, 743). When the premiere issue of the periodical *Hitel* (Trust) was published, its authors denied connections to the MDF, despite the fact that eight out of nine of the founders of the party also sat on its editorial board. In the first issue, for example, the claim was made that "the events of 1956 had to be revaluated" and that this should not be done on the streets but politically, in "workshops" (NSZ 03/11/1988).

Contrarily, FIDESZ made a break with the past when they argued in the founding document that present young generations bear no responsibility for the wrong decisions made in the past nor for their consequences, which are now evident (MPÉ 1988, 713). In November of 1988, FIDESZ held its first congress and took a favourable position toward the establishment of a free economic market. However, in February of 1989, the party organ, *Népszabadság*, also connected FIDESZ to '1956', noting that emigrated Hungarians consider FIDESZ as an inner resistance, which continues the work of the 1956 generation, and defined its members as "quiet freedom fighters" (NSZ 21/02/1989).

Furthermore, in November of 1988, the former Smallholders' Party declared that it had never formally been banned – last time after the 'uprising' – and continued its activity. Now the revival was carried out in Café Pilvax (MPÉ 1988, 731) an historical milieu, in which Sándor Petőfi and the other youngsters had met on 15th March, 1848. The party once again embraced the old party program from 1930, because the "majority of it was still of current interest". In the beginning of January 1990, the party clearly dissociated itself from cooperation with the Socialist Party. The leader of the party, József Torgyán, stipulated that the party demanded the withdrawal of Soviet troops, reckoning with the Communists and the return of land owner-ship to the level of 1947 (MH 22/01/1990).

In the beginning of February 1990, the MDF also unequivocally announced that the former Socialist Workers' Party, the Socialist Party and the organizations close to them were the political opponents of the MDF (NSZ 05/02/1990). Until then, the MDF had been the most cautious of the parties, and was the last to make the tactical turn. For example, in November, *Magyar Nemzet* had questioned whether the coalition with Socialists would actually materialise (MN 20/11/1989).

Prior to the first round of elections, András B. Hegedűs from TIB pointed out that 1956 was a national matter which surpassed the political parties and which they should not use in their policy (MH 02/03/1990). TIB also focused on the relation to politics in a statement published two weeks before the first round. TIB defined itself as an organization, which would not organize itself into a party, although its founding members included persons who had been active in various parties in 1956. Therefore, it was considered natural that they were active in the new parties, too. TIB was satisfied, because all the political groups as well as the former ruling party had recognized that a revolution had begun in Hungary on 23rd October, which ended in a fight for freedom. According to TIB, it was generally acknowledged that the new democratic Hungary was impossible to create without revaluating the year 1956. Moreover, the aims of the revolution were actually considered relevant: a democratic multiparty system, a representative political system, an independent and sovereign Hungary. Members of the TIB held the view that the spirit of 1956 was a unifying tradition; the parties had to preserve the ideals which unified the entire nation. In the statement, it was also stressed that no party should 'own' the memory of the martyrs and the drama of 16th June (MH; NSZ 10/03/1990).

Thus, there were no considerable parties wanting to continue directly where 1956 had left off, but rather '1956' appeared indirectly as a model to return to and the last 'link' before 1989. There were, however, a few exceptions: In July of 1989, a *Magyar Október Párt* (Party of the Hungarian October), was founded. It attempted to carry out the entire programme of the 1956 revolution and fight for freedom (MPÉ 1990, 297). Their idea was, for example, to propose Sándor Rácz, who had led the Central Workers' Council in 1956, as a candidate for Presidency (Ibid., 313). Moreover, there was a group called *Magyar Radikális Párt* (The Hungarian Radical Party), which, together with the October Party, painted and 'soiled' street signs in the Summer of 1989 (see the next chapter). These parties did not reach the second round of elections and, moreover, on 10th April, TIB dissociated also itself from the '56 Association. It did not recognize the elections, because "real decisions" were made behind closed doors, and it urged the "real opposition" to withdraw from the elections (MN 03/04/1990).

A few demonstrations took place prior to the elections, for example, a "Christian Democratic Union without Communists" organized a demonstration led by László Romhányi (MH 16/02/1990; MPÉ 1991, 461). On the same day, there had been an incident in what was then Leninváros (later became Tiszaújváros), in which demonstrators attacked Károly Grósz, who had participated in a local TV-conversation. A local chapter of MDF had organized a demonstration, and supporters stayed and waited for Grósz, jostled him and shouted slogans against him. According to Grósz, the demonstrators resembled fascism, in 1944 and in Miskolc on 23rd October,

1956. The parties generally condemned the incident, although András Bozóki (FIDESZ) also noted that everyone has the right to speak in public about those, who in the past have compromised themselves (MH 16/02/1990).

'1956' was not specifically present in the election campaign, however, a temporal dimension was clearly discernible: SZDSZ had a poster in which a sign was pointing toward Europe, the road to the horizon was characterised by the slogan "For a Clean Future", and "With a Clean Past". The MDF promised a "Big Spring Cleaning", and amongst the debris in the poster were pictures of Mao and Lenin and the statue of Lenin. Moreover, FIDESZ asked people to choose; in the upper picture, Brezhnev and Honecker kissed and in the bottom picture a boy and girl repeated the act. FKGP had a corn in the old poster with the text "God, Country and Family, Peace, Wheat And Wine". Contrarily, the Socialists unambiguously concentrated on the future and, in the slogan "With the Socialists for Tomorrow", a pair of hands and a small baby were represented in the images (MPÉ 1991, 62-67; A magyarok krónikája 1996, 787).

Among the symbols, flag with the hole in the centre, the symbol of '1956', was seen in the background of an image of József Antall, who was photographed with Valery Giscard d'Estaing. Another traditional symbol was also used by the MDF: the old crown coat of arms was shown as breaking under the gray socialist coat of arms in the party's advertisement (MH 03/03/1990) – and was accompanied by a line from the Lord's Prayer "thy kingdom come" (MPÉ 1991, 67). The SZDSZ advertisement included 12 paragraphs, which the party promised it would put into practice in the government. The first dealt with beginning negotiations to hasten the withdrawal of the Soviet troops, and, for example, also included the suggestion of a bill which would be based on Imre Nagy's declaration on 1st November, 1956, i.e. to leave the Warsaw Pact (MN 03/04/1990).

In the first round of elections, however, no single candidate won a majority in more than five constituencies, and therefore the proper power struggle was left to the second round of elections. Because the focus here is on how the past was used in current policy, the most important document was the announcement published on 28th March, 1990 in *Magyar Hírlap*. In it, the MDF wanted to dissociate itself from its rival, SZDSZ, against whom the attack was targeted in the first place.

First, it was noted that the Free Democrats accused their opponents of being amicable with the Communists. This was followed by the old slogan, which SZDSZ used in a new, altered form: "He Who is Against Us is With Them" (*Aki ellenünk van az velük van*). The MDF itself denied being against anyone, stating that it was in *favour* of the nation (*Mi nem mások ellen, a nemzetért vagyunk!*) (MPÉ 1991, 62). Thus, the opponent was associated with stalinism, while the 'positive' concept of nation was also simultaneously harnessed for political purposes.

Representatives of the MDF estimated that the forum was rooted in Hungarian traditions and built on the experiences of previous generations. An attempt was made to solve the question "who were 'we' in history" through a chronological chain of great men, who hardly had anything in common: Dániel Berzsenyi, Ferenc Kölcsey (poets), István Széchenyi, Sándor Petőfi, Lajos Kossuth, Ferenc Deák, Pál Teleki (Horthy's Prime Minister), Endre Bajcsy-Zsilinszky, László Németh and István Bibó. In addition to these men, two other examples were sited: the responsible and non-extreme politicians of 1945-1947 and 1956.

The MDF came to the conclusion that they need not forget the past, with its noisy anti-communism, because 'we' are:

> "...not Marxists, not at the moment but not only a decade or two did not turn against the communist dictatorship either. We continue the parties, which between 1945-1948 fought against the singleparty dictatorship, which in the revolution of 1956 tried to end it, who because of it were imprisoned and... who during the Kádár era always made up the silent, inner opposition."

The MDF attempted to avoid associating itself with the Kádár era, first by referring back to the years prior to the singleparty system. Secondly, the opposition during the dictatorship was stressed as having existed throughout its duration as the German *"innere Emigration"*. Yet the metaphor "silent, inner opposition" is problematic with regard to whether a silent opposition can be defined as an "opposition" at all. For example, in the United States, Richard Nixon argued that the war in Vietnam was supported by the "silent majority", which, however, according to Murray Edelman (1977), was impossible to prove, precisely because of the fact that it was silent. Moreover, in autumn of 1988, the MDF itself rejected being branded as an opposition group, nor were they defined as such by the ruling MSZMP.

Next, the MDF asked for the respect of the ideas and political courage of those who had rejected the background of the communist family, their own Marxist, sometimes Marxist and Trotskyist, convictions or the MSZMP experience that only "in the 1970s did the principles of liberal democracy begin to be accepted. Many of them are members of SZDSZ today." Thus, the value of the Democratic Opposition was recognized politely, "although there are moderate and more silent fighting popular or bourgeois, [non-leftist, *polgári*, HN] writers and other intelligentsia, whose remarkable role of never believing in the socialist-communist utopia or the revolution of 1956 had revealed the previous bolshevist lies. More than one current leader of SZDSZ has retained his communist past and mentality." Finally, it was concluded that the Free

Democrats "only with great difficulties could identify with national aims" (MH 28/02/1990).

Representatives of the Free Democrats replied to these accusations (MH; MN 30/03/1990) in an advertisement, in which they found it to be untrue that the leaders of the SZDSZ were communists who had 'reversed their coats'. It was mentioned that only that particular party had accused them, a party which the previous year had twice its current amount of members, i.e. the Forum and the Communist Party. Furthermore, the Free Democrats argued that they continued the work of the Democratic Opposition, which for 11 years had fought for civil rights. Other statements were also quoted, which represented the moderate dissociation of the MDF from the ruling party in a comical context.

Hence, the struggle between the leading parties and intellectuals shifted during the second round of elections to a struggle of the past in the style of "I was not for them I was against them". Thus, prior to May of 1990, '1956' was more generally 'a link in the chain' from the past to the present. Moreover, one corner stone appeared as early as the party conference in October 1989. There, historian Mária Ormos requested that the congress salute the memory of "martyrs of historical events", such as Batthyánys, Dessewffys, Rajks, Imre Nagys and Imre Mezős, who were not only victims, but who had struggled on behalf of their own great ideas (NSZ 07/10/1989). The successor party still also laid a wreath at Köztársaság tér on October 30th (MPÉ 1990, 322).

Thus, the successor party, the Hungarian Socialist Party, also used the same style of historical argumentation in a draft of their program, which was published after the elections (NSZ 26/04/1990). In the draft, the Socialists were defined as the legacy of all those who had thought in the best interest of the nation: Széchenyi, Kossuth, Deák (they did not want to go further into the past), Ady, Bartók, Kunfi, represented the generation ranging from Jászi to the poet József, Bibó as well as the national and middle class (*polgári*) writers. Moreover, the 'chain' was built in relation to the communist movement and its reformers. However, the final version was eventually shortened and the names were left out (Ibid., 28/05/1990).

# Identities of Parliamentary Politicians and 1956

In 1990, the newly elected parliament became a representative forum of educated Hungarians and was nicknamed "the doctors' parliament". The education level was the highest it had ever been, because 90% of its members had university level degrees. There were 100 teachers, 77 lawyers, 47 economists but only three workers, as was pointed out by *Magyar Hírlap*

178

(MH 02/05/1990). Moreover, there was a significant group of humanists and specifically 27 historians, and even the new government might be called the "historian government" (cf. Youth and History 1997, 282; Szabadon választott 1990).[50]

In the parliamentary calendar, *Szabadon választott* (Freely Chosen), the new members were given a chance to introduce themselves. 16 out of 165 in the MDF, 13 out of 44 in the FKGP, seven out of 91 in the SZDSZ, two Christian Democrats, one of the six independents and one of the Socialists specifically mentioned their activity in 1956 in the calendar. 1956 was openly considered as a merit, especially in the Smallholders' Party, in which almost a third (29,5%) had something to do with the revolutionaries.

Only 14 members had been reelected from the previous parliament, however, conversely, here was also *a longer* continuity: five MPs, mainly in the Smallholder's Party, had been MPs already right after the Second World War (MH 02/05/1990). A typical member of the parliament was a man born in 1944, which was also the average age of members of the largest party, the MDF. In three of the parties the average age was higher: in the Socialist Party (1938), in the Christian Democratic People's Party (1935), and the Small-holders' were the oldest (1932). Conversely, the SZDSZ typically represented the "beat-generation" (1948). The Young Democrats, FIDESZ, had an age limit of 35 in their membership guidelines, and an ideal FIDESZ MP was born in 1962.

If we continue to use Iván Völgyes's categorisation (1987) that an identification to political generations occurred at a rather young age, especially between 13 and 20 years (Völgyes 1987, 191-197), then FIDESZ was completely a product of the late Kádárian era: its members did not have personal experiences from 1956. For the SZDSZ, the important years had been between 1961-1968, although it is conceivable that they might possess personal memories from 1956. A typical MP of the MDF was also close to the beat-generation, however, their experiences typically referred to the early Kádár era of 1957-1964, the period during which the reprisals had taken place.On the other hand, the representatives of the three other parties, MSZP, FKGP and KDNP, belonged to those generations born between 1926-1940 and, according to Völgyes, were in a key position in Hungarian political culture.

Thus, a typical MP had been 12 years old in 1956, and thus it seems that the majority of the new MPs did not have personal, but rather mediated experiences from 1956. Nevertheless, all of the parties also included prominent members, who had personal experiences and who beamed in the forefront of the first post-communist parliament. The year 1932 is of particular significance in itself, in that a total of three party leaders were born in 1932; they were: József Antall (MDF), József Torgyán (FKGP) and Gyula Horn (MSZP).

179

Moreover, the tradition of 1956 had played a significant role in the life of the new President, author Árpád Göncz, of SZDSZ. In his first interviews after being elected, Göncz noted that he had acknowledged '56 in court, and that he viewed himself as a lawful trustee of the revolution (MN 04/08/1990). Furthermore, two Ministers in the new government had been directly involved in 1956. The new Prime Minister, historian József Antall, had held the chair of the Revolutionary Committee in Eötvös Gimnasium of Budapest. The Minister of Defence, historian Lajos Für, had been a Secretary of the Revolutionary Committee in the department of Hajdú-Bihar (Szabadon választott 1990).

However, József Antall, for example, had also had a prominent career during the Kádár era. In 1964 he had become the Vice-President of the Semmelweiss Medical Museum, of which he has been the director since 1974, and he also received a highly prestigious Work Decoration in 1982 (Antall 1994, 640). In 1992, Antall told how he had taken politically persecuted '56-ers into his medical institute (NSZ 02/05/1992) and recalled his personal experiences of, for example, how he had been at the 23rd October demonstration with his pupils (MN 04/07/1992).

Thus, the new parliament belonged to one of the forums, in which 1956 was discussed in the years between 1990 and 1994. In the first place, there were several debates concerning actual political issues and interpretations, in addition to which the parliament was responsible for the creation of several laws, which both directly and indirectly impacted the ways of dealing with the past. Thirdly, the Members of Parliament, as well as the President of the Republic, maintained several commemorative rituals, such as laying wreaths, and represented the country through the practice of these public rituals. Moreover, in 1993, a few members close to the government attempted to establish a specific "'56 Circle" within the parliament (MN 31/08/1993).

Therefore, it is assumed that '1956' in the parliament was still a part of the experience, which also had an impact not only on commemorations but also on laws, on the new identity and on the relations between new parties. The traditions of all previous generations weighed on the mind of the living, although not necessarily as a nightmare, as Karl Marx formulated it in the *Eighteenth of Brumaire* (1973, 146). The space of experience did not yet belong only to historians, but both new and old politicians were also constructing the past, the politics of memory. The peculiar character of Hungarian political culture had contained several system changes, and the last 'revolutionary crisis' had taken place precisely in 1956.

All in all, in 1990, 1956 became one of the new elements in official public, in which journalists and politicians trusted. The leader of the Smallholders', József Torgyán pointed out that he had joined the '56 Party (MH 06/07/1990) and when the Foreign Minister Géza Jeszenszky spoke in the UN, at first he obliged to the audience in the name of the Hungarian people for the support for Hungarians in 1956 (MH 04/10/1990). When the withdrawal from the Warsaw Pact was discussed in the parliament in June 1990, 'the old '56-ers', Miklós Vásárhelyi, Imre Mécs, Béla Király and József Antall, referred to analogies and to the example of '1956' (NSZ 27/06/1990). For Antall, the dismantling of the Warsaw Pact was also an issue of personal importance: he was not only the son of the Smallholder Minister following the Second World War, but József Antall senior had also belonged to the delegation whose task it was to negotiate Hungary's resignation from the Warsaw Pact in 1956 (cf. 1956 kézikönyve (I) 1996, 185).

## The First Law

When the new parliament held its first session in May of 1990, it enacted a symbolic law. The bill was prepared by TIB and dealt with the historical significance of 1956.

> "This freely elected Parliament regards as its urgent task to codify the historical significance of the October Revolution of 1956 and its struggle for freedom. This illustrious chapter of modern Hungarian history can only be compared to the 1848-1849 Revolution and war of independence. The Revolution of 1956 lay foundation for the hope that it is possible to achieve a democratic social order, and that no sacrifice for our country's independence is made in vain. Although the ensuing suppression reinstated the old power structure, it could not eradicate the spirit of 1956 from people's minds.
>
> The new Parliament assumes the responsibility to preserve the memory of the Revolution and the ensuing struggle for freedom.
>
> The Parliament underscores its determination to do everything in its power to secure multiparty democracy, human rights, and national independence by proclaiming in its first session the following law:
>
> (1) The memory of the 1956 Revolution and its struggle for freedom is herewith codified.
>
> (2) October 23, the day of the outbreak of the Revolution of 1956 and the beginning of the fight for freedom, and also the day of the proclamation of the Hungarian Republic in 1989, shall henceforth be a national holiday." (The Hungarian Revolution... 1996, x).

The first paragraph concentrated on several matters. Firstly, it codified an event into law. Secondly, it canonized a certain name – or precisely two names – of an historical event. Thirdly, the law made an analogy to the past and compared one event with another. Finally, the law dealt with memory, simultaneously canonizing it.

As a whole, an historical event was now defined by a law and thus, the Hungarian parliament began its task of examining the past. The act, quite rare occurrence in a western democracy, however, becomes partly understandable from the aspect of history culture. When we focus on the Hungarian penal code, we are able to locate several examples of such laws. As mentioned earlier, 1848-1849 was enacted into law on its 100th anniversary, although this is merely one example among many (cf. for example the memory of Saint Stephen in 1938). Moreover, since 1848 several memorialised deaths were codified, such as József Nádor (1848), Ferenc Deák (1876), Francis Joseph (1916) and Josef Stalin (1953). The memory of Stalin was decanonized, however, no earlier than 1989, by the reform communist government as a part of the democratization process.

The purpose of the first law in 1990 was to commemorate an important historical event and create an important basis for the future, as the Speaker of the Parliament, György Szabad, mentioned in his opening address (MN 03/05/1990). However, *de facto*, the first law also canonized an interpretation, which until then was a compromise between the 'Revolution Party' and the 'Fight for Freedom Party'. Until 1990, these 'parties' had superseded the two others, i.e. the 'Party of Counter-Revolution' and the 'Party of Uprising'.

Moreover, since the spring of 1990, this canonization also seemed to open a new space for candid political argumentation; 'all' Hungarians 'became revolutionaries', and the successor party to the MSZMP, MSZP, also shifted and began using the terms "revolution and fight for freedom", as did the newspapers. Since 1990, the double name has survived as the most commonly used term. Nevertheless, there is at least one case in 1993, during the year of "incertitude", when an attempt was made to substitute the term "revolution" with the term "fight for freedom" as the only acceptable name (MH 15/05/ 1993).

In addition to the first law, in July, the new parliament requested that the Soviet Union condemn the intervention of 1956. The request was directed to the Supreme Council of the Soviet Union:

"In October of 1956, the Hungarian people took arms in order to liquidate the Stalinist tyranny and in order to achieve the independence of the country. The revolution and fight for freedom was quelled with ruthless violence by the unlawfully [already] located, as well as with the later in-rolled Soviet troops.

During the 90 day period following the entry into force of the Austrian Peace Treaty, the Soviet troops should have left the country, which did not happen. There was no legal basis for their presence past this point. Their military intervention in 1956 was merely a contemptuous act against the country's sovereignty and a serious crime against the Hungarian people.

Therefore, the Hungarian parliament requests that, in a revaluation similar to that of the situation in Czechoslovakia in 1968, the Supreme Council of the Soviet Socialist Union should deem unlawful and condemn the 1956 military intervention by the Soviet Union. This step would strengthen the Soviet Union's commitment to have respect for the sovereignty and independence of the Hungarian Republic, would contribute to the creation of amicable relations between our people, and would be a sign of encouragement to the Middle- and East-European people with regard to the hastening of the democratic system change." (MH 24/07/1990; MPÉ 1991, 476). (Transl. HN)

The appeal was also a parliamentary document that dealt with history; Members of Parliament interpreted the past, named it and found reasons why specific events occurred. On the following day, Gennadi Gerassimov commented that the intervention was "unpardonable" and agreed with the request (MH 25/07/1990). The final answer was delayed until after the 1991 coup in the Soviet Union and took place in December, when Prime Minister Antall signed of several bilateral treaties in Moscow and Kiev. During that visit, Mikhail Gorbachev declared that thirty-five years earlier the Soviet Union had intervened in the internal affairs of Hungary (MH 07/12/1991).

However, until September of 1990, there had been two clear signs of emerging differences between the government and the opposition. First, in the end of August, a detailed *Justitia* plan was introduced into the public (NSZ 28/08/1990). Secondly, in the beginning of September, the SZDSZ took out page long political advertisements in both *Magyar Hírlap* and *Népszabadság*, in which the party evaluated the first hundred days of the government. According to the Free Democrats, the moral, economic and social conditions of the country were worse than they had been during the elections. In one paragraph they argued that the government was finding less and less continuity to the years 1956 and 1947, and more and more to the great deadlock of Horthyite Hungary (MH; NSZ 03/09/1990).

"Fears rise about the undisguised nostalgia, which the parties of the governing coalition feed in the direction of Hungary prior to 1945. The spirit of the coalition recalls [idéz] the Hungary between the two World Wars. The governing parties decreasingly admit the continuity to 1956 and 1945-47, and increasingly refer to our historical deadlock of Horthyite Hungary. It alarms everyone who wishes the system change not to bring back to the vanished world of upper classes [úri világ] but towards to the democratic Europe in the turn of the millennium." (Ibid.) (Transl. HN)

Even though the quotation is taken from a political advertisement, it is astonishing for reasons other than the style of argumentation. First, there is the question of continuity and certain symbolic years. Secondly, there are the questions of "return" and "restoration", i.e. whether the past was past at all in post-communism. We might ask how far the new republic could delve into the past, or from how far back the past could be "rehabilitated"; nationalism, revisionism etc. also existed in the Hungarian space of experience. Therefore, we must also focus on the general left-right dimension in post-communism and its relation to '1956' and other identities.

## Left and Right or Wrong?

In 1990-1991, Hungarian political scientists developed two ideal types with which to describe the new political scene. Parties were divided either into a triangle or in the left and right axis. Mihály Bihari, himself a member of the Socialist Party, suggested a tri-polar political centre: a) the National Conservative, Christian Democrat political centre (MDF, FKGP, KDNP), b) the Social-Liberal centre (SZDSZ, FIDESZ) and c) the Euro-Socialist, Social Democratic centre (MSZP) (MPÉ 1991, 38-46).

According to András Körösényi, classical definitions of left and right had lost their meanings in Hungary only in economic dimensions, i.e. between employees, trade unions or proprietors and the middle class. However, Körösényi stressed that left and right were clearly separated in the ideological-political sense, noting that the current government followed these ideological lines. He characterised the government as belonging to the right and the opposition to the left. The opposition was described with adjectives like *international, secular, town, industrial, working people, "softer" and "liberal"*. The political right was described as *national, religious, country-side, peasant, "harder" and "conservative"*. (MPÉ 1991, 77-79).

However, these classifications are problematic with regard to their 'objectivity' i.e., for example, not everybody in 1990 accepted Socialists as "Euro-Socialists" (Socialist International nominated the MSZP for membership in December 1994, which was subsequently carried out in 1996). Hence, besides political scientists, it could be asked how citizens and politicians identified political actors or themselves on the left-right axis. Therefore, I have chosen two polls, made in March 1990 and between 2nd and 21st October, 1992. There, to some extent, leftist, centrist and rightist tendencies were found in all parties. (NSZ 25/11/1992; MH 07/03/1990).

*Népszabadság* interpreted the 1992 numbers with the headline "Direction Toward the Centre" (NSZ 25/11/1992). It seems evident that in 1992, the centrist image had strengthened in all parties. However, if we also examine the rightist and leftist images and compare them to 1990, it seems that the

184

leftist image has decreased in all parties with the exception of the MSZP, in which the image had stayed the same (46%). There is also one significant exception in the right-wing images: the leading government party, MDF, had begun to lose its leftist character (from 21% to 6%) and began to appear more clearly as a right-wing party (22% considered it as a right-wing party in 1990 and 32% in 1992).

However, another reading is also possible, because both in 1990 and 1992 the 'largest party' was composed of those who could not utilise the left-right dimension. The amount in all of the parties was nearly 40%. This is in part due to the system change, i.e. the political milieu of a system of many parties was still something new. For example, in the middle of 1991, 30% (N=1500) did not know which party Antall belonged to, and every fifth did not recognize the parties in the parliament (NSZ 29/07/1991). Secondly, the identities of the parties were still unclear, partly to themselves and partly to the citizens.

Thus, the identities, the 'roots' had to be 'created' and 'reactivated'. Therefore, we must continue the analysis of how the parties defined themselves in terms of the past, and how an emotional 'event' such as '1956' was a part of this struggle. As I have mentioned earlier, the parties did not come from vacuum, they did also 'have to' "invent a tradition", a process in which various struggles of naming between the parties were essential. For example, in 1990, the word "conservative" was not yet politically correct in defining self-identity.

Thus, prior to the elections József Antall's "national liberalism" included István Széchenyi, Lajos Kossuth, Ferenc Deák and Loránd Eötvös, whose liberalism, according to Antall, also represented social ideals which were contrary to the Manchester liberalism. Secondly, Antall classified national-populism, which was rooted in writers Gyula Illyés, László Németh, Imre Kovács and István Bibó – compared to 1989 the Petőfi Party in 1956 was also added to the list. Thirdly, the People's Party/Christian Democratic world view was mentioned, of which there were also traces in Hungary after the Second World War (MN 27/01/1990).

However, Zoltán Bíró, who was expelled from MSZMP in April of 1988 on the basis of his connections to Lakitelek, left MDF in November of 1990 and accused the party of shifting toward the right (MN; NSZ 16/11/1990). Two other members also criticized that MDF was no longer liberal (168 óra 27/11/1990). Moreover, János Dénes, who had a background in the workers' councils of 1956, also left the fraction in November. According to him, 1956 was made a mere decoration and the new laws did not succeed the first symbolic law, which directly dealt with the revolution and fight for freedom (NSZ 24/11/1990).

In October of 1991, István Elek argued that MDF was a *conservative* party, which had won the election with a *liberal* program (NSZ 14/10/1991), although he later revised that characterisation by saying that in fact MDF was a *conservative liberal* party (NSZ 28/10/1991). It is interesting to notice that Antall worried about the characterisation of MDF as conservative, because according to Antall, the word "conservative" does not sound as bad in the West as in Hungary, where the political opponents had shaped the word (MH 22/06/1992). When Antall explained the current political situation to foreign journalists, he concluded that MDF represented *traditional* Hungarian *centrist* politics (NSZ 25/04/1992). Minister of the Interior, Péter Boross, clarified the front lines with the past, because Ferenc Szálasi had belonged to extreme right, while Horthy's Prime Ministers István Bethlen, Miklós Kállay and Pál Teleki had not (MH 06/10/1992).

However, Antall's traditional centre rubbed shoulders more with the right, if we examine the caricature published by *Magyar Hírlap* during the media demonstrations. It was an illustration of a darts game, in which Antall sat in the middle of number ten. However, the round dart board was twisted out of shape in such a way that the right side was some three times closer than the edge on the left. (MH 22/09/1992).

The existence of the left-right dichotomy resurfaced following the elections, when the parties had to decide where they should sit in parliament. In 1990, the seats were distributed as in Britain, however, in 1994, the winners did not want the right side. Following the decision of the Socialists, the representative of the SZDSZ wanted to be seated beside them. Finally, FIDESZ agreed to be "the farthest right" (NSZ 10/06/1994), but criticized that the decision was not made according to historical tradition, but rather on ideological grounds (NSZ 11/06/1994). When FIDESZ won the election in 1998, they returned to the custom of 1990, which meant, for example, that the SZDSZ was forced to sit beside the "national radical" MIÉP, thus the extreme-right.

Therefore political struggle was also struggle about concepts and concepts, which were essentially bound to past experiences. In Hungary, liberalism had two natures: on the one hand, there is the *national liberal* character, which is rooted in the 19th century Hungarian leading politicians. On the other hand, there is *liberal* character which is rooted in the beginning of the 20th century (*polgári radikalizmus*) as a critic of the former. Thus, according to Miklós Szabó, an historian and a Member of Parliament (SZDSZ), everybody declared their politics "liberal" – "except MSZP which 'confess' to being Social Democratic" (MN 24/06/1992; Szabó 1995, 13).

For example, immediately following the 1994 elections, Imre Mécs made an interesting interpretation of left and right in an interview with Béla Kurcz's: "The last freedom fighter in the parliament: Imre Mécs. Did '56 once again fall?" By this, Kurcz supposed that Mécs was the last freedom fighter, because

186

three (Darvas, Vásárhelyi and Király) had withdrawn and Dénes and Zimányi had not won seats in parliament. According to Mécs, their *current centrist* view in 1956 seemed to appear leftist within the context of the 1990s. Mécs argued that in 1956 they were perceived as having been more liberal (*szabadabb*) and pluralist, yet as a society which would stand on a socialist basis. (MN 23/06/1994).

The dichotomy of left and right was also seen in several expectations of the future. In 1992, the government considered the left more dangerous than the right (MH 06/05/1992). Moreover, since 1993 it began to be apparent that the government would not win the elections (NSZ 18/05/; 04/10/1993). The Minister of Defence, Lajos Für (MDF), warned of a "leftist danger" that "the past, although not as such, might return" (MN 19/02/1994). In addition, the MDF leaned on the recipients of compensation and also *Recski Szövetség*, political prisoners prior to 1956, promised to support the MDF (MH 14/02/1994).

In conclusion, the concepts of left and right were frequently used during the first post-communist years, and tended to be accepted in a traditional and even 'unchanged', 'universal' sense. Several analogies were made in the debate, and this 'analogous', repetitive past will be discussed next.

# IX  ANALOGIES AND SYMBOLS

By this point it has become evident that certain years were used quite frequently and broadly in Hungarian political argumentation. In 1956, 1848 was brought into the present, but 1918-1919 and 1945 were also mentioned. Furthermore, in the first programmes SZDSZ analogised all three. On the other hand, with regard to 1848 and 1956, the representative of the Ferenc Münnich Association was of the opinion that the use of the term "uprising" was humiliating to the year 1848.

However, after the superseding of János Kádár it was possible to perceive that something new and different was happening in Hungary. Hence, one political question was of how to interpret this new situation; as a totally new phenomenon or as a reincarnation of the past. For example, in September-October, a few members in the Central Committee were of the opinion that a counter-revolutionary situation had existed and others compared the new movements to the Petőfi Circle of 1956 (Nagy 1989, 116). Moreover, in November of 1988, Károly Grósz spoke about "white terror" and also compared Leninváros in 1990 to Miskolc in 1956. Those who were familiar with his background also knew that he had been in Miskolc, where a few lynchings also took place (1956 kézikönyve (I) 1996, 105, 131).

A slew of analogies were made prior to the reburial of Imre Nagy. For example, president Mátyás Szűrös found connections between the present and the events of 1956 in Italian television: a transition to parliamentary democracy is parallel to the researching of the white spots of the past (NSZ 22/05/1989). Moreover, a radio reporter posed the analogy to Imre Nagy made by Imre Pozsgay, who felt that the same basic questions as in 1956 could be solved now and a peaceful transition could be achieved (168 óra 13/06/1989). Historian Miklós Szabó (SZDSZ) argued that the year 1956 was comparable to the present, because those who participated in the revolution despise those who for more than thirty years considered it a counter-revolution and vice versa.[51]

Thus, up until this point, two kinds of political analogies have emerged: one between two historical events and the other regarding whether it was possible to analogise the past to the present. Moreover, historical analogy seemed to have been quite a common way of interpreting the present in Hungarian political culture. For example, when national minded intellectuals met in Lakitelek (1987), one of the speakers speculated as to whether they were already symbolically approaching 1847-1848 or only in 1825, i.e. the beginning of the reform era (Lakitelek 1991, 82).

Both the Czech reformers in 1968 and Polish opposition leaders in the 1980s also had the Hungarian 1956 on their minds (The Hungarian Revolution... 1996, 167). Therefore, it could be assumed that similarities could also have been found in the 1980s from 1956 to present Hungary. Thus, for alternative organizations, 1956 had become an analogy for the present on two levels. First, they were familiar with the space of experience and had learned their lesson from their failures; Hungary should not hurry toward a multiparty system as it had in 1956 (MN 31/12/1988). István Csurka was of the opinion that the MDF had drawn the conclusion from 1956 that democracy must be built on deliberate reconciliation and moderation (Ibid.).

Secondly, many of the demands made in 1956 were not fulfilled until now: the multiparty system, the Kossuth coat of arms, rehabilitation, the 15th of March as a national holiday and the withdrawal of the Soviet troops. Thus, an 'analogous' situation existed and a political problem arose as to how to reactivate and 'repeat' the 'best parts' of the past in order to avoid earlier mistakes. However, there is at least one exception. In 1956, numerous parties emerged, while in 1988 different *organizations* came into being.

Three types of analogies will be separated here. First, there are analogies which politicians, researchers etc. used themselves in their speeches. Secondly, there are analogies which showed a sense of drama and symbolically tried to 'repeat' the past in the same places or with the same actions etc. In this sense, *lieux de mémoire*, such as the statue of Petőfi and Batthyány Memorial Light, are essential – in 1987, an artist group called Inconnu even attempted to name the light the Lajos Batthyány – Imre Nagy Light (1956 kézikönyve (I) 1996, 347). Finally, there are the analogies which I have specifically separated and constructed for this study, in which 1956 is compared to other political changes.

We can assume that analogous argumentation did not cease in 1990 either. There were typical analogies used in political speeches which dealt with 1956. For example, there was no script such as the Pilvax boys had (MN 21/10/1990), no such revenge since the days of György Dózsa (MH 09/03/1991), Ferenc Deák, the tolerance of liberalism and 1956 (MH 13/04/1991). Moreover, the 4th of November was compared to the execution of the 13 generals in Arad and Mohács in 1526 (MN 04/11/1992). In general, all of these examples expressed a strong sense of dramatic 'sacredness' in representing the past. The glorious, but also dramatic past became a part of the present and people were deeply conscious of their elders.

However, 1956 also brought other pasts and analogies to the present. For example, Prime Minister József Antall showed how the only picture he had hung in his office was of Lajos Batthyány. Not only because the executed Batthyány was the first Prime Minister, but also because, to Antall, he symbolized moderate centrist politics (NSZ 31/12/1991). In another interview, Antall revealed that the headquarters of the MDF was chosen, because in 1956 he saw a flag with a hole in the middle hanging from the building, which was being used as a barrack at that time. According to Antall, the square – Bem tér – not only symbolizes Bem, but also the barrack, in which soldiers sympathised with the revolution. Antall reminisced about the great opportunity he had to sign the dissolution of the Warsaw Pact, which would also have been one of the targets of the negotiations in 1956 (MN 04/07/1992).

In addition, analogies have also been used pejoratively. For example, it was argued that the press was still bolshevist and there continued to be a dictatorship (MH 27/11/1990), i.e. the opponent still represented a 'rejected past'. Terms like "Antall-system" (MH 25/05/1992), balkanization (MH 02/06/1992), Right-Wing People's Front (MH 16/05/1992), trumped-up charges (MH 02/12/1992), White Books (NSZ 12/06/1993) and national agit prop (MH 11/03/1994; 168 óra 29/03/94) were increasingly used in the speeches while the relations between the government and the opposition worsened.

After the MSZP victory, someone suggested a "goulash-capitalism" (MN 01/06/1994) and another argued that a situation like the end of the Kádár era was continuing (NSZ 21/09/1994). Thus, in the argumentation good concepts were associated with 'us' and the bad ones transferred to 'them'. In 1945 Communists had compared the land reform to a new conquest (*honfoglalás*), but in 1992, it was compensation that was raised to the level of a new *honfoglalás* by a member in the cabinet (MH 03/04/1992). Especially István Csurka used several analogies. Béla Kun's reign of terror was compared to the present media (MN 03/04/1992) and Trianon to 1956: in Trianon, the large country had to be given away, in 1956 it was freedom and that Hungarians are alone (NSZ 06/06/1992).

In 1991, András Körösényi illustrated a few stereotypes that were connected to the MDF. Firstly, there was the idea of returning to the past, which meant that the party was not conservative in a western sense, but rather referred to Hungary between the World Wars. National symbols and upholding historical tradition had also been popular themes. Liberals and the left used the traditions of 1848, 1918 and 1956, "discontinuity" and the "future", while the government was really building on continuity, religion and tradition (MN 13/05/1991).

190

Nevertheless, these stereotypes were not entirely inaccurate, because a few months later, historian and MDF-ideologist András Gergely noted that returning to the old past is not an entirely bad idea (*régi múlt*) (168 óra 20/08/1991).

Analogies accepted in a certain political context are, thus, a part of political argumentation, and they attempt to keep the *Geschictskultur* in the present, connect the past to the present and vice versa. In the following subchapters I would like to discuss national holidays, the coat of arms and national decorations, reburials, memorials and street names. All of these are part of the analogies on the national level, which appeared following the autumn of 1956, and which then reappeared in the post-1988 period. They also all had their own patterns in the earlier space of experience, but were not necessarily remembered and analogised in the post-1988 period. Other analogies could also evidently be found, but the following became also symbols representative of the idea of the new, post-communist Hungary.

## National Holidays

The new Hungarian Republic was declared on 23rd October, which was also the day on which the mass student demonstration took place in 1956. In current Hungary, the day is celebrated as a national holiday, and here I relate national holidays to other important days and political debates. The day was already declared a holiday in the first law enacted by the new parliament, which, thus made an analogy between '1848' and '1956'. It later became known that Imre Nagy had also declared 23rd October a national holiday in a speech he made in front of the parliament on 31st October, 1956 (1956 kézikönyve (I) 1996, 160).

Already in the first paragraph of the French Constitution of 1791, it was declared that "national celebrations will be established to preserve the memory of the French Revolution" (Le Goff 1992, 86; cf. Ozouf 1976). Later, for example, French Republican Léon Gambetta noted that a free nation needs national celebrations (Le Goff 1992, 86-87). With a few exceptions, every state has a national holiday (cf. The Universal Almanac 1996). However, the question of why an annually repeated national holiday, a TimeSpace, is remembered, alternates in different countries. Although the celebration of independence day is the most common in the world, there are many others national holidays, such as 'the celebration of great men', constitution day etc. (Ibid.).

In 1956, Prime Minister Imre Nagy reestablished 15th March as a holiday as one of his first initiatives. In 1988 it had belonged to the demands of the opposition and the government declared it as a holiday in December. Thus, on 15th March, 1989, *Magyar Hírlap* reminded its readers of the background of 15th March. The idea was first proposed in 1898 by the national minded opposition, thus, near the 50th anniversary of 1848. The government, however, supported the policy of the Dual Monarchy and 11th of April was chosen, because in 1848 it had represented the provisional compromise made with Austria at that time. Nevertheless, the day could not compete with March, and the 15th of March was canonized by law both after the Chrysanthemum Revolution in early 1919 and during the Horthy regime in 1927. According to the journalist Béla Beller, the latter had been Pharisaiac, because the current opposition accused Horthy of falsifying the legacy of the revolution and war of independence. Moreover, on 23rd April of 1945, the provisional government once again reinstated the day as April 4th (Liberation Day) and May 1st (Labour Day) (MH 15/03, cf. NSZ 15/03/1989; 168 óra 15/08/1989).

A week after the declaration of the establishment of the multiparty system in February of 1989, the independent organizations published a manifest, which included twelve points – as in 1848 and 1956. They argued that the Hungarian people would like to have a free, independent and democratic Hungary, a multiparty system, free education, the right to strike and free markets. In the two last paragraphs, national integrity was demanded, as were the disclosure of the truth about 1956, honour to the martyrs and finally the abolition of the holidays of 7th November and 4th April (MH 20/02/1989). The manifest also challenged the invitation of Patriotic People's Front, which wanted to celebrate the national holiday *under the same* flag, i.e. together.

However, the independent organizations dissociated themselves from these organizations, and wanted to invite people to *an independent celebration of 15th March and a peaceful demonstration*. The alternative organizations gathered at the Petőfi statue, marched to Freedom Square, where the actor György Cserhalmi read the twelve points (MPÉ 1990, 278; cf. Hofer 1992). Unofficially, both occasions were indicators of the popularity of both camps: the opposition succeeded well and was ready to continue their political activities.

The next symbolic struggle emerged prior to the reburial of Imre Nagy. *Magyar Hírlap* published a statement, in which the MSZMP characterised the day of the reburial as *a day of national reconciliation*. However, in the same paper, the alternative organizations published an invitation to *a national mourning and commemoration day* (MH 02/06/1989). The division, however, was quite as black and white. On 8th June, the widow of Imre Mező wrote that: "it was only with great difficulty that we were able to see the reconciliation through" (NSZ 08/06/1989). When Miklós Vásárhelyi answered her, he stressed that for her, the day would also be one of reverence, mourning, remembering and reconciliation (NSZ 13/06/1989). Finally, the day was defined as both a day of national mourning and reconciliation or commemoration (NSZ 17/06/1989; MPÉ 1990, 293).

The third struggle dealt with the expectation of 23rd October; should it be celebrated, reconciled or commemorated? In the summer of 1989, the Budapest Committee of the MSZMP introduced an initiative that the day be celebrated as *a day of reconciliation* (NSZ 19/07/1989). The committee defended their initiative on the basis that, in 1956, the majority had acted in support of socialism. The Ferenc Münnich Association opposed the idea, because the days "ended in bloody white terror and to the persecution of communists and progressive people" (MN 26/07/1989) – and concluded that it did not serve the idea of national reconciliation (MPÉ 1990, 301).

In September it became public that a 23rd October Committee had been established, which prepared the celebrations of the day. The committee included several parties, although notably absent were FIDESZ, SZDSZ and TIB. Miklós Vásárhelyi (TIB) criticized the exclusion and demanded that the day be a *free holiday and a national celebration*. At the same time, TIB dissociated from aspirations which attempted to use the day or to monopolize it. According to Vásárhelyi, the TIB did not want to celebrate with MSZMP or those party members who had participated in reprisals after the 4th of November. Therefore, *Népszabadság* reminded its readers that TIB itself was making an attempt to own the day. A few days later, however, the organizations worked together, condemned the intervention and the reprisals after 4th November (MH 19/09/1989).

In October, the committee made a statement that the day should be a *day of national celebration,* not a *commemoration* (MN 11/10/1989). The successor party of the MSZMP, MSZP, was not considered a suitable partner for the committee either, because even after the congress they still only wanted a reconciliation day (NSZ 11/10/1989). At the same time, the committee put forth the idea to switch off the lighted red star above the parliament precisely on 23rd October (Ibid.). The idea did not materialise, because two days later it was reported that the leader of the parliament office had already carried out the act (NSZ 13/10/1989).

It had been no secret that there had been contradiction within the ruling MSZMP, and the separation finally took place in October. A few days later, the successor party accepted a statement in which it preferred the day as *a national commemorative day* to commemorate the injustices of all dictatorships (NSZ 11/10/1989). Moreover, the parliament did not prefer a national holiday either (1956 kézikönyve (I) 1996, 380), and the government had considered it a *national memorial day* (*nemzeti emléknap*) (NSZ 05/10/1989).

Thus, on one side was the day of reconciliation and a national commemorative day, and on the other side was the holiday and the celebration. As a compromise, President Mátyás Szűrös noted that we should "let the day of the 1956 uprising be *a common celebration for national reconciliation*" (NSZ 18/10/1989).

All in all, the symbolic struggle of the past had become significant not only because the parties tried to define the meaning of the day or were frightened that 'the other' could use and own it. In addition, 23rd October also had real direct political meanings in 1989 in another sense, as well. For the first time, the day was officially taken into consideration and even in an historical way, because the space of experience was not only opened or reopened for research work, but also the new Hungarian Republic, a new basis for legitimation, was proclaimed on that day. Therefore, an historical analogy was taken from 1956, and the significance also lay in the positive or negative meaning given to the past. The old government still managed to declare 23rd October a holiday on 19th March, 1990, thus, before the elections.

The discussion of the national holidays of the new republic actually took place in March of 1991. In the Law (VIII/1991), 23rd October was defined as "the day of the beginning of the 1956 Revolution and the fight for freedom, as the day on which the Hungarian Republic was declared in 1989". The day, thus, had a double meaning and, if one doubted the older meaning, (s)he might remember the latter. For example, in France, Catholics and nationalists added a double meaning to 14th July, the celebration of Joan of Arc Day and the Republican Day (Le Goff 1992, 87).

In March of 1991, a total of three alternatives were suggested (NSZ 23/02/1991) and the parliament was forced to decide which of the three national holidays would be promoted to state holiday (NSZ 06/03/1991). Government circles tended to supported the Saint Stephen Day and argued that the day best expressed the ideas of the Hungarian state and Constitution. Christian Democrats added that the day was also a Christian day. Miklós Szabó (SZDSZ) and Zsolt Németh (FIDESZ) preferred 15th March and argued that the day represented the unity and ideas of democracy (MH; 06/03/1991; 168 óra 14/03/1991). In the final vote, the winner, 20th August, was supported more in the ranks of the government and 15th March by the opposition (August 155 (for), 57 (against), 60 (absent), March 131-78-61, October 124-61-93) (NSZ 06/03/1991).

Although a national holiday refers in other countries to a King or the Royal Family, in Hungary, the most important day of the 'state' refers to medieval history, more specifically, to the first King to whom the Hungarian Kingdom is connected. In addition to this, 20th August also had actual political significance in 1991, because it connected also connected the Hungary of the present to conservative traditions which were used prior to 1945 and, therefore, also strengthened the prejudices of the opposition regarding the basic ideals of the new republic. Earlier, the 20th of August had been chosen as a national holiday in 1938, on the 900th anniversary of Saint Stephen's death.

Moreover, in the struggle of political memory the medieval King had

194

defeated revolutionary and modern political movements. A peculiar solution was to separate the state and the nation, because the celebration of the state (*állami ünnep*) takes place in August, while the two other holidays refer to the nation (*nemzeti ünnep*). We may conclude that 15th March and 23rd October have a place in the 'national pantheon' and narrative, but the first King is representative of the 'state'. In 1989, the day of the constitution and new bread had once again celebrated as the day of the first King Stephen.

## The Coat of Arms and National Decorations

A coat of arms is a logo which is used to show things like the old army standards and flags, to which the rank and file belonged. Moreover, it is a sign of the property of the state and represents symbolic, 'sacred' values as borders of universal community in everyday life (cf. Giesen 1998, 34). Whether people remember those represented historical and political values, the coat of arms is an essential part of public space, in which the aesthetic is defined as political.

During political upheavals, coats of arms are often changed and moreover, they are the part of the change which is most visible. For example, only a few days after the 1991 coup, the Russian eagle was seen in front of parliament (NSZ 27/08/1991), and in Poland, the old crown was returned to the head of the eagle etc. The Austrian Republic was declared in 1918, at which time the Habsburg eagle was "democratized": the other head was cut off, the crown was substituted with bricks (bourgeoisie) and the royal apple was replaced by a sickle (peasants) and hammer (workers). The discussion reached Austria in 1992 as to whether the eagle should be modernized by abolishing the sickle and hammer. They had previously been abolished in 1934, but were subsequently restored in 1945 (MH 06/01/; NSZ 11/01/1992). Therefore, the discussion in Hungary is not original, however, as a vanguard of the reforms, the question of the new coat of arms also emerged at an early stage in Hungary.

When the coat of arms is eventually changed, there is still the problem of whether a new one will be chosen or an old one restored. In Hungary, both the 1949 coat of arms and the current 1957 model were new, while in 1956, Imre Nagy had restored the 'Kossuth Emblem'. Furthermore, if a restoration is chosen, there is the question of what parts of it should be restored. An extreme example can be seen in the former Yugoslavia, in which the new Croatian state symbol actualized the memories of the Ustasha-terror, and at Knin in 1990, the Serb police refused to use new uniforms, which were decorated with the 'new-old' Croatian Emblem.

In 1989 in Hungary, the question was one of restoration, and the 'Kossuth Emblem' was initially preferred throughout the reform communist government. When the initiative was published on 23rd January, 1989, it was argued that the model had also been used by Ferenc Rákóczi (with a crown) in the beginning of the 18th century, in 1848, 1918 and between 1945 and 1949; 1956 was not mentioned in the newspapers at that time. Later, in October, there was talk of organizing a referendum on the issue, and three alternatives were presented: the current socialist star-model, the Kossuth-model and the old crown-model, which was used, for example, in the Dual Monarchy and between the World Wars.

Historian György Litván wrote in October of 1989 that a coat of arms was not only an heraldic, but also a political question. According to Litván, there was the question of choosing either an historical tradition, an imperial or republican one. Litván included himself in the category of supporters of the republican tradition, in which he among others included Lajos Kossuth, Sándor Petőfi, Mihály Károlyi, Oszkár Jászi and István Bibó (MN 30/10/1989).

There had been some criticism voiced during the discussion as to whether the question should be included in the referendum of 1989 or decides during the presidential election. In June of 1990, *Medián* published a poll made the previous November (N=1000). According to the poll, 49% preferred 'the crown', 34% 'the Kossuth Emblem' and 15% the current coat of arms with a star. Among young citizens, more educated people, residents of Budapest and among Protestants and atheists 'the Kossuth Emblem' was more popular, while older people, Catholics, less educated people and people in the 'countryside', i.e. outside Budapest, preferred 'the crown'. (MH 23/06/1990).

However, in the new parliament, 'the Crown Party' had already won a majority over 'the Kossuth Party', although in the first vote, held on 19th June, the crown did not receive the necessary constitutional majority of two thirds. For example, Miklós Szabó (SZDSZ) had speculated that the crown alternative might be interpreted abroad as representative of an attraction to the pre-45 period (NSZ 20/06/1990). The government once again suggested 'the crown' on 3rd July. However, Ferenc Kőszeg (SZDSZ) made a counter-proposition that in certain sites and on certain occasions the 'Kossuth Emblem' could be used, while the crown would be used on more solemn occasions. Prime Minister Antall replied that there are many republics, which have a crown in their coats of arms, citing San Marino as an example (MN 05/07/1990). The coat of arms with a crown was eventually selected (258 for, 28 against and 35 abstaining) (NSZ 04/07/1990). Moreover, the present Hungarian coat of arms is defined in the Constitution, as were its predecessors. The national anthem *Himnusz* was incorporated into Constitution already in October of 1989, and was even supported by the old parliament.

However, in the Hungarian political discussion of that time, the coat of arms became another concrete example, which was possible for the SZDSZ to interpret in feeding its undisguised nostalgia for the direction of Hungary before 1945, in which the traditions of 1848 and 1956 had been defeated. In the summer of 1991, historian András Gerő concluded that on both occasions the majority of parliament had chosen a conservative, rank oriented symbol, as opposed to a modern (*polgári*) freedom oriented one (MH 08/06/1991). The crown was also included in the symbol of estates and feudalism, while Kossuth was the symbol of modernization (*polgárosodás*) – similarly to the difference between 15th March and 20th August. The old idea of possessing the crown legitimated the power, and an attempt was made to nourish timeless symbolic continuity (Ibid.).

In addition to the coat of arms and national holidays, Gerő mentioned two decorations, *Magyar Corvin Koszorú* (the Hungarian Corvin Wreath) and *Szent István Rend* (Saint Stephen's Order) (Ibid.). In September of 1990, Saint Stephen's Order, which was established by Maria Theresa in 1764, renewed by the Horthy regime in 1938 and eliminated in 1945, was chosen as one of the new decorations of the republic. The Hungarian Corvin Wreath was established in 1930 (the other two had been established in 1946). From the state socialist period only Széchenyi and Kossuth rewards remained – "older decorations instead of the old", as the headline in *Népszabadság* defined it (NSZ 29/09/1990).

At the same time, the government decided to prohibit the use of the *Munkás-Paraszt Hatalomért* (For the Workers' and Peasants' Power) and *Szabadság Érdemérem* (Medal for the Merits of Freedom) decorations (Ibid.; MPÉ 1991, 483). Both had been distributed in 1956 and 1957 by Kádár and his supporters to the first loyalists of the new government. As of the late Kádár era, the decorations had *de facto* lost their substantiality and it became a 'dubious' distinction, if the rewarded persons even had the nerve to bear the decoration. However, instead of a more liberal solution, the government chose a stricter alternative and prohibited them altogether.

There are also a few decorations, which directly had to do with rewarding '1956' itself in the new democracy. Near the 35th anniversary in October of 1991, on the initiative of the Prime Minister, the President granted decorations "for services rendered in the service of the nation and in the defence of the Fatherland during the 1956 revolution and fight for freedom". Individuals were decorated for service to the nation on five levels: the Merit Order of the Hungarian Republic with the great cross and '56 decoration, with the middle cross and star, with the middle cross, the plain Merit Order of the Hungarian Republic and finally the '56 decoration, which was also granted posthumously (NSZ 24/10/1991). The Merit Order of the Hungarian Republic and the cross were also to be distributed annually on 20th August (MH 10/07/1991). The decoration which carried the Great Cross was granted to Prime Minister József Antall by president Árpád Göncz shortly before his death in December of 1993 (NSZ 13/12/1993).

In 1991, the first '56 decoration was also granted to two current Ministers, Bertalan Andrásfalvy and Péter Boross, and was granted posthumously to Péter Mansfeld, who was executed after his 18th birthday in March of 1959. At that time, the relatives of a total of 94 martyrs also received the 1956 plaque. On the contrary, Imre Mécs (SZDSZ) dissociated himself from the homage (NSZ 25/10/1991), because he disagreed with the ongoing initiative, which dealt with the possibilities of solving the question of historical justice through a retroactive law.

Nevertheless, these decorations became an important part of the new rituals of the republic in the 1990s. In 1995, there was a discussion regarding distributing the plaques for the last time, but the change also required a change in the law. At that time there were some 2,000 applications to receive decorations, of which one third was rejected by the organizations of 1956 (NSZ 18/09/1995). Finally, the image of Imre Nagy himself had become part of the motif of a few medals and plaques. In May of 1989, TIB published a plaque with the profile of Nagy to finance a particular memorial on Section 301. There was also a special Imre Nagy medal, which was awarded to two Kings who visited Hungary. In 1990, it was granted to the King of Belgium (MH 14/06/1990) and in May of 1991, Erzsébet Nagy delivered the medal to the King of Sweden (MH 31/05/1991).

# Reburials

If we take Napoleon, Frederic the Great or Polish General Sikorski as but a few examples, it becomes clear that Hungarians are not alone in the practice of reburials. However, we find such a plethora of examples from Hungary that it is possible to argue that reburial has been a part of the Hungarian space of experience and, thus, a part of the political culture until the middle of the 1990s. Although the reburial of Imre Nagy was perhaps the most popular of these events, it had both several predecessors and also successors in the first half of 1990s.

Among Hungarian reburials, András Zempléni has found two ideal types: first, there is the hidden martyr, and secondly, the exiled patriot (MH 23/07/1994). Thus, Imre Nagy in 1989 or László Rajk in 1956 are not the only examples. The space of experience also includes the Prime Minister, Lajos Batthyány, who was shot in 1849 and reburied in 1870, i.e. after the 1867

*Ausgleich*. In 1906, Imre Thököly, Ferenc Rákóczi II and a few others were also brought from Turkey and reburied. Moreover, it is interesting to examine the fate of the Hungarian Jacobins executed in 1795: Sándor Petőfi had searched their graves in his poem and Kossuth, Deák and the year 1848 had kept the question on the agenda. Finally, in 1914, they were found with the help of an old map of Budapest. Their reburial was delayed as a result of the World War, but was put into practice after the Chrysanthemum Revolution, in March of 1919 (A magyar jakobinusok... 1919, 59-172). The first President of the Republic, Mihály Károlyi, was also reburied in Hungary – as early as 1962. In 1988 the mortal remains of Béla Bartók were brought to Hungary.

In general, death seems to be well remembered in Hungarian political culture. Someone deceased could be claimed as ones' 'own' (*saját halottjának tekinti*), thus, an institution, for example, a work place, could consider that person as if (s)he had been a relative and memorialise them accordingly. Moreover, in 1988, John Lukacs surmised that perhaps All Saints Day was taken more seriously in Hungary than elsewhere because of the "Hungarian soul". Not even ten English words were sufficient to translate strictly the expression "*temetni tudunk*" ("We can bury") (Lukacs 1991, 19). In 1998, when *Hoffmann Research International* polled the importance of holidays among Hungarians, All Saints Day was considered the second most important holiday of the year, second only to Christmas (NSZ 09/04/1998). A particular example could be mentioned already now, because when the dissident and founder of the October Party, György Krassó, died, three different years were written on his coffin: 1932-1956-1991 (NSZ 12/03/1991).

However, for example, during war time, the honourable last service is impossible to carry out and sometimes a public tomb is even denied. Occasionally, punishment seemed to also concern the body, as was the case after Nuremberg, when the ashes of the leading Nazis were secretly sprinkled in a river, or Eichmann's ashes being spread in the Mediterranean (cf. Burton 1982, 182; Arendt 1963/1965). Moreover, Hitler is said to have finally been annihilated in 1970 after several burials in 1945 (MN 25/07/1992), and Ferdinand Marcos' reburial in the Philippines was only possible by permission from his successor, Aquino (MH 11/09/1993). The roots of de-canonization, 'nameless memory', go as far back as the medieval church (cf. Le Goff 1992, 72-73).

In the case of Imre Nagy, there was the idea that if the corpse does not exist, then there can be no grave or pilgrims. After their executions, Nagy, Maléter and Gimes had been temporarily buried inside the prison walls, and because newspapers had reported their executions, graves could be identified and direct burial might have caused demonstrations. In February of 1961, their coffins were exhumed and taken to the cemetery at night, even though the gates were normally kept locked. The operation was well-prepared, because different names were written in the cemetery records (MN 03/06/ 1989). Thus, a good question is, in which sense those people, who carried the act, 'knew' the possibility of reburials and their essence in Hungary.

At least, it is striking that several burials of the 'great men' since Vörösmarty (1855) were seen though the paradigm of national resistance and, thus, we may assume that in the Nagy's case the idea was to get rid of the 'repetitive' past forever. However, during the reburial of Imre Nagy in 1989, different expectations of public political memory reached László Rajk and Lajos Batthyány. For example, the editorial of *Magyar Nemzet* ran the headline of "Resurrection", which referred to both political and moral resurrection. The exhumation of László Rajk from Gödöllő in the autumn of 1956 was mentioned as an analogy. Moreover, a journalist and a veteran of 1956, Áron Tóbiás, mentioned an analogy in a speech he made in Kaposvár, where Nagy was born. Thus, after the execution in 1849, the former Prime Minister Count Batthyány was first taken to Rókus Hospital, then buried in an unnamed grave and finally reburied in 1870 (MH 16/06/1989).

Therefore, to see a non-conformist political symbol in Nagy was still an essential part of Hungarian political culture, as Máté Szabó (1991, 991) has formulated it. Although a deceased person could be claimed as ones' 'own', the question of to whom Imre Nagy belonged was much more difficult to answer. The party distrusted the opposition, the opposition distrusted the party, former revisionists suspected that the party and the right wing suspecting all others. Thus, the reburial became an enormous issue in the argumentation, in which there was a sense of fear that someone might use the funeral politically, as had earlier been done.

The new First Secretary, Károly Grósz, first mentioned the idea of private reburial by the relatives in the summer of 1988. The private sphere was also the main issue when the Ministry Council granted the permit on 27th January, 1989. At that time there had still been no official discussion as to when the burial would take place. Nevertheless, in April, György Litván from TIB reminded that Imre Nagy was used for ideological purposes in the ruling party, and that the funerals should be left to those to whom the deceased belonged (MN 11/04/1989). Whether Nagy finally belonged to political parties and organizations, the official funeral and invitation were organized by them. There were, thus, the relatives, TIB, the former political prisoners, *Recski Szövetség*, the People's Party, Social Democrats, Republicans, the New March Front and five of the parties, which became represented in the parliament in 1990.

Although we may speak about a human action and consensus among the opposition in the act of reburial, it does not reduce the political character of the action. The past was literally dug up, and the following questions had to be addressed: whether Nagy would be privately or publicly reburied, whether Nagy would also be rehabilitated and whether the burial meant only Nagy's burial or the burial of the entire communist system. Having a specific standpoint on these questions meant also taking a political stand, and it labelled front-lines in Hungary in the spring of 1989. For example, the opposition declared that the reburial meant also the burial of state socialism and, thus, presence at the funeral also became an essential question (cf. Bruszt 1990).

The government also made a declaration, in which they noted that Imre Nagy had been an excellent statesman. The government invited people to commemorate and act moderately. The reformers also sent an open letter to TIB on 3rd June, in which they stated their wish to lay a wreath on the occasion. According to the reformers, an attempt was made to make the entire party appear to be the guilty party. An agreement was finally reached between the TIB and the government on 8th June, in which President Mátyás Szűrös and Prime Minister Miklós Németh would participate in the reburial (NSZ 09/06/1989).

In 1989, there were two other reburials on a local level, and the newspapers mentioned that a representative of the MDF was also present at these ceremonies (MN 07/10/1989). Furthermore, Péter Mansfeld, who was sentenced to death under the age of 18 and executed eleven days after his birthday in 1959, was reburied in 1990. The inscription on the coffin read: "the last honour to the youngest martyr of 1956" (MN 22/06/; NSZ 23/06/1990). Later, Mansfeld's image has been present at commemorations of a political nature, for example, at the Buda Castle in October of 1994. When Anna Kéthly was reburied on 3rd November, 1990 in Hungary, some political leaders, such as György Szabad and two other Ministers, took part in the mass (MH 05/11/1990).

In a country with such a high level of emigration as Hungary, many reburials were dependent upon the last will of the person in question. In his last will and testament, Cardinal József Mindszenty requested that he be temporarily buried in Austria (MN 06/10/1990). Radical liberal Oszkár Jászi requested that he be buried in Hungary only after the system change (MN 11/04/1991). Thirdly, Horthy's ex-Prime Minister, Miklós Kállay, who died in New York in 1967, was later brought to Rome in 1987 and then to Hungary in 1993. According to Kállay's last will and testament, he was to be buried home, during a time of no foreign occupation (NSZ 19/04/1993).

Even though all three also have political significance, the actual political meaning of their reburial cannot be compared with Imre Nagy or Admiral Miklós Horthy. However, there was a small incident involving Mindszenty, when a few demonstrators had taken his last will and testament literately

201

and had chained themselves to the crypt: not all of the Soviet soldiers had left Hungary, and the resignation of current leaders of the Hungarian church was also demanded (NSZ 02/05/1991). In the case of Jászi György Litván, estimated that he was more contemporary than ever and that he continued the traditions upon which the present and future could be built with safety. In the same interview, Litván also noted: "I did not want that kind of horse" (NSZ 11/05/1991).

Common interpretation of 'horse' in Hungarian politics refers to November of 1919, when Horthy rode to Budapest at the head of the National Army. Since 1920, Horthy has been seen not only as a regent, but also as a symbol of the entire era, which officially was not remembered positively after 1945. In February of 1991, *Népszabadság* had posed the question "Horthy in Hungarian Soil?", because the Hungarian Association for Sea Officers and Municipalities of Kenderes wanted to bring Horthy back to Hungary. The newspaper mentioned also how the burial of Lajos Kossuth had turned into a social demonstration (NSZ 01/02/1991).

According to President Árpád Göncz, Horthy had the right to "rest" in his motherland, but if he were to be buried officially, it would also be an acknowledgment of his policy (NSZ 25/06/1991). In October, Minister of Justice István Balsai (MDF) denied juridical rehabilitation, but considered it obvious that political rehabilitation was only a matter of time. According to Balsai, it was unlikely that Horthy's tomb in Estorial "would continue to be acceptable in Hungarian public opinion". The end result would be the same regardless of whether it was carried out by the government or any other organ (NSZ 21/10/1991). Socialists made an interpretation: "A democratic human system" would not want Miklós Horthy to be buried in Hungary. When Prime Minister Antall answered, he stressed that because Horthy had not been sentenced, he would not be rehabilitated or reburied by the state either (NSZ 13/11/1991).

However, in August of 1992, Antall and Horthy's widow met, and it seemed that the reburial would be organized by the family in accordance with ecumenical ceremonies as opposed to being organized by the state (NSZ 19/08/1992). However, when the reburial finally occurred in 1993, the relationship between the government and the opposition had deteriorated and, in part as a result of the sharpened conflict in the electronic media. As in the case of Imre Nagy, the struggle over what was "private", "official" or "public" became actual and no particular sense of rhetoric was needed to define the ideas and prejudices of 'repetition' or of 'cyclical time'. Tamás Bauer (SZDSZ) argued that if there were a private funeral, the state should not coin a medal, the national television would not broadcast it, and Ministers would not reveal beforehand whether or not they were planning to attend (MH 25/08/1993).

Gyula Horn (MSZP) was of the opinion that nationally broadcast state television makes a private event to political (MH 27/08/1993).

In the government, the Horthy-criticism fell upon deaf ears and was left behind his patriotism by József Antall. Antall, for example, had noted that "we do not expect western or international history writing to want to place Miklós Horthy in his correct place" (MH 23/08/1993). Ministers had to explain their intentions. For example, Foreign Minister Géza Jeszenszky phoned Bucharest to explain why they were going to attend the reburial as private persons (NSZ 21/08/1993). Critical comments were issued from Slovakia, by Ferenc Fejtő and from Bucharest (MH 06/08; 02/09; 06/09/1993). The Slovak Vice-Prime Minister, Roman Kovác, noted that six Ministers who attend a public function cease to be "private persons" (NSZ 09/09/1993).

It was already possible that up until 1993 the opposition had held their own symbolical funerals. Iván Vitányi (MSZP) wrote that they did not want to resurrect what was already gone, but to give to the memory the last service, which it deserves (NSZ 30/08/1993). Thus, a day before the reburial they held an hour long program, which was directed by Miklós Jancsó "*Végső búcsú a Horthy-rendszertől* "(The Last Goodbye to the Horthy System), which also bid farewell to Horthyism (MH 04/09/1993). In addition, there was a small demonstration in Budapest and Social Democrats commemorated two editors, Béla Somogyi and Béla Bacsó, who had opposed white terror in 1919 and been killed (MH 06/09/1993). Earlier, the SZDSZ leader Iván Pető had announced that he would commemorate in Pécs the striking miners who had been killed in the volleys shot by the Horthyiete gendarmes in 1937 (NSZ 31/08/1993).

However, according to anthropologist András Zempléni, reburial is not "dangerous", because, although it first appears that figures are resurrected, they are eventually buried. Zempléni also pointed out that political parties could not use the reburials, because the MDF victory followed Nagy and the victory of MSZP followed Horthy (MH 23/07/1994). However, accepting this practical view would mean that politics is seen from the winning *telos*, even though as a *praxis*, politics included a *telos* in itself, i.e. politics as a current struggle of symbolic power must be taken into consideration. Moreover, time is an important entity: for example, Wladislaw Sikorski was reburied in Krakow only a few days before the general elections (NSZ 17/09/1993).

In Hungary the Ministers were playing with dangerous expectations, and particularly in a situation, in which two neighbouring countries had collapsed and there were speculation about historical, 'revisionist' analogies even as 'a possible' policy. A public reburial was not only an attempt to acknowledge Horthy's policy, but simultaneously expressed his personal contradictions and his way of dividing Hungarians. Thus, the reburial might have been a certain political "Thermidor" of the system change, because the support of the MSZP began to rise in autumn of 1993. Finally, on the basis of the Slovak and Romanian comments the act was certainly far from helpful. Hungary's neighbours had not only considerable Hungarian minorities but their own *tisos* and *antonescus* to widen the existing tensions between the countries as well.

According to Zempléni, in Hungary, reburial has to do with the Hungarian patriotic character of misfortune. It is also quite striking that all of the political wings had buried someone after 1989. A total of 13 reburials had taken place as of July of 1994 – some of them already having been buried three or four times (MH 23/07/1994).

## Memorials and 1956

Reinhart Koselleck (1994) has noted how the modern political cult of death has become a part of political culture since the obelisk for the fallen revolutionaries of Tuileries. For example, the inscription of names on the memorials became common after the First World War, in accordance with the democratic idea of not forgetting anybody, i.e. the idea of an unknown soldier. Moreover, memorials also have domestic political effects, for example, both sides of the Spanish Civil War were commemorated in Franco's Valley and through the mediation of the state church (Koselleck 1994, 9-20).

According to Koselleck, a political constellation change was needed before enemies of a civil war could be brought to the cult of memory. As an example, Koselleck mentions 'the reds' in Finland prior to 1945 (Ibid.). Although there were a few memorials before the war, the actual 'boom' began after 1945, continued into the 1960s, although even in 1998 newspapers might report that for the first time *all* the main political parties had laid a wreath at the prison camp in Tammisaari (Helsingin Sanomat 14/06/1998). Hence, on the one hand, there is a temporal period which is necessary in order to make the past into history – implicitly a generation, on the basis of Koselleck's examples of the US and French civil wars. On the other hand, there is politics and policies themselves, i.e. the acts carried out during that time period.

In Kádár's Hungary, official commemoration was focused only on the winners. Other official memorials of 1956 simply did not exist – they were erected abroad by emigrants from America to Australia. In Hungary, a total of 128 memorials were erected, of which 25 were in Budapest – of them, more than half, 72, were memorial tablets (Boros 1997, 10). Commemoration belonged clearly to the rituals of the 'winner', and 'integrative' memorials were unheard of. The lack of memorials recognizing the Second World War or Jews was discussed in the Central Committee as late as February of 1989

(A Magyar Szocialista Munkáspárt központi... 1993, 105-107). In other words, certain parts of memory were left in the hands and ideologies of the non-conformists.

Finally, the system change implied also a system change of statues – according to Béla Kurcz, a statue system change (*szoborrendszerváltás*) had taken place (MN 04/04/1992). However, not all of statues erected in Hungary during the Rákosi or Kádár era were changed or removed either, and those which were, had to be selected through political decision. Therefore we will first discuss new memorials erected during the system change. Secondly, there are a few examples of demanded memorials, which were never actually carried out. Finally, we will focus on those memorials which have been abolished or relocated since 1989.

After the Kádár era, some 400 memorials dealing with 1956 have been unveiled. Of these, *kopjafa*, a wooden monument resembling a totem pole, is the most typical, despite the fact that it actually has nothing to do with 1956. However, it is commonly considered an old and 'ancient Hungarian symbol', which contains myths of wars, resistance and traditions. In Hungary, a total of 154 *kopjafa*s were erected between 1989-1996, 90 of which were erected during the three first years (Boros 1997, 81-85). Among the first *kopjafa*s was the one in Tököl, which was dedicated to the memory of Pál Maléter by the MDF of South Pest (MH 06/11/1989).

Other common themes in the memorials are crosses, various stones, the flag with the hole in the centre and memorial tablets, which a metropolis such as Budapest has in profusion. For practical reasons the commemorative texts in the memorials remain brief. Some contain the text *"pro memoria"* the names of the deceased or the year 1956. However, some memorials also have other years inscribed on them, such as 1848, 1914, 1939, 1956 or even 1703-1711. Géza Boros (1997) referred to the last one as a combined memorial, because some parts of the statues or tablets were built in connection with an older memorial – occasionally even in connection with the memorial of liberation, by changing the red star or the socialist coat of arms. The reason for a combined memorial could be practical, sometimes there is also the inherent idea of stressing historical continuation and the survival of the nation (Boros 1997, 141-152). In other words, the memorials attempted to connect '1956' to part of a larger mythical narrative of identity and nation building, of being "Hungarian".

However, the tablet also tends to include the name of the donor and, therefore, one could not always be 'sure' of 'who' is actually being com-memorated. Earlier, town councils had frequently been agents, who actively remembered, and this old idea was followed by the opposition. For example, during the reburial of Imre Nagy a tablet was unveiled with the *names* of the opposition parties and organizations, as were tablets in memory of the Hungarian revolution at Zsigmond Móricz Square, at Kossuth Square and at Széna Square, which were all are signed by the MDF. Sometimes the text is also changed afterwards, perhaps covered, like the memorial of Mindszenty.

Thus, the memorials have many political dimensions, and political values frequently surpass artistic ones. Erecting memorials has also united citizens as a group working together. Furthermore, they also canonize historical events, but also to help to occupy political space for 'us'. In Hungary, since 23rd October, 1989, several tablets were unveiled, and the act of unveiling memorials was quite common during the first years of the new republic (cf. NSZ 05/11/1990; MN 28/10/; NSZ 09/11/1991). The statue of Imre Nagy was first planned to be unveiled on his home town of Kaposvár and the second in Giromagny, France (MN 21/05/; 15/09/1993). In Budapest it was planned to be unveiled in 1996, on the 100th anniversary of his birth. A Canadian businessman had made an initiative, contributed 200,000 dollars to fund its construction, and a foundation was also been founded. The statue would be on Vértanúk tere (The Square of Martyrs), The Memorial Committee of '56 also suggested Kossuth Square as a suitable place (MH 07/12/1994; NSZ 31/12/1994).

In the 1990s, the 40th anniversary on 1956 in 1996 had been on the horizon of expectation. In October of 1994, Béla Kurcz asked if the '56 Memorial would be erected in Budapest at Vérmező (Field of Blood, refers to Jacobins 1795). Several organizations jointly organized a bronze statue, which would symbolize the patriotism and freedom of the nameless heroes of 1956 (MN 18/10/1994). According to the first plan, the statue would have inhabited the empty corner of the abolished Béla Kun memorial at Vérmező, and with the help of the American emigrants the memorial would have been an exact replica of "the biggest Hungarian monument in the Free World", i.e. an obelisk with a Turul-bird on top. However, the plan was changed and the statue, which used a statue in Los Angeles as an exact model, was erected near the Buda Castle in Tabán (Boros 1997, 146-147; NSZ 19/10/1996).

The most 'inconvenient' debates concerning the memorials took place in 1992, in the "year of polarization". Since 1989, the Committee for Historical Justice, TIB, had progressively built up the idea of erecting a memorial at Section 301 at Rákoskeresztúr. The competition of who would build it was won by György Jovánovics, whose avant-garde artwork was sculpted in rustic stone and commemorated with terms like 'timelessness' and 'eternity', like the plot itself (Boros 1997, 42-43). In 1991, Jovánovics received the financial support, and the work was in progress until the summer of 1992, at which point the National Foundation, *Nemzeti emlékhely alapítvány*, was able to express its gratitude of the finished statue (MN 28/07/1992).

However, in the summer of 1992, the government and the opposition actually held their commemorations on successive days. Jovánovics' memorial was unveiled on 15th June as opposed to the 16th, which was the proper anniversary of the execution. On 4th June it had become clear that a joint-action (including the President, Prime Minister and Chairman of the Parliament) would not follow and that instead the President would send a message for the occasion (MN 04/06/1992). At that time, the President participated in the Environmental Congress in Rio, which ended on the 14th (NSZ 15/06/1992).

Imre Mécs argued that the national consensus which had existed three years earlier had faded away. András B. Hegedűs had no idea who had scheduled the ceremony and the idea of waiting until the President could attend was also rejected by the authorities (Ibid.). Hegedűs also reminded that the original bill of the symbolic law written in 1990 also included Imre Nagy's name, but it was removed at the last minute. According to Hegedűs, a political tendency to reduce the significance of '1956' existed. In the same article, Tibor Erdélyi argued that the government did not find continuity with 1956, but rather from Horthy and Bethlen – 1956 was more unpleasant for the government, as *Népszabadság* concluded in its headline (Ibid.).

Thus, present confrontations were also projected into the past and, vice versa, the past was used as a legitimate message for the present. On 16th June, the subtext of the front page picture in *Magyar Hírlap* briefly revealed the contradictions: "Árpád Göncz stressed the 1956 unity of the nation; according to József Antall, the unity was only a temporary state" (MH 16/06/1992). When Antall made a speech on the occasion, he noted that everyone considered his own revolution as the true one. Whether or not the struggle had failed, there should be no illusions that the weeks and months had not brought the differences to the fore (Ibid.). Antall interpreted that some had longed for something better, a more democratic form of socialism, while others wanted a western type parliamentary system as early as October (MN 16/06/1992).

On the 16th, *Magyar Hírlap* also published a declaration which had been signed by the founding members of the TIB. They noted that in three years, the political expectations of 1956 had yet to be realized. Although Soviet troops had withdrawn etc., the country was divided, cultural and moral progress had become stagnant and economic changes had hardly begun to occur. Miklós Vásárhelyi argued that scheduling the commemoration had been the most important reason for the declaration: it was impossible to commemorate 1848 on the 14th of March (MH 16/06/1992).

Finally, on the 16th, there was a silent commemoration at Section 301, at which politicians from the SZDSZ and the FIDESZ were present. On that same day, Pofosz held a commemoration at the new Nagy Imre tér and two

Ministers, Péter Boross and Mihály Kupa participated in the ceremony (MH 17/06/1992).

In general, not only had the government presented more radical means of dealing with the past until 1992, but the extreme right, too, had risen in the headlines. In Budapest, those neo-fascist groups rallied around *Jurta*[52] theatre and wanted to erect a symbolical gate at Rákoskeresztúr. In addition to Nazi symbols, the groups used symbols like the Turul-bird, the flag with the hole in the centre and a particular székler gate, which was taken from old Transylvanian cultural traditions. The gate was built close to Sections 300 and 301, but it was primarily built for Section 298, in which executed persons were buried, but mainly from the communist period prior to 1956. In a political situation in which the government had also comfortably understood and advanced old traditions, the act strengthened the impression that the government did not judge the political actions of the extreme right with a sufficient amount of explicitness.

The case became public when the mayor, Gábor Demszky (SZDSZ), wrote a letter to the director of the cemetery and pointed out that the construction of the gate was done without permission and that it disturbed the new conception of Jovánovics (NSZ 28/05/1992). A few days later the gate was unveiled, which happened as part of the commemorations of the newly revived "Heroes Day" – heroes of the First World War had been commemorated on the last Sunday in May during the Horthy era. According to *Magyar Hírlap*, they had argued in *Jurta* that if the gate was to be torn down by Demszky, he would effectively be signing his own death sentence. The present rulers were branded as leftists and its replacement with the union of right-wingers was demanded. Gergely Pongrátz, a commander at the Corvin Theatre in 1956, declared that the time of reform Communists was over (MH 01/06/1992).

Thus, a small yet visible radical right began to collaborate with skinheads and the extreme right. Moreover, the extreme right, too, was building an "honourable and trustful past" by the act of commemoration, as the other political wings had done before them. Nazi-symbols began to appear and the old debate of the existing anti-Semitism once again resurfaced. At the end of August, two quite sizable stars were drawn on the work of art at Section 301 (NSZ 28/08/1992). The székler gate itself was relocated to another site on the plot prior to the unveiling of Jovánovics' piece (MH 13/06/1992). Originally the gate had been located only 50 metres from the statue, and had been inscribed with the words: "Entered only with a Hungarian spirit" (NSZ 15/06/1992).

Thus, the first memorial category contained new memorials, and the second contains those monuments which were never actually erected. Initially, in the autumn of 1990, Foreign Minister Géza Jeszenszky (MDF) was opposed to the idea of reestablishing the statue of Trianon (MH 10/09/1990). The debate, however, continued later, because the only Soviet liberation memorial left in Budapest had been built on the same spot (cf. Prohászka 1994, 73-74). One idea was to substitute the memorial with an original relic of the Hungarian flag. According to Gergely Pongrátz, they were backed by 90% of the population and thus would not allow the liberal cosmopolites and the reform Communists to steal the revolution (MH 02/11/1992). In the January party conference, the MDF also demanded the abolition of the statue (NSZ 27/01/1993).

However, the most important idea in the second category was *Megbékélés Emlékmű Alapítvány* (The Foundation of the Reconciliation Statue), which since 1991 had planned a memorial on Köztársaság tér. The original idea was to build another memorial for the *martyrs*, which would be located beside the existing statue of the *victims* who had died in the coup of the party headquarters building, thus, for the fighters on both sides of the barricade. However, in October of 1991, some art historians rejected the idea, and with the signature of the leader of the Budapest Gallery, himself a member of the parliament in the leading government party MDF, they expressed their doubts about the existing consensus and the function of the memorial (cf. Boros 1997, 150). At that time the government did not support a reconciliation, but had prepared a retroactive law, which will be discussed in the following chapter.

Some of the innovators included aforementioned individuals such as Iván Vitányi (MSZP) and András B. Hegedűs from TIB. Hegedűs argued that we must finally honestly confess that we do not know what happened on the square in 1956 (NSZ 04/11/1991). Moreover, there were Free Democrats and Socialists behind the foundation, who since 1991 had begun to reach a sort of understanding with one another and came to oppose the government's ideas of punishment. In October of 1992, the foundation was brought out by inviting people to commemorate Kossuth Square 25th October, 1956. The commemoration would take place at the memorial stone at the same square, but instead of the more logical date of the 25th October, the day of commemoration was now the 2nd of November (NSZ 31/10/1992).

The plan of the joint-monument did not materialise, and the memorial which had been erected in 1960 was abolished in September of 1992 (MH 23/09/1992). In November, the memorial-issue reached the parliament floor, when the chairman of the radicalised TIB, Tibor Zimányi (MDF) condemned the idea. According to Zimányi, nowhere in the world was it possible for the fallen of both sides to be included in the same memorial. The case of Spain is not a suitable example, because the country had not fallen under foreign rule (NSZ 10/11/1992). Alajos Dornbach (SZDSZ) responded that a black and white division between killers and revolutionaries was impossible, because both sides also had innocent victims and passersby (Ibid.).

During the first half of the 1990s, an atmosphere of 'peace' did not exist, the foundation stone was laid but the memorial was not constructed. In 1995, when the atmosphere had partly cooled down, Zimányi continuously rejected the idea (NSZ 23/02/; MN 20/06/1995). In Zimányi's thought, Russians and Francos could not be compared, and that as opposed to a civil war, the struggle had been directed against foreign occupation and for the restoration of national independence. According to Zimányi, "our predecessors never had to face a situation, in which they had to erect a joint memorial for the *kuruc-labanc* war, the 1848 Hungarian volunteers or the Habsburg-troops or forced labour and the guards" (MN 20/06/1995).

Thus, Zimányi seemed to use an historical argument quite conservatively, i.e. continuity with analogies will dominate. An exception, a discontinuity, was not possible in a democracy either. Frankly speaking, following the defeat in 1994, the Hungarian right had fallen into a crisis and had to decide what it was building continuities with. To some extent, 'rightist' Viktor Orbán (FIDESZ) used old 'leftist' arguments against the present 'left' when he spoke on 23rd October, 1994. According to Orbán, two traditions existed, i.e. 23rd October "the tradition of national independence, freedom and citizens' [bourgeois] democracy [*polgári demokrácia*], while 4th November was the tradition of high treason, dictatorship and terror. One must be aware of both traditions, in the sense that images of Francis Joseph and the martyrs of Arad cannot be hung beside each other on a wall" (MN 29/10/1994).

Finally, the third category of memorials includes memorials and statues which were torn down. The phenomena, known at least since Vendôme 1871, reached the Baltic States and the Soviet Union (NSZ 26/; 28/08/1991) or Caucasus, in which a statue of Lenin was blown up prior to a visit by Yeltsin in 1993 (NSZ 06/12/1993).

In Hungary, however, Lenin was to be restored. Already before Imre Nagy's reburial it was noted that the high statue of Lenin had been removed for restoration. According to the Buda Gallery, repairs which had been planned for a long time were now to be completed. It was promised that the statue would be returned once the repairs were completed (NSZ 01/06/1989). However, the restoration was postponed and in February of 1990, *Magyar Hírlap* printed the headline "Lenin On the Floor", because the statue remained in the yard until it was repaired. The vice-manager of the Buda Gallery, Edit Müller, said that "exceptionally, the work was not interrupted because of a lack of funds, but rather because 'lower forums' were wanted". Müller estimated that the work would not be finished before the elections in March (MH 22/02/1990).

The cautious act in the summer of 1989 was among the first destructive acts within former Eastern Europe (in Salgótarján, however, unknown persons had toppled Lenin's bust one night in March of 1989 (MPÉ 1990, 279)). The legendary statue of Stalin faced its destiny in October of 1956, and in June of 1989, it was Lenin's turn.

Nevertheless, the question remains as to whether the tearing down of a statue symbolizes or also constructs the change, because statues, if understood like brands of companies, actually tend to be consequences of certain changes. For example, Finns did not remove the 'Good Russian Czar' from the central square in Helsinki, although they gained independence from Russia in 1917. Contrarily, in the Hungarian space of experience, removals had belonged to earlier history and the question also became actualized during the first years of the new democracy.

In 1991 the statues continued to occupy public spaces, and in October, the Minister of the Interior, Péter Boross (MDF), reminded mayors of this fact in a letter. According to the Minister, innumerable public statues and street names still "proclaimed the memory of a system, which denied democracy and served a foreign power". Therefore, he demanded the removal of certain statues and changes in street names throughout the country. One of his arguments included the forthcoming 35th anniversary of 1956 a few weeks later (NSZ 10/10/1991) – thus, 1956-rhetoric was also used to help to put actual claims into practice.

However, the director of the Budapest Gallery, Attila Zsigmond, was sceptical and considered Boross' letter unrealistic, because it was simply impossible to move the statues in such a brief period of time. For example, the removal of the Soviet soldier from the Gellert Hill would cost 20-30 million forints (MH 11/10/1991). Moreover, according to the information provided in *Népszabadság*, the extreme right planned violent removals on 23rd October. The list included the memorials of Béla Kun, Mihály Károlyi, a few Soviet memorials etc. (Ibid.) The removals never actually happened, but on 23rd October, the statue of Béla Kun was covered by a cloth (NSZ 26/10/1991) – on which someone later painted a Star of David.

Mechanically, they began by tearing down a Soviet obelisk in March (MH 10/03/1992), but there were *de facto* only promises until September of 1992, thus, prior to the demonstrations at the radio station. In August, Gergely Pongrátz had given an ultimatum, according to which the statues would be torn down if they were not removed by September 1st (NSZ 08/08/1992). According to *Magyar Nemzet*, Pongrátz had, however, asked veterans to exercise patients, and the abolition "of the politically unwanted statues" would begin after 15th September (MN 08/08/1992). That day, a list of the statues that were to be torn down was published and it was reported that they would be relocated to a special statue park (MH 08/08/1992).

The idea for the park had come about when, in December of 1991, the Budapest City Council had decided on the fate of the statues. They would not be destroyed,[53] but would be placed in a special statue park, which would be built in the 22nd district. Certain statues would be deported from the centre of the city, however, their relocation to other districts would be possible (MH 06/12/1991). The cost of the park eventually rose to 62 million forints, and it was opened in 1993. The mayor of Budapest, Gábor Demszky, had feared extreme reactions (MH 28/06/1993) and repeated the sentiment that the statues had to be removed before fanatical anti-Communists had blown them up.[54] For Demszky, the statues not only represented the communist world and ideology, but they were also in poor taste (MN 13/09/1993).

Historian János Pótó was interviewed during the removals, and he considered the events "very similar to events following the war". For an historian dealing with statues, the present actions appeared to be a political substitution (*pótcselekvés*). District politicians wanted to do something that they thought would satisfy the people (MH 23/09/1992).

Whether or not the threats made by the extreme right were legitimate, they did help to legitimated the removal of the statues. A noticeable resistance did not emerge either, even though, for example 100-150 persons bid "farewell to philosophers" Marx and Engels (NSZ 07/10/1992). Thus, the only statue park in former Eastern Europe was established in Hungary and it became a reserve into which unpopular statues were removed in a civilized manner – although, into a suburb far from the city centre.

All in all, it was the last time that the same phenomenon occurred as in 1956, but in the 1990s, the way of dealing with the 'inconvenient statues' diverged significantly. Contrary to Stalin, the statue of Lenin was not broken. As such, tearing it down meant a much more profound change, and a special park was eventually established. A noisy 'minority' did want to abolish the statues quickly, however, there was no significant resistance either. It seems that in most cases the 'majority' would have done nothing or perhaps even supported the idea of the park. This conclusion could be made on the basis of a poll of *Medián* (N=1200) (NSZ 16/10/1992).

|  | Destroy | Store-house | Statue-park | Nothing |
|---|---|---|---|---|
| Lenin | 9% | 12% | 46% | 33% |
| Soviet heroes | 7% | 9% | 42% | 42% |
| Marx & Engels | 6% | 12% | 40% | 42% |
| First Soviet Republic | 4% | 9% | 38% | 49% |

| | | | | |
|---|---|---|---|---|
| Communist victims before the WW II | 4% | 10% | 37% | 49% |
| Communist victims under communism | 4% | 8% | 37% | 51% |
| Communist victims of 1956 | 4% | 8% | 34% | 54% |
| Non-communist left-wing politicians | 2% | 7% | 33% | 58% |
| Anti-fascist | 3% | 6% | 31% | 60% |
| Osztapenko | 5% | 7% | 29% | 60% |

The desire to remove the statues also corresponded to political views and to the ages of the respondents. Among the parties in the government, the eagerness was to some extent higher than in the ranks of the opposition. One the basis of age, half of the right-wing citizens older than 62 years wanted these changes, as did the third of them who were younger than 36 years. Simultaneously, only 15% of left-wingers older than 62 agreed. Persons between the age of 36 and 47 – i.e. the beat generation, (HN) – tended to support the removal of the statues (NSZ 16/10/1992).

The last name in the table is Osztapenko, who was one of the Soviet soldiers who fell in the siege of Budapest. The removal of his statue from the edge of town also raised a few critical voices. First, Osztapenko had already lost political significance (MH 06/12/1991), and secondly, the question was not only of a person but of a space; a place (NSZ 21/12/1991) which had became a famous landmark, for example, for hitch hikers.[55]

## Street Names and 1956

In the same survey in which the fate of the statues was questioned, the relations to changes of street names was also questioned. According to the poll, 10% would have preferred that more street names be changed than had occurred. Among those who wanted extensive renaming and who revealed their political views, MDF-supporters were the most supportive and MSZP-supporters were the weakest group. The 'majority', 57%, was of the opinion that too many of the names had already been changed, and according to 33%, the amount was appropriate. According to Népszabadság, the re-baptising disturbed more left-wingers, while right-wingers were less disturbed about the actions (NSZ 16/10/1992).

In Hungary, several 'waves' of changes in street names had occurred and therefore, the period of 1956-1957 is only one link in the politics of street names, which has become widely prevalent in former Eastern European countries after 1989 (cf. Nyyssönen 1992). Moreover, the names themselves – like stamps or banknotes etc. – appear as indicators of political and social changes and frequently offer space for a national pantheon (Speitkamp 1997, 7-9). The street names which remind of historical events and persons also create a certain picture of the canonized history of the national past (Azaryahu 1997, 138) – and also always exclude something. Maoz Azaryahu (1991) has studied the street names of Berlin since *Kaiserzeit* and has divided symbolical changes into de-canonization, canonization and re-canonization. For example, Nazis de-canonized signs of the Weimar republic, re-canonized, i.e. restored Königsplatz, and, for example, canonized Horst Wessel and Adolf Hitler (Azaryahu 1991, 29-40; 1997, 140).

In Hungary, there are two points that I would like to raise here. First, street names in Hungarian – similarly to memorial tablets – "guard a memory" (*emlékét őrzi*), thus stressing the commemorative point. Secondly, naming has clearly been considered a political act. Thus, politics and naming have been inter-linked, and these actions have been thoroughly repeated also in the 1990s. Mostly older names have been restored, although changing street name also has the potential to open a new space for politics; there was discussion in Berlin as to whether *Otto-Grotewohl-Straße* should be restored to *Wilhelmstraße* or named *Toleranzstraße* (cf. Azaryahu 1997, 138-147).

In Budapest, between 10th April, 1989 and 30th March, 1994, a total of 342 street names were changed (Budapest Atlasz 1995, 54-57). Among them there are also names belonging to '1956', but finally, for example, Habsburg-House was restored to the former Lenin Boulevard – an act which was given much attention in the White Books. One of the best-known examples is the present Andrássy út, which in 1957 was named after the People's Republic. When, on 14th March, 1990, Foreign Minister Gyula Horn established a memorial tablet for count Gyula Andrássy, he argued that it would not be long before the street would once again be Andrássy.

However, in the summer of 1989, the establishment of Imre Nagy streets was demanded in the 5th, 6th and the 14th districts of Budapest. Furthermore, the Budapest Committee of the MSZMP proposed an initiative on 19th July, which stated that the as yet unnamed square inhabited by the Batthyány Memorial Light would be named after Imre Nagy (MN 31/07/1989; cf. MPÉ 1990, 291). In August, *Magyar Függetlenségi Párt* (The Hungarian Independence Party) suggested that The Boulevard of the People's Democracy be named for Imre Nagy and that Lenin körút would become Pál Maléter Street (MH 16/08/1989). In September, the published initiative of the MDF stated that Pesti út (Pest road) would be renamed Pál Maléter Street.

Finally, Imre Nagy Square was unveiled in front of the Ministry of Foreign Affairs during the 35th anniversary in 1991. In an illustration in *Magyar*

*Hírlap*, Prime Minister József Antall was making a speech, the new name had yet to be unveiled and the old name had a red tick on it (MH 04/11/1991). The earlier 'owner of the square', Elek Bolgár, had been the Vice-Commissar of Foreign Affairs in 1919, after which he become an emigrant, a professor in Rostov and after 1945 a Hungarian diplomat and professor in ELTE. Thus, there were similarities between his and Imre Nagy's background, although he never acquired any status within the government.

There was a red tick painted over the old name, and indeed, in 1989, a few organizations tried to make symbolic statements in the streets. In July, *Magyar Október Párt* (The Party of the Hungarian October) and Radical Party had painted and glued the signs of Ferenc Münnich Street and wanted others to follow the action, which was based on the fact that they had not received a reply from the council regarding change its name. The party considered itself of the legacy of the October Revolution (thus, not 1917, HN) and defined themselves as openly anti-Communist (MH 28/07/1989). In a radio interview they included the revolutionaries and freedom fighters of 1956 to their ranks and reminisced about 1956, because the revolution had taken place in the streets (168 óra 04/07/1989). Later, during the election campaign, the party once again took action by painting the statue of Ferenc Münnich red on 21st March. The necessity of the act was stressed by the fact that Münnich had no place on such a busy street (cf. Dalos 1991).

In practice, the street names and signs were changed during the MDF-regime (Ibid). In Budapest, however, a committee of the City Council had already proposed changing more than 300 names at the end of January of 1990, i.e. prior to the elections (MPÉ 1991, 459-460). That summer, 55 new names were introduced in the newspapers, decisions from April and June were mentioned (MH 03/07/1990) and a list of changed names was published (MN 03/09/1990). During the course of this whole process a few of the old signs had been left on the walls and were usually 'vandalised' with a red cross painted over them.

On the whole, the changes in street names took place on three levels. First, there were spontaneous acts, such as the case of Ferenc Münnich, in which citizens themselves took an initiative. Secondly, there were cases of a political decision-making process in a town or community organs, which took time to be carried out, i.e. for a new street sign to appear. Finally, the second stage led to the third, state level. When, in October of 1991, the Minister of the Interior, Péter Boros (MDF), hastened mayors with a letter, in addition to statues it also concerned street names.

In the letter, the Minister wrote not about new names, but about the restoration (*visszaállítás*) of old ones. Boros described that the abolition of symbols and restoration of old historical names is a duty (*feladat*), in which

215

local municipalities need all moral support. Names which were reminiscent of the dictatorship should be changed (NSZ 10/10/1991). However, the historicity of the old names was not defined further, and there were also cases in which a plurality of older names existed. However, at this point, restoration usually meant going back to the period of Austria-Hungary, which was also harmonious with the current national-liberal ideology of the leading party in the government.

Furthermore, after 1989, canonization also meant Azaryahu's de- and re-canonization. The names of the three persons, who had died in the attack at Köztársaság tér and who were considered martyrs by the Kádár regime, were removed from the street canon: Éva Kállai became Alföldi utca (Street of the Hungarian Plain), Imre Mező was restored to Fiumei út – Orczy út (Street of Fiume (Rijeka in the old Italian form); Orczy was a baron in the 18th century). Finally, János Asztalos Park would remind of Baron Orczy and the street would be named Aladár utca.

In addition to Imre Nagy Square, two new names were established: Ötven-hatosok tere (Square of '56-ers), earlier Chlepko tér, and Október huszon-harmadika utca (Street of 23rd October), earlier Zoltán Schönherz, an underground Communist activist, who was prosecuted and executed for high treason in 1942. Finally the statue of Imre Nagy was erected at Vértanúk tere (Martyrs' Square), which during the Kádár regime was named after Endre Ságvári, a young Communist resistance activist, who in 1944 was shot by the gendarmes. Nevertheless, the name of the Martyrs' Square is plural, and we may imagine that it also includes Ságvári, who lost six out of eight streets named after him.[56] Individuals like Cardinal József Mindszenty, István Bibó and Pál Maléter do not have streets named for them in the capital (Budapest Atlasz 1995, 26-53).

In general, the changes in the street names did not raise significant opposition, nor did it inspire a flood of letters to the editor. Rather, they were experienced as a part of the system change, which required financing and also caused practical problems; the primary function of a street name is an address. However, in one of the few critical letters, József Hlavács suggested that there be small signs clarifying all the names and meanings in temporal order, because also Horthy, the coalition government, Rákosi and Kádár had played with street names, and the same thing was going to happen now (MN 21/02/1991). The de-canonization of Hungarian Stalinists, were not problematic, but there were a few other problematic street names, among them, Endre Ságvári and the First of May (cf. MN 17/07/1990).

Moreover, the new street names were an attempt to create a presentable picture and to show 'us' in an acceptable and 'European' light for the future. On the other hand, the phenomenon, the street names themselves, have

216

constructed new identities, which in addition to restoration have been a part of contemporary political argumentation. For example, in 1990, it was suggested that Marx tér be replaced by Európa tér (MN 12/07/1990). The idea was never realized, although the new name, Nyugati tér (Western Square) in front of the Western Railway Station, once again reflects the present political aspirations of the country. Before Marx the square was Berlini tér.

## The Restored Past for the Future

In this chapter we have focused on national holidays, coats of arms, decorations, reburials, memorials and street names, which were all symbolic actions belonging to the change. As history politics people were motivated by these actions, the actions unified the opposition and also canonized certain interpretations of the past. Moreover, these actions concerned all citizens, and most of the decisions were made on the national level. In this sense, even such a trifle phenomenon as new license plates – bigger, brighter and with a small national flag on the edge – constructed expectations of the change. The new license plates were introduced for the first time in July of 1989 (MH 20/07/1989).

Actually, symbolic history politics can frequently be connected and are an essential means of nationalism, because through these actions the state – or the nation – appears not only to the citizens, but also to other countries. In post-communism politicians have looked backwards and restored the past for the new beginning. Although the Hungarian system change has belonged to one of the less painful tumultuous periods, it is not impossible to think that these symbolic actions also influenced more radical actions and movements in neighbouring countries as well. The phenomena rose most extremely in the former Yugoslavia, in which national symbols were interpreted through the fears of the Second World War.

All in all, here, we may separate three basic symbolic acts in Hungary, which have taken place during the system change. First, the acts of de-canonization, secondly, re-canonization and thirdly, symbolic politicking, particularly with 1956 symbols. In 1989, de-canonization initially dealt with the question of who could switch off the star of communism. Thus, also forthcoming positions were struggled over with the help of the past. However, symbols did not yet imply a formal change in the power structure, because some of the symbols were already changed by the old regime. For example, the 15th of March was mentioned both in 1956 and 1988, prior to the formal argument in favour of a multiparty system.

Secondly, national holidays and decorations such as street names could be

217

mentioned as examples of re-canonization, which also helped to create the change. The first change, found in this study, took place, when in November 1988 the Teacher's Training College in Eger gave up the name Ho Chi Minh in honour of the local writer, Géza Gárdonyi (MPÉ 1988, 457). However, if we relate the re-canonization of street names, for example, to the Soviet Union, in this sense, Hungary was not a clear forerunner. In January of 1988, Gorbachev had opposed the idea, but a few weeks after the 29th Party Conference in June, a Council of Toponomy was appointed, which approved a proposal that the historical names should be restored to Soviet towns and other places (Davies 1989, 158).

Outside Hungary, one of the most well-known symbols of 1956 is the flag with a hole in the centre, which has later become popular also in the 'revolutions' of the DDR, Romania and the Soviet Union. In Hungary, the MDF had used it at least once during the election campaign in 1990, and the flag was also present during the demonstration of the Democratic Opposition, as is visible in the pictures from the 15th March. Furthermore, when István Csurka lost the battle in the MDF and established his own organization, *Magyar Út* (Hungarian Road), the flag hung on the wall and beside it was a picture, in which two rivers (Danube and Tisza) could be understood as representing a Hungary without borders (!) (MH 15/02/1993). According to Csurka, "the last reform attempt had ended in Hungary on 4th November, 1956" (NSZ 15/02/1993).

# X  THE STRUGGLE AMONG CONTEMPORARIES IN POST-COMMUNISM

In recent transitions in Latin America and Southern Europe, a primary concern has been the future of civil-military relations. On the contrary, most investigations dealing with the former state socialist countries have primarily been concerned with individuals who have been repressed by state police or security officials. On the one hand, the issues were quite similar across the region, and on the other, policy initially differed widely, while there was considerable agreement in politics. In general, Communist Party officials and members were subject to prosecution only if they had collaborated with state security agencies, or if they had been involved in criminal activities.[57]

However, purges and legal procedures are only one way to deal with the past. These different alternatives in the Hungarian post-communism and their relation to '1956' will be discussed now. I have separated both 'positive' and 'negative remembering', which in addition to symbolic actions, were concrete laws. They either rewarded and recompensed an individual, or were used as an attempt to punish and exclude individuals. In the first category, there are several compensation laws, which defined those who were entitled to receive compensation in post-communism. However, most of those laws mainly concentrated on the pre-56 period, and since my case deals with a particular historical event, I will concentrate more on 'negative remembering' in this chapter. The Hungarian discussion concerned two main issues: whether crimes committed during the communist regime could be punished *afterwards,* and the screening of high officials and Members of Parliament. In connection with 1956, the point is that both laws deal indirectly with the 'revolution'. Moreover, these debates not only concerned the parliament, but also several '56 organizations, as well as other current issues like the Hungarian electronic media.

In post-communism it could be said that the whole Hungarian past-oriented politics culminated into the word *igazságtétel*, making justice. *Igazság* means both truth and justice, and thus, two meanings are entangled in one word; ontological truth is frequently connected to moral truth to distinguish between right and wrong, even if justice could be used without truth, and truth without justice (cf. Kenyeres 1995, 84-87). Furthermore, the ending – *tétel* in *igazságtétel* – means the act of making (ÉrtSz 1960, 446). The truth from 1956 also meant justice for 1956, and it became an issue in the hot-tempered political debate on how to deal with the past.

## The *Justitia* Plan and its Consequences

At the end of August 1990, a detailed *Justitia* plan became public (NSZ 28/ 08/1990). In eleven paragraphs, the plan outlined settlement with the past, finding responsible persons, and taking legal measures against the leaders of the old system. Representatives of the MDF had given the plan to the Prime Minister in June, but it was not made public until August (MPÉ 1991, 277).

In March 1991, the Attorney General, Kálmán Györgyi, answered one interpretation and said that the punishment of 'communists' crimes' was not possible unless parliament changes a law and declares that crimes committed during the communist era have no statute of limitations (MN 06/; 08/03/ 1991). On the basis of this statement, for example, József Torgyán (FKGP) considered punishment possible (MN 08/03/1991) and László Surján (KDNP) stated that it was necessary to close the past. However, those who participated in the reprisals of 1956, and those who broke down the economy, must be named (MN 18/03/1991).

In the summer of 1991, MDF again incorporated the *Justitia* plan into its political agenda. Also, the other government party, KDNP, had supported re-opening past crimes made (*feltárás*) (MN 08/07/1991). The National Committee of the MDF during its discussion requested that White Books be prepared in every province and town. The books would research illegalities during the last decades, and name those who had committed homicide, and those who were disloyal and guilty of treason. Moreover, a bill would deal with the period of 1944-1990. According to the piece of news, Dr. István Varga argyed that no "show trials" (*koncepciós perek*, 'draft actions') would take place since they wanted to avoid the "bad" model of Nuremberg, where several sentences had no lawful base, and "Wehrmacht officers who had only obeyed orders, were sentenced". Varga considered the execution of Prime Minister Bárdossy in 1946, as a juridically justified murder. (NSZ 15/07/1991).[58]

The whole plan of punishment was revealed by *Népszava* on 5th September. The basic idea was that those who were responsible for the present situation should not be in better positions than those who had suffered as a result of the system. The plan had to be carried out, although the majority of society might not have agreed with it. According to Imre Kónya (MDF), the idea belonged to the political philosophy of the party.

Practically, it meant supporting the Zsolt Zétényi's initiative of the retroactive law, reduced pensions on the basis of activity in certain organizations (MSZMP, KISZ, HNF etc.). Moreover, historians and lawyers should investigate illegalities occurring after 1956, and the Chairman of the Academy of Sciences should provide information concerning them at the request of the Prime Minister. Moreover, the time had come to create justice and to thoroughly change the spirit of the Hungarian radio and television. In Kónya's view, the change had been too risky to carry out earlier. Secondly, the Soviet coup was interpreted a sign of how stratums of the old system had begun to reorganize, and how even inside the MDF, there were ideas of a "second compromise" (Népszava 05/09/1991).

The radical populist wing of the MDF argued that they would back the plan with pleasure (MN 16/09/1991). István Csurka declared "them" to be frightened, but is not concerned with those who were only party members (MN 04/09/1991). On the other hand, Népszabadság wondered if the whole Justitia was dead, because a national presidium of MDF promised to stand behind the Constitution (NSZ 20/09/1991).

In October, Szonda Ipsos published an opinion poll (N=1000) on "how to face the past". According to the poll the 'majority', i.e. 57%, wanted to hold the former leaders of the country responsible. Moreover, 58% agreed with an allegation that historical justice demanded this responsibility. However, 43% agreed, and 45% disagreed, when it was postulated that the question only turns focus away from the country's present problems. Of the supporters of parties, 63%-67% supported responsibility to some extent, but in the MSZP the opponents had the majority, 53%. When the question was asked whether or not concentration should be on the future and not on the question of former leaders and their responsibility, the majority, 64%, preferred the future, and 22% did not. (NSZ 07/10/1991).

The representatives in the press bureau of the MDF immediately criticized the results, and denied the notion of a retroactive law (NSZ 09/10/1991). Instead, the question should have been whether people wanted to see those, who for political reasons were not prosecuted for their actions which, at the moment of the act, had been punishable, held responsible. According to the MDF, an inquiry based on this question would have given another result (NSZ 09/10/1991).

However, at the end of October, a discussion concerning homicide, treason, and disloyalty, was brought into parliament. Ágnes G. Nagyné Maczó (MDF), accused that "the government had failed in the possibility of reckoning, but that guilty people such as Aczél, should be catch up with". Tibor Zimányi

(MDF) argued that this question was outside party interests. Imre Kónya's opinion concerned the future: "A bill which will not make one who is guilty, and one who is not guilty, equal in the future, must be passed." Iván Vitányi (MSZP) stated that the law awakens a spirit of reprisals, and that moral judgement belongs to society, not to parliament. Viktor Orbán (FIDESZ) argued that the judgement must be based only on law, and not on emotions (MH; NSZ 30/10/1991).

Finally, the Zétényi-Takács law was accepted in parliament on 4th November, i.e. on the anniversary of the second Soviet invasion in 1956. The proposal dealt with homicide and treason committed between December 1944 and May 1990, and parliament accepted it with a vote of 197 for, 50 against and 74 abstaining. Gábor Fodor (FIDESZ) requested open vote, because the bill was not compatible with Hungary's international agreements. Delegates from the government parties, KDNP and FKGP, voted for, as did the MDF. From the ranks of the MDF, one voted against and seven abstained. Contrarily, from the opposition, FIDESZ and MSZP (one absent) voted against. The majority of SZDSZ was absent, four of them voted for and two against (MH; MN; NSZ 05/11/1991).

After the vote, President Árpád Göncz made the decision to turn to the Constitutional Court to clarify the content of the law (NSZ 19/11/1991). Another veteran, Imre Mécs (SZDSZ), considered the bill harmful from every point, and also promised to turn to the Constitutional Court (NSZ 18/11/1991). In addition, close relatives of the deceased, i.e. Ferenc and László Donáth, Ágnes Hankiss, Ferenc and Katalin Jánosi, Anna Losonczy, László Rajk, Júlia and István Szilágyi and Júlia and Mária Vásárhelyi made a statement, in which they did not accept the government's proposal. Instead, the real criminals should be named in public, with the full extent of their actions (NSZ 19/11/1991).

Until then the debate had continued and spread out. In November (MN 13/11/1991), the Chairman of the Human Rights Committee, Gábor Fodor, stated that the criminals of the dictatorship should be punished only within the framework of a rule of law. Moreover, ex-veteran Miklós Vásárhelyi condemned the law, which brings uncertainty; and elsewhere, ex-veteran János Dénes (ex-MDF) in his speech in parliament (NSZ 22/11/1991), had demanded hangings.

Finally, the Constitutional Court made its decision in March, and found all paragraphs of the Zétényi-Takács law against the Constitution. According to the decision, the paragraphs were not clearly defined, and a law must already be enacted before a crime is committed. When President Árpád Göncz commented on the decision, he reminded everyone of two principles: every nation has the right to know its past, and "legal responsibility" does not mean that the state should not re-open events of the last decades, i.e. the question also deals with people's sense of justice. Gábor Fodor argued that a rule of law had won, and Zoltán Gál (MSZP) noted that the democratic state structure was functioning. From the MDF, Zsolt Zétényi argued that in the European value structure and Judeo-Christian culture, crime and punishment could not be separated. Moreover, Imre Kónya agreed with the decision, but reminded that it does not discuss finding other lawful means of carrying out historical justice and restoring moral order. (MH; NSZ 04/03/1992).

The competence of the court was questioned in parliament by János Dénes, who argued that the court was created during the party state. On the 12th, Tibor Füzessy (KDNP) said that the government would formulate a new bill (NSZ 13/03/1992). Thus, in September, *Népszabadság* reported that the government was preparing a new bill, which was based on the Law VII/1945, concerning war crimes. The model was taken from Czechoslovakia, in which legal proceedings were to be modeled on the basis of the law enacted in 1950. According to the newspaper, lawyers had advised Prime Minister Antall two years previously that it would will be extremely difficult to get convictions (NSZ 22/09/1992). A few days earlier, both the Hungarian Martial Court in Budapest, and the local Martial Court at Győr, had refused to prosecute in the case of Mosonmagyaróvár in 1956. They argued that prosecuting would mean the death of constitutionalism, because in Hungarian law, manslaughter has a statute of limitation of fifteen years, which had run out in 1971 (MH 17/10/1992).

Thus, the discussion had culminated with the word *igazságtétel*, which emerged, for example in *Magyar Hírlap* (MH 21/10/1992). The paper commented on the opinion poll made by *Medián* with the headline "Doing Justice is Not the Most Important Task". *Medián* had polled by telephone on 15th October, 264 people from Budapest:

Those who had used their power to secure a glorious life:

| | |
|---|---|
| 52% | wanted the names published |
| 25% | wanted nothing |
| 20% | some other punishment |
| 2% | did not know |
| 1% | wanted to condemn them in prison |

Those who had persecuted people on the basis of opinions:

| | |
|---|---|
| 53% | wanted the names published |
| 26% | wanted nothing |
| 5% | some other punishment |
| 7% | did not know |
| 9% | wanted to condemn them in prison |

Those who had committed political murders in 1956:

| | |
|---|---|
| 28% | wanted the names published |
| 10% | wanted nothing |
| 8% | some other punishment |
| 7% | did not know |
| 46% | wanted to condemn them in prison (MH 21/10/1992) |

Naming names seemed to be sufficient to satisfy most people's sense of justice, except in the case of political murders committed in 1956. In the parliament, however, there were several more radical propositions, and Zsolt Zétényi and a few other members of parliament asked for an investigation on the basis of the law from 1956 dealing with war crimes committed in 1956. Because the law still existed, the Attorney General ordered the investigation (NSZ 22/10/; MN 24/10/1992).

This particular debate took place in parliament not only "in the year of polarization", but also around the 36th anniversary of 1956, when the skinhead incident against the President at the Kossuth tér occurred. On the 24th, the Minister of the Interior, Péter Boross, mentioned that "perhaps a Socialist Hungarian Nuremberg is not a bad formulation". "A Socialist Nuremberg" was also in the headline of *Népszabadság* and *Magyar Hírlap* on the same day, when it was reported that in Germany, the trial of Erich Honecker would begin on 12th November (MH; NSZ 24/10/1992). Finally, there were four different proposals, and three of them were accepted on 16th February, 1993. Socialists opposed the bill; Free Democrats and FIDESZ opposed the Zétényi's new version but abstained from voting on the government version (Juhász 1993, 38).

However, in March of 1993, President Arpád Göncz once asked solicited the viewpoint of the Constitutional Court before he would sign the bill (NSZ 08/03/1993). The court made its statement in the end of June, and again declared the bill unconstitutional (NSZ 30/06/1993). If the punishment for the crime had been more than five years at the time when the crime was committed, either a statute of limitations would not apply or would only partially apply (MH 30/06/1993). The final statement was released in October: there is no statute of limitations on a crime against humanity. The Geneva Treaty of 1949, which protects victims of war, also defines international armed conflicts and forbidden actions as not considered international armed conflicts.

Thus, according to the Constitutional Court, the formula of the present bill, "any action against the breaking of peace after the war," could not be defined as a war crime, i.e. it should be valid at the moment of occurrence. Therefore, the first paragraph of the 1992 bill was considered unconstitutional, although the second was not (NSZ 13/10/1993). After complicated juridical sentences, the message became clear: crimes committed in 1956 were not considered war crimes, but crimes against humanity.

The Minister of Justice ordered a few dozen legal proceedings to be heard (MH 14/10/1993). A week later, the 1956 Association of Mosonmagyaróvár demanded the arrest of frontier Colonel István Dudás (NSZ 21/10/1993). However, critical voices were also heard: Lajos Bodman wrote that the decision surprised many, because international agreements usually do not justify punishments, and international treaties are not definitions understood in the legal sense. The qualification of a crime is sufficient if an international agreement declares it so, provided that the state has signed the declaration (MN 17/11/1993).

In February of 1994, two suspects were arrested in Mosonmagyaróvár and two in Salgótarján (MH; NSZ 12/02/1994). After 35 investigations, there were to be proceedings in five cases: Berzence, Eger, Mosonmagyaróvár, Salgótarján and Tiszakécske. Except in the case of Eger and Salgótarján, the cases were to be handled by the military courts (NSZ 01/04/1994). In August, Attorney General Kálmán Györgyi reported on the ongoing process, stating that it had been possible to verify slaughter, and that the actions are based on the Geneva Treaty. According to Györgyi, a juridical problem had emerged, which neither Hungarian nor European law had looked directly at until now (MH 13/08/1994).

In Salgótarján, the proceeds began on 23rd June, when three of the twelve accused were questioned. According to the indictment, on 8th December, 1956 a crowd had demanded the release of two prisoners, two men had shot into the air and then some had fired volleys (sortűz) into the crowd without having been ordered to do so. According to the prosecutor, at least 46 people had died and 93 were wounded. (MN; NSZ 24/06/1994) (see also epilogue).

The Budapest Court heard several people, among them, Béla Biszku and Gyula Uszta (MN 08/07/1994). Other high officials from 1956 were interrogated as witnesses: ex-Minister of Defence Lajos Czinege, and László Földes, both of whom denied that an order had been given to open fire (MH 21/09/1994; NSZ 12/10/1994). In November of 1994, István Dudás and three other border guards were prosecuted for crimes at Mosonmagyaróvár. According to the indictment, on the 26th of October, 1956, men had shot from, and in the front of the barracks, causing the death of more than fifty people. Furthermore, Dudás had ordered increased defence alertness and had given the order to fire by moving his hand (MH 12/11/1994). At the end of the year, one more case was opened in Tata, against Lieutenant-Colonel K. János, who had retired from active service (MH 29/12/1994).

In conclusion, as of 1989 there were two levels in the juridical-political discussion dealing with the past: *rehabilitation*, i.e. undoing former juridical decisions – in several cases carried out before May of 1990 by the old parliament – and *punishment*, from autumn of 1991 onwards. In it broadest form, the retroactive law (1991) dealt with the temporal period from 1944 to 1990, i.e. cases which were not put before the court in the former political system. The character of the retroactive law was evidently political, in that its purpose was to settle old injustices, and particularly to reach those who had participated in the political restrictions after November 4th, 1956.

## Screening Law

In an historical perspective, all the rapid system changes which occurred in Hungary in the 20th century – and also 1848 – had contained purges as well. According to István Deák, these purges also legitimized the power of new rulers and their goals. For example, after the Second World War, so-called "A- and B-lists" were used in addition to direct purges. A three member commission (the Prime Minister, the concerned Minister and the representative of the Trade Unions) decided, who could remain on the A-list, and thus not be discharged. Although the main task was to reduce the number of officials, a view of separating with the Horthyite past seemed obvious, too (Deák 1998, 65). Thus, in which sense has the question of purges become real in post-communism?

Hereafter, a screening has more to do with reconciling with the past than the particular law mentioned in the preceding chapter. In this study, it is impossible to concentrate on the lustration in general, to define an agent or who was purged after 1990. Nevertheless, the main point in this chapter is that in Hungary, the screening law also deals with 1956. Hence, on 8th March, 1994 a law "for the persons chosen for certain important positions" was enacted in parliament and would enter into force on 1st July, 1994. The law not only dealt with official and secret members of the former counterintelligence III-III, but went further to the past, also persons in the armed forces (*kárhatalom*) (1956-1957) and members of the Arrow Cross before 1945.

According to critics, the timing of the law prior to the May 1994 elections suggested that its motivation was to damage the government's major political rival, the Socialist Party, which was leading in the polls (Welsh 1996, 422). However, the discussion had already begun in the autumn of 1990, when the Free Democrats had their own version of the law, but it was rejected in the parliament (MH 05/09/1990). In May, 1991, 12 Smallholder MPs had asked requested their own lustration on moral and political grounds. On the 31st of May, Prime Minister Antall gave them their files in envelopes (MPÉ

226

1992, 432-433). They speculated that there could be 50 spies in a parliament, and wondered whether the publishing of names could be used for political purposes (MH; MN 13/05/1991).

In the discussion, Minister of the Interior, Péter Boross (MDF), referred to a forthcoming law and a commission (Prime Minister, President, Chairman of the Parliament and Chairman of the Constitutional Court), which would uncover whether a person had been a member of the III-III, the armed forces between 1956-1957, ÁVH, or had something to do with the cases before 1956 (NSZ 11/05/1991). The Minister speculated that the results would be secret, or would be published after consultation with the person; in June the III-III archives were declared state secrets (MN 13/06/1991).

In October of 1991, Boross made a statement that it would investigate whether someone had been a member of III-III, ÁVH or in the armed forms in 1956-1957 (NSZ 14/10/1991). Zoltán Gál (MSZP) called it "the little brother" of the Zétényi-Takács law. Properly, this III-III problem had not been not "negotiated" in the roundtable in 1989 (MH 14/11/; NSZ 27/11/1991). Doubts had also been voiced, because the government had found Minister József Torgyán's (FKGP) file selective – concerning his doings in 1957 i.e. during the reprisals (MH 01/11/; MN 11/11/1991; NSZ 24/02/1992).

Thus, quite soon it became apparent that the question was not only about the former members of the MSZMP or counterintelligence, but it was a far deeper problem in which the past could also be used to compromise someone in the present. In 1993, István Csurka, for example, assumed that his name might be on the list because after 1956 "during the internment [after 1956] he had signed 'this and that', but had never worked for the department." *Népszabadság* speculated that the MDF had probably known about the information, because after the SZDSZ initiative in 1990, the MDF had torpedoed the idea of organizing the ranks of the party (NSZ 17/06/1993).

On the other hand, there were also ideas about ousting persons who were "on the wrong side in 1956" from politics. Minister of Justice István Balsai (MDF) argued that the government was going to further restrict those who had belonged to organizations like the armed forces from public action. Socialist leader Gyula Horn interpreted that the law was directed against active politicians such as himself. Moreover, Imre Kónya's speech was directed at him when he said that any person who had participated in the reprisals, could not lead the Committee of Foreign Affairs (MH 09/12/1992).

In February of 1993, the latest version of the bill outlined several categories of co-operation: A secret informer, documents provided and signed by hand, an informer, and the most essential here, belonging to the armed forces between 1956-1957. On the basis of the draft, the law would touch a large number of people: Members of Parliament, those nominated for office, those who would take an oath, the government, political secretaries, judges, lawyers, ambassadors and the President and Vice-President of the National Bank. (NSZ 13/02/1993). The discussion in parliament finally began in October of 1993, in the shadow of the events on Hungarian television. The bill was referred to as a 'fluoroscopy' and also had the nickname *pufajkás* law (NSZ 17/01/1994), thus, according to *pufajkás*, who was a man who aided the Soviet army after November 4, 1956.

Finally, in March of 1994, parliament accepted the "Agent law" in the midst of the purge atmosphere at the Hungarian Radio. According to the screening law, the files of the security services would not be made available to the public until 1st July, 2030, i.e. 30 years after the lustration process will have ended (Welsh 1996, 418). 177 members of the parliament voted for, 12 against, and 50 abstained. From the Free Democrats, only Béla Király supported the bill. The others abstained. Ten Socialists voted against, and the remaining two votes came from SZDSZ and independents (NSZ 09/03/1994).

In July of 1994, the screening judges began their work by requesting a list of the Members of Parliament. Had someone worked with internal security or been in the armed police forces, the judges would ask the person to resign. Whether or not they did resign, their names would be published in official paper and given to the news agency MTI. It was estimated that the law in its present form would apply to some 10,000–15,000 people (MH 21/07/1994). However, voices critical of the possibilities of putting the law into practice, were heard (MH 30/06/; MN 27/07/; 03/12/1994), and the National Association of Judges remarked that the screening work had political dimensions (MH 10/12/1994). In December, the Constitutional Court changed the law, limiting it scope, and thus universities, state owned companies, banks and the media were exempt (MH; NSZ 23/12/1994). The timing also became a problem, because, instead of completing the screening process by June 1995, only 40 members of parliament were lustrated in March (NSZ 25/03/1995).

However, according to András Domány, the law had not achieved its original goal, not in the restricted form from 1996 either, i.e. to reveal former political secret service professionals and secret officers and agents. Only one organized member was found until 1998. He resigned, and therefore there are doubts about a special kind of punishment which concerned the well-known leaders of the old system and the Socialist Party. In fact, all the politicians belonged to the reform Communists, and, on the basis of their positions were able to view the III-III material, whether they used it or not. (NSZ 31/01/1998).

In conclusion, a specific problem of reckoning with the past also existed in the 1990s and not only in Hungary. For example, President Václav Havel argued that if we do not reckon with the communist past in a civilized way, then we show the way to the extremists who want revenge instead of justice

(MH 11/12/1992). Also, the Czechoslovakian case became problematic and, for example, the ILO and The European Council considered the law as discriminatory (NSZ 11/03/1992). Moreover, the Polish case in 1992 led the government into crisis and to the election of a new Prime Minister (MH; NSZ 06/06/1992).

However, it is astonishing how strongly Hungarian law was bound to 1956. The *past,* the political past until the 1940s, was put first while, for example, the economic commitments were left out. However, it is embarrassing for a Prime Minister to leave the government on the basis of allegations of his having been an agent as has happened in Poland in the 1990s. Moreover, in the Hungarian case, "Duna-gate" must be remembered, i.e. the Secret Service covered the opposition after 23rd October, 1989. After the scandal, the Secret Service destroyed a portion of the material in 1990.

## Commemorative Organizations and 1956

In the previous chapters we have concentrated on the parliament and on two particular laws dealing with 1956. However, there are also several organizations and interest groups, and commemorative organizations, which played a role in the creation of the aforementioned laws, but which also tried to define post-communist politics in general.

The most important of the '56 organizations, *Történelmi Igazságtétel Bizottság* (The Committee for Historical Justice), TIB, was founded in June of 1988. Some 40 persons, mainly veterans and relatives of those executed, signed the founding letter, which, according to Miklós Vásárhelyi, the news agency MTI did not publish (MN 08/02/1989). Up until the first free elections, the members were frequently interviewed in the newspapers and, for example, they played an essential role in the reburial of Imre Nagy. Following the elections, activity was transferred partly to the parliamentary level, because six member of TIB became Members of Parliament: Iván Darvas, Árpád Göncz, Imre Mécs and Miklós Vásárhelyi represented the largest opposition party, Free Democrats, and Tibor Zimányi and Gyula Fekete represented the leading party in the government, MDF.

In September of 1990, for example, members of TIB were not satisfied with the system of compensation. According to Zimányi, the government did not do enough in the name of those who were libelled, and the compensation law should have been among the first to enter into force. Another member of TIB, Elek Nagy, complained that those who beat them receive 15,000-20,000 forints while he received only 5,600 forints a month (MN 24/09/1990). Moreover, Miklós Vásárhelyi noted the necessity of the

TIB, because the spirit of 1956 had yet to win a worthy place in common knowledge (NSZ 23/05/1991). In other words, members of TIB attempted to keep the memory of 1956 in the fore and, on the other hand, to promote the interests of those "calumniated by the dictatorship but who have yet to receive their 'sedatives'" (cf. MH 02/01/1991).

However, over the course of 1991 there had been varying views between the parties on finding the means and extent of compensation. Finally, in June, the first compensation law was accepted government vote. Already in May it was questioned whether TIB was at a crossroads, and if so, could it become a mass organization (MH 31/05/1991). As early as November there were beginning to be signs of a split and, for example, József Tittman criticized that the leaders of TIB were "on the side of the brakemen of the system change" and that TIB wanted to own the ideas and values of 1956 (NSZ 11/11/1991). Moreover, the chairman of the TIB, Miklós Vásárhelyi, refused to run as a candidate, arguing that he had been labelled a Bolshevik for his support of reconciliation. Vásárhelyi explained his decision by stating that he was tired, that passions have been let loose during the last months, that public life has radicalised and politics moved to the right. Vásárhelyi argued that reconciliation had been the most important achievement of the system change until then (MH 09/12/1991).

In December, the annual meeting of TIB was postponed until March. József Tittman commented on the existence of different political directions in 1956, noting that even today we cannot form similar opinions in dealing with, for example, compensation and even the whole 1956 (MH 13/12/1991). Thus, towards the "year of polarization" the debate in parliament reached the TIB also and *vice versa*.

Moreover, after the decision in the Constitutional Court in 1992, a committee, which prepared the meeting of the TIB, condemned the decision in the name of the entire organization. On 23rd March, another declaration, "This is Not the TIB Which We Founded," came into being. The document was signed by 23 original members of the TIB and it included current and present (opposition) politicians, researchers and relatives of the victims. They stated that the meeting held at the end of March 1992 was illegal and accused the organization of misusing it for political purposes. They also noted the delay of compensation and denied the argument that an individual could represent "the true spirit of 1956", because the revolution was considered a national matter (MH; MN; NSZ 23/03/1992).

In the opening session on 29th, Tibor Zimányi interpreted that the members were not satisfied with the present leadership. András B. Hegedűs considered the meeting illegal and argued that they would create an organization that is independent of the parties and the government. According to Hegedűs, the storm began when "extreme right-wing groups gathering near The *Jurta* Theatre like to tend to a fold" i.e. use the organization for their own purposes. On the other hand, Tibor Zimányi concluded in his answer that the earlier meeting in December had been illegal (MH; NSZ 30/03/1992). Finally, a communique was accepted which defined TIB as "a tradition saver [*hagyomány örző*] and an interest defending organization, and simultaneously an organization with a national, over partial [*összpárt*] character". Moreover, "compensation for victims of the past system was as desirable as the punishment of the criminals." From that point on, TIB had three Vice-Presidents: Tibor Zimányi, József Tittman and Gyula Erdész, and Imre Nagy's daughter Erzsébet Nagy was appointed an honorary chairperson (NSZ 30/03/1992).

However, Erzsébet Nagy also left the organization and her resignation took place during the media demonstrations in the autumn. At that time, she argued that the camp of 1956-ers had broken and extremists were alien to the spirit of 1956 (NSZ 21/09/1992). Moreover, already in the beginning of April, the widow of Pál Maléter, Judit Gyenes, was fired from the Medical Historical Library and Gyenes herself interpreted that there were political implications to her firing (168 óra 07/04/1992). However, in both cases, Tibor Zimányi denied the political arguments, and in Nagy's case interpreted that radio newspaper *168 óra* had only provoked argumentation (MH 15/04/; 25/09/1992).

Both the former police-chief of Budapest and another main figure of 1956, Sándor Kopácsi, resigned from Zimányi's led TIB. Kopácsi did not leave the soldiers' department, which functioned within the TIB and, according to Kopácsi, had the '56 companion of arms and was loyal to the achievements of democracy. Kopácsi commented on Nagy's resignation, which was in part due to health reasons, but also because of political declarations by the extreme right and an increasingly tense atmosphere (MH 30/09/1992). In November, Sándor Kopácsi, Erzsébet Nagy and a few others founded a new organization called *Nagy Imre Társaság* (The Imre Nagy Association) (NSZ 12/11/1992).

Thus, from 1991 onwards, the TIB had lost visible members and the radicalisation tendency was also visible in the organization. The debate concerned the past in the present: What should the role of the TIB be in the new Hungarian democracy, and what should be the relation of the organization to the present political government? What kind of legitimization in present political matters should be given to veterans on the basis of a certain past political experience? Moreover, the question started to reach the more principal question of the significance of 1956 in general: *whose* revolution was it and who has the right to speak in the name of '1956'. In 1993, for example, Tibor Zimányi concluded that the TIB was no longer a Politburo or representative of an (former communist, HN) elite, but that it was an organization for the people and those who fought on the streets (MN 11/01/1993).

*Pofosz*, the Association of Political Prisoners, is the second of the essential interest groups, which dealt with 1956 and presented current political demands. In February of 1991, Pofosz had the opinion that the real system change had yet to take place. According to Jenő Fónay, the sentences were not revoked, compensation had not yet been paid and serial killers went free. In April of 1991, Fónay connected the TIB to the Free Democrats and promised that "after 30th June we will rule", i.e. after Soviet troops have left Hungary (MH 16/04/1991; 168 óra 23/04/1991). After the parliamentary vote on 4th November, 1991, Mária Wittner and Jenő Fónay sent a letter to members of the MSZP and FIDESZ, who had opposed the Zétényi-Takács bill. In the summer of 1992, Fónay was even chosen also as one of the three Vice-Presidents of the *Magyarok Világszövetsége* (The Hungarian World Association) led by the writer Sándor Csoóri (MN; NSZ 22/08/1992). Fónay supported punishments, demanded the opening of the archives of the secret police and criticized the delay in the distribution of compensation and finally criticized entire system change (MH 07/12/1992).

There were also other organizations: In June of 1991, the old resistance organization, The Association of Hungarian Resistance and Anti-fascists (*Magyar Ellenállók és Antifasiszták Szövetsége*, MEAFSZ) was split – or more precisely, a rival organization, MESZ, came into being without the criterion of antifascists (NSZ 12/06/1991). The old association had included members who had participated in the armed vigilante squads in 1956 and who had been taken into the organization in 1957. Iván Vitányi (MSZP) chose a double membership, explaining that some 250-300 were welcomed as members of the MEAFSZ, because they had been rewarded by the medal "pro workers-peasant power" after 1956 (NSZ 22/06/1991). A year later the successor, The Association of Hungarian Resistance (*Magyar Ellenállók Szövetsége*, MESZ), which was also led by Tibor Zimányi, received one million forints from the government. The amount was taken from the old association by reducing its budget to zero. The decision was defended by the view that the old organization had served the old system until its end (NSZ 11/05/1992).

On 6th October, 1990, The Association of 1956 ('*56-os Szövetség*) held its first congress. During the election campaign the association had made a statement in which it did not recognize the elections, because the most important decisions had been made behind closed doors (MN 03/04/1990). In the autumn of 1990, the association declared that it would function in the spirit of 1848-1956 and collected nationally minded (*nemzetben gondolkodókat*) members in the organization. Of the five leading fellows, three had been first sentenced to death and then imprisoned, "spending 54 years in the prisons of Muscovites" (MN 08/10/1990). The organization later changed its name to *1956-os Magyarok Világszövetsége* (The 1956 Hungarian World Organization), the goal of which was to bring the ideas of 1956 into peaceful victory (MH; NSZ 21/10/1991). In 1992, after the release of Csurka's pamphlet, the '56 Association declared its support of Csurka (NSZ 08/09/1992).

The association was led by a former freedom fighter at the *Corvin* film theatre, Gergely Pongrátz, who in 1991 had returned to Hungary after emigration to the United States (cf. MN 28/10/1993). One of the goals of the association was to provide a house for veterans, considered the second "Corvin" (MH 04/03/1993). The real estate, an old barrack used by the Soviets, was restored in 1993 with the help of a particular association for freedom fighters, led by the Minister, Péter Boross. Above the outer door was the text "Everything for the Fatherland", and veterans were ready to move into the estate in July (NSZ 17/04/1993). Moreover, in October of 1993, Pongrátz had a 'plan' to organize a World Congress, in which the priest László Tőkés would bless the flag which would be laid beside The Holy Right of the First King Stephen in Saint Stephen's Church (NSZ 14-16/10/; MN 28/10/1993).

On the whole, these organizations were the most essential interest groups of the contemporaries dealing with 1956 in the system change. They were, however, not the only ones, and in autumn of 1995 a weekly magazine, HVG, listed nineteen organizations and four parties, which had something to do with 1956 (HVG 21/10/1995). The majority of the (small) organizations had emerged in Hungarian politics between 1990 and 1992. The organizations mainly tried to organize themselves as interest groups and tended to be concerned with compensation.

However, it looks as if these organizations were not always able to distinguish '56 from daily governmental politics – rather, they attempted to outline the entire system of Hungarian politics on the national level. In addition, either party politicians or emigrants led the organizations and, therefore, they slowly began to either defend or oppose the present government. Thirdly, there are also signs that the current government attempted to "own" the matter of the veterans. In June, József Torgyán argued in a press conference that the Smallholders' Party represents 1956 and political prisoners in the parliament, and how he as a lawyer had defended those prosecuted after 1956 (MH; MN 07/06/1991). Moreover, prior to the elections of 1994, Prime Minister Péter Boross reminded these organizations of which party to vote for (MN 12/03/1994) and the *Recsk*, political prisoners before 1956, promised to support the MDF (MH 14/02/1994). According to Boross, the government had tried to punish the killers and traitors from the beginning, and if it did not happen today then it would happen tomorrow, and if not tomorrow then the day after tomorrow. Boross drew that conclusion back in 1989, because at that time too many compromises had to be made in order to avoid "waking up the sleeping lion" (NSZ 23/08/1993).

# The Media War

In 1956, Hungarian Radio and its programme policy had been the focus on 23rd October, and in post-communism the electronic media also became one of the centres of political struggle. Already in November of 1990, The Association of '56 criticized that the system change has not taken place in Hungarian television and demanded the resignation of TV-leaders. The state television was criticized for practising censorship and especially because it had not focused on the associations' "international congress" in the media (NSZ 07/11/1990). From the ranks of the government, István Csurka and Imre Kónya had also criticized the media (NSZ 09/07/; MH 10/10/1990) Csurka continued to do so, accusing the radio of not serving the interests of the MDF or SZDSZ, but some third party (NSZ 07/02/1991).

Moreover, *Sajtószabadság Klubja* (The Free Press Club), which in the autumn of 1991 emerged within the Hungarian Journalists' Association (MUOSZ), complained that radio, television and some newspapers had not paid enough attention to the 35th anniversary of the 1956 revolution and fight for freedom. Csaba Gombár was mentioned specifically, because he had denied to put the plaque of Otto Szirmai, an executed martyr of the Free Hungarian Radio in 1956, on the wall of the radio building (NSZ 26/10/1991). István Csurka also argued that radio and television had sabotaged the memory of the revolution and fight for freedom and that reform Communists are ruling in the newspapers (NSZ 30/10/1991).[59]

Similar phenomena also took place towards the year of polarization and in the midst of the punishment debate. On the 16th of November, 1991, Imre Kónya (MDF) and Iván Pető (SZDSZ) participated in a television programme in which they debated the question. An audience was present in the studio, too, and there was an atmosphere of partiality and the sense that the reporter also supported Kónyas views. On the basis of the mixed reception, it was decided that the programme was to be re-broadcast in November. In the beginning of December, *Népszabadság*, whose position was critical to the government, published a opinion poll of *Median* made by the order of *168 óra*: the studio audience had supported Kónya (66%), although the television viewers had favoured Pető (55%) (NSZ 03/12/1991).

On the 15th of March, 1992, the Mayor of Budapest, Gábor Demszky, felt "cold winds blowing" and according to him, television was also in danger. Elsewhere, the leader of Pofosz, Jenő Fónay, pointed out that the Hungarian media showed ways of living that were "alien to the nation". "Jewish papers" and anti-Semitism were also included in the argumentation, and the rival journalist organization, MUK, came into being on that day (NSZ 16/03/1992).

In one of its headlines, *Magyar Hírlap* reported on "The Feeling of Lynching in Front of the Television" (MH 16/03/1992).

In October of 1991, Christian Democrats had demanded the resignation of Hankiss, and the MDF had demanded the resignations of both Hankiss and Gombár in February of 1992. In May and June, both Gombár and Hankiss were heard in front of the Cultural Committee of Parliament. By a majority vote of governing parties the removal for both of them was demanded. In the case of Gombár, Prime Minister Antall demanded that his position be filled by the Vice-President (NSZ 09/05/1992). President Göncz refused and received support from IPI (NSZ 21/05/1992).

In other words, the demands in the government began to be parallel to the aims of the more radical outer-parliamentary organizations. At this phase, people involved in politics began to understand and sympathise with either one or the other old 1956-er. In 1992, the struggle over the media, also known as the "media war", culminated between the Prime Minister and the President of the Republic. On the one hand, Imre Kónya accused the President of violating the constitution, while *Magyar Hírlap* and *Népszabadság* published a political advertisement, which was signed by 26 public persons, who condemned the political pursuit and concluded that Árpád Göncz and demo-cracy in Hungary are synonymous (MH; NSZ 25/05/1992). Moreover, the MDF concluded that they did not consider Göncz as a president above the parties (NSZ 07/07/1992). The '56 Association also complained about the decision, which, according to the association, was reminiscent of the period of dictatorship and openly bound the president to the politics of the opposi-tion (MH 03/07/1992). Thus, towards the autumn of 1992, the political situation in Hungary had polarized in the sense that the '56 Association might threaten other demonstrations unless the radio and television leadership were removed.

First, a small '56 anti-fascist and -bolshevist group had demonstrated in front of the radio station (MH 15/08/1992), after which Pofosz and The '56 Association organized a demonstration (MH 25/08/1992). The demonstrators in front of the radio station demanded that their declaration be read in the Kossuth news at eight o'clock – as a direct parallel to 23rd October, 1956. Moreover, Gergely Pongrátz declared "that which we did not achieve with weapons, we can achieve with a broom" which implied the removal of servants of alien (*idegen*) interests and liberal "bolshevist mafia" in the press. *Magyar Hírlap* also recognized three members of the leading government party in the demonstration (Ibid.).

On 19th September of 1992, *A Szabad Magyar Tájékoztatásért Bizottság* (The Committee for Free Hungarian Information) organized a demonstration against the media leaders. According to István Csurka, the entire system change would collapse, if there were no free media. Someone accusingly stated that it was because of the media that Hungarians lack national consciousness; the resignation of President Göncz was demanded; rock musician Feró Nagy sang a few songs and national anthem *Himnusz* was sung (NSZ 21/09/1992). Once again, historical events were used, because in the demonstration a declaration entitled "What Do the Hungarian People Want?" was read (MH 21/09/1992). Among the 26 organizations that supported the demonstration were *'56 Világszövetsége* ('56 World Association), *'56 Antifasiszták és Antibolsevisták* ('56 Antifascists and Antibolshevists), *'56 Szövetség* (The '56 Association), *Nemzetőr szövetség* (The National Guard Association), *Fehér Megyei Munkástanács* (The Worker's Council of Fehér Department) and *MDF '56 köre* (The '56 Circle of the MDF). According to newspapers, between 10,000 and 15,000 participated in the demonstration (MH; NSZ 21/09/1992).

The situation was absurd: as a party the MDF had dissociated itself from the demonstration (NSZ 16/09/1992), yet members of the party were present at the demonstration and Csurka was one of the main organizers (NSZ 21/09/1992). According to *Népszabadság*, Antall advised his party that it would not change leaders when the opposition would demand it (NSZ 03/09/1992), thus, he might have had the communist "salami tactics" after the Second World War on his mind.

Political purity and 'we' in the electronic media were, however, complicated to explain. On the one hand, it was reminded that Csurka was surrounded by many Communists, and even Csurka himself was twice rewarded by József Attila Prize (NSZ 15/09/1992). On the other hand, as early as1990, some journalists did not want to work with the journalist József G. Pálffy, because he was considered to be too close to the MDF (MN 29/08/1990). Moreover, TV-leader Elemér Hankiss had claimed that no other communists remained in the leadership except Lajos Chrudinák and Pálffy, who were supported by the demonstrators (MH 15/09/1992). Csurka replied that although there were allies who had been in the party, their "work of today and yesterday" had certified their place among us (MH 21/09/1992).

However, the point here is that all three of these men, i.e. both sides of the debate (Hankiss, Chrudinák and Pálffy) found '1956' to be one of the points with which to defend their present positions. Hankiss pointed out that the 1956-ers were demonstrating for those who had previously been on the other side; Hankiss reminded of his own imprisonment after 1956, too (MH 15/09/1992). On the other hand, Pálffy found his party career quite limited and stressed how they had criticized him for being nationalist and *narodnic* at that time (MH 16/09/1992). Chrudinák wrote how he was imprisoned in 1957 and deported from the university on the basis of representing Imre

Nagy's ideology, after which time he was finally brought to the television station in 1972 (MH 18/09/1992).

On the day of the demonstration, Iván Vitányi – also a participant in 1956 – presented a challenge: he who is against fascism is not a Bolshevik agent – as the leader of Pofosz had argued (NSZ 15/09/1992), although the question is about general defense of democracy. Thus, The Democratic Charter organized a counter-demonstration and their supporters argued that their demonstration was not a demonstration of the opposition but a referendum of Csurka's Hungary (MH 23/09/1992). Of the parties, MSZP and SZDSZ listed themselves as supporters of the demonstration (NSZ 23/09/1992). According to political scientist Attila Ágh (MSZP), a grey civil war had begun (MH 18/09/1992).

According to Népszabadság, several tens of thousands of people had gathered at the statue of Petőfi and marched to parliament (NSZ 25/09/1992). Imre Mécs (SZDSZ) demanded that the government dissociate itself from the extremists, and Vitányi argued that democracy belongs to everyone. The Hungarian national anthem was sung, but the gathering was cut short by a bomb threat (MH 25/09/1992). On the same day, Hungary was discussed in the House of Representatives in Washington, D.C, in which the Csurka-essay was translated for the members of Congress. According to István Balázs (MDF), who was present at the Congressional session, the events in Hungary were partly theatrical and partly a struggle for the next elections (NSZ 25/09/1992). No doubt, politics had the dimension of a spectacle – even the world forgatókönyv (script) is common in Hungarian politics. But the play had begun to turn to tragicomic. The public role of different actors had slowly but surely confused the audience about the style and name of the play.

The incident at Kossuth Square on 23rd October of 1992, when skinheads shouted President Göncz down, could also be connected to the "media war". The question was about the role of the skinheads and their activity in a political situation, in which the government was not on good terms with the President. However, the debate primarily concerned whether the information of the event corresponded with "the reality" or was manipulated and, thus, whether a "fascist danger" had been "exaggerated".

After the incident, the opposition and critical intellectuals ran wild: The Democratic Charter took out a full-page political advertisement, which included two pictures. The upper presented Buda Castle during the Szálasi Arrow Cross regime on 20th October, 1944, and the second referred to Kossuth Square on 23rd October, 1992. The text asked "Once Again? No." (MH; NSZ 28/10/1992). Furthermore, on the previous day Magyar Hírlap had published a caricature, in which an old woman asked two men whether they were celebrating the 15th or 23rd October; one had a flag with a hole in the middle in his hands and the other was drawn with an Arrow Cross ribbon on his arm (MH 27/10/1992). The title of the caricature was: "The Regrettable Events of October", which directly referred to first interpretations of 1956 made by the Kádár regime.

Moreover, the incident was filmed and it became one of the elementary documentaries over the course of the media war. Since 1993, the journalistic organization MUOSZ argued about purges in the radio and television (MH 14/01/1993). In October of 1993, Vice-President Gábor Nahlik suspended reporter András Bánó from his office, i.e. announcing the show *Egyenleg* (Balance). According to Nahlik, the reason for the suspension had to do with Kossuth Square in 1992, on the basis of an investigation conducted by Sony. Sony had made a conclusion that the tape had been cut later, and thus 'manipulated'. However, political doubts were laid on Bánó's successor, who had previously been fired from the TV station and belonged to the council of the new journalist association, MUK (MH; NSZ 27/10/1993). On the following day, *Egyenleg* was suspended and ten more journalists had to leave on the grounds of "working problems" (NSZ 28/; 30/10/1993).

Once again, the television and Kossuth Square were the arenas of political demonstration. The Democratic Charter had asked people to come to a "demonstration for freedom of the press" and slogans like "once again the media has become a weapon of the government" were used. Another incident concerned a radio cabaret, which was "censored" a few days later, i.e. not broadcast again. Listeners had complained that Imre Nagy was made to look ridiculous in a satire, which pleaded for the return of communism (NSZ 11/11/1993). Right after TeleMedia asked 2,000 people, if they agreed with the discipline against the cabaret and the reporters: 83% disagreed and 8% agreed (MH 12/11/1993).

According to Gábor Nahlik, a media war did not exist (MN 13/11/1993). However, in March of 1994, IPI's former director, Péter Galliner, wrote in the *Times* that the media war had already begun two years earlier when an attempt was made to remove non-communists. Galliner also used an analogy to 1956, noting that everyone should be anxious, because they were reminded of the suppression which followed after 1956 (NSZ 18/03/1994). Lurking in the background was the "Black Friday" in the Hungarian radio, which referred to the removal of 129 journalists (NSZ 05/03/1994) – illegally, as the court pronounced in its sentence (MN 23/04/1994).

*Le Monde* wrote of a new step toward the total control of the media, and that the removals had crossed the Rubicon (NSZ 07/03/1994). The opposition highlighted everything from the scandal and, for example, SZDSZ made a statement that there is no example of this kind of political purges since the revolution (1956) (MH 05/03/1994). Iván Pető argued that once again people were removed in such great numbers that no similar examples existed since the 1956 revolution. Elsewhere, Béla Csépe (KDNP) considered the comparison unworthy, because, according to him, it hurt the memory of the martyrs (MN; NSZ 08/03/1994). Moreover, among the ranks of the government, there was great difficulty to condemn the events. For example, the leader of the MDF, Sándor Lezsák, spoke only of respecting the independence of the electronic media (MH 07/03/1994).

The hands belonged to Esau but the voice to Jacob, i.e. the removals were carried out merely two months before the general elections. In *Magyar Hírlap's* caricature, an owl with the face of Prime Minister Péter Boross peeped from the window and asked if you (the reader) were searching for Radio Free Europe on the radio again (MH 08/03/1994). A few days later the statue of Petőfi and lantern of Batthyány were once again the sites of a demonstration by the Democratic Charter (MH; NSZ 16/03/1994).

## 1956 in Television and Film after 1989

Since 1989, '1956' has not only emerged in the present in political argumentation, in the repetition of an historical spectacle in the media and on anniversaries, but also through the mediation of television and film. The state owned television programme policy mostly worked on two levels: On the one hand, there were actual commemorative programmes and on the other hand, there were programmes which presented the historical 1956 itself. During the 35th anniversary, The Free Press Club had complained that the electronic media had neglected the commemoration. Thus, it was announced that the following year, television would begin to be broadcast live as of 23rd October (MH 20/10/1992).

During the 35th anniversary, every evening a fifteen-minute-programme, *Ez történt akkor* (Happened At That Time), was televised. The television programme repeated old documentary films from each day 35 years earlier until 4th November. However, the proper turn began in the era of Vice-President Gábor Nahlik in 1993. Thus, from September to November a new six-part series, *56 perc 56-ról* (56 Minutes from 1956), was televised (MH 02/09/1993). Secondly, in November, a mammoth-series was broadcast under the title: *Magyar félmúlt – a törvénytelen szocializmus* (The Recent Hungarian Past – Illegal Socialism). Together, the series were comprised of 38 parts (until July 1994), and it already began to be re-run in January of 1994, when the first presentation was still being broadcast. According to *Népszabadság*, the average Hungarian saw 5.4 parts of the series; in the afternoons the programme had 80,000–500,000 viewers and between 400,000 –1,200,000 in the evenings (NSZ 18/05/1994).

The headline *fél* (Half) *múlt* (Past) provided an excellent description of the meaning of recent history; something which on the one hand was temporally already in the past, but which, on the other hand, had yet to be dealt with, debated and written away, turn into history. Also, the term "illegal" was 'provocative', because it was left ambiguous whether the entire system was illegal or whether it simply referred to the illegal activity occurring within that system. However, the series did not spawn any great debate in the newspapers, although the cameraman, László B. Révész, had already dissociated himself from the introduction trailer in November. In the trailer, a clip of pictures from the Workers' Guard were, for example, followed directly by pictures from Mosonmagyaróvár and by strong symbolic coats of arms and the removal of the communist statues. According to Révész, one of the alternative clips was accepted but then considered "too soft" and revised, but was eventually replaced with another logo that was seen on television (MH 28/01/1994). For Révész, nothing like this had happened during his 28 years in party television, and he viewed the clip as being in bad taste and as falsifying history (Ibid.). Criticism also came from László Varga, who argued that television showed a legend as a reality. Arguments had been presented in the programme that Imre Mező had been shot by his "own men" at Köztársaság tér (MH 03/05/1994).

Because the series ended in July of 1994, it was also seen during the election campaign and during the elections themselves. On 3rd May, the fate of Péter Mansfeld, the boy who had to wait until his 18th birthday before he was hanged, was seen on television. According to the director, Mansfeld became a victim of a show trial and his judge was named in the programme. On the same day, Béla Kurcz wrote in *Magyar Nemzet* about the well-natured Mansfeld, who had only hijacked a policeman in front of the Austrian Embassy and driven him by a car in the edge of town, taken his pistol and a half an hour later let him go (MN 03/05/1994).

Within the scope of this study it is impossible to check the validity of all of the arguments presented in the series or in the press debate concerning the debate. It is sufficient to note the timing of the series. Although it could be a coincidence, the series and, thus the Mansfeld-section, was televised less than a week before the general elections. Moreover, it occurred in a situation in which the Socialist Party, led by Gyula Horn, a participant in 1956, was the predicted winner[60]. Three days prior to the election there was a discussion in *Magyar félmúlt* as to whom the history belongs (MN 05/05/1994).

In conclusion, the main 'problem' was not whether the new TV-leadership also saw '1956' and their work through Lenin's theory of the press. Instead, the result, the series itself, was in some places so weak that it might have turned against the original political purposes, if there were any. On 16th

May, after the first round of elections, *Népszabadság* wrote about plans to take legal action against the programme, because material from a documentary film had been used without permission. The older film was described as having been made from the point of view of a victim, when the criticized programme looked for guilty persons. In addition, the programme was accused of publishing false details, which were in harmonious with articles published in right-wing news magazines (NSZ 16/05/1994). Thus, the quality was substituted with repeated quantity to such an extent that the word propaganda is not far from defining the result.

Proper films were not finished until the end of 1994 and, for example, on the 35th anniversary old documentary films – both Hungarian and non-Hungarian – were shown in cinemas. However, in 1992, Minister of Education and Culture Bertalan Andrásfalvy (MDF) informed journalists about the possibility to support historical documentaries dealing with the "questions of Hungarian misfortunes". The revolution of 1956 was particularly stressed from three points of view: First, there was the 1956 revolution itself, secondly, the path leading to it and thirdly, social continuities produced through the revolution. Among other themes, the Minister introduced the fate of Hungarians living outside the borders and also changes in the quality of life during the last fifty years (MH 27/08/1992).

In February of 1994, *Magyar Történelmi Film Alapítvány* (The Hungarian Historical Film Foundation) was founded. Historian Sándor Szakály stated in a press conference that they would particularly focus on producing historical movies, documentaries, manuscripts and current documents. The foundation received 350 million forints and on the basis of the headline in *Magyar Nemzet* its target was clear: "1956 Documentation is the Aim" (MN 10/02/1994). Until 1996 their efforts were yeat to come: in the1956 kézikönyve (1996) there were three films in the film category: *A gólyák mindig visszatérnek* (Storks Will Always Come Back, 1992), *És mégis* (And Still, 1992) and *Az asszony* (Wife, 1995). On the other hand, there were also a numerous amount of documents (Ibid. 219-236). There were also several series: in 1992 three, 1993 ten, 1994 one, 1995 and in 1996 13 series, all of which dealt with 1956 (1956 kézikönyve (II) 1996, 219-250).

## Reckoning and Polarization

In this chapter we have discussed political and juridical consequences, which '1956' had in post-communism. Radical politicians connected the entire system change to punishments, i.e. there is the question of *when* the system has changed. In the Hungarian historical space of experience, there had existed also show trials, purges and punishments, reprisals and settlements (cf. Társadalmi Szemle 1989). Moreover, there are several examples of political changes in Europe, for example, France between 1944-1945, and of violent confrontations carried out by new rulers against the old and their collaborators.

Thus, particularly during political changes, the question of what should be done to the past still exists and past is a part of present actions. To some extent, people had, however, learned their lesson in Hungary, because even most of the radicals formulated that instead of settling (*leszámolás*), pay-offs (*elszámolás*) should follow. In this sense, the Hungarian system change was "negotiated" and peaceful, if it is compared, for example, to Yugoslavia.

Nevertheless, as in the "media war", there seemed to be signs to 'repeat' a certain space of experience. It seems evident that in 1991, many Hungarians, and the majority of the MPs, were convinced that the communist system, or more precisely representatives of that system, did not punish their 'own' men. However, another question is the political conclusion of this conviction: Whether these problems should be 'forgotten', and 'close' as a specific sign of 'reconciliation', either to be studied or incorporated into a political agenda.

All in all, in addition to representation there have been four ways of dealing with the past in this chapter: compensation, rehabilitation, naming and punishment. When we look this complex phenomenon from the point of view of whom it will reach personally, punishment and naming belong to the categories of 'negative' remembering. Punishment is the strictest of these and its commemorative influence is restrictive and juridical. Naming could also restrict, although in the Hungarian case it was more liberal, because its supporters denied punishment and preferred moral judgement.

The two others, compensation and rehabilitation, are more 'positive', because they recompensate and dismantle earlier actions affecting a person. In the strictest sense of the word, rehabilitation, as punishment, is juridical, although there was also talk in Hungary of political rehabilitation. Finally, compensation usually requires political decisions and implies economic concessions and support as well.

In my argumentation, the first phase of the Hungarian discussion contained rehabilitation, and then from 1991 onwards, the discussion of punishment was the key topic. For example, a few weeks after the rehabilitation of Imre Nagy and his companions, *168 óra* interviewed Ferenc Vida, who had been the judge in Nagy's case and had also condemned many other '56-ers. In the interview, Vida argued that had he not been convinced of the "four reasons" of the party, he would not have judged. According to Vida, consensus had existed about the sentences and they were made on the basis of current law (168 óra 25/07/1989).

Although people could appeal wrong and unjust sentences after decades,

Vida's sentences were not only repealed but nullified *during* the system change. Moreover, the other post-communist examples which we have discussed in this chapter, raise the question of punishment in relation to political power. Although crimes concerning 1956 had taken place in the former political system, they were officially discussed during and after the political system change. However, it is not unique that within a given political system a blind eye is turned to the activities of the supporters of that system. For example, in Finland, the executions carried out by the 'winners' at the end of the civil war in 1918 were not prosecuted afterwards (Kekkonen 1991, 102-103).

However, contrary to the Finnish case, we are discussing juridical-political processes *after* or *during* a system change. Although Hungarian politicians did not particularly follow the ongoing discussion in other post-communist countries, as of the end of 1991 they knew a few details based on what they read in the newspapers. In November of 1991, the Spanish example came up for discussion at a conference which dealt with problems of justice (MH 11/11/1991). In Poland, (martial law of 1981 was declared illegal), and there were thoughts of bringing the Polish leadership before the court. In the autumn of 1992, General Jaruzelski took full responsibility for his actions in front of the Sejm. (NSZ 04/01; 03/02/; 11/02/; MH 14/02/; MN 23/09/1992).

However, punishment was not the only alternative, and it could be said that the previous examples were also the most political – as well as the most emotional – issues during the first years of post-communist Hungary. On the whole, the discussion of punishment evidently cleansed the atmosphere in the long run, but it *also* essentially widened the gulf between the government and the opposition, to those who better understood the views of the government, and to those who identified with the current views of the opposition. The Democratic Charter was not established as an instrument for the forth-coming social-liberal government, as Imre Kónya with a hindsight interpreted it (168 óra 50/1994), but it came into being in 1991, some two months after the renewal of the *Justitia* plan to progress the democratic 'transition'.

Although the atmosphere at that time is difficult to describe, 'everything was connected to everything', the leading government party did not always remember that it was more than a Hungarian forum, and the western idea of law seemed not to be clear enough for everyone. Law VII/1945 had also been retroactive and had declared that political murders which were impossible to punish between 1919 and December 1944 – thus until the provisional government – did not become obsolete (cf. Juhász 1993, 32). Punishment seemed to be extremely essential to the government, which was afraid of losing its "historical opportunity" in the forthcoming elections and, thus, it seems that the proceedings were quite hurried.

However, research is frequently seen as a way of dealing with the past so that "clarifying the past also serves the future". Therefore, in the next chapter we will discuss history writing in post-communism first generally, and then concentrate on its relation to current debates. The aforementioned political situations created the context in which the dimensions of 1956 have been studied and analyzed.

# XI RESEARCH AND THE POLITY

In the previous chapters it has been clarified how the past has been a part of current politics both during the Kádár era and after. On the one hand, we could speak about the political use of the past and on the other hand, we could discuss the impact that the past has on people's minds and their thinking. Furthermore, in the short run there could be direct political effects, purposes and expectations regarding why something should to be studied in the present, why history should be written and by whom.

From the viewpoint of history culture, research also sustains the past in the present, and thus researchers, too, are considered a part of the current political discussion. They have their own specific skills and are able to influence the debate as specialists. In Hungary, research work did not taken place in a 'political vacuum' either, but rather within a specific social and political context – which since 1988 has been in the midst of the change of the entire political system. Hence, in the following chapters the role of the historians, their acting in public and their research work will be focused on in greater detail. Hereafter, the focus will be on studying 1956 during the period of post-communism, as well as its relation to current political debates, which I have described in previous chapters.

In 1994, historian György Litván concluded that as early as the Kádár era it was possible to write reliable works concerning the Horthy period. For example, Miklós Lackó argued in the late 1960s that the base of fascism had been in the working class. In addition, there was a larger amount of freedom within research institutes than in the universities, which were under stricter ideological control. According to Litván, it was impossible to tell the whole truth, in the context of which 1956 and the post-1956 period were the biggest problems, "real taboo themes". During the 1970s and 1980s, however, Hungarian historians possessed international authority unparalleled in the socialist world. (NSZ 16/09/1994; cf. also Fischer 1982).

Litván's words in 1994 have been cited, although until then – and to some extent also after – it was not evident *who* and *whose* history would be adequate specialists in post-communism. It has earlier been argued that until 1989, the history of '1956' had belonged to the history of winners and that politicians have used the issue both prior to and following 1989. However, also historians used recent history in their political argumentation and had demands concerning of the opening of the recent past. Therefore, in Hungary, the research of '1956' has also been connected to the system change.

There is at least one example of "history writing following the fashion", from January of 1994. László Eörsi criticized in *Magyar Hírlap* the historical works of General Mihály Berki, whose latest book had just been published by *Magyar Fórum*, a publishing house close to the Csurka-wing of the MDF: In 1988 there had been the counter-revolutionaries, in 1989 the rebels and now the revolutionaries (MH 06/01/1994). Furthermore, in 1994, Konrád Salamon (MDF) wrote a text-book and argued that it had been impossible for him to do so earlier, because he would have been unable to write that '1956' was a counter-revolution (MH 26/09/1994).

Although the terminology had changed and although these arguments were mostly directed to tantalize political opponents, the question of research work in relation to current political power was still valid. Who should have the opportunity to write the recent history after a political change? Did the 'history of winners' continue after the change, and if so, on what level has it taken place? Does a regime change imply merely the replacement of one version of the 'history of winners' with another? Or does the politics of history (and of historians) achieve a greater independence than the politics of the general polity?

## Power, Political Debates and Research

György Litván outlined the present research problems in a paper presented at the University of Tampere, Finland in March of 1993. According to him, "a general and clear-cut confrontation" existed on three levels: in the 56-organizations, on the political scene and on the level of historical research. First, the general rift in the organizations emerged between the former armed fighters and politicians, between the ex-Communists who supported Imre Nagy and the anti-Communists. Secondly, there was confrontation on the political scene concerning the problems of historical justice and how to face the past in general. On the research level, some veterans and historians accused current historians of the falsification and distortion of the history of 1956. (Litván 1995, 5-12).

According to Litván, the struggle "about and for 56" had suddenly broken down towards the end of 1991, and only minimal communication and comprehension existed between the two fronts. There were two 'reasons' for this, the *political* one belonging entirely to the present and the *historical* one to both the past and the present. Litván also noted the current polarization process of political life, in which "almost everybody is forced to accept a collective view and to confront another". The other factor was more complicated, because the revolution was a result of very different, in some cases even antagonistic forces, which were temporarily united against a common enemy (Ibid.).

There are three implicit topics in Litván's paper, which I will discuss in greater detail. The most common topic has been the role of the "reform Communists" in 1956 (in fact, the question was about the party opposition, revisionists, who were thrown together with communist reformers in the 1980s.). The second debate concerned the question of *who* made the revolution. Particularly in post-communism, several political groups entered the legacy of 1956 – as did a great number of the members of the MSZMP in 1989. The third problem dealt with the question of the aims and character of the revolution: was it socialist or bourgeois-democratic.

The standpoints of all of these questions also had concrete daily-political consequences. The past was seen through present eyes, the past was connected to the present and 'radical' interpretations also legitimated actions done in the present. There, 'we' was rebuilt, and in the radical views there was no room for everyone, on the basis that those who were against 1956 would not have 'anything' to say after 1990. Therefore, not only the naming, i.e. "we cannot negotiate with the successors of the counter-revolutionaries" (cf. Bruszt 1990), became the focus, but also the question of who were the 'legitimate' heirs of 1956 and the 'true' conquerors of stalinist communism.

At the conference in Tampere, Litván denied allegations "mostly rightist elements – not historians" that the ex-Communist group, 'revisionists', were against the revolution. According to Litván, the followers of Imre Nagy "had a decisive role *before* the revolution, in undermining and paralysing the one-party system." However, in October, 1956, the leading role was taken from them first by the radical, patriotic students and then by the young workers in the armed uprising and struggles. Moreover, Litván argued that the reformist intellectuals "played a *mediating* role between Nagy and the fighting groups during the first days of the uprising, and had an important role again after the Soviet invasion..." (Litván 1995, 11).

Thus, secondly there was the question of who created the revolution. As early as 1990, György Litván had lectured at a second meeting of historians under the tittle "Whose 1956". At that time, the dichotomous concepts were politicians and scientists, "reform Communists" and conservatives, students or workers (NSZ 25/08/1990; Litván 1991). Since 1990, the theme "Whose 1956" has frequently been repeated in discussion and has also been connected to the debate on historical justice. For example, in another interview, "Whose Revolution?", Litván distinguished between the historical and moral judgment of 1956 (i.e. made by the historians and by the citizens, HN). Although a few 56-ers demanded a partial writing of history, there was no official interpretation, nor was one even necessarily essential (MH 03/01/1992).

In addition to the question of 'whose 1956', there also emerged a problem of owning and monopolizing the past (NSZ 25/08/1990; 21/10/1993), which already dealt with the third problem i.e. the aims of 1956. In 1957, the ruling party had, for example, declared its representation of the legacy of 1848. Since 1989, a plurality of new parties have come into existence and in founding their identities have distinguished themselves from other parties. Thus, the past was also seen in different ways by different organizations. Until the end of 1992, Ervin Csizmadia might argue that liberal, conservative and populist interpretations existed (NSZ 04/11/1992). Indeed, they did exist in the present and they did utilise the legacy of 1956, but did they also exist in 1956? The problem brings us to the third research question brought up in György Litván's paper, i.e. the character of 1956. According to Litván:

> "...there is a tendency for new assessments. While in the past most of the friends of the Hungarian revolution emphasized its socialistic and democratic features and its enemies pointed out the bourgeois characteristics, nowadays many politicians and even a few historians want to strip the socialist clothing from 56, asserting that it was only due to fear and mimicry: the people rejected every form of socialism, and it was only a question of time that the genuine, conservative or bourgeois character of the revolution would prevail." (Litván 1995, 11.)

First, there is the question of temporal distance. What did the people think at that time and what did they believe within the context of system change? Since 1989, '1956' had not only not been resurrected, but there was also a clear tendency to view the past through present experiences: in 1992, workers' councils had nothing to say and the MSZP was also 'beaten'.

Historians, however, argue that the past should be seen within the framework and from the viewpoint of its own age. If one had supported 'socialist construction' in 1956, did he 'really do so', and if so, did he agree with it in the 1990s? Thus, there is the problem of what individuals 'really' wanted in 1956. Free, open speech was impossible during the Kádár era and since 1989 the whole political context had changed. Although it is difficult to refer to the "will of the nation" etc., in 1956 there were the students, who represented a certain collective in the demonstration and were later supported by the workers. The most essential was the current polarization of 'us' and 'them': the category of 'other' comes later. The core was that the rebels did not want the present existing Stalinist model of state socialism and the presence of Soviet troops.

According to György Litván, "...revolution was the work of very different, in some cases even antagonistic forces which were united only temporarily by the common enemy, the Stalinist party and police apparatus." Litván himself identified four political trends: the most significant, "at least at the beginning", was the concept of reformed socialism represented by Imre Nagy and his followers, but also by a great number of students, intellectuals and workers. Furthermore, there was the national-democratic wing, which István Bibó claimed, was represented by the leaders of the Peasant Party and other politicians from the 1945-1948 era. The third direction appeared more in the streets and is referred to as the Christian-Conservative wing. This wing preferred private ownership and property and was symbolized by Cardinal József Mindszenty and followed by many old bourgeois elements and many insurgents. They were suspicious about the government but accepted it temporally. Finally, an extreme right-wing political trend began to emerge on the streets. It was the most intolerant of the groups, and wanted to drive out all other convictions, especially those of communists and socialists (Litván 1995).

Twelve days were not enough to bring these differences to the fore, although they did exist – at least in rudimentary form – and were manifested during the last days. Later, all these wings had representatives during the imprisonment, in emigration and even some who were still present in the 1990s (Ibid.). However, only a *few people* have noticed this fact until now, according to Litván, because in

"...front of the Communist slandering campaign, national and democratic solidarity suppressed the memory of the rightist excesses. In the Western press and historical literature the role and the information of the exiled leftist intellectuals were rather dominant. The rightist ones kept silence cautiously and prudently. Now they can afford speaking again." (Ibid., 10.)

A critical reading of history books during the Kádár era would have produced the same result, but it seems that it took a former opposition activist to say it out loud (the different 'wings' were also specified in the report of the Pozsgay Committee in 1989). Thus, the problem was not with the past itself, but with historians and their audiences in a specific present. Not everybody was ready to accept the contradictions and uncertainty of 1956, but rather found an ideological argument in opposing existing the communist power. "The most beautiful revolution in the world" also included the Köztársaság tér.

When the character of 1956 in Hungary is in the focus, there is also the more or less speculative question of 'what would had happened if' – if the Soviet troops had not have intervened for the second time. We cannot give 'a final answer' *de facto*, because it did not happen and because one different move might have also changed the game as well as the entire space. Although different plans could be found, it is not definite that the outcome would have been the same as planned – the other players in the game might also think differently. Therefore, two possible consequences will be separated in the history of possibilities: possible consequences which were known at the moment of decision making and those which will only be known later.

These possible histories open an interesting perspective in political science, because they construct and legitimate political views and actions. One might speculate on 'what would have happened if the Kennedys had not been shot' or, for example, consider Richard Nixon, who expressed in his memoirs that if he had not been forced to resign, North Vietnam would have not attacked the South (Nixon 1978). In Hungary, in discussions with György Aczél, Kádár had often pondered what the extent of the bloody reprisals would have been had he not done what he did (NSZ 28/01/1993).

During the Kádár regime, party historians tried to 'prove' that the restoration *would have continued* and that Imre Nagy and his followers were superseded de facto during the second week of the counter-revolution. On the other hand, a right-wing emigrant, Emil Csonka, had parallel views in 1981: The true change *had only followed after* the elections. From the perspective of possible histories there was too little time to formulate concrete programs. The alternatives of "finlandisation" or the Austrian pattern (Kende 1996, 169) are possible views, although Hungary did not have the same democratic, protestantic traditions as Finland already before the Second World War – if it has something to do with 'economic miracles'.

However, it seems clear that until 4th November, the Hungarian economic structure remained "socialist". Although there were signs of the unraveling and reorganization of economics, "the bourgeois characteristics" of '1956' were mainly based on the historically imaginative idea of 'what would have happened if'. Embittered people were taught to fight, they had weapons and, for example, Mindszenty had promised the return of "restricted private property". It could be doubted, whether the possible question of retribution and reorganization of the economy would have gone. Would it have gone as peacefully as it had after 1989?

Thus, on the basis of the current documents, we can only imagine how the entire picture of Cold War Europe would have changed, if one piece had redefined the game. However, while Cold War Europe ended in 1990, the 'ideologisation' of the past did not cease. In addition, it was not merely the recent past that was seen from a new political present and perspective. Since 1989 there has also been a similar tendency to 'continue' from 1956 as if nothing had happened. The withdrawal of Soviet troops in June of 1991 was often understood as a reincarnation of the possible history after 4th November, 1956. The idea was expressed, for example, by the Prime Minister Antall: if Soviet troops had not intervened for the second time, until January, we would have experienced the same conflicts, which currently signify public life (NSZ 02/05/1992).

Although the past itself cannot return, nor can history repeat itself, there were still people who attempted to repeat history and use the past in political argumentation. Indeed, following the communist reformers of 1989, Imre Nagy was 'walked' towards 1992 (cf. also Rainer 1993), after which came Horthy as an object of reincarnation. Astonishingly, other persons also emerged who recognized themselves as *hungarists* (NSZ 29/01/1994), arguing that Ferenc Szálasi had been the last legal leader of Hungary (NSZ 28/04/1994). Moreover, since 1989 only a few politicians have wanted to make a clear cut with the past and have longed for a 'Golden Era'.

In the middle of a debate concerning the extreme right, Péter Kende (1992) posed the question: "Back – But to What Kind of Traditions?" in his article. In this sense, a few researchers of 1956 also became defenders of the past, although of the 1956 past in relation to the 'other pasts' (cf. Kende 1992; Litván 1995). These debates took place in part on a personal level (MN 09/07/1993) and in part, according to the participants, did not do any good for the "legacy of 1956" (MN 21/10/1993).

However, György Litván, the academician, is not entirely 'impartial' in these debates either. Similarly to Péter Kende and András B. Hegedűs, Litván had been a member of the old Hungarian Working Peoples' Party until 1956. Moreover, they had belonged to the party-opposition surrounding Imre Nagy and had been sentenced to prison (except Kende, who emigrated) after 1956. Of course, this does not mean that they should be remembered only for this, but their backgrounds also evidently influenced *expectations* concerning them both before and after 1989 in Hungary.

Furthermore, Litván and Hegedűs had participated in the activity of the Democratic Opposition and in the elections held in spring of 1990 Litván ran as a candidate for the SZDSZ in the national list (MN 02/03/1990). However, in this case, both men also led the most important research institute, The Institute for the History of the 1956 Hungarian Revolution. More important than to reveal party memberships is, however, to notice that the Institute functions in the Hungarian Academy of Sciences.

# Institutes and Researchers

In May of 1989, historian László Varga suggested that an institute be founded, the function of which would be to conduct research on the past 45 years. A national institute, which would be independent from parties, was considered necessary in order to avoid the problem of national history becoming a battle-field of party politics. The naming of the institute made a splash in current political discussion: Varga's original idea was that the institute's name was to have been the Imre Nagy Institute. However, over the course of the summer of 1989 the name was abandoned, and it was announced in September that an "Historical Documentation and Research Institute of the 1956 Revolution" was under construction. Thus, not only did the ongoing political changes on the national level encourage research work, but also the research itself partly constructed expectations of these changes.

Thus, the most important organization in the attempt to solve research problems has been The Institute for the History of the 1956 Hungarian Revolution. According to a leaflet (1996), the Institute *"considers itself primarily the successor of the Imre Nagy Institute of Sociology and Politics, which operated in Brussels between 1959 and 1963, and of other western emigrant organizations and writers that maintained the inheritance of the Hungarian Revolution for more than three decades"* (The Institute... 1996, 2). The Institute's 'predecessor' in Brussels had concentrated on leftist and socialist movements and tried to open possibilities for the principles of humanist and democratic socialism (Borbándi 1989, 456; Litván 1992, 7).

According to a leaflet (1996), the preparatory committee and temporary international board of trustees were formed in 1989, the day after the reburial of Imre Nagy and his fellow martyrs. Prior to the first elections on 1st March, 1990, the institute and its foundations were registered, and on 16th March, on the initiative of Domokos Kosáry, the Hungarian Academy of Sciences formed the Academic Documentation and Research Group for the History of the 1956 Hungarian Revolution. Until 1995 the Institute worked as a social organization, after which time it was given the official status of a public foundation by the government of Hungary. (The Institute... 1996, 2). For example, in 1991, 3,5 million forint of the budget was coming from the Hungarian Academy of Sciences (MTA) and 500,000 forint from the Ministry of Education and Culture (MH 25/04/1991).

In 1996, the board of trustees included several ex-56-ers and other prominent influential Hungarians. The political scientist Péter Kende held the chair, and among the 15 trustees were members of the Hungarian Academy of Sciences such as Rudolf Andorka, Domokos Kosáry and György Szabad. Furthermore, there were historians and sociologists who had become Members of Parliament after 1989: Iván Vitányi (MSZP), Miklós Vásárhelyi (SZDSZ), Miklós Szabó (SZDSZ), György Szabad (MDF). In other words, the allegation that in the 1990s the Institute represented "reform Communists" was quite an exaggeration. However, the majority of those in positions of authority belonged to the generation which had personally experienced or participated in 1956. In this sense, they also had their own memories and space of experience connected to 1956.

In the 1950s, some of those individuals had been members of the ruling party, while, for example, some others had been re-settled. After 1956, a few also had experiences of being imprisoned (Litván, Hegedűs, Vásárhelyi, Andorka, Kosáry), and Kosáry, who, for example, had led the Revolutionary Committee of Historians, was set free in 1960. In general, many of these people had difficulties in the 1950s and 1960s, but since the late 1960s they had been able to participate in intellectual activity and had also achieved success in the Kádárian society. The activity concentrated mainly on the human and social sciences: in 1970, Szabad became a professor in ELTE, and Andorka followed in 1984. Kosáry worked in the Academy of Sciences from 1968-1989, as had Litván since 1971 and Vásárhelyi 1972. Since 1982, Hegedűs, economist and sociologist, had been a researcher at the main university of Budapest, the Karl Marx University of Economics.

In addition, the majority of the trustees possessed another essential experience, which dealt with the system change. Historian János M. Rainer, for example, had researched the amount of executions after 1956 by comparing census lists of the different Budapest districts. Prior to 1989, he had also published a book under a pseudonym "Fényes Elek" (MH 30/11/1992). Moreover, the system change offered intellectuals both in- and outside the ruling MSZMP a 'once in a lifetime' chance. When new organizations began to emerge, historians joined them in addition to other intellectuals. There were several historians in the leading parties, such as Miklós Vásárhelyi and Iván Pető in the Free Democrats and József Antall and György Szabad in the MDF etc.

As of the end of 1997, the institute has published ca. 50 books. Among them are seven books dealing with the debates of the Petőfi Circle in 1956, which were published until 1994. In addition, there are five yearbooks, several handbooks, memoirs, two volumes of material from international conferences and books dealing with events in the countryside and outside Budapest. Several biographies were also published: Mindszenty and Pallavicini (1994), Pál Maléter and István Bibó (1995 and 1996) and Imre Nagy (1996). The roles of writers, police and the parties have been researched, as have the history of the Miskolc Student Parliament and emigrant student movements.

In 1992, the institute published the minutes of the lectures and discussions in the first underground conference near the 30th anniversary in 1986. Four years later, the discussions held at the Budapest University in late 1988 were edited as well. Near the 40th anniversary in 1996, works were produced which concerned on international politics (Csaba Békés), decisions in the Kremlin (Vjacseszlav Szereda and János M. Rainer) and the Polish documents concerning the revolution (János Tischler). Moreover, among the first publications was a textbook published in 1991, the expanded version of which was translated first into German (1994) and then into English (1996) (Évkönyv V. 1996/1997, 393-399). In autumn of 1991, the institute solicited people to write autobiographies dealing with 1956. In 1993, 11 of some 200 texts were selected (MN 18/06/1993).

An Oral Historical Archive was also established at the Institute of 1956. It was founded in 1985 on the basis of a conception that the "second liners" of history also be interviewed. At that time, these people were enduring both economic problems and problems which were related to the actual political atmosphere, i.e. they did not want or dare to speak. In 1993, András B. Hegedűs s argued that they were not looking for heroes, but that those inter-viewed could speak without fear. According to Hegedűs, the researchers were more interested in how the apparatus worked than who informed against whom. Despite the fact that the archive held a real political significance, according to Hegedűs, there had not been any major attacks. The majority of the surviving witnesses are still sitting at home (MN 09/07/1993; The Insti-tute... 1996, 9-10).

In assessing the results of the new research work, György Litván, for example, said that especially outside Budapest, the picture focused as opposed to changed (NSZ 06/09/1991). Until then, the former Soviet archives had not yet been opened, and in the beginning of 1992 Litván spoke about "the first swallow of the spring". At that time, Novoje Vremja 49/1991 had estimated the number of deaths as higher than Hungarians had ever done before: 4,000 as opposed to the earlier estimate of 2,700 (MH 31/01/1992). Moreover, in the autumn of 1992, President Boris Yeltsin visited Hungary and brought with him as a gift documents dealing with the Soviet decisions concerning 1956. Earlier, Russia's new leader had given written documents to the Poles, among which was information on the decision regarding the shooting at Katyn on 5th March, 1940. In Hungary, Yeltsin apologized to Hungarians for 1956 and also visited the Section 301. (NSZ 15/10/; NSZ; MN 12/11/1992). Moreover, in September of 1993, Yeltsin also gave the so-called "Suslov File", which Foreign Minister Géza Jeszenszky had requested the previous December (MN 18/09/1993).

The so-called "Yeltsin File" contains 62 Russian documents, which are currently preserved at the National Széchenyi Library and were published as book in 1993. According to György Litván, the file was a selection from the Presidential Archives and from the Russian Ministry of Foreign Affairs. Evidently, the collection was put together in Moscow during a short time as a gesture of friendliness toward Hungarians. According to the preface by President Árpád Göncz, the material did not bring any sensational news, although it did make the existing picture more credible (A "Jelcin-dosszié" 1993, 11-14).

For example, the documents confirmed that seven death sentences (Nagy, Losonczy, Donáth, Gimes, Maléter, Szilágyi, Király) were prepared as early as September of 1957 (NSZ 19/11/1992), and that the Hungarian Politburo had accepted the plan for the later trial of Nagy (NSZ 08/01/1993). Moreover, it confirmed that Gerő had requested the troops for the first invasion, but that the Soviets had initiated the second invasion. Kádár and Münnich were taken to Moscow by an airplane on the morning of 2nd November, while Rákosi, Gerő, Hegedűs and Révai had already traveled on 28th October (MH 29/01/1993; NSZ 28/01/1993).

Although a special ad hoc institute was founded in order to research a specific event, it did not have a monopoly in research work. At the same time as the 1956 Institute edited the "Yeltsin File", "missing papers" from 1956 were published by the Mora publishing company, a case which, for example, György Litván was unaware (MH 28/01/1993). Moreover, TIB had demanded as early as January of 1991 that the archives be opened during the audience with the Ministry of the Interior, Péter Boross. It became clear in the discussion that some 200 researchers had already requested permission to view the documents (MN 24/01/1991). However, the Ministry of the Interior feared that someone might destroy the documents concerning the Kádár era. Therefore, Boross promised that only researchers recommended by the Hungarian Academy of Sciences would receive permission in the near future (Ibid.).

In December of 1992, the material, which until then had been in the possession of the Socialist Party, was declared state property. In January of 1993, they sealed the material in the former Institute of Party History – an act which came too late, i.e almost three years after the free elections. According to historian Laszló Karsai, it was impossible to study earlier, but now it was equally as difficult, because any official in the Ministry could prevent it (MH 11/01/1992). In May of 1994, András B. Hegedűs also relayed his own experiences and had the view that the Ministry of the Interior was once again hiding documents. For example, in his own case, the trial of Ferenc Mérei, which he had reviewed several times over the last three years, was once again declared top secret (MN 26/05/1994).

However, the minutes which dealt with the 1956 provisional Central Committee of the new Hungarian Socialist Party were published in four volumes. The work was begun in 1991 by the former Institute of Party History, now operating under the name the Institute of Political History. Historian Sándor Balogh signed the foreword of the first volume on 11th March, 1993. Three out of the four books were published in 1993 and the fourth came out in 1994 (a fifth volume eventually came out in 1998). The first volume began from the session on 11th November, 1956 and the fourth ended on 24th June, 1957. According to the researchers, the minutes of every session were present with the exception of those from 7th November, 1956 (A Magyar Szocialista... 1993 I, 7). When, for example, *Népszabadság* reported about the books, it put in its headline the detail that people surrounding György Aczél had tried in vain to reach a compromise and considered the events as a democratic mass-movement (NSZ 24/03/1993).

Thus, the aforementioned documents concerned events which took place more than 35 years ago, yet continued to have actual significance in daily politics. However, up until the end of 1993, documents also newer that five years old, thus which already dealt with the system change, were published. Hence, in 1993, the Hungarian National Archive began to publish the minutes of the Hungarian Socialist Workers' Party, the first volume beginning with 1989. The first document concentrated on the new interpretation of 1956 and the principal acceptance of the multiparty system in February of 1989.

From the perspective of archives and secrecy, the material could be described as ultimately 'fresh'. Secondly, the question of timing was once again present; there was less than six months until the next elections. Evidently, the political purposes of the timing were highlighted in the newspapers. The editorial staff of *Népszabadság* provided information that the leader of the archive, János Lakos, would be a candidate for the parliament under the colours of the MDF. Lakos himself denied that the publishing had anything to do with the election campaign. According to him, party material was state property and it was the responsibility of the Minister of Education to deal with its secrecy (NSZ 24/02/1994).

Member of Parliament András Tóth (MSZP) criticized the publishing of the 1989 minutes and argued that it was not a mere coincidence. According to Tóth, it was also no coincidence that the Socialist Party had suggested a three-member *kuratorium*. It would consist of a member from the Academy of Sciences, a specialist and a political representative. All the material, including the negations in the national roundtable, should be dealt with simultaneously (these minutes came out in spring of 1999, HN). According to Tóth, the idea had been rejected by the Ministry (NSZ 24/02/1994).

In other words, an expectation existed which dealt with the continuity of the 'history of winners'. Once again the current government seemed to 'rule' through the documents and through its position of granting permissions only to "trustworthy researchers". Earlier, for example, political scientist Mihály Bihari had accused one researcher of writing "bolshevist history": the book in question had been a typical example of bolshevist type history writing, because it contented an interpretation that "everything was leading to the present MDF-leaders" (MN 24/09/1991). The past was evidently only a half past (félmúlt) and was unfinished (befejezetlen múlt), as the periodical Beszélő often described it between 1991 and 1993.

All in all, when 1956 is the specific focus of attention, it plays a certain role also in several other books dealing with the recent past and were written after 1989. For example, newspapers frequently interviewed historian Péter Gosztonyi, who had served as an officer in the Kilián barracks in 1956, emigrated and became the leader of the Eastern European Library in Bern (MN 04/05/1993). Furthermore, there was a text-book, Magyarország története 1938-1990 (Hungarian history 1938-1990), which was written by Tibor Seifert at the request of the Ministry of Education and Culture.

## Research and the Discussion of Punishment

Although there are arguments and demands that human and social sciences are and should be independent and autonomous, there are also innumerable connections, expectations and  wishes concerning concrete studies. These expectations not only come from 'the society', i.e. from 'outside', but also from 'inside', thus, also from the side of researchers themselves, whose task it is to convince certain audiences. In post-communism, the whole '56 theme might bring opportunities and honour to researchers, but there were also clear expectations and demands, which will be focused in this chapter.

For example, when in 1992 the Ministry of Education and Culture granted money for the preparation of historical documents, three specific subjects were particularly stressed: the 1956 revolution, the path leading to it and social continuities produced through it. Among other themes taken to the fore by the government were, for example, the fate of Hungarians who resided outside the borders as well as the changes in their state of living during the last fifty years (MH 27/08/1992). Moreover, President Árpád Göncz had argued earlier that 1956 did not enjoy the dignity it deserves in Hungary (MH 01/06/1991).

However, the question of historical justice reached the level of research work and researchers. A week after the rejection of the retroactive law in the Constitutional Court, President Árpád Göncz made a proposition to found a special committee (feltáróbizottság) to 'dig up' the events (NSZ 10/03/1992). This initiative failed to make progress and, in fact, was buried in the confrontation between the government and the opposition.

Already in the summer of 1991, the chair of the Hungarian Academy of Sciences, Domokos Kosáry, draw a line towards the expectations expressed by the leading government party, MDF. Up until then the government had not only founded a commission within the parliament to deal with the issue of punishment, but that summer the party got the idea for the so-called new White Books – a certain 'analogy' to 1957. At that time Kosáry made a statement that the MTA would not partake in the "recording of crimes", i.e. would not write White Books from the communist era (NSZ 20/07/1991).

From the perspective of the government, the idea of punishment was in a head wind, nor was the government satisfied with the media. As of January of 1993, one man, Frigyes Kahler, began to occupy the Hungarian newspapers (in November he introduced himself to the department director in the Ministry of Justice (MH 04/11/1993)). First, in January, Kahler argued that the events of 1956 had been a war and, thus, strengthened the notions echoed from the government side. According to historian Sándor Balogh, the statement was absurd, because if a war had taken place, then who was it who made peace. Kahler estimated that less than 100 persons would be held responsible, and that common soldiers would not be. (MN 26/01/; MH 18/02/1993). In May it became apparent that the Attorney General was interested in investigating five volley firings and that military courts would investigate three other cases (NSZ 07/05/1993).

In May of 1993, it was noted that a secret research group existed on the behalf of Frigyes Kahler. Indeed, the existence of the group was kept secret until it was revealed by the weekly journal, HVG. According to *Magyar Hírlap*, the group was one-sided and, for example, one of the researchers had nothing else to do with the case other than the fact that he had connections to the Prime Minister and Minister of Foreign Affairs (MH 13/05/1993).

Kahler and his group focused especially on volley(firings) (*sortűzek*), which they considered terrorist actions planned in advance (MH 04/11/1993). The word *sortűz* has also been repeated several times in this of research and if translated literally, it means a "line fire". The dictionary definition of *sortűz* is "the simultaneous totality of shots fired from several rifles, cannons or some other firearms". In the specific military sense, it refers to "the totality of a fixed duration of simultaneously fired shots from several guns [cannons, HN] armament [artillery] or weapons formation" (ÉrtSz 1966, 1247). In addition to police operations, it relates to an execution, like in the famous picture of Count Lajos Battyány's execution in Pest in 1849. The word itself is quite common in Hungarian and has been used, for example, to describe the events which took place in Beijing or in Tbilisi (cf. NSZ 06/06/1989; /08/ 01/1992). Moreover, it has been a common word in legal actions concerning 1956 and in the punishment debates.

According to Frigyes Kahler, one of the main results of their research work was the creation of a definition for the word *sortűz*. Volleys occurred "when an armed, uniformed formation or a half-regular gathering open fire in the defined aim of gathering an unarmed civil crowd, also into with unarmed groups together being unarmed but in uniforms." On the basis of the definition, the committee found volleys in three categories: volleys during military operations, volleys to defend objects and intimidated and reprisal volleys. They found 25th October, 1956 to be a watershed: the first firings before the 25th were classified in the first category, the 25th October (excluding Kossuth Square) belonged to the second category and after the 25th October, the rest belonged to the third category (NSZ 23/11/1993).

Kahler also clearly expressed and defined his views. When, for example, the Constitutional Court declared in October of 1993 that the statute of limitations on crimes against humanity would not run out, Kahler commented that a great breakthrough had taken place in the Hungarian history of law. Kahler subsequently estimated that there would be an investigation into 50 cases and some dozen trials, according to the Minister of Justice (MH; NSZ 14/10/1993). Moreover, the committee assembled some 400 death sentence cases, primarily those based on the drumhead court marshals (MH 28/03/1994). By April of 1994 they had already found 65 volleys; according to Kahler, the reprisal following 1956 had been incomparable to any other (MN 22/04/1994). Their research work seemed to already include characteristics of studying the past in the sense of 'charging' (compare also the second stage in the category of Donald Cameron Watt).

In this chapter, moreover, the current rhetorical position of Frigyes Kahler and their research in connection to the debate of punishment is the main focus. Not only a weekly journal had revealed the research group but it seemed that Kahler did not only work in the Ministry, but was also on good terms with the existing government and even with its present policy. Whether or not all of the results were eventually used in court, at least in November of 1993, the Minister of Justice handed the results of Kahler's Commission to the Attorney General (MN 21/12/1993) – after which time the first arrests were carried out the following February. Frigyes Kahler himself argued that only the material interested him, not the party politics (MN 22/04/1994). In May, the journalist of *Népszabadság* questioned his political connections and Kahler denied having anything to do with the present elections (NSZ 13/05/1994). The explanation might be true, but directly following the elections (30th May), Kahler was chosen as a judge in Veszprém (NSZ 10/06/1994).

In July, the new Minister of Justice, Pál Vastagh, revealed that the committee had been established by a decision of the previous government. Therefore, the (new) government had to decide about its future (NSZ 20/07/1994).

However, new Ministers met with Kahler and, according to Kahler, agreed that the committee should remain active. Both Kahler and Vastagh had shared the opinion that the society has the right to know what happened regardless of the current government (NSZ 18/08/1994). In spite of this dialogue and interpretation, the committee was suspended and the last session took place in December (NSZ 23/12/1994).

When the Minister of Justice explained the decision, he argued that research work would continue, but that it belongs primarily to science and not to the ministry. At the same time, it was revealed that the government had established the commission through a secret decision on 21st January, 1993, and awarded it ten million forints (NSZ 28/12/1994).

Thus, it seems evident that studying the past not only had political impacts in the long run, but also in the near future. The past was still strongly bound to the immediate present and the debate of historical justice reached historians as well. For example, in November of 1993 (thus, after the interpretation of the punishment law), András B. Hegedűs, one of the men behind the TIB, the idea of the reconciliation statue and the first law of theparliament, noted that it was time to stop. According to him, it was strange that András Hegedűs (Prime Minister 1955-1956, not related), who had been a dissident for 30 years would be the first to go to court. In an special interview, András B. Hegedűs also told about his own experiences in prison, during which time he had an opportunity to meet real war criminals, who were released after fifteen years in the amnesty of 1960. Although he did not sympathize with them, he also did not view their release on 4th April as unjust. According to Hegedűs, the lesson was that one should possess the courage to say that we must now stop (MH 29/11/1993).

Hegedűs preferred amnesty in the discussion and noted that historians seemed to be ignored in the debate (Ibid.). Moreover, János M. Rainer said that he did not believe that actions like those taken in Eger would dig up the real dependencies. As an historian, his work was to examine the degree to which the documents could be cleared of charges or had played a role in the actions. The men who put the decisions into practice are the weakest links in the chain and their responsibility is a much more complicated question. (MH 08/02/1994). For the researchers in the '56 Institute and to academic research in general more essential was to discover how the entire apparatus worked (cf. MN 09/07/1993).

Following the elections, Hegedűs pointed out that at the moment the most important task was to separate two discussions: research and punishment (MN 26/05/1994; NSZ 16/06/1994). According to Hegedűs, it was absurd – not in a political but in a dramatic sense – that President Árpád Göncz, who was imprisoned after 1956, was asking Gyula Horn to form a government.

Hegedűs had participated in the happening of the Democratic Charter and wondered the present situation: in the late eighties they demonstrated with Csurka against "Vilmos" (imagined metaphorical name) and now already with "Vilmos" against Csurka. (NSZ 16/06/1994).

However, research work continued in the institute and in October of 1994, the rest of the discussions in the Petőfi-Circle were published (NSZ 05/10/1994). A new year book, partly revising Kahler's volley firings, was also forthcoming (MH 20/10/1994).

In conclusion, a Truth Commission like the one in South Africa never existed in the Hungarian newspapers. However, political and moral problems of how to deal with the past frequently had much in common with the ideas of such commissions. In this chapter we have discussed problems and expectations concerning research work: who has the right to study the past, or more precisely, who is 'credible' enough to do so. Not all of the researchers belonged to the category of 'winners' prior to 1989, although in practice all of them had lived in Kádárian society and sooner or later went on to hold intellectual jobs. In 1990 '1956' became a part of official public experience and the 'history of winners'. In the 1990s, the former 'losers' wrote history *as* 'winners', but not necessary the 'history *of* winners', the lattter emerged more in speeches for occasions. Contrarily, also the new 'losers' went on to write history, although the 'history of losers' concerning 1989 has not yet realized in the 1990s. In general, the main point has been nationally centred, and has focused on adding '1956' to a national metahistorical narrative (cf. Kende 1993), and former counter-revolution had come under brackets.

Although there were expectations of a new history of winners, the new polity offered a broader basis for historians. The former experience created possibilities for a certain "open society" in a Popperian sense. Also, the new government noticed this in 1994, and it would have been political suicide to cease research work. Open research also became a part of the new policy (cf. Ferenc Glatz's application to the Academy of Sciences (Glatz 1991), particularly when the right-wing government had shown certain signs of using 'old methods'.

However, in the discussion of polarization prior to 1994, it was not always evident which questions had already resulted from the *system* or *regime* change. If we look solely at the rhetorical position of the parties of the new 'winners', SZDSZ historians belonged to the supporters of the current opposition, while MDF-historians already 'defended' the government. Rhetorically, Litván and Hegedűs were connected to the current opposition, and there was also some criticism that their text-book (1991) was "reform communist" (cf. Litván 1995, 9). On the other hand, *Népszabadság* might have run the headline "Official History Book", when it reported the news that Tibor Seifert's textbook had been published. Historian Ernő Raffay (MDF), who had scrutinized the book, simultaneously worked as a Political Under-Secretary of State in the Ministry of Defence. (NSZ 08/12/1992). Some might also remember his radical 'revisionist' views: in 1990, Raffay was asked to chair an association to restore the *irredenta* memorial at *Szabadság tér* (Freedom Square), which between the World Wars had been a reminder of the territories lost in Trianon (NSZ 03/09/1990).

Moreover, an ambiguous thin line separated Kahler's Commission from the aims of the current government, and in this sense the old notion of an intellectual supporting the present aims of the government was repeated or, if you will, continued. There were also expectations of writing a new 'history of winners', but the Academy of Sciences did not agree with demands directed from outside. In conclusion, it might be said that the research helped and also indirectly legitimated trust in the young democracy. People had the moral right to hear the arguments used in the decision making which directly concerned them. The legitimization was also achieved by making a distinction from the Kádár era, which is also implicitly mentioned in the leaflet (1996); the "history of the Revolution had been and to some extent is still obscured by distortions and falsifications of the Kádár regime" (The Institute for... 1996, 2). Even if research did not bring consensus until 1994, in the long run research has been helpful in the process of 'leaving' the past behind. It does not mean forgetting per se, however, it could imply taking events from memory and changing them into historiography, thus, turning the past into history.

# XII CONCLUSION: ATTEMPTS TO TURN THE PAST INTO HISTORY

In this study we have focused on one essential Cold War event, namely, the process of how the Hungarian '1956' is becoming history. This "Hungarian Bastille" has had innumerable long-lasting political impacts on several levels, similarly to Lüsebrink and Reichhart found from the original Bastille. In Hungary, these examples can be found mainly on three levels: the system change itself, political culture and the specific uses of the past in politics.

In this sense my study could contribute to three discussions: the transition in Eastern Europe, political culture and problems of history writing. The first level includes a 'microscopic analysis' of two historical processes, '1956' and "the system change", both of which have already been the subject of numerous studies, pamphlets and political interpretations. In addition, I have argued that these discussions were not only entangled, but also that various political agents even joined them together and used the past in the present. Therefore, my starting point has been to view these two debates as one political struggle of the past and, thus to reach the presence of the past in present politics.

In general, great and upsetting events are watersheds in people's minds and will be presented in public for a long time. On the one hand, these experiences are connected to political generations, although a part of them are also mediated over those generations. Therefore, two levels could be separated up until this point: mediating historical experiences and attempts to turn those experiences into history. Both of these levels can be found in '1956', although the temporal period until the 1990s has tended to favour the latter, to turn the past into history.

Actually, the political systems in European history in the 20th century have more "discontinuities" than "continuities". Countries like Finland, Sweden, Britain or Switzerland are in fact a minority with regard to their not having endured foreign occupations or gradual system changes. Hence, for example, questions of continuity and discontinuity in Hungary have been essential also in a political sense. For example, Gerhard Seewann (1987) examined several "failed revolutions" in Hungary, "memento mori" and continuity "after all", which have been essential for the self-consciousness of the small country (Seewann 1987, 706; cf. Rév 1994).

Thus, it would be said that people even build these continuities and discontinuities, they are not "natural". For example, on the 250th anniversary of the Rákóczi fight for freedom in 1953, an historians' congress put Rákóczi on the same "line" (*sor*) as the years 1848, 1919 and 1945 (A magyarok krónikája 1996, 680). In the 1990s, the same continuity building can be discerned in several '1956' memorials. In 1956, the legacy of 1848 was brought into the present analogously and symbolically. However, the phenomenon evidently reaches further into the past in Hungarian political culture than 1956. For example, the tradition of 1848 was already used in the Dual Monarchy and Horthy era. There are also other examples of how the past has been used in the present, i.e. the idea of the 1000 year Hungary and the 400 year fight for freedom (cf. von Klimó 1998).

Thus, in this sense '1956' is beginning to settle as a part of Hungarian history, although not only as part of history with a small "h", but also History with capital "H". In the 1990s new national identities have been constructed simultaneously to the attempt to thoroughly research and document the problematic question into history. Even if the question has dealt with the past, current political aims have also been mixed in with the discussion. Since 1989 there has been a quarrel as to whom the legacy of 1956 belongs, i.e. continuity with the certain past has appeared to be more essential than breaking with it.

In this research work I have argued that instead of "history repeating itself", there exist people who have located repetitive signs from the past and who even more or less seriously want to "repeat" history. There are numerous examples and include Hitler had his Compiegne, Honecker and his Moabit prison etc,. In Hungary there are so many astonishing 'similarities' that they cannot be coincidences.

Rather the mythical picture of '1848' was already "ripe" in peoples' minds prior to 1956. For example, because of the heroic myth of Petőfi, he held the fore throughout several generations and political systems (cf. Márai 1992, 185-186), it is possible that the poetic, glorious past was the space of experience, which was present in 1956 and was seen at an early stage in revolutionary speeches. The "youth of March" was not only used in 1956, but was during the Kádár era also connected to October and continued to be present throughout the system change of the 1990s.

Here, the attempts to "repeat" history should not be understood only in the sense of Karl Marx, i.e. as a farce – although in the Hungarian case there have also been signs of that – but also as attempts to sustain the past in the present. These actions belonged to several identities on national and other levels as well. Identity, however, was partly even found from controversial traditions, and people might have fears and question if and how the past is returning. Therefore, the public history culture has strong political dimensions – it is the symbolic and spectacular dimension of politics seen everywhere.

Thus, on the one hand, the 'similarities' in Hungarian history are astonishing, but it is even more astonishing how analogies as opposed to differences were frequently used in political argumentation. Although during historical "breaks" and "upheavals" the past could be used more in political argumentation, it is astonishing how Hungarian political jargon is full of tips and hints related to earlier history and certain key-figures. It is quite typical to speak in the name of the "nation", and particularly in conservative speech, the term nation has continued to appear as an organ with a soul and a memory and, after 1989, as an organ whose wounds would be healed (*orvosol*).

Different experiences of the past were still so strong in post-communism that their rhetorical dimension remained unnoticed. Indeed, memory (*emlék*) and legacy (*örökség*) are typical words used to deal with the past in Hungary. Moreover, the present was also frequently interpreted through concepts of the past, i.e. , for example, changing Leningrad to Saint Petersburg was interpreted in the headline of *Magyar Hírlap* as "Back to the Past in Russia" (MH 23/09/1991). Furthermore, in a book dealing with the Horthy era written in 1995, the author had to argue that it did not mean "rehabilitation" of the era (NSZ 10/05/1995).

However, I have argued that the struggle regarding the past has occurred essentially during the Hungarian system change. It is interesting to notice how the political programme of 1956 soon began to compete with other political pasts (i.e. identities) (cf. Péter Kende, MH 11/11/1992). Initially, '1956' was viewed by most – with the exception of the 'conservative' Communists – as an adequate basis for a new beginning. However, to a certain amount of Hungarian politicians 1956 was considered too "socialist" and, therefore, other traditions were also soon rehabilitated by the parties and organizations. In other words, the question of returning also existed and, thus, political expectations were found in which political tradition should be chosen.

Moreover, the left-right dimension was broadly based on the past and the shift toward the right in the 1990s meant going further into the past and rehabilitating it. For example, an historian and "MDF-ideologist", András Gergely, said that reverting back to the old past (*régi múlt*) was not a bad idea (168 óra 20/08/1991). However, an attempt was also made to reawaken the Arrow Cross leader, Ferenc Szálasi (MH 19/01/1994), and elsewhere "conservative youngsters", who denied being skinheads, commemorated Trianon along with the '56 Association and Pofosz (MH; MN 05/06/1993). Whether these phenomena were essential and dangerous is not the point here, because simply acknowledging their existence after decades was sufficiently astonishing.

Thus, in this study I have concentrated on the Hungarian system change, particularly from an historical perspective. There, people act as historical human beings through their experiences, memories etc., which have to do with their motives, present views and actions. The 'inside' story of the system change leads to the other two levels: to the questions of political culture and to different stratums of time, which also belong to the category of the problems of history writing.

Hence, how to deal with the past in a certain present is a crucial universal question. According to William Faulkner, the past never dies, it is not even past. Nevertheless, there have been at least a few attempts in this study to attempt to "solve", i.e. to move the problem from the daily agenda. On the one hand, politics is always necessary in order to "close" a case, but it is also needed to reopen them. Therefore I began by discussing past oriented politics, after which I have named these attempts to turn the past into history. In this study, political dimensions were found in concrete situations of how people deal with the past: whether they attempt to get rid and dissociate from it, build continuities, remember and forget or even try to repeat and return to the past.

The simple fact that revolution has been a general concept in modern politics (Koselleck 1984, 655-656) makes it one of the most controversial terms. Revolution is primarily an historical event, although it is impossible to purify the concept analytically, because it summons together a cognitive muddiness and the spell of a revolution (cf. Dunn 1989). In Hungarian, and especially in the Marxist political vocabulary, revolution has been a positive and progressive concept. Thus, in Hungary, revolution (*forradalom*) was remembered and considered a  positive concept as a fight for freedom / war of independence (*szabadságharc*): people rebelled against foreign occupation, tyranny and oligarchy. Conversely, the term counter-revolution has been a part of negative remembrance since 1945 – the Horthy era became an "anti-period", as Ferenc Glatz (1991) called it.

Hence, the entire debate on '1956' was discussed in the symbolic terms of the past: revolution and fight for freedom referred to 1848, counter-revolution to 1919. In 1956, the changes in the naming of the present were directly connected to the current events of that time. As of 4th November, 1956, two-revolutionary governments "existed", which fought over possession of the same concept. At that time, revolution became a canon in the name of the Kádár's government, and the era was known as a consolidation. After the first months of hesitation, the term counter-revolution was established. Later, for example, János Molnár defended the term by writing that the current actors themselves did not have an exact picture of what was going on (Molnár 1967, 245-250).

It is my contention that in February of 1989, the decision to implement a multiparty system was done in the shadow of the new interpretation of 1956. When the rewriting (*Umschreiben*) began at the end of 1988, it appeared especially in naming: counter-revolution became an uprising. At that time, a breakthrough from above took place, because the Central Committee had to do something to save face. Until then, the discussion of the past had been inspired by the way Imre Pozsgay used the public and the results of his committee. It was a jump into the dark, but at the same time it opened new political spaces and chances.

Therefore, contrary to Kende (1993, 9), I consider naming to be politically significant, particularly the debate of naming. In Finland, for example, as late as the beginning of the 1990s, a seminar of historians was organized in which the topic of discussion was whether there was "a correct name" for the "war" which took place in Finland in 1918 (Historiallinen... 1993, 97; Yli-kangas 1993, 521-526). Until the 1960s, the interpretation *war of independence* had dominated, which was launched by the 'whites', who had won the "war". The interpretation considered the motives of the 'reds' criminal and treason-able, and, thus, the name was also symbolic. In the 1960s, the name *civil war* became more popular also in academic literature and, indeed, justified the losers, too (cf. Jussila & Hentilä & Nevakivi 1996, 103-105). Later, it was common to speak about a war which began as a war of independence but ended as a civil war. Over the last few years there have been attempts to restore the name war of independence, although, on the other hand, people can use different names on the basis of their own experiences and traditions.

Thus, the question was not only of the 'right' name, but also of names and naming as symbolic actions (cf. also Edelman 1971; 1977). In Hungary, the reformers of the old regime first tried to compromise by renaming 1956, after which they were ousted from power and the discussion of the content of 1956 began. Therefore, I would like to argue that the entire system change 'culminated' into naming. Up until the end of 1988, counter-revolution was the official term used, after which came uprising, and in May of 1990, revolution and fight for freedom were established by law. The 'parties' of the counter-revolution and uprising were ousted in May of 1990 and replaced by a the 'parties' of revolution and fight for freedom. Following the compromise came the struggle over the content.

To some extent the past is always reinterpreted, and in principle all history writing is *Umschreibung*. The Hungarian case, however, is more complicated, because in principle the whole legitimation of the Kádár regime was based on a specific naming and an interpretation of the past. Moreover, there are also two temporal periods: the period of quiet survival, i.e. the 'period of the history of winners', which lasted until 1988, and the 'period of resurrection', which has existed since 1988. During the system change there was no systematic attempt to separate the past and present. On the contrary, 1956 became the basis of a new legitimation, in which the government, the parliament and parties all interpreted history and to some extend based their identity on the past.

During the Kádár era recent history was represented by the experience of winners and was also written into history by the winners. The so-called White Books were published already in 1957 and *Fortschreibung*, writing forward, began in the 1960s. Furthermore, history writing legitimated the experiences of a winner, more precisely, the experience of a particular generation among the winners. Using Völgyes category (1987), all of the people who wrote history and who have been focused on here had the essential experience of fascism, a new beginning (1945) and stalinism (1956). All of them were born between 1921 and 1930: Berecz 1930, Balogh 1926, Jakab 1926, Hollós 1923, Lajtai 1921 and Molnár 1927. However, even more amazing is that many of the outstanding figures of 1956 – Maléter, Gimes, Losonczy, Szilágyi, Vásárhelyi and the most important cultural politician of the Kádár era, György Aczél – happened to be born in the same year, 1917.

For example, Ervin Hollós and Vera Lajtai indicated moralist experiences by writing that it had not been easy to write, because the counter-revolution ruled openly during the first half of the century. In an historical context, they understood the existing system better when the comparisons were projected into the past, to the Second World War and fascism, not to the present rival political systems. According to János Molnár (1967), the question was about the struggle between two worlds, in which also Cuba, Indonesia and South America had their own places between the communists and against the Pope, Dulles and Eisenhower.

However, only trusted researchers in the archives and 'their' language connected them to the current power and caused them to lose their rhetorical credibility. When *ethos* and *pathos* were lost, the trustworthy elements of history writing were left in the shadow of distortions, and researchers became outlets of reliable information. Therefore, the defence of the existing alternative led to an alternate goal than was intended: the politics of memory included the idea of unity and the dream of an explicitly better future, had the 'revolution' ended differently. Recent history became a political argument either defending or accusing the present, and at the end of 1980s, the question and the compromise of Kádár was openly politicized.

According to Konrád and Szelényi (1974), whether an intellectual chose not to pursue dangerous issues or began a career as a dissident was primarily dependent on the intellectual him- or herself. Konrád and Szelényi argued that such dangerous issues were those concerning the fundamental issues of the social structure and having strong political meaning (Konrád & Szelényi 1979, 199). Evidently, the process of 1956 belonged to this category, because of the genesis of the present power structure. Therefore, an intellectual might have consoled herself with the idea that the case is still too recent to be studied.

Thus, the history of winners was also connected to memory and experiences, thus to the experiences of winners. However, the main problem in history writing is how to deal with the past, which had many other symbolic, moral, political and juridical dimensions. In the beginning of this study I isolated six categories of remembering and reminding, which also occurred in the case of '1956'. Remembering and forgetting (I) were more passive and contingent, while reminding and making to forget (II) require more public political activity. In addition, there is positive and negative remembering (III), as well as positive and negative forgetting (IV). Finally, I have separated reconciliation (V) from compromise (VI), which are the fifth and sixth categories, i.e. positive and negative means to remind and to make to forget. In comparison, there are many ways of making to forget, while also the negative features can be openly reminded and dealt with in reconciliation.

At first, it is very difficult to discern whether during the Kádár era "the nation", "the society" and "the majority" remembered or forgot '1956', or whether citizens remembered of forgot its positive and negative features. However, there were signs of reminding and making to forget, such as statues, a few street names, censorship, locking the copying machines or the preventive acts prior to the 25th anniversary. Moreover, public remembering and commemorating simultaneously remind of something. Contrarily, ending certain rituals, moving the statues etc. were all attempts to make people forget, although it is not self-evident that those persons or ideas will be forgotten.

During the Kádár era, the entire official picture was negative, which can be seen, for example, in text-books. However, there were also a few examples of positive remembering, such as the commemoration on 30th October or various decorations. Reconciliation did not exist, although there was a compromise from above, in which there was an attempt to make people forget both the positive and negative aspects of the 'tragedy of 1956'. In psychological terms, reference has been made to a "national amnesia" (The Hungarian Revolution... 1996, 147) – the term is also used later in reference to the Horthy era. Questions of deconstruction were in all practicality ousted from the daily agenda, because people also had other aims for their every day lives.

However, not everyone forgot the positive and negative features of '1956'. Later, in the end of the 1980s, the positive heritage of 1956 came into the Hungarian public and during the change of the system became a part of the new identity of the state. This process includes many examples of all six categories. The period between 1989 and 1992 might be referred to as a 'period of memorial tablets and statues', i.e. '1956' was reminded in the city-text of Budapest and other communities. In addition to the statue of Petőfi, Batthyány Square has also continued to be an essential space in the politics of memory (cf. MH 29/07/1991).

In this sense, anniversaries are important TimeSpaces of remembering and reminding. Anniversaries are days for which people prepare themselves beforehand, have many kinds of expectations, keep the past in the present and commemorate it. During the system change, old political anniversaries were superseded and were made to be forgotten, some new ones were created and some of the old ones were rehabilitated.

Of the new anniversaries, 23rd October has been the most important in this study. Moreover, in the present Hungary it represents a totally new day; not a repetition but a new beginning. Until the end of the Kádár era, 23rd October was officially 'meaningless'. In 1988, commemoration was still prohibited, however, in 1989 the whole symbolic system change was synchronised with the anniversary. The naming of 23rd October as a national holiday was an attempt to start something new, which had never existed in Hungary, while at the same time to remind on the basis of a certain past. Two important discussions are connected to this day, which are, for example, present in juridical spheres and have formed a basis in which the relation of the past and the present is dealt with.

During the Kádár, era 4th November was also 'meaningless', although in 1986, on the 30th anniversary, the government was the main issue in the party newspaper. During the 1990s, not only have these two days been com-memorated as the new ideologies of the state, but also the time between them has become a specific period of the new democratic canon. There, the phenomenon of parliamentary democracy has come to the fore, and of less significance have been the worker's democracy and soviets, which were essential after 4th November, 1956.

Two other kinds of anniversaries must also be mentioned, which express the political character and features of making to forget an anniversary. 4th April had lost its official position in political ceremonies, while the tradition simultaneously came closer to the character of a party anniversary. After 1989, the Workers' Party has continued and has reminded about the tradition. However, their actions, too, have not only commemorated the past but have also assembled and united the supporters of the party. According to them, the party would honour the parliament enacted on 23rd October, but would prefer to lay a wreath on 30th October (MH 19/10/1990).

Secondly, the anniversary of János Kádár's death has had similar political meanings, i.e. political statements concerning the present and the future have also been made. On the first anniversary, Gyula Thürmer said that the party

270

would maintain the lasting values of the tradition (MH 07/07/1990), and in the 1990s, commemoration has taken place annually. For example, on the second anniversary 10,000 people gathered at the Kerepesi Cemetery, where Valéria Benkené Kiss pointed out that behind the democratic scenery conservative Horthyite power is on its way (NSZ 08/07/1991). Two years later, Gyula Thürmer noted that they were not mourning, but were making a political statement in which they demanded the end to privatisation (NSZ 05/07/1993).

Thus, several political actions have been timed to special anniversaries in the 1990s as well. The famous pamphlet of István Csurka was published on the 20th of August, and the newly founded MIÉP wanted to publish its new program, "a program of real change", on 23rd October (MN 06/08/1993). Furthermore, the new journalist organization, MUK, was established on 15th March, as was a new newspaper close to the views of the government, *Új Magyarország* (168 óra 19/03/1991) – the name was the same as the organ of the Petőfi Party in 1956. In addition, there was discussion among a few parties as to whether the election campaign of the municipal elections should begin on 20th August (NSZ 08/08; 15/08/1990) and, for example, in the summer of 1998, it was announced that the new National Theatre would be opened on 23rd October, 2000 (NSZ 29/06/1998).

In conclusion, the anniversaries have been important in the timing and spacing of politics. During the period I have focused on in this work, anniversaries, specifically in the month of October, had not lost their political character. On the contrary, October had become so clearly political that in an opinion poll the question of what possible incidences could disturb the day was posed (NSZ 21/10/1994).

In general, the laying of wreaths and the bestowing of decorations have been one of the most essentials annually repeated rituals. The bestowing of decorations has been another typical way of remembering the positive - and also the negative, because the pro workers power medal from 1957 was declared illegal. Since the system change, people have been decorated, and have been decorated by the state on 23rd October, 16th June and on 20th August.

In post-communism, the laying of wreaths in the previously ousted Plots 301 and 21 at Kerepesi Cemetery became also a part of the new commemorative ideologies. Moreover, these actions have been a part of the protocol as symbolic political openings, similarly to what Willy Brandt did in the Warsaw ghetto. Therefore, especially during the first years of the new democracy, commemorations were incorporated into the programs of several foreign politicians: Alexander Dubcek, Mario Soares, Francois Mitterrand, Václav Havel, Dan Quayle, George Bush, the King of Sweden, the President of Cyprus and the Dalai Lama. When the third Hungarian Word Congress – the first since the Second World War – took place, wreaths were laid at the statue of Bem and at Plot 301. (MN 08/02/; 21/08/; MH 25/07/1992).

If wreaths and anniversaries were commemorative actions of remembering someone and maintaining their memory in the present, were the others then forgotten or made to be forgotten, and if so, by whom? For example, in the letters to the editor in 1991, it was pointed out that no one had laid wreaths on the twentieth anniversary of the death of György Lukács (MN 25/06/1991). Moreover, János Kádár became an inherent part of the 'counter-culture' of the Workers' Party. On the state and municipal levels he was negatively remembered and made to be forgotten. In 1993, the purpose of his residence was also changed and his personal property was sold by auction (168 óra 23/02/1993; MH 09/02/1993) – his villa would later be used as a children's rehabilitation centre (NSZ 03/05/1995).

Whether or not the life of "a soft dictator" might be of interest to some people, the idea for a museum was not taken seriously at that time. Although surprising, in an opinion poll made in 1999, János Kádár was considered the most positive person in Hungarian history since 1920 (the poll, however, was clearly divided, because altogether five out of nine persons, Kádár among them, were also on another list, which contained the most negative persons in recent Hungarian history) (HVG 10/07/1999). Thus, both the memory of Kádár and the entire era in general are contradictory.

Temporally, the era was the closest to post-communism, but similarly to the Horthy period earlier, during the system change it also became an "anti-period" (cf. Glatz 1991). Although the period after 1956 was not unequivocally remembered in a negative sense, in public its positive features were forgotten and for a while were made to be forgotten. In 1992, György Litván even noted that there were signs in the current debate, which made it appear as if the Kádár era had not existed at all (MH 03/01/1992). Hence, during the system change the 'socialist' Kádár era was on people's minds, but it was politically correct to radically dissociate oneself from it, and there was an attempt to make it forgotten.

Furthermore, there are also attempts of reconciliation and compromise, which require many other public actions than trustworthy history writing. In the summer of 1990 formal attempts to apologise were made, such as the one by the University of Miskolc, which requested forgiveness for the discrimination within the university following the revolution and fight for freedom (MN 11/06/1990), or the apology by the Council of Pécs (MH 04/07/1990). On one hand, these are merely formal gestures, however, even these gestures might take decades to become realized: in 1995, for the first time, the Japanese Prime Minister asked forgiveness for of sufferings and damages caused in South-East Asia by the Japanese during the Second World War (NSZ 16/08/1995).

Thus, public apologies are significant rhetorical gestures of reconciliation – as the examples of Truth Commissions indicate – but a more difficult question to answer is whether a formal apology, which could be interpreted also as a form of public humiliation, is sufficient in order to reach a compromise or a reconciliation. For example, in one interview, the leader of the Socialist Party, Gyula Horn, asked forgiveness from the Hungarian people. The forgiveness encompassed everything that had happened in 1956, and in spite of that, the MSZP would have nothing to do with it (MN 27/09/1993). Although Horn has done more for democracy than many other East European politicians, it has not been enough for his political opponents, who have tended to favour reminding people of his past.

After the 1994 elections there were clear signs of reconciliation from the government side, which were partly accepted by the organizations and partly rejected by the parties in the opposition. Gyula Horn was present during the commemorations on 16th June, and the new Foreign Minister, László Kovács, defined the tradition as belonging to everybody who wants reconciliation instead of revenge, and not belonging to the extremists who endanger the stability of the democracy (NSZ 24/10/1994). Moreover, the '56 Memorial Committee was founded in October of 1994, and it attempted to avoid actual politicking in which all the directions were represented (MN; NSZ 19/10/1994).

We then come to the question of what kind of reconciliation is needed. Those who attempted to suggest a memorial for the reconciliation in 1991 were evidently too early with their proposal. According to Miklós Vásárhelyi, his support of the reconciliation was one of the reasons why he was "bolshevised down" and did not want to run as a TIB candidate (NSZ 16/11/1991). In 1994, the new Minister of the Interior, Gábor Kuncze, (SZDSZ) spoke at the commemoration at the Kerepesi Cemetery and said that it was not a reconciliation, but rather an attempt to forget, which brought consolidation after 1956 (MN; NSZ 05/11/1994).

Moreover, remembering and forgetting have also represented advantages and disadvantages, which 1956 itself has brought to individuals. In the beginning of the Kádár era the winners were honoured while, in addition to being imprisoned, the losers were stripped of their pensions and had difficulty finding work. During the system change the tables were turned and participation in 1956 became an advantage. Therefore, one essential question in post-communism, also elsewhere than Hungary, has been how to compensate former suffering and how to deal with former winners.

Where as positive remembering could bring recognition or economic appreciation to someone, negative remembering was an attempt to deprive someone of these attributes. In this discussion, essentially dealing with 1956 but also with the whole post-1945 period, there have been several levels:

The most essential discussion of the negative remembering – positive for many Hungarians but negative for the targets themselves – has been the debate of punishment. It has been the strictest way of dealing with the past, and its commemorative influence is restrictive and juridical. Naming could also be restrictive, but in the Hungarian case it was more liberal, because its supporters preferred moral judgment instead of punishment.

The two other levels, compensation and rehabilitation, were more 'positive', because they recompensed and dismantled earlier actions which affected a person. In the strict sense of the word, rehabilitation, as punishment, is juridical, but in Hungary there was also discussion of political rehabilitation. Finally, compensation usually requires political decisions and results in economic concessions and support.

On the level of history writing, these actions belong to the second level in the category of Donald Cameron Watt. They were characterised by guilt, innocence and a period of actual trials and legal proceedings (Watt 1991, 13-20). Temporally, the period from 1988 to 1991 was dominated by the discussion of rehabilitation and then by the debate of punishment. It seems that these discussions were necessary in order to building the future, although at the same time it seems that the question of historical justice has also made neutral discussion more difficult.

Thus, I am not sure whether the 'resurrection' of '1956' in the late 1980s was an unequivocally positive sign for the historical event itself and its critical study. According to Reinhart Koselleck (1979), the gap between experiences and expectations is widening and, thus, less and less of the future can be interpreted with the past. In Hungary, 1956 had been a complete experience, and there are several examples of attempts to define the present on the basis of 1956. In post-communism the question not only meant the recognition of the memory of the losers, but also an attempt to built a state on the symbolic principles of morality and history.

Finally, it is difficult to conclude the historical significance of '1956' in the present Hungary. On the one hand, several demands were fulfilled at the turn of the decade (free elections, the multiparty system, the withdrawal of the Soviet troops), but there remains ambivalence and unanswered questions. Moreover, on the basis of the Hungarian example it is difficult to generalize the relationship of history and politics. In which sense is the case of Hungary an exception, or can there only be exceptions?

I would like to conclude research work with two notions: history as a science of the present and politicking with history. Traditionally, history has been understood as temporally concentrated in the 'past', however, I would categorise history more to the sciences of the 'present'. As necessary as it is to know the past itself, I have found a context in which the past has been signified. Thus, I have analyzed history as a part of the problematic concept of the present – not as the 'past', but a present political discussion, of which historians as specialists are also a part. In this type of debate, history does not 'mechanically' influence or motivate people, but rather what is interesting is the complicated process in which the past has been 'used' and 'misused', depending on the person, in political argumentation.

The past is not only clarified by historians, but it is simultaneously a political implement. In 1968 in Paris, they shouted "we are all German Jews", and used the tradition of their opponent to open new political perspectives with the past. In Hungary, however, not only the arguments of the opponent were used and fulfilled, but the threats constructed by that same opponent. The debate was taken rather seriously and therefore, playing with the past also includes several risks. It also provokes strongly ideological politics, because everyone does not agree with the memory.

However, the question of what should be dragged from the past remains, because a person who denies his/her past is a prisoner of the past, as well. Hungarian historians tried to argue that the "legacy of 1956" belongs simultaneously to a nation, a logical demand and a problematic argument. On the one hand, it is true that the political debates did not do any 'good' for the "legacy", but on the other hand, one might question whether there is such a concept as national history at all. Rather, different identities in a sort of "national fiction" (for example, the walls of the headquarters of the MDF are full of pictures of Hungarian writers) competed with each other, and '1956' was an essential part of this political debate.

Finally, it is interesting to notice that the revision of the past was also connected to the changes in the present. Evidently, an enlivened discussion of the past also disclosed changes in the present and the way in which new ideas began to spread. Moreover, a further conclusion or open question can be posed: the question was not only of a connection and enlivened discussion, but the past was also used in order to produce changes in the future. Normally, it could be said that an historian is also always making politics through revising the past, i.e. finding new arguments and documents, which in the long run also change people's political thinking.

However, the case of Hungary was not such a 'liberal' and relative. An authoritative and official interpretation existed until 1989, and there was one party which controlled publications. Thus, a good follow up question is, in which sense does a re-writing of history also provoke a system change? Not only in Hungary but, for example, in the Soviet Union during perestroika, the discussion of the past became quite enlivened. In the spring of 1988, the Politburo openly recognized that the reconsideration of the past, particularly the 1930s and 1940s, was essential to perestroika (Davies 1989, 179-193).

Thus, if it is not only in hindsight, in which sense might an enlivened discussion of the past (and history) also forebode and encourage social changes, because debates on the past are also symbolic struggles of the future?

There are at least several examples of how also the opposition also juxtaposed the present demands with demands concerning the past. Moreover, even if the implementation of a new (MSZMP) party programme was merely an attempt to get rid of the past, it did not succeed. Still, it would be wrong to deny that changing the picture of the past – history writing included – did not have something effect on the game in the system change. Further studies, however, are needed in order to strengthen the hypothesis of how history culture and history politics influence people's political thought. Their role is particularly interesting in the collapse of communism, in a political system which was based on the idea that a philosopher's task was not to explicate the word but to change it.

# XII EPILOGUE

When I write these lines ten years after 1989, it would be wrong to assume that '1956' has been ousted or no longer impacts daily politics. Although the intensity is not as impressive as ten years ago, the past does appear in the daily political agenda.

For example, in January of 1999, the Budapest Military Prosecutor's Office brought an action against the leader of the Central Archive of the Minister of Defence. The indictment was based on the information that the file of former Prime Minister Gyula Horn had disappeared from the archives. (NSZ 11/02; 24/02/1999). Horn had also played a role in 1956 and in his autobiography he had written that he had participated in the armed forces beginning on December 15, 1956. However, copies of documents seem to refer that he had been a member already on December 6th, and therefore might have participated in the executions of civilians at the Budapest Western Railway Station (NSZ 23/01/1999). Horn himself denied the accusations and argued that the date of December 15th had already been confirmed by the judges who screened his and all other parliament members' backgrounds in 1997.

Moreover, there has been another fresh case, the political dimensions of which were discussed in 1998 and 1999. In the state-budget, the Institute for the History of the 1956 Hungarian Revolution lost over 90% of its public financial support. In 1995, the official status of a public foundation was granted to the institute by the government (The Institute... 1996, 2). This means of financing functioned until 1998, at which point the new FIDESZ-led government reduced all the grants to the Institute of Political History and over 90% from the '56 Institute, i.e. *de facto* suspended the support alloted from the state budget (NSZ 05/02/1999).

Altogether, 102 French and German historians protested the decision, particularly because a new institute, the Institute of 20th Century History, was simultaneously established. Protesters noted that research work was taken to the level of party interests. The leader of the new institute was at the same time one of the advisers to the present Prime Minister, and the institute was thus close to the government. (NSZ 05/02/1999). In the summer of 1999, the city of Budapest, in which the SZDSZ and MSZP had a majority, came to the rescue and granted 15 million forints for both the Institute of Political History and the '56 Institute (NSZ 25/06/1999).

In the parliamentary elections held in May of 1998, FIDESZ had grown to the strongest party. After a four year period of socialist-liberal government, FIDESZ formed a government with Smallholders and the MDF. In the 1994 elections FIDESZ had introduced a radical 'discontinuity' campaign (cf. Mpé 1995, 72). However, after their defeat they broadened the party's name to FIDESZ – The Citizen's (Bourgeois) Party (FIDESZ – *Magyar Polgári Párt*). Indeed, in the summer of 1997 they celebrated the memory of the Opposition Declaration from 1847 (cf. BW 16/1997), which rather seemed to be a new TimeSpace to bring the Hungarian right-wing together. Moreover, according to Viktor Orbán, Hungarian liberalism had divided in 1918: FIDESZ represented "national liberalism" while the governing SZDSZ was the heir of Mihály Károlyi (NSZ 25/11/1997). A big picture of István Széchenyi hung in the background in the part of the campaign film taken from 15th March, 1998.

In his first statements the Prime Minister also appealed to the legacy of the Antall government. Orbán had also interpreted that Hungarians had demanded the reestablishment of their bourgeois (*polgári*) traditions in 1956. Finally, in the opening speech of the new parliament, the new Prime Minister also mentioned in the context of 1956 the *polgári* revolution and fight for freedom (NSZ 08/07/1998). Thus, it is no wonder that in a conference held ten years later in Vienna, Orbán had words with other participants. Orbán said that they would celebrate the tenth anniversary in 2000, because they consider the elections in 1990 as representing a distinct change. (NSZ 28/06/1999).

Moreover, several of the themes which I have discussed in this study continued to be of current interest. Although the new media law was born in December of 1995, the electronic media has been a constant issue on the political agenda. For example, in June of 1999 a new boss chairman was chosen for TV-news, which the opposition leader interpreted as a sign of a new media war. Considerable personal changes were expected to occur within the news, and the International Press Institute (IPI) has also expressed its anxiety that the government is intervening in media issues (NSZ 02/06/; 29/06/; 07/07/1999).

In the summer of 1999, three volley cases remained open. The Hungarian Supreme Court changed its former decision and, thus the volley fires of Tata, Tiszakécske and Kecskemét will be investigated again. In November of 1998, the cases were closed on the basis that the statute of limitation had run out. However, the Military Supreme Court considered them as crimes against humanity, which have no statute of limitation (NSZ 26/06/1999). In the new decision of the Hungarian Supreme Court, a non-international conflict had taken place between the period of 23rd October and 4th November, 1956, which falls within the guidelines of the Geneva Convention. Therefore, the courts were mistaken and those acts could be interpreted as crimes against humanity (NSZ 29/06/1999).

In the autumn of 1995, investigations had been ordered in a total of 38 cases, more than 2,000 witnesses were questions, 48 persons were under suspicion, and seven legal actions were taken against 28 persons (NSZ 28/10/1995). The first sentences had been passed in the case of Salgótarján in January of 1995, when two members of the ex-armed forces were sentenced to five years in prison. The court had to investigate whether the accused had been in front of the Council on 8th December, 1956, and if they had fired shots into the crowd. The court was convinced that the two men had consciously used weapons against the demonstrators. Earlier, the other defendant, Lajos Orosz, had confessed to being near the fire, while the other, Ferenc Toldi, was found guilty, because in 1984 he had demanded his pension to be increased on the basis of being "in lions share" in Salgótarján. A total of twelve persons were accused, of whom seven were released, while the rest were asked to close. (NSZ 01/02/1995).

However, in 1995, the law itself was found unconstitutional (NSZ 24/11/1995). In September of 1996, an announcement was made that current valid laws must be used in sentencing, and that the Geneva Convention 1949 merely provides direction to the decisions (NSZ 04/09/1996). In January of 1997, the Supreme Court made its decision that after 4th November, 1956 *an international armed conflict* had begun in Hungary. All in all, three men were sentenced on the basis of war crimes and crimes against humanity. Two of them were sentenced to two years in prison and Lajos Orosz's sentence remained five years. At this time, Ferenc Toldi was released based on a lack of evidence (NSZ 17/01/1997).

Furthermore, in February of 1998, juridical processes began in Eger, where five men were accused, one of whom had already died. According to the prosecutor, they had committed a war crime and consciously killed several people on 12th December, 1956. The armed forces had opened fire against an unarmed group assembling on the street resulting in 24 deaths and almost 30 people being wounded (NSZ 05/02/1998). In June, the Heves County Court of Justice acquitted all four men, based on a lack of proof regarding whether two of the men had even been present at the scene and whether the other two had, in fact, shot into the crowd (NSZ 12/06/1998).

In the case of screenings, the Constitutional Court made a decision in the summer of 1999, which keeps the amount of screened persons unchanged. Political Secretary István Balsai (MDF) would have liked to have increased the amount, which was reduced to 500-600 persons in 1996 (NSZ 30/06/

1999). The present screening law concerns persons who take an oath in front of the parliament, the President and the government. Screening will continue until the year 2000, and concerns persons who were born prior to 14th February, 1972, i.e. had not been more than 18 years old prior to February of 1990 (NSZ 22/12/1995; 04/07/1996). The current right-wing opposition would liked to have also checked judges, layers, high ranking military and police officials (NSZ 07/02/1996).

The screening process officially began in October of 1996, when people were called to Nagysándor József Street and told whether or not their names were found in the archives. In cases in which the person had been a member of the III-III, ÁVH or Arrow Cross Party, the commission will ask that person to resign, and if that person refuses to do so, the material will be published (NSZ 26/09/1996). Finally, the year 1997 was the actual screening year, and newspapers also occasionally published the letter in turn. A total of 13 contempt cases were found, and among them were six Members of Parliament (NSZ 23/05/1998).

Two out of the 13 had to do with the period of 1956-1957: on the basis of Prime Minister Gyula Horn's fluoroscopy they were able to verify that he had participated in the armed police forces in 1956. From 15th December, he had been a member of the Budapest Police Headquarters Armed Forces Regiment János Hunyadi. According to the information, he had kept guard over bridges and prisons from outside and eventually resigned in the summer of 1957. In addition, Horn had received secret information while working as a political secretary between 1985 and 1990 (NSZ 02/09/1997). The law did not force persons to resign and, Prime Minister Horn argued that all the details of his past were already known prior to the 1994 elections and therefore he had no moral or legal reason to resign (NSZ 02/09/1997). The other case was exposed in May of 1998, when a former member of the Christian Democrats had co-operated with the Ministry of the Interior to compensate his imprisonment (NSZ 08/05/1998).

At the same time as the parliament reduced the amount of screenings, they established a special institute, the Historical Office (*Történeti Hivatal*) (NSZ 04/07/1996). The office was finally opened in September of 1997, and it offers the possibility for citizens to view their own files. The new Historical Office, however, does not contain all essential documents (NSZ 29/04/1998), which is in part due to the fact that the Secret Service destroyed some of the material following the "Duna-gate" scandal in January of 1990. As of the end of 1998, 2,800 persons had requested to view their files and about a quarter of them had been granted to do so (NSZ 29/06/1999).

Commemorative rituals have mainly continued on three levels: the state, local and organizational levels. The laying of wreaths, opera, decorations etc., have all become repeated commemorative acts on 16th June, 23rd October and 4th November. State rituals were represented by the President and the government of Socialists and Liberals until 1998. They frequently stressed the need for national unity, thus, without 1956 and its unity, there would be no free Hungary (cf. NSZ 17/06/1995; 24/10/1998). Other 'messages' regarding the present can also be found in the speeches: there was no exclusion in 1956, we need a unity similar to that of 1956 (MH 24/10/1995), it is time to carry out national unity (MH 24/10/1997) etc.

On the organizational level, particularly opposition parties have had their own commemorations, especially on different *lieux de mémoire,* like Corvin, Széna tér or the Bem statue. These speeches also included 'messages' regarding present policy, and the opposition was particularly critical toward the idea of reconciliation. Prior to 16th June, 1995, Jenő Fónay said that they would commemorate a day earlier, noting that it was impossible to lay a wreath together, because they (the government) have not make their excuses and asked pardon from '1956' (NSZ 09/06/1995). Moreover, in October, MIÉP wanted 12 points to be read in a television broadcast, which, however, was rejected. István Csurka also encouraged people toward national resistance (NSZ 24/10/1995). In 1996, Viktor Orbán interpreted that instead of reconciliation, Hungarians were condemned to peaceful coexistence (NSZ 24/10/1996).

On the 40th anniversary in 1996, the main commemorative event was moved from the cemetery in front of the parliament (MH 19/10/1996). Among memorials, stamps etc., for example a "flame of the revolution" was built and unveiled in front of parliament (NSZ 24/10/1996). President Árpád Göncz both lit the symbolic fire on 23rd October and put it out on 4th November. The same ritual was repeated in 1997, but in 1998 it was became an eternal light (NSZ 24/10/1997; 05/11/1998).

The year 1996 was also the 100th anniversary of the birth of Imre Nagy. During the first years of the new democracy it had become evident that in 1990, Nagy's name had been ousted at the last moment from the draft of the first law. When the centennial birthday was celebrated in 1996, the Socialist-dominated government prepared a memorial bill in honour of Nagy's memory. Among those who opposed the bill in parliament, a member of SZDSZ argued that Francis Joseph and Stalin both had their names in Hungarian laws, too. Moreover, among the opponents, historian and Chairman of the SZDSZ, Iván Pető opposed the fact that the parties were dealing with history (NSZ 14/05/1996).

However, in June the parliament enacted a law commemorating the memory of Imre Nagy. The results of the final vote were 177 for, 77 against and 64 abstained from voting (NSZ 09/03, 04/06, 26/06/1996). According to a part of the long text:

"...the appointment of Imre Nagy as Prime Minister on October 24th expressed the will of the people... . The second freely elected parliament considers Imre Nagy as a national martyr, an outstanding person in Hungarian history and therefore enact a law for his memory." (Törvények és rendeletek... 1996, 345-346).

Among other plans was the construction of a museum, the foundation of which has existed since 1996. Thus, the foundation emerged in the same year when, for example, several memorials were unveiled, children had illustrated their thoughts about the revolution and the Open Society Archive had organized an exhibition based on newspapers and photographs, i.e. regarding how the event was represented between 1956 and 1989 (NSZ 05/11/1996).

# NOTES

1 According to Rosenberg (1995), *Geschichstaufarbeitung* means the "working through of" and "*Vergangenheitsbewältigung* ...the business of getting the upper hand on the past." (Rosenberg 1995, 306).

2 I use quotation marks for '1956', when it is used as a political symbol and not only as numerically representative. Similarly, I use quotation marks when mentioning the different names used for the 'events of 1956'.

3 For example, in the NATO debate politicians have used Hungary's neutrality aspirations in 1956 in arguments both for and against membership (NSZ 08/07/1998). The extreme right, MIÉP, eventually voted against joining, arguing that under no circumstancces should Hungary abandon the 1956 efforts at neutrality (NSZ 10/02/1999).

4 Two Hungarian words could be translated as 'national': *országos* and *nemzeti*. However, the word *ország* means country, land or empire and *nemzet* refers to a nation more in the ethnic sense. In the political sense, *ország* could be connected to the present borders, while frequently *nemzet* has also referred to Hungarians living outside the geographical borders. Thus, *Népszabadság* itself refers to "*országos* daily", which I, for lack of an English counterpart, have translated into 'national' or 'nationwide'.

5 The circulation of the newspapers is difficult to prove. *Népszabadság* has been described as 'the biggest and most beautiful', and in the first half of 1996 it was also the largest, with some 808,000 readers daily. The next on the list were mostly boulevard and sport papers; *Magyar Hírlap* was the seventh largest with 139,000 readers, and *Magyar Nemzet* the ninth largest with 101,000 readers. (A Magyar Újságírók Országos Szövetségének Évkönyve 1997). Another yearbook (1991) has information only from *Népszabadság*, which published 330,782 daily copies. In all likelihood, *Népszabadság's* circulation was not as great from 1990-1994.

6 Moreover, the *International Encyclopaedia of the Social Sciences* (1968) uses the name "revolutionary uprising" in referring to Berlin in 1953, Poznan in 1956 and Budapest in 1956. Contrarily, a political dictionary from the GDR (1982) connected Hungary to the pattern of counter-revolutions including the GDR in 1953, Czechoslovakia in 1968, Poland in 1981 and Chile in 1973. In the Soviet use, however, the concept counter-revolution was more or less exact

and was also used to describe events occurring in Afghanistan, Nicaragua and Guatemala (cf. Zemtsov 1991; Nyyssönen 1997, 22-26).

7 The word had emerged in a dictionary already in the sixties in the form of *rendszerváltozás* (ÉrtSz 1961, 992). There, it refers to a political and social system, one state inverting to another. ("*Vmely politikai v. társadalmi rendszernek, állapotnak másikkal való felcserélődése.*").

8 For example, Carr (1961) referred to how historians of the Rankean school used different names for the 'common people' in Paris: *les sanculottes, le peuple, la canaille, les bras-nus*. For those who know the current rules of the game, all of these names represented political views and interpretation. (Carr 1963, 27). However, Carr cannot avoid naming and interpretation either!

9 The definition in Hungarian is as follows: "*...az emberiség, vmely nép, nemzet, ország v. ennél nagyobb közösség életében történt fontosabb események egymást követő sorozata... ezeknek az eseményeknek a tényeket illető en hű , időrendbe szedett, írásba foglalt elbeszélése ezeknek az eseményeknek megismerésével, rendszerezésével, bísálatával és hatásaival... foglalkozó tudomány... tantárgy... a jövendő, az utókor... .*"

10 "*Es ist jedenfalls innovativ, denn es rückt in eine bewußte Opposition zur bisher berichteten oder geschriebenen Geschichte. Daraus läßt sich vorläufig folgern, daß ihm ein Erfahrungswandel korrenspondiert, der einer Neuerfahrung gleichkommt.*" (Koselleck 1988, 37).

11 "*Geschichtskultur – das ist eine Sammelbezeichnung für höchst unterschiedliche, sich ergänzende oder überlagernde, jedenfalls direkt oder indirekt aufeinander bezogene Formen der Präsentation von Vergangenheit in einer Gegenwart. Sie ist nichts Statisches, sondern permanent im Wandel... .*" (Hardtwig 1990, 8-9).

12 "*...politische Nutzung von Geschichte in der Öffentlichkeit, um mobilisierende, politisierende oder legitimierende Wirkungen in der politischen Auseinandersetzung zu erzielen.*" (Wolfrum 1996, 377).

13 For example, in *Oxford Advanced Learner's Dictionary of Current English* (1995) the word nation is still connected to "a large community of people, usu[ally] sharing a common history, culture and language, and living in a particular territory under one government" (Oxford Advanced... 1995, 773). One might also question whether the lack of such experiences necessarily implies that the community would fail (Smith 1995; Mikkeli 1998).

14 In Finland, Kari Palonen (1993) has used the term *menneisyyspolitiikka* ('past-politics') (cf. also Nyyssönen 1997). In Germany there is the concept *Vergangenheitspolitik* used by Frei (1996), who has studied how Germany dealt with its Nazi-past after the Second World War.

15 The whole text in Hungarian is as follows: "*Budapesten a városligetnek az Andrássy-ut és a tó közötti részében a honalapító Árpádot és a nemzet egész történelmi multját megörökitő emlékm űvet állit.*"

16 In December 1991, for example, the Hungarian Institute for Pulic Opinion Polls, *Szonda Ipsos*, re-circulated a questionaire from 1947, which dealt with

the Hungarian 'great men'. The top four remained the same, although the order had changed: István Széchenyi had substituted Lajos Kossuth as the first. Next on the list there were Kings Stephen and Matthias, earlier in reverse. (NSZ 05/02/1992). Széchenyi's succes might be partly based on the fact that 1991 was the 200th anniversary of his birth and his policy was widely present in the public.

17 The film *Föltámadott a tenger* (The Sea Has Risen) is one of the greatest examples of Stalinist cultural policy. It was based on the novel of peasant writer Gyula Illés and directed by Kálmán Nádasdy. Minister of Education József Révai personally supervised the preparations and selected the actors. The plot does not end with Hungary's capture by the Russians, but rather with the earlier defeat of the Austrians.

18 Since 1989 there have also been a few attempts to establish parties whose names refer in some way to 1848 and 1956.

19 Folklorist István Győrffy wrote about Kun-Hungarians, an ethnic group in Hungary, and when they spoke of politics (*politizálnak*) they used the verb kossuthing (*kosutozik*). According to Gyula Ortutay, Hungarian people considered political thinking as synonymous to the politics of Lajos Kossuth, i.e. there was only one true and good politics – Kossuth's politics. (Ortutay 1949, 16; cf. also Magyar szókincstár 1999, 707).

20 The number of victims of this white terror is astonishingly inexact. One of the textbooks I use in the fourth chapter refers to 5,000 victims (Jóvérné Szirtes 1985, 84), while another (1998) reduces the number to a mere thousand (Konrád 1998, 49).

21 The bridge was finally reopened in 1949, on the same day on which the first bridge over the Danube was opened by Haynau in 1849 (NSZ 11/02/1999).

22 Cf. *a Pallas nagy lexikona* (1893-1897), *Révai nagy lexikona* (1911-1926), *Új lexikon* (1936), *Új idők lexikona* (1936-1942).

23 "...*alkotmány erőszakos megváltoztatására irányuló mozgalom. A forradalom a jogfolytonosság megtagadása... ."* (Új idők lexikona 1938, 2522).

24 "...*forradalmi úton, tehát erőszakos eszközökkel, ill. államcsinnyel uralomra jutott kormány és államberendezés ellen irányuló mozgalom. Az ellenforradalom célja a régi törvényes rend biztosítása és ilymódon a megzavart jogfolytonosság helyreállítása... ."* (Új idők lexikona 1937, 2011).

25 "...*kizsákmányoló osztályok reakciós harca, rendsz. fegyveres felkelése a forradalom vívmányai ellen a forradalom előtti állapotok, saját uralmuk visszaállítása érdekében."* (ÉrtSz. 1960, 217).

26 "...*elnyomott osztály (1) v. osztályok, ált. a társadalom többsége által megkísérelt v. végbevitt erőszakos, többnyire fegyveres felkelés a fennálló kormány vagy (társadalmi) rend megdöntésére... ."* (ÉrtSz 1960, 899).

27 In the first meaning *felkelés* is 'getting up' (ÉrtSz 1960, 668). A modern meaning connects the word to rebellion, revolt and uprising, although in Hungary

it seems to have appeared only after the Second World War (Nyyssönen 1997, 29). The 'half-feudal' meaning of the term is found, for example, in the vocabulary of 1938, during which time it refers to nobles going to war. (Új idők lexikona 1938, 2357).

28 "...osztálytársadalmak fejlődésében az a törvényszerű bekövetkező szakasz, amelyben a fejlettebb társadalmi-gazdasági alakulat rendsz. fegyveres felkeléssel megdönti és felváltja az elavult társadalmi rendet."

29 In fact Hungarian word dolgozó is broader concept than worker, munkás, which refers clearer to class and as German Werktätiger might include also intelligentsia. Frequently in western literature party's name is translated to Hungarian Workers' Party, although Information from Hungary (1968) uses the form Hungarian Working People's Party (cf. also Balogh & Jakab 1986). In fact the party broaded its basis to the 'petty bourgeois elements' and thus not only to the 'pure' working class.

30 In March 1956 the speech was published in Poland but in Hungarian it came out only in November 1988. However, details of the speech reached Hungary already in spring 1956.

31 In the same September the MDP made also a decision that streets should not be named after living persons.

32 On 15th March members of Történelmi Emlékbizottság (Historial Memorial Committee) had gathered at the statue. The event has became famous as an attempt to oppose Hungary's participation in the Second World War.

33 Bem tér has also a connection to 1848, because Polish general József Bem had helped Hungarian troops in 1848-1849. The statue of Bem was established in 1934 to Pálffy tér, which in 1938 was also named after Bem.

34 In the source material there are several versions from the speech although the basic information is the same: 1956 plakátjai és röplapjai (1991), A forradalom hangja (1989) and one from collection of documents in Egy népfelkelés dokumentumai (1989).

35 The term was testvérháború i.e. test (body), vér (blood), (=brother or sister) and háború (war). In the following I have put the Hungarian term in brackets, otherwise the case is about more general civil war (polgárháború).

36 A text emerged on the remains of the Stalin statue, which named the square to Csizma tér (Boots Square). On November 1st Magyar Világ told that Múzeum körút was changed to the Road of the Rebellions (Felkelők útja).

37 The Hungarian word honvéd comes from poet Károly Kisfaludy and refers to 1848-49, when honvédség was used from Hungarian soldiers. Moreover Magyar Honvéd was even printed in the press of Október huszonharmadika (October 23rd).

38 However, Mindszenty's position did not prevent him to make a statement against the German occupation, to intervene to the parliamentary elections of 1945 or to oppose the establishing the republic and the new school system.

39 However, Révai's possibilities were destroyed at the party convention of the summer of 1957, when the plan to oust Krushchev failed and Molotov was dismissed (1956 kézikönyve (I) 1996, 299).

40 Beside Király there were two other persons, Imre Nagy and József Dudás, who had their 'own chapter' in the White Books. In emigrant literature several of these notions were denied. From Király *Az igazság a Nagy Imre ügyben* (The Truth about Imre Nagy Affair, 1959) reminded that he was also nominated as a general in the People's Republic, too and became a victim of stalinism (1989, 75).

41 Former Arrow Cross members had to sign a paper, in which they repented their mistakes and conviced their loyalty to the new Communist Party (Lahav 1985, 233-235).'Crypto-communism' i.e. occupying legal parties by communists had belonged to the former tactics of the Communist Party.

42 Membership in the state-party rose from 37,818 members in December to 345,733 in June 1957 to 500,000 until 1962 (1956 kézikönyve (I) 1996, 298).

43 Compare Mikes 1957, Fryer 1956, Fossati 1957, Lasky 1957, see also Bain 1960.

44 In his memoirs Gorbachev (1995), however, does not particular deal with Hungarian 1956 although he valued Hungary 1956 as Czechoslovakia 1968 and Afghanistan 1979 as Pyrrhic victories (1997, 484).

45 The "Yeltsin File" from 1992 seemed to confirm that it was Ernő Gerő who requested the troops for the first intervention (MH 28/11/1992).

46 Moreover, Ferenc Glatz, the director of the Historical Institute of the Hungarian Academy of Sciences, defended the new name in the last issue of the periodical *História* in 1988. It seems that Glatz raised the modes of production as a revolution into the fore, because according to him, "ruling political elements between 23rd October and 4th November did not want to intervene in the structures of society [*a társadalom alapjaiba*]." Thus, "...October of 1956 was not a 'revolution', because it did not touch on the bases of the social system. At the same time, it was not a 'counter-revolution' either, because it did not want to overthrow revolutionary relations from 1945-1948... it was not revolution and it was not a counter-revolution but an uprising against the stalinist system." (Glatz 1988, 2).

47 In the Soviet Union, a few revaluations and rehabilitations had taken place already in 1987. However, on 13th June 1988, The Supreme Court of the Soviet Union annulled the cases of Zinoviev-Kamenev and Pyatakov-Radek. Bukharin, Tomsky and Rykov followed on 10th July. (Davies 1989, 134-158).

48 These problems have been raised more to the fore in the "media war" since 1992. The core was in the problem of what kind of influence could a present government have in the electronic media. For example, in March of 1989, the ruling MSZMP held the view that the Hungarian Radio, Hungarian Television and the Hungarian News Agency MTI were "national institutions under the supervision of the government" (MPÉ 1990, 280).

49 The public opinion poll made a brave and current conclusion in the headline. "Today we would live better, if the rebels had won." According to this poll, those who supported counter-revolution were frequently disinterested in the events, or thought they already possessed sufficient knowledge about history. Researchers came to the conclusion that contemporaries had a more positive picture of 1956 than those who had acquired their information from the teaching of history and from the media. (MN 09/11/1989).

50 On the other hand, the number of women members was quite low at only 28, i.e. 7,25%; the percentage of female members was the highest in the Socialist Party, 15%, thus five out of 33 (Ibid.).

51 Nevertheless, an ongoing change was taking place, as the argumentation of Roland Antoniewicz from the Ferenc Münnich Association made clear. Many people used the situation in the "wrong" way, 'they' sent money from Austria as had been done in 1956, the red star from János-mountain was removed and the Lenin körút no longer existed (168 óra 20/06/1989). According to Antoniewicz, the crisis had a counter-revolutionary nature, which he focused on through the analysis of symbols: red stars were removed, the People's Republic was to be changed to a republic, and even the Hungarian coat of arms was to be changed (Ibid., 16/09/1989). In December, Antoniewicz confessed that he had helped to create and deliver leaflets on the rebirth of the Arrow Cross Party (MPÉ 1990, 338).

52 One particular theatre, Jurta, became one of the most essential "birth-places" of the opposition. It was opened in April of 1987 "for a forum to debate about questions of national fate", which had to do with the radical populists. Moreover, the MDF and political prisoners had gathered there. In November of 1988, SZDSZ was founded there as the Independent Party from 1947 (1989). Since 1992, skinheads have also gathered there, and in the summer of 1992, the director of the theatre, László Romhányi, was arrested on charges of suspected murder (NSZ 22/07/1992).

53 In January of 1992 it was reported that the old statues from the 1940s had not been destroyed either, but had been stored in a village store near Budapest by the Budapest Gallery: Stalin, Habsburgs, Dimitrov etc,. According to Magyar Hírlap, some of the statues would not be returned to their original places (MH 31/01/1992).

54 The official opening was planned for August, but "the national meeting of socialist statues" was held in June, which also indicated a humorous point of view of the whole process. Actor Róbert Koltay belonged to the organizers, as did director Péter Bacsó, whose film A tanú (Wittness) is one of the most popular political satires made during the socialist era (MN 04/06; MN; NSZ 28/06/1993).

55 When Osztapenko was removed another incident took place. There, a man declared the statue under a protection in front of the "national guards of 1956", who were celebrating its removal. An independent Member of the

Parliament, János Dénes, argued that the removal belonged to historical justice (MH 25/09/1992).

56 The first Imre Nagy Street was established in Hódmezővásárhely in June of 1991 (MN 28/06/; 01/07/1991). Outside of Hungary, there is an Avenue of 23rd October in Novi Sad in ex-Yugoslavia (MH 01/12/1990). Moreover, Péter Mansfeld has both a street named after him and a plaque in Poznan (NSZ 24/10/1991), as does Imre Nagy in Belfort, France (MN 20/03/1992).

57 The major exception was the former Czechoslovakia, in which former communist functionaries from the township level up were barred from holding certain positions. In Czechoslovakia and East Germany, any kind of political collaboration with the state security service was sufficient to exclude office-holders from public service. Moreover, in July of 1993, the Czech parliament passed a law declaring the past communist regime "illegitimate" and the legislation suspended all statutes of limitation between 1948 and 1989. In the beginning of 1993, the German parliament decided that in certain cases, crimes which were not punished in the GDR have no statute of limitations (HVG 06; 27/02/1993). The shootings at the Berlin Wall were in part analogous to the Hungarian debate (HVG 03/08/1991). In Poland, special screening commissions investigated former security officials, and in Bulgaria, former senior Communists were not allowed to occupy government positions in universities and research institutes (cf. Welsh 1996, 414-415; Rosenberg 1995).

58 Unusually, Népszabadság added a comment that the principle in modern criminal law is that the act must be punished in accordance with current laws. Moreover, Bárdossy had been sentenced to death because he had declared war against the Soviet Union in 1941 without asking for parliament's approval. (Ibid.).

59 When Sajtószabadság Klubja was established in January of 1992, György Fekete (MDF) said that there has yet to be a system change in the press and "it has to be fight for the national television", thus, according to them the present TV was not enough 'national'. They argued in a press conference that Catholic journalists supported the club and that the old MUOSZ was a bolshevist organization (MH; NSZ 20/01/1992).

60 A week before the elections another TV-programme, Panoráma, presented a refugee from Sweden, who told about his journey from 1956-1957 and claimed that he recognized Gyula Horn as one of his beaters (MN 30/04/1994). Horn denied the claim and accused the television station for weeks of slander and of using false witnesses. Horn wanted to confirm that neither in 1956 nor after has he insulted anyone or done anything illegal (MN 04/05/1994).

# SOURCES

## Documents

1956 a forradalom kronológiája és bibliográfiája. László Varga (ed.), 1986, 3. ed. Budapest: Századvég Kiadó, Atlanti Kiadó, 1956-os Intézet 1990.

1956 a sajtó tükrében. 1956 október 22 - november 5. Lajos Izsák & József Szabó (eds.). Budapest: Kossuth Könyvkiadó 1989.

1956 plakátjai és röplapjai. Budapest: Zrínyi Kiadó 1991.

1956 sajtója. Ernő Nagy (ed.). Budapest: Tudósítások Kiadó 1989.

A "Jelcin dosszié". Szovjet dokumentumok 1956-ról. Budapest: Századvég Kiadó & 56-os Intézet 1993.

A Magyar Demokratikus Ellenzék (1968-1988). Dokumentumok. Ervin Csizmadia (ed.). Budapest: T-Twins Kiadó 1995.

A Magyar Szocialista Munkáspárt határozatai és dokumentumai 1956-1962. Henrik Vass & Ágnes Ságvári (eds.). Budapest: Kossuth 1964.

A Magyar Szocialista Munkáspárt határozatai és dokumentumai 1980-1985. Henrik Vass (ed.). Budapest: Kossuth 1988.

A Magyar Szocialista Munkáspárt ideiglenes vezető testületeinek jegyzőkönyvei I-III. Sándor Balogh (ed.). Budapest: Interart 1993.

A Magyar Szocialista Munkáspárt ideiglenes vezető testületeinek jegyzőkönyvei IV. Sándor Balogh (ed.). Budapest: Interart 1994.

A Magyar Szocialista Munkáspárt ideiglenes vezető testületeinek jegyzőkönyvei V. Balogh Sándor (ed.). Budapest: Napvilág Kiadó 1998.

A Magyar Szocialista Munkáspárt központi bizottságának 1989 évi jegyzőkönyvei. 1 kötet. Anna S. Kosztricz & János Lakos & Karola Némethné Vágyi & László Soós & György T (eds.). Budapest: Országos levéltár 1993.

Döntés a Kremlben, 1956. A szovjet pártelnökség vitái Magyarországról. Budapest: 1956-os Intézet 1996.

Kenedi, János (ed.): A forradalom hangja. Budapest: Századvég Kiadó és Nyilvánosság Klub 1989.

Korányi, Tamás G. (ed.): Egy népfelkelés dokumentumaiból 1956. Budapest: Tudósítások Kiadó 1989.

Lakitelek 1987. A magyarság esélyei. Budapest: Antológia-Püski Kiadó 1991.

Molnár Erik kiadatlan tanulmánya: Nemzeti-demokratikus felkelés vagy burzsoá ellenforradalom? Társadalmi Szemle 4/1989.

Report of the Special Committee on the Problem of Hungary Vol 1-2. Published on Demand by University Microfilms International Ann Arber, Michigan USA – London England 1977.

Társadalmi Szemle. Különszám 89. Budapest 1989.

Tetemrehívás 1958-1988. Párizs-Budapest. Párizs: Bibliotéka Kiadó 1988.

Ötvenhatról nyolcvanhatban. Az 1956-os magyar forradalom előzményei, alakulása és utóélete című 1986. december 5-6-án Budapesten rendezett tanácskozás jegyzőkönyve. András B. Hegedűs (ed.). Budapest: Századvég Kiadó & 1956-os Intézet 1992.

# Collections of Laws

1875-1876. évi törvénycikkek. Budapest: Franklin-társulat.

1896. évi törvénycikkek. Jegyzetekkel ellátta Dr. Márkus Dezső. Budapest: Franklin-társulat 1897.

1927. évi törvénycikkek. Jegyzetekkel ellátta Dr. Térfy Gyula. Budapest: Franklin-társulat 1928.

1930. évi törvénycikkek. Jegyzetekkel ellátták Dr. Degré Miklós, Dr. Várady-Brenner Alajos Gyula. Budapest: Franklin Társulat 1931.

1938. évi törvénycikkek. Jegyzetekkel ellátták Dr. Degré Miklós, Dr. Várady-Brenner Alajos Gyula. Budapest: Franklin Társulat 1939.

1946. évi törvénycikkek. Jegyzetekkel ellátták Dr. Vincenti Gusztáv, Dr. Gál László. Franklin-társulat kiadása 1948.

1948. évi törvénycikkek. Jegyzetekkel ellátták Dr. Vincenti Gusztáv, Dr. Gál László. Franklin-társulat kiadása 1949.

Törvények és rendeletek hivatalos gyűjteménye 1989. 1. kötet. Közzéteszi az Igazságügyi Minisztérium és a Minisztertanács Hivatala. Budapest: Közgazdasági és Jogi Könyvkiadó 1990.

Törvények és rendeletek hivatalos gyűjteménye 1990. 1. kötet. Közzéteszi az Igazságügyi Minisztérium és a Minisztertanács Hivatala. Budapest: Közgazdasági és Jogi Könyvkiadó 1991.

Törvények és rendeletek hivatalos gyűjteménye 1991. 1. kötet. Közzéteszi az Igazságügyi Minisztérium és a Miniszterelnöki Hivatal. Budapest: Közgazdasági és Jogi Könyvkiadó 1992.

Törvények és rendeletek hivatalos gyűjteménye 1992. 1. kötet. Közzéteszi az Igazságügyi Minisztérium és a Miniszterelnöki Hivatal. Budapest: Közgazdasági és Jogi Könyvkiadó 1993.

Törvények és rendeletek hivatalos gyűjteménye 1993. 1. kötet. Közzéteszi az Igazságügyi Minisztérium és a Miniszterelnöki Hivatal. Budapest: Közgazdasági és Jogi Könyvkiadó 1994.

Törvények és rendeletek hivatalos gyűjteménye 1994. 1. kötet. Közzéteszi az Igazságügyi Minisztérium és a Miniszterelnöki Hivatal. Budapest: Közgazdasági és Jogi Könyvkiadó 1995.

Törvények és rendeletek hivatalos gyűjteménye 1996. 1. kötet. Közzéteszi az Igazságügyi Minisztérium és a Miniszterelnöki Hivatal. Budapest: Magyar Hivatalos Közlönykiadó 1996.

# Newspapers and Magazines

*168 óra*
  1989 April - 1994 December.
*Budapest Week (BW)*
  16/1997
*Helsingin Sanomat*
  1998 June 14.
*HVG*
  1991 Augustus 3.
  1993 Februar 6, Februar 27.
  1995 October 21.
  1999 July 10.
*Magyar Hírlap (MH)*
  1988 May - 1994 December.
  1995 October 24.
  1996 October 19.
  1997 October 24.
*Magyar Nemzet (MN)*
  1988 May - 1994 December.
  1995 June 20.
*Népszabadság (NSZ)*
  1957 January - December.
  1961, 1966, 1971, 1976, 1981, 1986, October - November.
  1988 May - 1994 December.
  1995 February 1, March 25, May 3, 10, June 9, 17, September 18, October 24, 28, November 24, December 1, 22, 27.
  1996 February 7, March 9, May 14, 18, June 4, 5, 26, July 4, September 4, 26, October 15, 24, November 5.
  1997 January 17, April 25, May 8, August 14, September 2, October 9, November 25.
  1998 January 31, February 5, April 9, 29, May 8, 23, June 12, July 8, October 24, November 5.
  1999 January 23, February 5, 10, 11, 24, June 2, 25, 26, 28, 29, 30, July 7.
*Népszava*
  1991 September 5.

# Dictionaries and Encyclopedies

A Pallas nagy lexikona 1-16. Budapest: Pallas irodalmi és nyomdai reszvénytársaság 1893-1897.

A rendszerváltás szótára. Budapest: Móra 1992.

Az Athenaeum kézi lexikona 1-2. Ignác Acsády (ed.). Budapest: Athenaeum 1893.

Carper, N. Gordon (1991): The Meaning of History. A Dictionary of Quotations. New York & Connecticut & London: Westport.

ÉrtSz. = A magyar nyelv értelmező szótára 1-7. A Magyar Tudományos Akadémia Nyelvtudományi Intézete (ed.). Budapest: Akadémiai Kiadó 1959-1962, 2. ed. 1966, 3. ed. 1978-1980, 4. ed. 1984-1986.

Geschichtliche Grundbegriffe. Historischer Lexikon zur politisch-sozialen Sprache in Deutschland. Herausgegeben von Otto Brunner & Werner Conze & Reinhart Koselleck. Band 1, 2 & 5. Stuttgart: Ernst Klett 1972 - 1984.

International Encyclopedia of the Social Sciences, vol 13. David L. Sills (ed.). The Macmillan Company & The Free Press 1968.

Magay Tamás & Országh, László: Magyar-angol kéziszótár. Budapest: Akadémiai Kiadó 1990.

Magyar szókincstár. Rokon értelmű szavak, szólások és ellentétek szótára. Gábor Kiss (ed.). Budapest: Tinta Könyvkiadó 1999.

Országh László (1953): Magyar-angol nagyszótár. Első kötet A-K, 3.ed. Budapest: Akadémiai Kiadó 1998.

Országh László (1963): Magyar-angol szótár, 7.ed. Budapest: Akadémiai Kiadó 1985.

The Oxford English Dictionary. Vol XIX., 2.ed. Oxford: Clarendon Press 1989.

Oxford Advanced Learner's Dictionary of Current English. Jonathan Crowther (ed.), 5.ed. Oxford: University Press 1995.

Révai nagy lexikona. Az ismeretek enciklopédiája 1-19. Budapest: Révai testvérek irodalmi intézet részvénytársaság 1911-1926.

TESz. = A magyar nyelv történeti-etimológiai szótára 1-3. Budapest: Akadémiai Kiadó 1967-1976.

Új idők lexikona 1-24. Budapest: Singer és Wolfner Irodalmi Intézet Részvénytársaság kiadása 1936-1942.

Új lexikon 1-6. Budapest: Dante-Pantheon 1936.

Uusi tietosanakirja 1-24. Helsinki: Tietosanakirja Oy 1961-1966.

Wörterbuch des Wissenschaftlichen Kommunismus. Erarbeitet im Auftrag des Rates für Wissenschaftlichen Kommunismus an der Akademie für Gesellschaft wissenschaften beim Zentralkomitee der SED. Berlin: Dietz Verlag 1982.

Zemtsov, Ilya (1991): Encyclopedia of Soviet Life. New Brunswick: Transaction Publishers.

# Maps

Budapest Atlasz, Atlas. Budapest: Cartographia 1995.
Budapest térkép, Kartográfiai vállalat Budapest 1987.

# Literature

1956 Die Ungarische Revolution der Arbeiterräte. Reihe internationaler Klassen-kampf. Dortmund: IAK 1977.
1956 kézikönyve I-III. Budapest: 1956-os Intézet 1996.
A burzsoá nacionalizmusról és a szocialista hazafiságról (Tézisek). Társadalmi Szemle 8-9/1959.
A magyar jakobinusok emlékezete. A vértanúk hamvainak feltalálása alkalmából kiadta Budapest főváros közönsége. Budapest: Főváros házinyomdája 1919.
A magyar országgyűlés története 1867-1927. Antall Balla (ed.). Budapest: Legrády nyomda és könyvkiadó részvénytársaság.
A Magyar Újságírók Országos Szövetségének Évkönyve 1991. Budapest: MUOSZ.
A Magyar Újságírók Országos Szövetségének Évkönyve 1997. Budapest: MUOSZ.
A magyarok krónikája. Összeállította, szerkesztette és az összefoglaló tanulmányo-kat írta: Glatz Ferenc. Budapest: Officina Nova 1996.
A vörös uralom áldozatai Magyarországon. Hivatalos jelentések és bírói ítéletek alapján írta és kiadja dr. Váry Albert koronaügyészhelyettes, (1922), 3 ed. Szeged: Nyomda 1993.
Ágh, Attila (1991): The Parliamentary Way to Democracy: The Case of Hungary. Budapest Papers on Democratic Transition N:o 2. Budapest: Budapest University of Economics, Department of Political Science.
Anderson, Andy (1964): Ungern 56 – den beväpnade sanningen (Hungary -56, (transl.) Ingemar E. Nilsson). Göteborg: Arbetarpress 1975.
Ankersmit, Frank R. (1992): On historiographical progress. Della storia Storiografia 22/1992.
Antall, József (1994): Model és valóság II. Budapest: Athenaeum.
Arendt, Hannah (1963/1965): Eichmann in Jerusalem. A Report on the Banality of Evil. New York: Penguin 1994.
Arendt, Hannah (1963): On Revolution. Harmondsworth: Penguin 1973.
Aristoteles: Rhetorik. München: Fink 1980.
Ash, Timothy Garton (1990): We The People. The Revolution of '89 Wittnessed in Warsaw, Budapest, Berlin & Prague. London: Granta Books & Penguin.
Az 1956-os magyar forradalom. Bázel: Marxizmus-Forradalom-Szocializmus, a Magyar Szocialisták Szövetsége - Külföldi Csoport 1964.
Az 1956-os magyar forradalom. Reform – felkelés – szabadságharc – megtorlás. Történelmi olvasókönyv középiskolásoknak. Budapest: Tankönyvkiadó 1991.

Az igazság a Nagy Imre ügyben, (1959). Századvég füzetek 2. Budapest: Századvég kiadó & Nyilvánosság klub 1989.

Azaryahu, Maoz (1991): Von Wilhelmplatz zu Thälmannplatz. Politische Symbole im öffentlichen Leben der DDR. Gerlingen: Bleicher.

Azaryahu, Maoz (1997): Zurück zur Vergangenheit? Die Straßennamen Ost-Berlins 1990-1994. In: Winfried Speitkamp (Hg.) Denkmalsturz. Kleine Vandendoek-Reihe. Göttingen: Vandenhoeck und Ruprecht.

Bain, Leslie (1960): The reluctant satellities. An eye-witness report on East Europe and the Hungarian Revolution. New York: Macmillan.

Balogh, Sándor & Birta, István & Izsák, Lajos & Jakab, Sándor & Korom, Mihály & Simos, Péter (1978): A magyar népi demokrácia története 1944-1962. Budapest: Kossuth.

Balogh, Sándor & Jakab, Sándor (1986): The History of Hungary After the Second World War. Budapest: Corvina.

Bangó, Jenő (1991): Die postsozialistische Gesellschaft Ungarns. Studia Hungarica; 39. München: Trofenik.

Békés, Csaba (1996): Az 1956-os magyar forradalom a világpolitikában. Tanulmány és válogatott dokumentumok. Budapest: 1956-os Intézet.

Berecz, János (1969/1981): 1956 Counter-Revolution in Hungary. Worlds and Weapons (Ellenforradalom tollal és fegyverrel 1956, (transl.) István Butykay). Budapest: Kossuth 1986.

Beszélő. Különszám. Társadalmi Szerződés, A politikai kibontakozás feltételei 1987 június.

Bihari, Mihály (1993): Az állampárti diktatúrából a versengő többpártrendszerig. In Mihály Bihari (ed.) A többpártrendszerek kialakulása Kelet-Közép-Európában. Budapest: Kossuth 1993.

Borbándi, Gyula (1985): A magyar emigráció életrajza 1945-1985 I-II. Budapest: Európa 1989.

Boros, Géza (1997): Emlékművek '56-nak. Budapest: 1956-os Intézet.

Boyarin, Jonathan (1994): Space, Time and the Politics of Memory. In Jonathan Boyarin (ed.) Remapping Memory. The Politics of TimeSpace. Minneapolis & London: University of Minnesota Press.

Bozóki, András (1990): Út a rendszerváltáshoz: az Ellenzéki Kerekasztal. Mozgó Világ 8/1990.

Bozóki, András (1993): Catching the Fleeting Moment. The Transition in Eastern Europe through Western Eyes. New Hungarian Quarterly 128.

Brown, Archie (1996): The Gorbachev Factor. Oxford: University Press.

Bruszt, László (1990): 1989: the Negotiated Revolution in Hungary. Social Research, (57) 2/1990.

Burton, C. Andrus (1969): A Nürnbergi Huszonkettő (The Infamous of Nuremberg, (transl.) Gyula Tellér). Ötödik, változatlan kiadás. Budapest: Kossuth 1982.

Carr, Edward Hallet (1961): Mitä historia on (What is History (transl.) Sirkka Ahonen). Helsinki: Otava 1963.

Collingwood, R.G. (1946): The Idea of History. Oxford: University Press 1963.

Comay, Rebecca (1990): Redeeming Revenge: Nietzsche, Benjamin, Heidegger and the Politics of Memory. In: Clayton Koelb (ed.) Nietzsche as Postmodernist. Albany: State University of New York Press.

Csizmadia, Ervin (1995): A Magyar Demokratikus Ellenzék (1968-1988). Monográfia. Budapest: T-Twins.

Csonka, Emil (1981): A forradalom oknyomozó története 1945-1956. München: Veritas.

Dalos, György (1991): Strassenschilderkampf. Kursbuch 104/1991.

Davies, R.W. (1989): Soviet History in the Gorbachev Revolution. Basinstoke & London: The Macmillan Press.

Deak, Istvan (1998): Revolutionäre oder Verträter? Politische Prozesse in Ungarn zwischen 1919 und 1958. In: Vom Neuschreiben der Geschichte. Erinnerungspolitik nach 1945 und 1989. Transit 15/1998.

Deigner, Anna (1988): Józsefvárosi utcák, terek és emléktáblák története. Budapest: Országos Műszaki Információs Központ és Könyvtár.

Dienstag, Joshua Foa (1996): "The Pozsgay Affair." Historical Memory and Political Legitimacy. History & Memory. Studies in Representation of the Past Vol 8, N:o 1, Spring/Summer 1996.

Dunn, John (1989): Revolution. In: T. Ball & J. Farr & L. Hanson (eds.) Political Innovation and Conceptional Change. Cambridge: University Press.

Dörner, Andreas (1995): Politischer Mythos und symbolische Politik. Sinnstiftung durch symbolische Formen am Beispiel des Hermannsmythos. Opladen: Westdeutscher Verlag.

Edelman, Murray (1965): The symbolic uses of politics. Urbana: University of Illinois Press 1985.

Edelman, Murray (1971): Politics as symbolic action: Mass arousal and acquiescence. New York: Academic Press.

Edelman, Murray (1977): Political Language. Worlds That Succeed and Policies That Fail. New York: Academic Press.

Ellenforradalmi erők a magyar októberi eseményekben I-IV. Kiadja a Magyar Népköztársaság Minisztertanács Tájékoztatás Hivatala, Állami politikai könyvkiadó Bukarest 1957.

The English Historical Review. Vol LXXX October 1965.

Enzensberger, Hans Magnus (1987): Ach Europa! Frankfurt am Main: Suhrkamp.

Fehér, Ferenc and Heller, Ágnes (1983): Hungary 1956 Revisited. The Message of a Revolution – a Quarter of a Century After. London: George Allen & Unwin.

Felkay, Andrew (1989): Hungary and the USSR, 1956-1988. Connecticut: Greenwood Press.

Fischer, Holger (1982): Politik und Geschichtswissenschaft in Ungarn. Südosteuropa, (31) 6/1982.

Fossati, Luigi (1957): Qui Budapest. Torino: Giulio Einaudi.

Frei, Norbert (1996): Vergangenheitspolitik. Die Anfänge der Bundesrepublik und die NS-Vergangenheit. München: Verlag C.H.Beck.

Fryer, Peter (1956): Hungarian Tragedy. London: Dobson.

Füredi, Frank (1992): Mythical Past, Elusive Future. London: Pluto Press.

Gadney, Reg (1986): Cry Hungary! Uprising 1956. London: Weidenfeld and Nicolson.

Gati, Charles (1990): The Bloc That Failed. Soviet-East European Relations in Transition. Bloomington & Indianapolis: Indiana University Press.

Giesen, Bernhard (1998): Intellectuals and the Nation. Collective Identity in a German Axial Age (Die Intellektuellen und die Nation, (transl.) Nicholas Levis and Amoz Wetsz). Cambridge: University Press.

Glatz, Ferenc (1988): Kérdőjelek 1956-ról. História 6/1988.

Glatz, Ferenc (1991): Az ún. Kádár-korszak kutatásáról. História 4/1991.

Gombos, József (1993): The Fiction of "Social Contract" in the Political Histography Covering the post-56 period. In: Paula Hihnala & Olli Vehviläinen (eds.) Hungary 1956. Tampere: Tampereen yliopiston jäljennepalvelu 1995.

Gorbachev, Mikhail (1995): Memories. London & New York & Toronto & Sydney: Doubleday 1997.

Gorlice, Josef (1986): Introducion to the Hungarian Democratic Opposition. Berkeley Journal of Sociology, (31)/1986.

Gosztonyi, Péter (1981): Föltámadott a tenger... 1956. A magyar október története. 3. átdolgozott és bővített kiadás. Budapest: Népszava 1989.

Gyarmati, György (1998): Március Hatalma – A Hatalom Márciusa. Fejezetek Március 15. ünneplésének történetéből. Budapest: Paginarium.

Gyurkó, László (1988): János Kádár. Porträtskizze auf historischen Hintergrund von László Gyurkó. Budapest: Pergamon Press-Akadémiai Kiadó.

Habermas, Jürgen (1986): Vom öffentlichen Gebrauch der Historie. Das offizielle Selbstverständnis der Bundesrepublik bricht auf. Die Zeit, 7. November.

Hankiss, Elemér (1989): Kelet-európai alternatívák. Budapest: Közgazdasági és Jogi Könyvkiadó.

Hardtwig, Wolfgang (1990): Geschictskultur und Wissenschaft. München: DTV.

Hegedűs, András B. & Baló, Péter (1996): 1956-ról a rendszerváltás küszöbén. Budapest: Széchenyi István Szakkolégium & 1956-os Intézet.

Hentilä, Seppo (1994): Jaettu Saksa, jaettu historia. Helsinki: Suomen historiallinen seura.

Hibbing, John R. & Patterson, Samuel C. (1992): A Democratic Legislature in the Making The Historic Hungarian Elections of 1990. Comparative Political Studies, (24) 4/1992.

Historiallinen aikakauskirja 2/1993. Helsinki 1993.

Hoensch, Jörg K. (1996): The History of Modern Hungary 1867-1994, Second Edition (Geschicte Ungarns, (transl.) Kim Traynor). London & New York: Longman.

Hofer, Tamás (1992) Harc a rendszerváltásért szimbolikus mezőben. 1989. március 15-e Budapesten. Politikatudományi Szemle 1/1992.

Hollós, Ervin & Lajtai Vera (1986): Drámai napok 1956. október 23.-november 4. Budapest: Kossuth.

Holt, Robert T. (1958): Radio Free Europe. Minneapolis: University of Minneapolis Press.

Horthy, Miklós (1953): Emlékirataim, 3. kiad. Budapest: Európa Könyvkiadó 1993.

Horváth, Csaba (1992): Magyarország 1944-től napjainkig. "Új magyar történelem". Pécs: Carbocomp.

Hruscsov, Nyikita (1988): A személyi kultuszról és következményeiről. Beszámoló az SZKP XX. kongresszusának zárt ülésén 1956 február 25, (transl.) Edvin Zalai. Budapest: Kossuth Könyvkiadó.

The Hungarian Revolution of 1956. Reform, Revolt and Repression 1953-1963. György Litván (ed.). London & New York: Longman 1996.

Hungary 1956. Paula Hihnala & Olli Vehviläinen (eds.). Tampere: Tampereen yliopiston jäljennepalvelu 1995.

Information Hungary. Ferenc Erdei (ed.). Budapest & Oxford: Akadémiai Kiadó & Pergamon Press 1968.

The Institute for the History of the 1956 Hungarian Revolution. Budapest 1996.

Irving, David (1981): Uprising! One nation's nightmare: Hungary 1956. London: Hodder and Stroughton.

Jóvérné Szirtes, Ágota (1976): Történelem a gimnázium IV. osztálya számára. A legújabb kor története. Negyedik kiadás. Budapest: Tankönyvkiadó 1985.

Jóvérné Szirtes, Ágota & Sipos, Péter (1976): Történelem a gimnázium IV. osztálya számára 1914-1945. Hatodik, átdolgozott kiadás. Budapest: Tankönyvkiadó 1989.

Juhász, Gábor (1993): A megnevezéstől a háborús bűnösségig. Igazságtételi törvényhozás Magyarországon 1990. február - 1993. február. Mozgó Világ 4/1993.

Jussila, Osmo & Hentilä, Seppo & Nevakivi, Jukka: Suomen poliittinen historia 1809-1995. Porvoo-Helsinki-Juva: WSOY 1996.

Kalela, Jorma (1993): Aika, historia ja yleisö. Jyväskylä: Gummerus.

Kalmár, Melinda (1998): Ennivaló és hozomány. A kora kádárizmus ideológiája. Budapest: Magvető.

Karjalainen, Erkki (1969): Normalisoinnin särjetyt tienviitat. In: Yrjö Länsipuro (ed.) Hullu vuosi 1968. Helsinki: WSOY.

Karlsson, Klas-Göran (1999): Historia som vapen. Historiebruk och Sovjetunionens upplösning 1985-1995. Stockholm: Natur och Kultur.

Károlyi, Mihály (1956): The Memoirs of Michael Karolyi. Faith Without Illusion, (transl.) Catherine Karolyi. Oxford: Alden Press.

Kecskemeti, Paul (1961): The Unexpected Revolution. Social Forces in the Hungarian Uprising. Stanford: Stanford University Press.

Kende, Péter (1992): Vissza – de milyen hagyományokhoz? Világosság 12/1992.

Kende, Péter (1993): Megmarad-e 1956 nemzeti hagyománynak? In: Évkönyv II. 1993. Budapest: 1956-os Intézet.

Kende, Peter (1996): Afterword. In: György Litván (ed.) The Hungarian Revolution of 1956. Reform, Revolt and Repression 1953-1963. London & New York: Longman.

Kenyeres Zoltán (1995) : Irodalom, történet, írás. Budapest: Anonymus.

Klimó, Árpád von (1998): Kampf um die nationale Geschichte. Die Auseinandersetzungen zwischen Kirchen und Kommunistischen Parteien in Ungarn und der SBZ (1945-1948). In: Kurt Imhof (Hg) Kommunikation und Revolution. Zürich: Zeismo.

Konrád, György (1985): Antipolitik. Mitteleuropäische Meditationen. Frankfurt am Main: Suhrkamp.

Konrád, György & Szelényi, Iván (1974): The Intellectuals on the Road to Class Power. New York: Harcourt Brace Jovanovich 1979.

Koselleck, Reinhart (1972): Einleitung. In: Geschichtliche Grundbegriffe. Historisches Lexikon zur politisch-sozialen Sprache in Deutschland. Herausgegeben von Otto Brunner & Werner Conze & Reinhart Koselleck. Band 1. Stuttgart: Ernst Klett.

Koselleck, Reinhart (1975): Geschichte. In: Geschichtliche Grundbegriffe. Historisches Lexikon zur politisch-sozialen Sprache in Deutschland. Herausgegeben von Otto Brunner & Werner Conze & Reinhart Koselleck. Band 2. Stuttgart: Ernst Klett.

Koselleck, Reinhart (1979): Futures Past. On the Semantics of Historical Time (Vergangene Zukunft. Zur Semantik geschictlicher Zeiten, (transl.) Keith Tribe). Cambridge, Massachusetts, London: The MIT Press 1985.

Koselleck, Reinhart (1979): Vergangene Zukunft. Zur Semantik geschictlicher Zeiten. Frankfurt: Suhrkamp 1989.

Koselleck, Reinhart (1984): Revolution. In: Geschichtliche Grundbegriffe. Historisches Lexikon zur politisch-sozialen Sprache in Deutschland. Herausgegeben von Otto Brunner & Werner Conze & Reinhart Koselleck. Band 5. Stuttgart: Ernst Klett.

Koselleck, Reinhart (1988): Erfahrungswandel und Methodenwechsel. Eine historisch-antroropologische Skizze. In: Christian Meier & Jörn Rüsen (Hg) Historische Methode. München: DTV.

Koselleck, Reinhart (1994): Einleitung. In: Reinhart Koselleck & Michael Jeismann (Hg) Der politische Totenkult. Kriegerdenkmale in der Moderne. München: Fink.

Kundera, Milan (1984): The Tragedy of Central Europe. New York Review of Books, April 26, 1984.

Körösényi, András (1990): Pártok és szavazók. Parlamenti választások 1990-ben. Mozgó Világ 8/1990.

Lahav, Yehuda (1985): Der Weg der Kommunistischen Partei Ungarns zu Macht I. Studia Hungarica 19. München: Trofenik.

Langewiesche, Dieter (1992): Geschichte als politisches Argument: Vergangenheitsbilder als Gegenwartskritik und Zukunftprognose – die Reden der Deutschen Bundespräsidenten. Saeculum 43/1992.

Lasky, Melvin (1957): The Hungarian Revolution: the story of the october uprising as recorded in documents, dispatches, eye-witness accounts, and worldwide reactions. London: Secker-Warburg.

Le Goff, Jacques (1978): Mentaliteterna, en tvetydig historia. In: Att skriva historia. Nya infallsvinklar och object. Stockholm: Norteds Tryckeri.

Le Goff, Jacques (1992): Memory. In: History and Memory, (transl.) Stephen Rendall and Elizabeth Claman. New York: Columbia University Press.

Lendvai, Paul (1988): Das eigenwillige Ungarn: Von Kádár zu Grósz. Osnabrück: Fromm.

Litván, György (1991): Kié 1956? Világosság 10/1991.

Litván, György (1992): Az 1956-os magyar forradalom hagyománya és irodalma. Előadások a Történettudományi Intézetben 19. Budapest: MTA Történettudományi Intézet.

Litván, György (1993): A Horthy-rehabilitáció csúszdáján. Világosság 8-9/1993.

Litván, György (1995): Research and Discussion on 1956 in present-day Hungary. In: Paula Hihnala & Olli Vehviläinen (eds.) Hungary 1956. Tampere: Tampereen yliopiston jäljennepalvelu 1995.

Litván György (1997): 1956-os kutatások és viták a mai Magyarországon. In: 1956 Évkönyv 1996/1997. Budapest: 1956-os Intézet.

Lomax, Bill (1976): Hungary 1956. London: Allison & Busby.

Lomax, Bill (1985): The Hungarian Revolution of 1956 and the Origins of the Kádár Regime. Studies in Comparative Communism vol. XVIII, No.273, Summer/Autumn 1985.

Lowenthal, David (1985): The Past is a Foreign Country. Cambridge: University Press 1988.

Lukacs, John (1988): Budapest 1900. A város és kultúrája (Budapest 1900. A Historical Portrait of a City and its Culture, (transl.) Klára Mészáros). Budapest: Európa 1991.

Lundestad, Geir (1986): East, West, North, South. Major Developments in International Politics 1945-1990, (transl. Gail Adams Kvam). Oslo: Norwegian University Press 1991.

Lüsebrink, Hans-Jürgen & Reichardt, Rolf (1990): Die Bastille. Zur Symbolgeschichte von Herrschaft und Freiheit. Frankfurt am Main: Fischer Tashenbuch Verlag.

Magyarország Politikai Évkönyve 1988. Sándor Kurtán & Péter Sándor & László Vass (eds.). Debrecen: R-Forma. (MPÉ)

Magyarország Politikai Évkönyve 1990. Sándor Kurtán & Péter Sándor & László Vass (eds.). Budapest: AULA-OMIKK. (MPÉ)

Magyarország Politikai Évkönyve 1991. Sándor Kurtán & Péter Sándor & László Vass (eds.). Budapest: Ökonómia Alapítvány – Economix RT. (MPÉ)

Magyarország politikai évkönyve 1992. Sándor Kurtán & Péter Sándor & László Vass (eds.). Budapest: Demokrácia Kutatások Magyar Központja Alapítvány – Economix Rt. (Mpé)

Magyarország politikai évkönyve 1993. Sándor Kurtán & Péter Sándor & László Vass (eds.). Budapest: Demokrácia Kutatások Magyar Központja Alapítvány. (Mpé)

Magyarország politikai évkönyve 1994. Sándor Kurtán & Péter Sándor & László Vass (eds.). Budapest: Demokrácia Kutatások Magyar Központja Alapítvány. (Mpé)

Magyarország politikai évkönyve 1995. Sándor Kurtán & Péter Sándor & László Vass (eds.). Budapest: Demokrácia Kutatások Magyar Központja Alapítvány. (Mpé)

Magyarország története 1918-1990. Ferenc Pölöskei & Jenő Gergely & Lajos Izsák (eds.). Budapest: Korona Kiadó 1995.

Magyarország történeti kronológiája III. kötet. Főszerkesztő Benda Kálmán, 1848-1944. Budapest: Akadémiai Kiadó 1982.

Márai Sándor (1937): Ihlet és nemzedék. (1946). Akadémiai Kiadó & Helikon Kiadó 1992.

Marosán, György (1989): A tanúk még élnek. Budapest: Hírlapkiadó Vállalat.

Marx, Karl (1852): The Eighteenth Brumaire of Louis Bonaparte. In: Karl Marx, Surveys from Exile. Political Writings Volume 2. Harmondsworth: Penguin 1973.

Middleton, David & Derek, Edwards (1990): Introduction. In: David Middleton & Derek Edwards (eds.) Collective Remembering. London-Newbury Park-New Delhi: Sage Publications.

Mikes, George (1957): The Hungarian Revolution. London: Andre Deutsch.

Mikkeli, Heikki (1998): Eurooppalainen identiteetti ja federalismi. In: Heikki Mikkeli & Juha Sihvola & Pekka Suvanto & Eino Lyytinen: Westfalenista Amsterdamiin. Helsinki: Eurooppa-tiedotus & Edita.

Miller, John (1993): Mikhail Gorbachev and the End of Soviet Power. New York: St. Martin's Press.

Molnár, János (1967): Ellenforradalom Magyarországon 1956. A polgári magyarázatok bírálata. Budapest: Akadémiai Kiadó.

Mylly, Juhani (1995): Narratiivista ja uushistoristista (lähihistoriaa)? In: Timo Soikkanen (ed.) Lähihistoria. Teoriaan, metodologiaan ja lähteisiin liittyviä ongelmia. Turun yliopiston Poliittisen historian tutkimuksia 1. Turku: Turun yliopisto.

Nagy, Tamás (1989): 1956 – revolution or counter-revolution? New Hungarian Quarterly 113/1989.

Nagytér, élettér, vezető nép. Szálasi Ferenc előadása. A nyilaskeresztes párt – Hungarista Mozgalom pártkülügyek értekezleteinek sorozatában: Budapesten A hűség háza nagytanácstermében 1943. június 15/16-án.

Nixon, Richard Milhous (1978): The Memoirs of Richard Nixon. New York: Grosset & Dunlap.

Nyyssönen, Heino (1992): Vain kadut ovat ikuisia. Kulttuuritutkimus, (9) 1/ 1992.

Nyyssönen, Heino (1997): Historia poliittisena argumenttina. Vuoden 1956 tulkinnat Unkarissa Kádárin ajasta monipuoluevaaleihin. Hungarologische Beiträge 10. Jyväskylä: Universtität Jyväskylä.

Ortutay, Gyula (1949): Művelődés és politika. Budapest: Hungária könyvkiadó.

Orwell, George (1949): Nineteen eighty-four. London: Penguin 1988.

Ozouf, Mona (1976): La Fête révolutionaire. Paris: Gallimard.

Palonen, Kari (1993): Politikointi – politisointi – politiikka. Tulkinta politiikan ajatusmuodon pelikieliaikatiloista. Teaching publications 1. Jyväskylä: University of Jyväskylä, Department of Political Science.

Parlamenti képviselő választások 1920-1990. Tanulmányok. György Földes & László Hubai (eds.). Budapest: Politikatörténeti alapítvány 1994.

Pekonen, Kyösti (1991): Symbolinen modernissa politiikassa. Jyväskylä: Nykykulttuurin tutkimusyksikkö.

Perelman, Chaim (1982): The Realm of Rhetoric, (transl.) William Kluback. Notre Dame: University of Notre Dame Press.

Pozsgay, Imre (1993): 1989. Politikus-pálya a pártállamban és a rendszerváltásban. Budapest: Püski Kiadó.

Prohászka, László (1994): Szoborsorsok. Budapest: Kornétás Kiadó.

Propaganda, persuasion and polemic. Jeremy Hawthorn (ed.). London: Arnold 1987.

Rainer, János M. (1993): Töprengések Nagy Imréről 1993-ben. Valóság 10/1993.

Rappaport, Joanne (1990): The Politics of Memory. New York: Cambridge University Press.

Rév, István (1994): Parallel Autopsies. Working Paper Series no. 10. International Institute University of Michigan.

Rosenberg, Tina (1995): The Haunted Land. Facing Europe's Ghosts After Communism. New York: Random House.

Salamon, Konrád (1998): Történelem IV. a középiskolák számára, 5. ed. Budapest: Nemzeti Tankönyvkiadó 1998.

Schlett, István (1996): A magyar politikai gondolkodás története, 1. kötet. Budapest: Korona.

Schöpflin, George (1977): Hungary: An Uneasy Stability. In: Archie Brown & Jack Gray (eds.) Political Culture & Political Change in Communist States, 2 ed. London & Basingstoke 1979.

Schöpflin, George (1981): Hungary Between Prosperity and Crisis. London: The Institute for the Study of Conflict.

Schöpflin, George (1989): The end of communism in Eastern Europe. International Affairs, (66) 1/1990.

Schöpflin, George (1991): Conservatism and Hungary's Transition. Problems of Communism, Jan-April/1991.

Schöpflin, George & Tőkés Rudolf & Völgyes Iván (1988): Leadership Change and Crisis in Hungary. Problems of Communism, Sept-Oct/1988.

Seewann, Gerhard (1987): Ungarische Mittel- und Osteuropaforschung. Ihre politischen und historiographischen Besonderheiten. Osteuropa, (27) 9/1987.

Seewann, Gerhard & Sitzler, Kathrin (1982): Ungarn 1956: Volkaufstand-Konterrevolution-nationale Trägödie. Offizielle Retrospektive nach 25 Jahren. Südosteuropa. Zeitschrift für Gegenwartsforschung 1/1982.

Seifert, Tibor (1992): Magyarország története 1938-1990. Tankönyv a középiskolák IV. osztályosai számára. 2. félév, 4 ed. Budapest: IKVA.

Seton-Watson, R.W. (1922): The Historian as a political Force in Central Europe. An Inaugural Lecture Delivered on 22 November 1922. Published by the School of Slavonic Studies in the University of London, King's College.

Siklós, András (1978): Magyarország 1918/1919. Események/képek/dokumentumok. Budapest: Kossuth & Magyar Helikon.

Smith, Anthony D. (1995): Nations and Nationalism in a Global Era. Cambridge: Polity Press.

Speitkamp, Winfried (1997): Denkmalsturz und Symbolkonflikt in der modernen Geschichte. Eine Einleitung. In: Winfried Speitkamp (Hg.) Denkmalsturz. Kleine Vandendoek-Reihe. Göttingen: Vandenhoeck und Ruprecht.

Standeisky, Éva (1987): A Magyar Kommunista Párt irodalompolitikája 1944-48. Budapest: Kossuth.

Szabad, György (1977): Hungarian political trends between the revolution and the compromise (1849-1867). Studia Hungarica 128. Budapest: Akadémiai Kiadó.

Szabadon választott. Parlamenti almanach 1990. Budapest: Idegenforgalmi Propaganda és Kiadó Vállalat 1990.

Szabó, Máté (1991): Kriterien des Gedenkens. Die Bestattung von Imre Nagy als politisches Symbolereignis. Ost-Europa. Sonderdrück 1991.

Szabó, Miklós (1995): Múmiák öröksége. Politikai és történeti esszék. Budapest: Új Mandátum.

Szabó, Péter (1996): Történelem II. a középiskolák számára. Budapest: Nemzeti Tankönyvkiadó.

Szalai, Erzsébet (1990): Elites and systematic change in Hungary. Praxis International, Vol 10 nos 1/2 1990.

Szűcs, Jenő (1971): Nemzet és történelem. Budapest: Gondolat 1974.

Tóbiás, Áron (1989): In memoriam Nagy Imre. Debrecen: Szabad Tér.

Toma, Peter A. & Völgyes, Ivan (1977): Politics in Hungary. San Francisco: W.H. Freeman and Company.

Tőkés, Rudolf (1990): Hungary's New Political Elites. Adaptation and Change. Problems of Communism, Nov-Dec/1990.

Tőkés, Rudolf (1996): Hungary's negotiated revolution. Economic reform, social change and political succession. Cambridge Russian, Soviet and Post-Soviet Studies: 101. Cambridge: University Press.

The Universal Almanac 1996. Edited by John W. Wright. Kansas City: Andrews and McMeel A Universal Press Syndicate Company 1995.

Vámos, Miklós (1994): Ha én Bródy volnék. Dunaújváros: AB OVO.

Vovelle, Michel (1990): Ideologies and Mentalities. Chigaco: The University of Chigaco Press.

Völgyes, Iván (1987). Political culture. In: Teil Ungarn, Südosteuropa Handbuch. Band V. Herausgegeben von Klaus Detlev Gnothusen. Göttingen: Vandenhoek und Ruprecht.

Watt, David Cameron (1991): Mitä oman ajan historia on? Poliittinen historia, Suomi ja muut. Seppo Hentilä & Timo Turja (eds.). Oulu: Pohjoinen.

Welsh, Helga A. (1996): Dealing with the Communist Past: Central and East European Experiences after 1990. Europe-Asia Studies 48, 3/1996.

White, Hayden (1987): The Content of the Form. Narrative Discourse and Historical Representation, 2 ed. Baltimore: Johns Hopkins University Press 1989.

White, Hayden (1978): Tropics of Discourse. Essays in Cultural Critisism. Baltimore. Baltimore: Johns Hopkins University Press.

Wolfrum, Edgar (1996): Geschichte als Politikum – Geschichtspolitik. Internationale Forschungen zum 19. und 20. Jahrhundert. Neue Politische Literatur 3/1996.

Ylikangas, Heikki (1993): Tie Tampereelle. Dokumentoitu kuvaus Tampereen antautumiseen johtaneista sotatapahtumista Suomen sisällissodassa. Helsinki: WSOY.

Youth and History. A Comparative European Survey on Historical Consciousness and Political Attitudes among Adolescents. Vol A. Description. Magne Angvik & Bodo von Borries (eds.). Hamburg: Körber Stiftung 1997.

Zinner, Paul (1962): Revolution in Hungary. New York-London: Columbia University Press.

# Abbreviations

ÁVH      *Államvédelmi Hatóság*
The Office of State Security

DISZ      *Dolgozó Ifjúság Szövetsége*
Alliance of Working Youth

FIDESZ      *Fiatal Demokraták Szövetsége*
Federation of Young Democrats

FKGP      *Független Kisgazda-, Földmunkás- és Polgári Párt*
Independent Smallholders' Party

HNF      *Hazafias Népfront*
Patriotic People's Front

KDNP      *Kereszténydemokrata Néppárt*
Christian Democratic People's Party

KISZ      *Kommunista Ifjúság Szövetsége*
Communist Youth Organization

MDF      *Magyar Demokrata Fórum*
Hungarian Democratic Forum

MDP      *Magyar Dolgozók Pártja*
Hungarian Working People's Party

MEFESZ      *Magyar Egyetemi és Főiskolai Egyesületek Szövetsége*
Alliance of the Hungarian University and College Associations

MIÉP      *Magyar Igazság és Élet Pártja*
The Party of Hungarian Truth (Justice) and Life

MSZMP      *Magyar Szocialista Munkáspárt*
Hungarian Socialist Workers' Party

MSZP      *Magyar Szocialista Párt*
Hungarian Socialist Party

SZDSZ      *Szabad Demokraták Szövetsége*
Alliance of Free Democrats

TIB      *Történelmi Igázságtétel Bizottsága*
Committee for Historical Justice

# Other SoPhi Titles

## KIA LINDROOS: NOW-TIME/IMAGE-SPACE
*Temporalization of Politics in Walter Benjamin's Philosophy of History and Art*

Kia Lindroos' book is a philosophical reconstruction on Walter Benjamin's thinking, and it elaborates a cairologic perspective on political and aesthetic time. As Benjamin's thinking has actualized especially in the 20th fin de siecle, the book opens a detailed view to his thinking. Kia Lindroos constructs an alternative interpretation on history, time, politics and art, approached through the moment of the Now (*Jetztzeit*).

"Kia Lindroos has been able to dig out of Benjamin's rather neological and hermetic terms new insights, and to show the stimulating originality of this thinker, often misunderstood as he and his work are."

Professor Wolf-Dieter Narr, Freie Universität Berlin
*1998, ISBN 951-39-0341-9, 303 pages, £14.95 pb*

## FINNISH YEARBOOK OF POLITICAL THOUGHT 1999

HOW DO CONCEPTS CHANGE? According to the usual view, Anglophone and Continental studies have developed incompatible paradigms on this topic. In the *FYPT 1999*, this view is relativised from different perspectives by Melvin Richter, Janet Coleman and Kari Palonen. In particular, Quentin Skinner assesses his own intellectual development, and also sketches his own rhetorical perspective on conceptual change.

HOW ARE WE TO DEAL WITH CONTINGENCY? Are novels better in understanding the contingency of politics than political science? Maureen Whitebrook combines a political reading of two contemporary novels with the discussion of contingency, and John S. Nelson argues that by reading John le Carré's novels we can learn of international political practices. Risto Eräsaari, however, tries to incorporate contingency into a socio-political *Zeitdiagnose*.

IN THE 'FINNISH SECTION' Eeva Aarnio and Kyösti Pekonen analyze the Finnish party programmes, and Mikko Salmela scrutinizes Finnish philosophers' views on totalitarianism during WW II.

*1999, ISBN 951-39-0432-6, 244 pages, £12.95 pb*

SoPhi is distributed by Drake International Services, Market House, Market Place, Deddington, Oxford OX 15 QSE, UK
tel. (+44) 01869 338240, fax (+44) 01869 338310, e-mail info@drakeint.co.uk

Please visit SoPhi Home Page at http://www.jyu.fi/sophi